LNER CARRIAGES

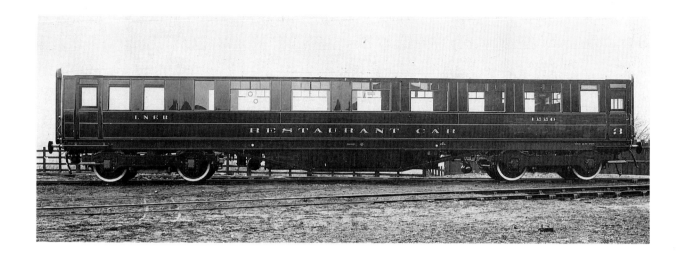

Above The down 'Silver Jubilee' passing Harringay behind 'A4' 4–6–2 No 4492 *Dominion of New Zealand*, probably not long after the addition of the eighth vehicle in March 1938.

Previous page Restaurant pantry car No 1226 (Built 1934 Dia 151, later No 9098). The pantry is to the left-hand of the body, the lavatory at the other end.

Below The 'Northern Belle' on Glenfinnan Viaduct during the 1934 season, with two 'D34s' at its head. This is the day portion, headed by an all-steel full brake, then GNR saloon No 46, toilet third No 1007, the two Dia 4 open firsts, kitchen car, sleeper third and brake first.

LNER CARRIAGES

MICHAEL HARRIS

David St John Thomas Publisher

an imprint of
THOMAS & **L**OCHAR
PO Box 4, Nairn IV12 4HU

With love,
for Carol who
cared enough to make
this book possible.

British Library Cataloguing in Publication Data
Harris, Michael
LNER Carriages
I. Title
625.230942

ISBN 0-946537-98-4

Typeset by XL Publishing Services, Nairn
Printed in Great Britain by
Butler & Tanner, Frome
for Thomas & Lochar
PO Box 4, Nairn IV12 4HU

CONTENTS

PREFACE   6

CHAPTER 1   Building and designing carriages – before Grouping   8

CHAPTER 2   Building and designing carriages – post-Grouping   16

CHAPTER 3   How LNER carriages came to be built   23

CHAPTER 4   The Gresley LNER standard carriage from 1923   32

CHAPTER 5   Gresley vestibuled 61 ft 6 in teak stock for general service   43

CHAPTER 6   Gresley non-vestibuled teak bodied stock   50

CHAPTER 7   East Coast stock from 1923–39   59

CHAPTER 8   GE section special vestibuled stock   73

CHAPTER 9   Gresley catering vehicles   79

CHAPTER 10   Gresley sleeping cars   89

CHAPTER 11   Steel, aluminium and plywood   94

CHAPTER 12   Post-war stock   101

CHAPTER 13   Non-passenger stock, saloons and LNER royal train   111

CHAPTER 14   Numbering schemes   118

APPENDIX 1   List of LNER carriages 1905–1953   121

APPENDIX 2   List of LNER telegraphic codes for passenger stock   157

ACKNOWLEDGEMENTS   158

INDEX   159

PREFACE

IT'S a summer morning in 1949 and we've just come over from Wix in Joe Wade's taxi to Manningtree for the train to London. Instead of the expected train, in comes the Glasgow to Colchester overnight service. We board an almost empty train, and it's like a moving rubbish tip. Impressionable eyes have never seen anything like it. Each carriage is strewn with the detritus of overnight occupation. But the carriages themselves have made an impact, for most are Gresley end door vehicles and they seem to soak up the mess and yet still retain some dignity.

Eleven years later and Manningtree has entered the diesel age. Little has changed and the station keeps its aloof atmosphere, a tranquil if windy outpost in the Dedham Vale, little disturbed other than by stopping and passing trains, the row of conifers complemented by a forest of signals, including the lofty up starter. The youth boards the first up Norwich to Liverpool Street train on a sunny August morning, not unlike the previous one. Behind the diesel locomotive is a Gresley carriage and, yes, I still have the number. It was Diagram 115 side-corridor E12666E, dating from 1938. The slanting sunshine highlights the treacly varnish on the teak panelling in the corridor, as well as the brass window rails, and the carriage travels with that steady, smooth gait that was so characteristic of the Gresley wooden bodied stock.

The third vignette is from a different decade, the date being 1974 and even Manningtree station has begun to change although a few years will elapse before its atmosphere has been lost for good, and the houses and car parks encroach on its surroundings of fields and poplar trees. In comes a London bound train from Norwich and there in the middle of the set of carriages is an old survivor, Gresley buffet car E9131E. Its interior has been tarted up a bit with plastic panelling but not all the characteristics have gone, the noises are still the same as the 37 year old carriage finds jointed track, 'fiddle de dee, fiddle de daa...'

Sentimentality if you like, but the interest in old carriages is bound up with past memories and perhaps they bring to life the numbers and arcane details that accompany the subject. Try as you may but there is not much character to find in today's trains. The mind pictures and smells of past days come flooding back. There was that odour of tea chests that seemed to accompany the teak-built stock. There was the idiosyncratic upholstery, the cherry, floral pattern, the fawn and greeny blue of the horseshoe design and the black, greeny grey and mauve of one of the first-class patterns. There were the aural effects such as the sighing sound produced by the compound bolster bogies when running, not entirely absent from today's railway, and also the screeching that sometimes accompanied heavy braking.

To anyone growing up in the early postwar years the world of the streamline trains was that of what grown ups called peacetime, a lost epoch. When the first edition of this book was being prepared in the 1960s the railway was still rooted in that time. Goodness, some of the Great Northern stations had hardly changed from pre-Grouping days and the procession of night sleepers through York may have had diesel locomotives at their heads but their

departure times had changed little from the heyday of the LNER. In revising the book – and, reader, you have almost a different work in front of you, thanks to the availability of archives that simply were not accessible over twenty years ago – it became clear that the changes between the 1960s and now were greater than those between 'peacetime' and over twenty years ago. More to the point, does it help in trying to assess the rolling stock featured in this work?

The story is dominated by Herbert Nigel Gresley. True, the majority of the vehicles described in this book were influenced by his tenure of offices in the Great Northern Railway and LNER, 36 years' span. But the postwar stock was influenced by the way that Gresley had done things and one can understand why some of his specialities were discarded in the difficult postwar days. There was an almost endless list of real achievements in the field of rolling stock that can be attributed to Gresley – the high speed trains that helped to lay the foundation of the InterCity services of today, apart from being technical marvels in their own right; the development of the compound bolster bogie which remains in service on Network SouthEast; articulation; electric cooking equipment; not least, the application of modern materials and processes in the manufacture of carriages. In the postwar days some of these achievements came to be discredited, in the same way that Gresley specialities on the locomotive side fell into disfavour. Hindsight, I think, enables us to see the true worth of many of them. Many of the specialities were perceived of as expensive, in first cost and maintenance. They were, but they offered advantages and were often the correct solutions. Gresley would have been treated differently in France where greater care with technical standards and maintenance would have ensured that 'the specialities' were given the facilities they needed. The superb competence of so many of the Gresley designed artifacts was only upheld by careful maintenance and plenty of manpower but who is to say that this was wrong and not the shabby and inadequate environment in which the equipment had to function in postwar days? Railway preservation has shown the true worth of the Gresley locomotive designs and suggested that the detractors of their progenitor's work were making excuses to cover their own deficiencies.

Perhaps it is enough to be reminded as Andrew Dow, Head of the National Railway Museum did when I was discussing this book with him that GWR meant something other than a railway with its foundations in London and Bristol: it stands for Gresley Was Right. It was difficult to resist a wry smile when visiting North Pole depot, built to serve the Eurostar super trains for the UK to France and Belgium workings through the Channel Tunnel. For here there are splendid facilities for servicing articulated trains with air conditioning, electric cooking, service of meals to seats, featuring light alloy materials... ... all developments that were championed or adopted by Gresley many years before.

To return to the LNER, many of the other specialities were not necessarily Gresley's in origin but the result of that company's combination of sound commercial judgment and astute understanding of public relations, despite its often impecunious circumstances. These specialities include the high speed trains, Tourist stock, cinema cars, observation cars, hairdressing saloons, the 'Northern Belle', radio on trains. Many were not profitable in themselves but they helped to stimulate the market for travel by the East Coast Route, the LNER seldom losing the opportunity to publicise the East Coast Route!

I have, I hope, given adequate acknowledgement towards the finish of this book to everyone who has helped me in work which has involved a thorough revision of the previous *Gresley's Coaches*, published in 1973 and its expansion to cover new material. One person has my profound gratitude and he is Norman Newsome, author of the renowned paper on Gresley's carriage and wagon design presented to the Institution of Locomotive Engineers in 1948, his work having been drawn upon for material in this book. He was also most helpful in the preparation of the present work and sagely suggested that I should think about changing some aspects of presenting the sequence of designs, as well as contributing much invaluable material.

There are one or two explanations to offer. In writing about the subject, does one talk of carriages or coaches, or prefer vestibules to corridors? The former has been chosen in both cases because that is how the LNER generally referred to them. There is no direct coverage in this work the of steam and diesel railcars operated by the company nor of the other self - propelled vehicles, the electric multiple - units. Something had to give way and whereas in 1973 there was no real reference in print, today there is, in the shape of the admirable *Locomotives of the LNER* Part 10B, published by the RCTS, which covers all these vehicles in detail. Similarly omited are those vehicles of Gresley inspiration built for the Great Northern Railway and East Coast Joint Stock, as well as the GN/NE Joint Stock. Limitations of space mean that no more than a brief mention can be made of the LNER royal train. There must also be an explanation for not including anything but brief mentions of the ranks of preserved LNER design carriages. It is now truly a subject on its own and I can do no better than to refer readers to the excellent work by my friends, John Lloyd and Murray Brown, entitled *Preserved Railway Carriages*, published by Silver Link Publishing Ltd.

It only remains to express the hope that you might find this book of interest and and as enjoyable as it was to write although I trust you will not have to stay awake quite as often until 3 am!

MICHAEL HARRIS
Ottershaw, Surrey 1993

CHAPTER 1
BUILDING AND DESIGNING CARRIAGES – BEFORE GROUPING

Background to design policy

THE requirements for the East Coast Joint Stock had a major influence on the carriage design policy of the Great Northern and North Eastern railway companies as, throughout the period 1880–1920, the ECJS set consistent standards for design and construction. Above all, what was supplied for the ECJS was la crème de la crème.

The provision of joint stock for Anglo-Scottish services originated from a scheme drawn up in June 1860 by the GNR. It was realised that it would be more convenient to maintain special stock for these services which would be paid for in proportion by the GNR, NER and NBR. Each company's share was estimated in proportion to the mileage covered on its metals by through Scottish trains. For the number of vehicles required for the first services in 1861, each railway paid a share of the total cost of that stock: the GNR 47.75%, NER 37.75% and the NBR 14.5%. In 1880, the proportions changed to GNR 40%, NER 35% and NBR 25%.

There was no separate ECJS capital account, and each company managed its share in its own way. For instance, the GNR capital account had a portion allotted to East Coast Joint Stock and when new vehicles were built the GNR (after 1880) contributed 40% of the cost and debited its capital account with that amount. When vehicles were withdrawn from the ECJS fleet, or otherwise disposed of, the GNR took 40% of the total or its equivalent and transferred the value of this 40% to the GNR carriage account. However, the ECJS vehicles stood in the respective companies' account at their original cost and no charge was made for their depreciation.

Until 1893, all ECJS carriages were built by the GNR at Doncaster but the Lancaster Railway Carriage and Wagon

Below Doncaster-built clerestory twelve-wheelers for the East Coast Joint Stock Nos 262–264, constructed in 1896/7. 'Ushered in the modern era of carriages with proper passenger comforts... but... obsolete in something like a decade'.

Company constructed the sets that entered service on the 'Flying Scotsman' in that year and, from then, vehicles were built by Doncaster, the NER's York carriage works and, to a lesser extent, by the North British Railway's Cowlairs Works.

The mid/late 1890s saw the evolution of a common style of twelve-wheeled carriages, 61–65 ft in length and produced at the three constituents' works which the late C. Hamilton Ellis fittingly described as 'Great Northern Decorated'. These vehicles were a triumph in many ways because they ushered in the modern era of carriages with proper passenger comforts but it is a measure of the pace of change in rolling stock design that they were obsolete in something like a decade.

The twelve-wheelers were followed by an experimental period in carriage design on both the GNR and NER, both companies having taken a close look at what was happening in the United States. Not least, this led to the austere, straight-sided ECJS carriages built at York. But a historic and significant meeting of East Coast general managers held in York on 10 November 1905 saw the adoption of the design features associated with the GNR and H.N. Gresley in preference to NER practice. The result was that Doncaster and York products began to conform in all but detail differences, the latter increasingly toeing the line, but not without some reservations, as we shall see in due course. But the participation of the companies in the ECJS was certainly a positive one in the adoption of design innovations such as the elliptical roof, buckeye couplings, steel underframes, electric lighting and steam heating for the railways' stock for internal services. Yet there remained a distinct difference in the characteristics of such internal stock until Grouping when the GNR standards became pre-eminent.

There is a danger of exaggerating the effect that the ECJS had on the carriage design of the East Coast companies when Doncaster and York had strong ideas of their own.

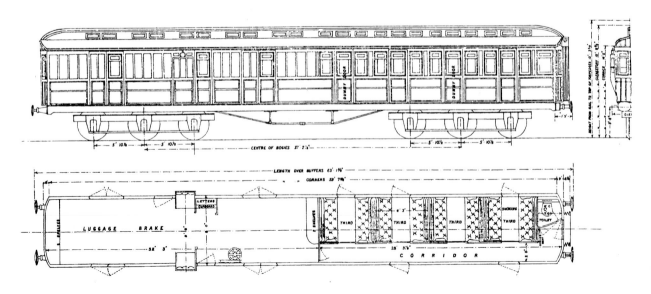

Resentment grew on the grounds that NER preferred practice was being passed over in favour of that originating from Doncaster and championed by Gresley. But this argument was about vestibuled stock and it should be appreciated that the fleet of such vehicles for purely NER services was small, abnormally so for a railway of its size. The Grouping saw the early standardisation of carriage design practice on the LNER and it proved to be much more thorough than was the case on the locomotive side. The different Areas on the LNER may have followed much of the practice of the pre-Grouping companies they succeeded but their managers obediently specified carriages to the Company's standard Gresley designs. That said, the Great Eastern managed a measure of independence until the late 1930s when it came to the length of vestibuled stock. Be that as it may, Gresley was a commanding personality with a particular initiative in carriage design matters and what Kings Cross said, went.

GNR carriage design policy to 1905 and the appointment of Gresley

Although Doncaster was set up as the main works for locomotive and rolling stock construction and repair in 1853, it was not until 1857 that the first Doncaster-built carriages appeared. Up until the late 1870s carriage and wagon design continued to be under the direct control of the locomotive superintendent for design policy, with the builders of carriages having much of the detailed design in their heads and hands. This period had seen the first GNR bogie vehicles built in 1874/5, the adoption of the three-centre round roof as standard from 1876 and the first British restaurant car in 1879, in the shape of the Pullman car (supplied by the Pullman company) that entered service between Kings Cross and Leeds in that year.

The increasing load on the locomotive superintendent led to delegation of rolling stock design and construction in 1877 to the newly appointed carriage and wagon superintendent, E.F. Howlden. Doncaster adopted the Smith vacuum brake in 1879 and introduced the first British side-corridor carriage (ECJS No 176) in 1882. The Gould centre-coupler and gangway were first introduced in 1889, the introduction of centre-gangway sleeping cars being agreed with the NER in 1893. Steam heating was fitted from the early 1890s and, by 1895, there were 209 GNR carriages so equipped. The use of steel for underframes was introduced from about 1902 and belt-driven dynamos from 1900.

Until the mid/late 1890s it is not unfair to say that the general run of GNR carriage design was not of a high standard, particularly when compared with the Midland or GWR, and was somewhat rough and ready. One thing was

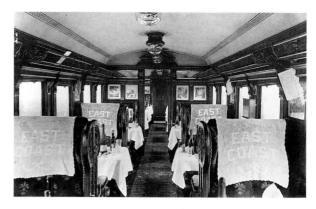

Above Interior of ECJS first-class dining car No 191, built by Lancaster C&W in 1893, 46 ft long over the headstocks and seating 24 diners in two saloons. This, and Nos 190/2/3, constituted the first ECJS bogie stock.

certain: the GNR was distinctly parsimonious when it came to its stock of carriages and we find F.P. Cockshott, the Superintendent of the Line, writing to the General Manager, Henry Oakley in May 1894 saying that at least 100 carriages should be added to stock. Patrick Stirling was both an individualist and reactionary when it came to the design of both locomotives and rolling stock. Writing to Oakley in January 1893 regarding Worsdell's sketches for a new ECJS sleeping car he said: 'I must however enter a strong protest against the bogie principle'. He preferred the rigid eight-wheeler and argued that the maintenance costs of the bogies themselves were excessive. Yet, by July 1895, Stirling had necessarily moved with the times and presented Howlden's designs for the splendid twelve-wheeled clipper-bodied, clerestory-roofed corridor stock, all three trains of which were delivered for East Coast service the following summer. But by then Patrick Stirling had died and the GNR had entered a new era.

That new era came quickly. At the end of the 1880s, even into the early 1890s, Doncaster was producing six-wheeled stock for the ECJS with the three-centre roof. They were technically backward and with undistinguished interior fittings. For this, Patrick Stirling must take responsibility. The nine six-wheeled composite sleeping carriages of 1889-92 with four berths arranged in parallel pairs were 39 ft 9½ in over buffers and weighed just over 15½ tons. But they looked poor alongside the GWR 'bay-window' sleeping cars

Below Elliptical roofed Gresley Doncaster-built brake thirds for the ECJS, EC Dia 49, Nos 97/8, 387–94 of 1908.

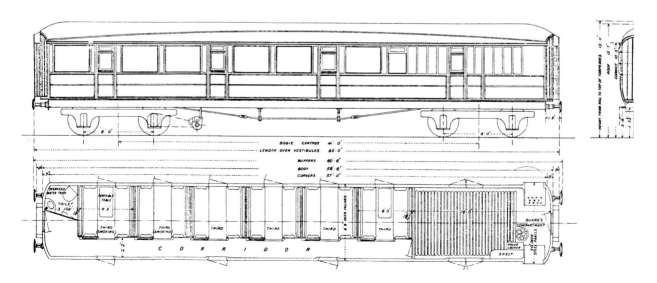

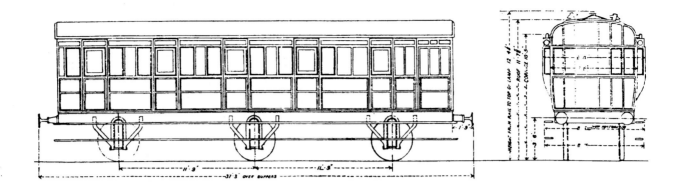

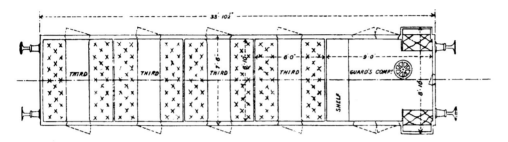

Above Doncaster-built, six-wheeled third-class brake for the East Coast Joint Stock dating from 1883, 'somewhat rough and ready'.

of 1890, for example. The change was to come with the first ECJS vestibuled sets built in 1893 by Lancaster Carriage and Wagon Company, Oldbury Carriage Co and other contractors, and maintained by York. These sets included 46 ft bogie dining cars, indeed the first ECJS bogie stock, but the rest of the vehicles, all gas-lit, were six-wheeled. The bogie vehicles ran on 8 ft wheelbase bogies, soon after adopted by Doncaster for GNR use. The example of the ECJS stock probably resulted in the building at Doncaster from 1895 of bogie carriages similar in general outline and with three-centre roofs.

Stirling tried to get the NER to accept rigid eight-wheelers for ECJS in 1893 but that company would not agree and, though the NER now moved to bogie sleeping cars, the GNR Board went ahead in the same year and approved Stirling's proposal for a corridor six-wheeled sleeping car. Yet, writing to the GNR Board Oakley admitted that 'most modern GNR carriages are not up to modern standard...' The initiative now passed to York so far as design is concerned and, certainly, the dining cars built at Doncaster in 1894 for the afternoon 'Scotsman' owed something to the designs of David Bain, the NER

Below Howlden GNR non-vestibuled brake third No 2589, built at Doncaster in 1897 and influenced in design by the ECJS low-roofed bogie stock of 1893.

carriage superintendent. When it was decided in 1895 to build new rolling stock for the '10 o'clocks', as they were usually known rather than the 'Flying Scotsman', the meeting of East Coast managers held on 20 June 1895 and chaired by Oakley came up with specifications that stood comparison with any others in Britain. These were for twelve-wheeled bogie stock, with bodies between 60–65 ft, clipper-built and with clerestories, corridor connections throughout the train and centre vestibules and sliding doors to the compartments. Meetings held by the East Coast managers in July 1895 took matters further and Howlden prepared something like three sets of drawings before satisfaction was reached. On 22 August 1895, Stirling was told by Oakley that he was 'to get on with the stock at once', the former having said that he could build all the three sets of carriages required for the summer 1896 service. By any standards this was an achievement and in view of Stirling's conservatism no less than a transformation in the way of doing things at Doncaster. The press run of the new stock took place on 29 June 1896, with two GNR dining cars attached to serve lunch. The return run was with two of the new NER-designed and built transverse sleeping cars added to the formation. It constituted an impressive step forward in the progress of the East Coast services. The new stock had Gould gangway connections and Gould automatic couplers.

From these came the 1900/1 stock for the Leeds service: all twelve-wheelers of 62–65 ft in length, with Gould couplers, Pullman gangways and with all third-class

accommodation in open saloons. H.A. Ivatt had led a party of other railways' officials to the United States in the spring of 1899. in the same way that this influenced GNR locomotive practice, the experience confirmed the decisions to adopt Pullman gangways, buckeye couplers and so on. A total of 79 generically very similar vehicles appeared for the ECJS services in 1902/3, built at Doncaster, York and Cowlairs. The basic design was produced by Howlden and, from this time, the appearance of the carriages was altered by extending the quarterlights up to the cant-rail. The York vehicles featured larger windows, producing a more harmonious and modern appearance. ECJS requirements for general service were met by vehicles to these general specifications turned out by Doncaster up until 1905. The very last examples were 64 ft 2½ in body composite diners Nos 196/7 and 352/3 and 65 ft 4¼ in length composite brake No 23. Yet York was once more moving ahead as stock built by the NER in 1904 for the ECJS comprised day and sleeping vehicles with elliptical roofs and flat, matchboarded bodysides.

In such a short time, the clerestoried twelve-wheelers had become obsolescent. Handsome externally, if overdecorated internally, they made up some of the most impressive trains in Europe. Headed by GNR or NER Atlantics they must have presented a truly satisfying spectacle. But obsolescent they were: they were neither mechanically efficient nor did they make the best use of their internal space. interior decor was not the equal of the contemporary Midland stock, for example. For its 65 ft length and 36 tons, the five-compartment brake composite No 23 of 1905 seated only 26 passengers in none too spacious seating. The underframes and headstocks of these carriages were wooden and the bracing and trussing were inadequate. Gresley writing to Raven in February 1919 characterised these twelve-wheelers as: 'expensive to maintain, very heavy and out of date'. He was, he said, very much in favour of scrapping all but the dining and sleeping cars and drew attention to their small lavatories and excessive luggage space in relation to the passengers carried. During 1918-20 a number were reconditioned, modernised internally and mounted on four-wheeled bogies. But sufficient has been said to show that radical changes were needed once more to bring GNR passenger

Above ECJS vestibuled locker third No 13, built at York in 1898 and seen in 1925 as transferred to GN section stock as No 41810. Sister vehicle No 12 is preserved in the National Collection.

stock to the same excellence as the company's locomotive design.

Very soon after his appointment in March 1905 as carriage and wagon superintendent, Gresley must have decided on a fresh approach to Doncaster's contribution to carriage design. The prototype carriage was a corridor composite No 2977 which featured the elliptical roof, electric lighting and the combination of side-corridor and saloon accommodation found in a number of GNR Gresley vehicles. in all probability it was originally to be built with a clerestory roof. First it had to be confirmed that elliptical roofed stock met the loading gauge of the East Coast companies and special gauging clearance runs were made between Kings Cross, Edinburgh and Aberdeen, and to Mallaig, in July and September 1905. The scene was being set for the evolution of the Gresley elliptical roofed carriage that was to be a feature of the East Coast main line for half a century or more. At this stage it is worth digressing to review the GNR's carriage building facilities at Doncaster.

Doncaster Works and carriages

The main carriage building shop at Doncaster Works was opened as a separate entity in 1889, the wagon works moving to Carr in 1890. The West carriage shop was brought into use in 1897 with alterations made in 1901 and 1913. This shop had two large overhead cranes. in 1913 the carriage building and repair facilities were grouped in three areas. The offices were in the long building adjacent to the station. The trimming shop was a continuation of the offices. Immediately behind the offices, adjacent to and north of the loco shops, was the sawmill 384 ft long and 132 ft wide. To the west of this shop lay the log-yard and timber drying sheds. The carriage building shop, part of the same block of buildings, was 300 ft long and 199 ft wide and had

Below Generally reckoned to be the first ordinary service elliptical roofed carriage built at Doncaster for the GNR, Dia 102 composite No 2977, with side corridor first-class accommodation and two third-class saloons.

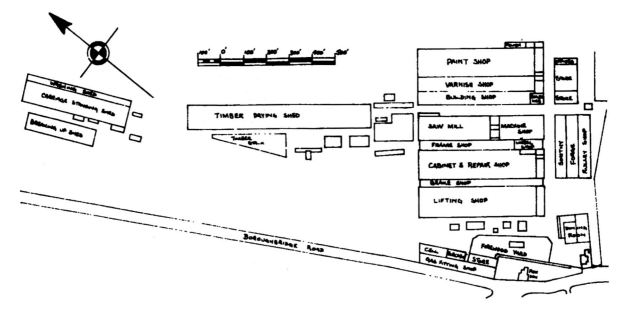

12 roads; a 60ft traverser was installed in 1906. Here the bodywork was constructed and lifted on to underframes which had been fabricated in the loco shops. The paint shop, a continuation of this same block, was 264 ft long and 180 ft wide and could stable 44 carriages on its twelve roads.

Alongside the River Don lay the West carriage shop, 593 ft long and 182 ft wide. This dealt with carriage repairs and was grouped into woodworking and lifting areas. in all, 24 bogie carriages and 48 six-wheelers could be accommodated. Finally, at the extreme north of the works, was the North carriage shed, 380 ft long and 110 ft wide with eight roads. Varnishing and light running repairs were handled there in addition to carriage washing facilities. Until the early 1960s the East Coast royal train was stabled in this shed.

The layout of Doncaster Works was reasonably modern and compact. in the same way that Churchward had modernised the machinery in the works at Swindon, so in 1913 Doncaster was equipped with all-electric machines. Nevertheless, the carriage works' facilities were primarily those of a woodworking factory, relying on the loco works and outside contractors for steel forgings and sections. By 1913, the 'Plant' as a whole covered 200 acres and employed 4,600 people. On the carriage side at maximum capacity it could construct 100 carriages annually and give 3,000 various categories of repair. But maximum capacity was not reached in the years before Grouping.

GNR carriage design from 1905
Returning to the appearance of the first Gresley carriages,

the standard was set by the Sheffield Stock sets of 1906 in terms of exterior design and a simplicity of interior finish. Both marked the departure from the overblown furnishings and style of the previous decade as well as representing Gresley's distinctive contributions to carriage design.

Carriage-builders were established craftsman in the early days of the century and, to a slowly decreasing degree, this remained until the onset of the mass-building techniques which came in with the aftermath of World War 2. Apart from the fact that the individual carriage was, in the days of small batches, very much a one-off job, the carriage-builders had no mean influence on the layout of the bodywork. The Doncaster carriage drawing office was small – and, as had become the case from Howlden's aegis, increasingly independent of the locomotive side – so Gresley was able to exert his influence effectively.

Over the next ten years, the Gresley carriage matured in design. Two important decisions had been reached in 1905. The Traffic Committee recommended that all new dining and sleeping cars should be fitted with electric lighting and, towards the end of the year, advocated that all new GNR carriages should be electrically-lit. This coincided with the meeting of the East Coast general managers at York on 10 November 1905 when various matters connected with the building of ECJS vehicles were considered and, to quote, 'it was agreed to adopt elliptical roofs curved downwards at the end, and curved side panels as a standard pattern for the future.' This was essentially a description of the GNR Gresley carriage which had now made its appearance.

There was a major building programme for ECJS stock in prospect. It had been discussed at least as early as March 1905. At the meeting of East Coast managers on 28 July 1905 it was minuted that: 'The GN representative would not agree to vehicles with matchboard sides, or elliptical roofs, unless constructed with sloping ends as present East

Coast clerestory stock.' So the outcome of the November 1905 meeting was not really too surprising!

So far as the archetypal Gresley carriage was concerned, there was the Gresley development of the Spencer-Moulton compound-bolster bogie which was increasingly used for GNR and ECJS stock from 1908. But one of Gresley's most distinctive developments was articulation and it was employed with varying success from 1907 until the last articulated carriages appeared during World War 2. As early as 1914, Gresley considered an all-steel carriage and possibly he was influenced by the increasing number of all-steel vehicles in the United States. The Pennsylvania Railroad had standardised on all-steel cars from August 1906 and, by 1912, some 2,000 were in service. But Gresley was not to move to all-steel stock, despite the construction of a number of vehicles during the late 1920s, and in his time on the LNER the teak-bodied carriage with a steel underframe was never seriously challenged. One of Gresley's alleged remarks was that he could design an all-steel carriage that would protect everyone in a collision but not the engine to pull it. in the last years up to the outbreak of World War 1 there were no particular developments of note in carriage design at Doncaster. More of interest was to come after 1919 with O.V.S. Bulleid's appointment as assistant carriage and wagon superintendent and the subsequent appearance of the Leeds quintuplet set and the twin-articulated sleeping cars for the ECJS.

In retrospect, the vestibuled carriages built at Doncaster for GNR service from 1907 onwards are curiously varied, with an often disconcerting lack of standardisation and widely differing dimensions. However, the chief mechanical engineer was not responsible for specifying which types should be ordered to meet the demands for new stock. That was the job of the passenger managers and operating staffs and they tended to think in terms of replacing like for like and the specific requirements of particular train services to be supplied with new stock.

NER design policy until 1922

The York carriage works was set up in 1880 on a site between Leeman Road and Poppleton Road and adjacent to the latter. The main design offices and chief mechanical engineer's headquarters were situated at Gateshead until 1910 and were then transferred to Darlington.

In the 1890s David Bain was the carriage and wagon superintendent. The standard NER carriage of the 1880s was a six-wheeled vehicle, but by 1895 clerestory bogie stock was produced in 45 ft and 52 ft lengths, together with 49 ft low-roof carriages. We have already seen how in the mid/late 1890s NER-built carriages for the ECJS were ahead of GNR practice and the Lancaster-built dining cars in the 1893 10 o'clocks are said to have been credited to Wilson Worsdell, the NER Locomotive Superintendent. He was certainly responsible for the five handsome clerestoried sleeping cars with transverse berths built at York in 1895/6. The 23 carriages built at York for the afternoon Scotsman sets in 1902 were to Howlden's designs.

With an eye on American practice, the stock built by the NER for the Tyneside electrification in 1903 had teak matchboarded lower body panels and slab sides. Elliptical roofed carriages with the straight sides and matchboard panelling were produced by York as the NER contribution to the new ECJS sets turned out for the summer 1905 timetable and also in the shape of dining cars for the GN/NE train set later the same year. in addition, there were three sleeping cars to the same slab-sided, high arched roof profile. They were not a brilliant exercise in carriage design. Though the corridors were wide, the compartments were somewhat cramped and it cannot be said that their appearance was anything but grim. The matchboarding was difficult to keep clean and no cheaper than large body panels but without their strength.

Above Spring flowers in the first-class dining car of the GNR Quintuplet set, photographed in LNER days. The Quintuplet for the Leeds service went into service in 1921.

The GNR's feelings about these NER vehicles has been recorded already and subsequently the York-built stock for the ECJS assumed more conventional lines; despite overall similarity, there were detail differences from the Doncaster product. Apart from ECJS requirements, the NER produced some very handsome sets for the Newcastle – Liverpool and Leeds – Glasgow services. These vehicles were of 53 ft 6 in body length – 65 ft for the restaurant cars – and had electric lighting and British Standard gangways. in comparison with the GNR stock, the bodies had a sleeker appearance, the roof was to a different more rounded profile and the bodyside mouldings and windows had radiussed corners. J.D. Twinberrow, chief draughtsman at Gateshead works, tried without success to obtain support for building ECJS stock with doors at the end vestibules only but was told by Raven in September that 'the Traffic people will not agree not to put doors in the compartments of corridor carriages.' Twinberrrow had cogently argued that the abolition of such doors would allow the body sides to be constructed with greater strength and with reduced weight and cost. This effectively illustrates the constraints placed on the engineers by the traffic departments.

In 1906 the 53 ft 6 in body stock built at York for the ECJS was the first not to have timber in the underframes except for the headstocks. The next year an all-steel underframe was introduced as buckeye couplers could be more easily incorporated and the headstock was also much stronger. Among the standard types of NER carriages built in the 1910s were the ubiquitous 49 ft semi-elliptical roofed compartment thirds with gas lighting, the 52 ft lavatory composites of the same general outline and 53 ft 6 in body corridor firsts and thirds with electric lighting. All these types ran on 8 ft wheelbase pressed-steel bogies. Their external appearance was characterised by wide-radiussed body mouldings and rounded corners to the windows. They looked neat and modern and indeed were built to much the same features up to and after Grouping.

Perhaps the most interesting York-built carriages of the period were the three all-steel kitchen cars deigned by Raven for the 1914 'Flying Scotsman' sets. As at that stage it was considered, to quote: 'difficult to procure sufficient current for efficient electrical cooking', the continued use of gas dictated fireproof construction, or as near as it was possible, with steel rolled angles, channels and T-sections for body

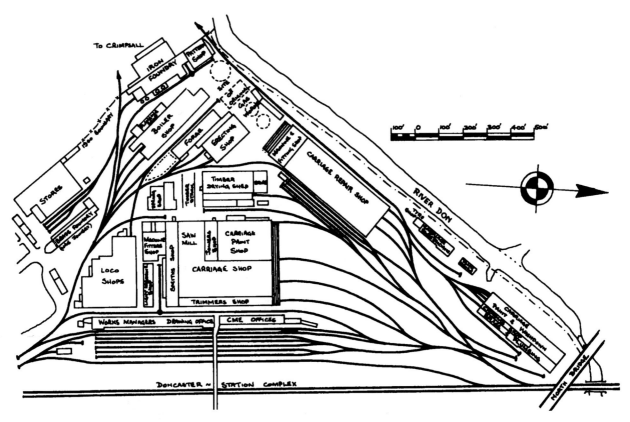

Above The layout of Doncaster Plant, after the alterations of 1913.

framing to which rolled steel plate was riveted. All flooring was of steel plating riveted to the underframe members. A penalty was paid with the tare weight of 36 tons for each vehicle but in view of public concern at the danger of fire on trains at the time, it was unavoidable.

Although the standard LNER Gresley carriage designs were produced so soon after Grouping there was construction of pre-Grouping designs, particularly of NER types, into 1925 under the 1923 Carriage Building Programme. in all, over 100 carriages were built at York in this way for other Areas. The 49 ft non-corridor vehicles were built for

Below York-built semi-open first for the ECJS – Nos 92 and 121 of December 1905. The NER's austere slab-sided, match-boarded design for elliptical roofed vehicles. The LNER transferred them from East Coast stock to the GN section.

the Southern Scottish Area and three types of the 53 ft 6 in corridor stock for the Great Eastern section – composites, thirds and brake thirds. This was in response for the GE's insistence on less than 61 ft 6 in carriages for general main line service, their requirement subsequently being met by the 52 ft 6 in vehicles otherwise to Gresley LNER standard. A limited number of NER corridor vehicles was also built for the Southern Scottish Area.

By 1908, the NER's carriage fleet was as follows:

	Bogie stock	Four/six wheeled stock	Total
Ordinary train sets	1,391	Nil	1,391
Excursion stock, spares, float carriages	183	2,365	2,548

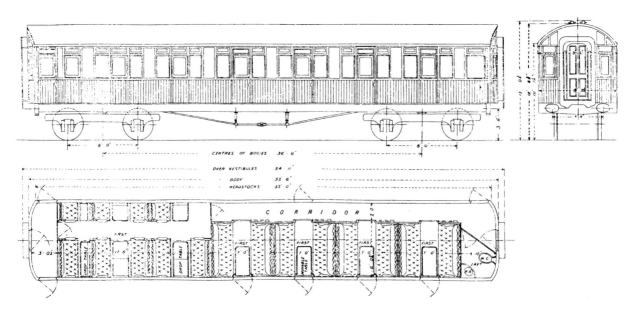

It reflected well on the NER as all scheduled trains were normally worked by bogie stock, although of the total less than 10% of the bogie carriages were vestibuled.

As to York Works, its maximum capacity for new construction was given in 1908 as 200 bogie vehicles annually, but in the years before World War 1 production never exceeded 80–90 carriages. in the heyday of British railways here was an instance of renewal programmes being slowed down, at a time when the book life of a carriage was taken as 28 years. Most of those built in this period at York lasted considerably longer. The York Works wages staff comprised 1,578 persons in December 1913, of whom 230 were engaged on new construction, the rest on repairs. Heaton (Walker Gate) employed about 120 men on heavy repairs but this category of work was transferred to York in 1935/6.

Other constituents

Though the pioneer of a number of passenger carriage innovations, at Grouping the Great Eastern Railway had nothing remarkable to contribute towards the new organisation in terms of design. There was nothing wrong with the neat and well-finished corridor stock, generally to a 50 ft length before 1914 and 54 ft thereafter. Many vehicles had been appropriated for wartime ambulance train service and their reconversion occupied the early postwar years. The North Eastern Area received two open thirds converted from such vehicles as part of the 1924 Carriage Building Programme. Construction of 54 ft suburban stock for the Ilford services continued at Stratford into 1923/4 and this marked the end of the Stratford designed carriages. At the very end of 1922, the GER approached the NER with a view to York Works building these eight-car suburban sets and, in their offer, the NER proposed changes to the design to facilitate production. The rolling stock contractors would have taken a dim view of such manufacture for a third party. Stratford Works continued to build carriages after Grouping but to LNER standard designs, both for its home section and for other Areas. Such work ceased after 1927 and the workshops were re-equipped in 1931 to serve as the major repair centre for GE section rolling stock, continuing as such until 1963.

The Great Central Railway's passenger stock was generally of 53–56 ft lengths, of conventional and handsome appearance and substantial in construction. Again, the immediate activity before Grouping was in the rehabilitation of former ambulance train vehicles. After the completion of outstanding orders for pre-1923 designs to complete Great Central section requirements, the works at Dukinfield turned to building to LNER standard designs. Dukinfield had been opened in 1906 and covered an area of 29½ acres where some 1,400 workers were employed. Facilities included a 700 ft by 60ft underframe shop, a bogie erecting shop and other main shops equipped with relatively modern tools and a 66 ft traverser. The capacity for overhauls was in the range of 400 carriages annually. New construction and heavy repair work ceased after 1939.

As regards the Scottish companies, the North British Railway produced no designs of particular note between 1919 and 1923, apart from the five massive Cravens-built twelve-wheeled steel restaurant cars of 1919; in railway terms these had a short life, being withdrawn in 1938/9. As on the locomotive side, new designs were probably vetoed after 1921, and in 1923 there was no new construction in hand at Cowlairs.

The Great North of Scotland Railway was latterly noted for its neat, low-roof carriages with toplights above the

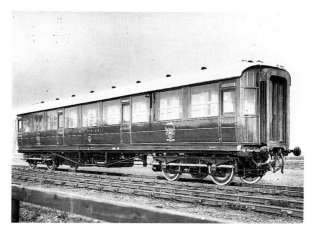

Top No 24, a York-built vestibuled third for the ECJS, dating from 1906. There were a number of differences between the Doncaster and York-built elliptical roofed vehicles for the ECJS, as explained in the text.

Above The GER was exercised before Grouping with the replacement of stock for the suburban services, such as this eight-coach train for the Ilford/Shenfield services, seen leaving Gidea Park for Liverpool Street behind 'N7' 0–6–2T No 69729 in October 1949 when there was mixed steam/electric working on this service.

windows. There were four thirds and four bogie brakes of this 48 ft type being built at inverurie Works in 1922/3 and they followed pre-1914 practice. Carriage building ceased at this establishment after their completion.

In summary, it was hardly surprising that Doncaster and York were to be the dominant centres as far as rolling stock was concerned in the newly formed LNER. Both had the experience of producing a full range of types for a variety of services and had the maximum of resources. The requirements of the ECJS had served to test the design staff and carriage-builders at the respective drawing offices and works. Yet, bearing in mind the outcome of battle of wills, as it sometimes seemed to be, between the GNR and the NER on the subject of ECJS design and building practices, and the fact that Gresley was now chief mechanical engineer, the direction that the LNER would take on carriage design was not in much doubt.

CHAPTER 2
BUILDING AND DESIGNING CARRIAGES – POST-GROUPING

On Grouping

THE LNER set up its general headquarters at Marylebone, but only a limited number of staff was based at these offices and, for example, the chief mechanical engineer's offices were at Kings Cross station. The new company's approach was not dissimilar to some modern management practices as its wide-flung railway empire was effectively decentralised in terms of day to day management, by retaining much of the identity of the constituent companies so far as the operating and traffic functions were concerned. Under the Chief General Manager, R.L. Wedgwood (recipient of a knighthood in 1924), there were four divisional general managers, each responsible for what was called an Area, the Southern Area being divided into two, with the divisional offices at Liverpool Street, York and Edinburgh.

Below Detail shot of vestibule brake third E16525 (Dia 178, built 1940 and originally No 57456). The E suffix is missing from the number while the G of its GE allocation, a short-lived feature of the early 1960s, has been excised. This close-up shows well the panelling, beading and roof profile of the standard Gresley vehicle, in this case awaiting its final journey, at Tring in 1967.

The result was as follows:

Southern Area	-Western	Great Central section (former GCR)
		Great Northern section (former GNR)
	-Eastern	Great Eastern section (former GER)
North Eastern Area		(former NER and Hull & Barnsley Railway)
Southern Scottish Area		(former NBR)
Northern Scottish Area		(former GNoSR)

The two Scottish Areas were later amalgamated

In this book, for easy reference the various entities will be referred to as the GC, GN and GE sections; the North Eastern Area; and Southern and Northern Scottish Areas. As described in Chapter 14, in dealing with numbering, each 'entity' was treated equally in terms of controlling its own passenger stock allocation.

From July 1921, the traffic superintendents and passenger managers from all the constituent companies, and including initially the Hull & Barnsley Railway, had met in committee to make recommendations on issues

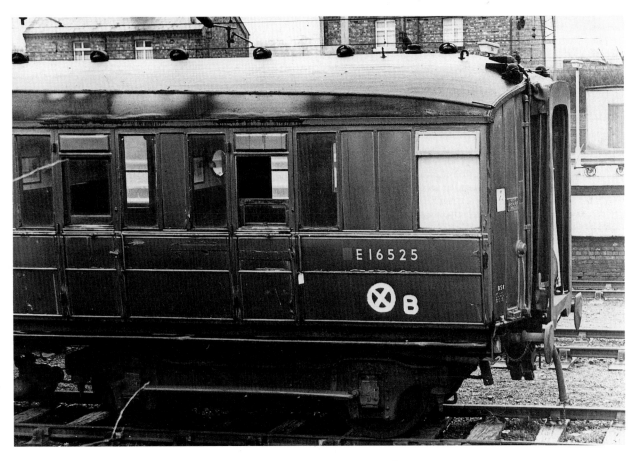

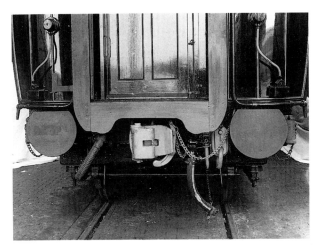

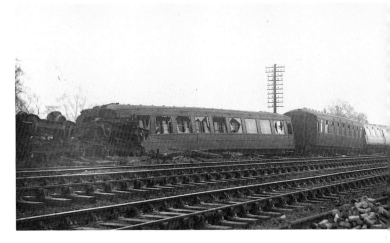

affecting passenger services and passenger rolling stock. The significance of their deliberations as members of the Superintendents' and Passenger Managers' Committee which met monthly from November 1922 until late 1947 is described in Chapter 3.The point of mentioning it now is to record that at the meeting on 2/3 January 1923 it was resolved that there should be no central control for rolling stock.

If highlighting this decision seems either prosaic or incidental, then the impression is false. It is not possible to understand how the LNER's policies towards passenger stock functioned without appreciating that each Area or section controlled its own vehicles and had an important say in the creation of the annual Carriage Building Programmes. The individual Area maintained the vehicles on its allocation. East Coast stock was controlled by the Southern Area but vehicles were designated for maintenance by Doncaster or York. Strictly speaking, carriages were not to be borrowed by other Areas but it did happen, and Area stock was routinely used at peak periods to augment East Coast sets, a state of affairs not rectified until after 1936 with the building of additional East Coast sets. The central distribution of coaching stock was not apparently discussed again until 1939 and the result was to reverse the decision of 1923 and establish all-line control. The abolition of the Area organisation came in August 1942, with the establishment of a central rolling stock control office at York, presided over by a rolling stock controller. It was this change almost as much as the retirement of Sir Ralph Wedgwood and the death in office of Sir Nigel Gresley and, indeed, the outbreak of World War 2, that marked a watershed in the passenger stock policy of the LNER.

Gresley as CME

After appointment as Chief Mechanical Engineer of the LNER in February 1923, Gresley established his office at Kings Cross station from the April of that year. O.V.S. Bulleid accompanied him as his personal assistant. Personnel from the NER's chief mechanical officer's department did not hold any position of great influence in the new company: Sir Vincent Raven became technical adviser but resigned in 1924 and although A.C. Stamer remained at Darlington, his title of principal assistant did not in fact give him the influence enjoyed by Bulleid. At Kings Cross, Bulleid assumed much responsibility for the carriage and wagon side.

In earlier days, the Kings Cross office had the job of co-ordinating work between the various works' drawing offices but, in 1936, Gresley set up the Central Drawing Office at Doncaster and all new design work was done there, the other works' establishments dealing with detail and residual matters. What has been described as the 'Gresley team' sums up the way in which operations

Above left The buffing gear, buckeye coupler and gangway face-plate of a Gresley vestibule carriage. The buffers are in the retracted position and the buffer sleeves stowed away.

Above right The aftermath of the Hatfield derailment of November 1946 with Dia 155 vestibule third No 1355 nearest. The Castlecary accident of 1937 was the occasion for an examination of the design strength of the standard Gresley teak bodied vehicles.

worked and emphasises the dominance of the former GNR/Doncaster influences. in his close friendship with, and support for Gresley, Sir Ralph Wedgwood did much to champion the latter's ideas and ensure the supremacy of the Kings Cross office. Norman Newsome expands on the managerial style of the LNER thus: 'One of the reasons why everything worked so well on the LNER of the time was that there was very close liaison between Gresley and the other chief officers.'

Of the coaching stock – including carriage trucks and horseboxes – 21,000 vehicles came under the CME's control in 1923 and of these 3,950 were electrically-lit carriages. Within the overall total were many four and six-wheeled carriages and some very poor vehicles could be counted among their ranks. in addition, the backlog of repairs resulting from the effects of World War 1 had to be overcome. Very soon after Grouping a series of standard carriage designs was evolved and these feature in more detail within Chapter 4. These designs for corridor and non-corridor stock lasted, with detailed modifications until 1941, seemingly because they served the purposes of the commercial and operating departments. in addition, a number of other designs were introduced progressively, such as the end-door corridor vehicles initially for East Coast service only but then built more generally. Yet the older standard designs continued to be specified.

By 1939, the Southern Railway was the only other member of Britain's 'Big Four' still building corridor vehicles with outer doors to the compartments. The LNER was certainly alone in continuing to build carriages with all-wooden bodies at this time. The LNER's policy in this respect was summed up in a letter received by the author in 1973 from T. Henry Turner, who had been Chief Chemist of the LNER. He said: 'Teak with multiple coats of first-class varnish wore well for many years. The old-fashioned teak carriages were safe in derailments because of the sturdy centre couplings of their welded steel frames. They were also quieter than modern all-metal carriages.' He went on to say, although I have no other confirmation of this, that 'in the 1930s we thought of having a crack train from Sheffield to London with carriages of stainless steel. But in the days before the Clean Air Act those carriages would have looked dirty.'

The practice of building teak bodied carriages was subjected to scrutiny by Lt-Col Mount, the inspecting

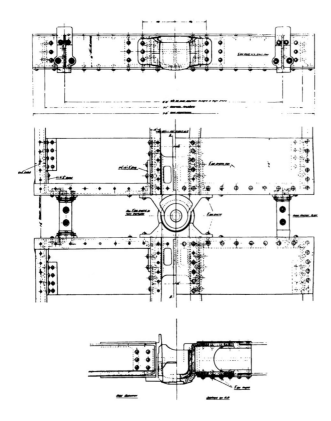

Above The twin coupler of LNER articulated stock, in this case the riveted version standardised from 1927/8 in which the coupler was secured to the headstock and longitudinal members by rivets, instead of by bolts as formerly.

Below The body of open third brake No 1738 of the high-speed stock (Dia 231) is lowered into position on the articulation bogie. Note the head-shaped bracket on No 1738 ready to engage with the cup-like chamber on No 1737, these being the major components of the twin coupler.

Officer at the inquiry into the extraordinarily destructive accident at Castlecary on 10 December 1937 when an Edinburgh–Glasgow express collided at speed with a stationary Dundee–Glasgow train, with the loss of 35 lives. Mount commented on current public criticism of wooden bodied stock but accepted the case advanced in Gresley's evidence to the accident inquiry that the shock of the collision was absorbed by steel underframe, buffing, drawgear and the Pullman type vestibule. He noted that the underframes and couplers of the modern Gresley vehicles had resisted telescoping. Mount accepted Gresley's view that a comparable collision between two trains of all-steel stock might not have prevented casualties. Noting Gresley's argument that for equal weight body framing of steel was not likely to be so strong as 'a massive teak structure', the inspecting Officer foresaw the day when high-tensile steels and welding might make possible lightweight all-steel construction; indeed such vehicles were being built in Britain by manufacturers such as 'English Electric'. Possibly an accident such as Castlecary might have prompted more critical comment on the teak bodied vehicles had it occurred a few years later. The inspecting Officer inquiring into the derailment at Goswick in 1947 pointedly stated 'my impression is that steel-panelled carriages are appreciably less liable to cause injury than timber panelled bodies'.

Gresley had looked at other means of constructing carriage bodies and as early as 1914 had proposed an all-steel vehicle. But it was doubtless the policy of the company that there should be teak-bodied and varnished stock for general service and, to that extent the CME had to provide what was specified. That was certainly true given the number of different designs for standard brake and composite carriages. These resulted from the operators specifying vehicles to suit the requirements of particular services or trains, frequently on a one-for-one basis as replacements of older vehicles. This practice served to encourage time-honoured ways of doing things and no doubt was frustrating for the CME and his able team, backed by resourceful and efficient main works.

None of the other 'Big Four' companies' CME depart-

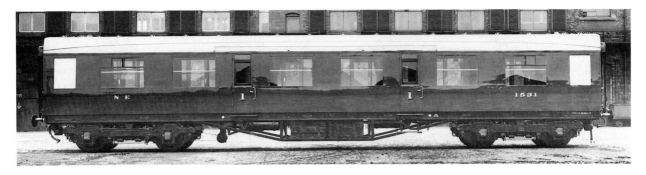

ments approached what Gresley and the LNER did in the way of innovations in the design of passenger carriages. Yet there are puzzles that serve to intrigue today. If teak-bodied carriages were the standard because they were the LNER's trademark, why were the high-speed trains of 1935–37 provided with steel-panelled stock? Why was so much effort and money spent on painting steel-panelled vehicles in fully grained paintwork to resemble teak? Why indeed were such vehicles steel-panelled at all if teak was the standard? Perhaps the answers are lost in the mists of time. What cannot be denied is that the LNER spent much of its existence watching its cashflow very carefully with the consequence that new construction was approved only after careful deliberation. Much effort went into sound housekeeping – watching what was spent – and equal attention paid to getting the detail right.

With the many inspired and important developments in rolling stock design inaugurated during the Gresley era, there were also what were known, even at Doncaster Works in the 1960s, as 'Mr Gresley's specialities'. Of these perhaps the most original was the articulation of passenger carriages. At a lecture to a railway debating society in 1928 Gresley explained that articulation originated from criticism he had had to face in 1907 or so from Lord Allerton, chairman of the GNR, as regards the poor-riding qualities of six-wheeled ECJS vehicles. There was no case for scrapping them and the only solution was articulation, placing the two bodies on three bogies. Gresley gave the following advantages for articulation: a saving in weight; lower first cost than two vehicles riding on four bogies; improved riding; less rolling resistance and greater safety in telescoping. All of these claims were – and are today – justifiable. in some applications, notably the suburban and high-speed trains, they were realised most successfully. However, maintenance costs and operating difficulties were increased by articulation. Gresley's system of articulation was protected by a patent accepted by the Patent Office in his name, No 4512 of 1908.

'I always felt that Gresley overdid articulation', comments Norman Newsome, 'it would have been better just restricted to twin-articulated vehicles. The savings in weight and cost were debatable. in the case of a triplet restaurant car set, so much weight was carried on the articulation bogie that both bogie and underframe had to be stronger, and the axles of larger diameter. There was often an unavoidable disparity between the weight of the bodies resting on the articulation bogies, particularly in the case of a restaurant car twin where one body had the kitchen with its extra weight.' While the manuscript of this book was being prepared, the North Pole international depot for the cross-Channel Eurostar trains was completed and it was possible to look at the facilities. There was an intriguing link with Sir Nigel Gresley and he LNER when the depot manager explained the maintenance procedures for dealing with – a fleet of *articulated* trains!

As to the other Gresley specialities, one must mention electric cooking, nowadays standard in catering vehicles, and the admirable application of pressure ventilation and double glazing to prestige stock. There were the

Above The prototype Newton vestibule carriage, first No 1531, outshopped in January 1945 and entering service the same month. The square shaped opaque windows on the corridor side were unique to this vehicle. Note also the abbreviated 'NE' and the compound bolster bogies, later examples of the first series of Newton or Thompson vestibuled stock had the all-welded single bolster bogies.

compound bolster bogies of Gresley design, still in British Rail service in the 1990s, and the use of aluminium and plastics relatively early in the world of transport. When collecting material for this book in the 1960s and more recently, one was struck by the continuing affection and respect for Sir Nigel Gresley. He has been described as an autocrat, but few who knew him ever doubted his professionalism and skill. A real esprit de corps distinguished the Gresley team.

Postwar developments

The LNER began its postwar development planning from January 1942, with the setting-up of the LNER Postwar Development Committee and a report was submitted to the Emergency Board of the LNER in September 1943. This did not consider rolling stock in detail, but as noted in Chapter 12 it set out guiding principles for postwar construction. The next step was in May 1944 at a meeting of the Emergency Board of the LNER directors when it was reported by the Chief General Manager that wartime losses and the deferred withdrawal programme meant that the postwar carriage building programme would have to make provision for the construction of 4,000–4,500 vehicles. in November 1944, the Chief General Manager, Sir Charles Newton set out proposals to the Emergency Board for postwar construction involving the building of 4,600 vehicles over a period of three years. The proposals intimated that postwar passenger carriages would be very different from what had gone before, Newton commenting that: 'Shortage of suitable timber will preclude our continuing our prewar construction of vehicles with timber bodies on steel underframes'. However, he believed that the first year's construction under the new programme would see vehicles built of the timber on hand, supplemented with steel. Thereafter, 'output will be in the form of vehicles principally constructed of steel.' Newton's report then went into detail on the characteristics of the new generation of LNER passenger stock.` Most of the features outlined by Newton were embodied in the prototype for postwar construction, Corridor First No 1531, built in early 1945 and sometimes referred to as the 'Newton coach'.

The initial calculations for postwar construction were considered by the Joint Meeting of the Locomotive and Traffic Committee in October 1945 which proposed an increased five-year building programme to begin in 1946 which would provide for the building of 5,500 vehicles, the majority by contractors. However, the LNER had to accept that the government's insistence that export orders must have priority and that only 3,400 carriages could be supplied by contractors over a three-year period.

With the emergence of No 1531, the LNER solicited

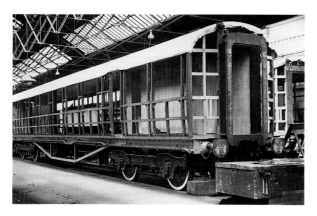

Above A Tourist stock buffet car under construction at York Works during 1933 and, from the chalked numbers on the solebars, the future No 43512 (Dia 168, later No 9146). Note the straight end to the roof, the teak body framing, oak body end members and roof canvas nailed down.

the advice of its passengers with the production of *Design for Comfort*, a brochure circulated widely to passengers during the latter part of 1945 and asking them to comment on the features of No 1531 and on aspects of rolling stock design generally. There were twelve questions for passengers to answer and they were asked to return the questionnaire to the Company. There was a healthy response to *Design for Comfort*. The LNER's postwar 'manifesto' *Forward the LNER*, distributed in 1946, set out the company's five-year plan for rolling stock construction, commenting that 'the LNER is in a particularly difficult position since both its York and Doncaster carriage shops have been destroyed by fire.' But *Forward the LNER* said that new carriages are coming into service and that 'they will follow a new design which was evolved in 1945'.

At this stage, it was still hoped to build all-steel passenger stock, but the realities of the postwar world soon became apparent. The quantities of new stock that the LNER was seeking to have constructed – and in view of the difficulties at its own works the majority would have to be ordered from outside contractors – were unacceptable to the Ministry of War Transport which considered the LNER's requirements to be in excess of its allocation of new vehicle construction. What then ensued was frustrating for all concerned as the Ministry intervened in the contractual negotiations between the company and the contractors. Add to this the prevailing shortages and delays, the limited allocation of steel supplies and the need to substitute alternative materials and something of the atmosphere of the times emerges. The postwar vehicles, sometimes referred to as Thompson stock, were inevitably a compromise, particularly when it came to their interior decor and fittings and the need to retain composite timber

Below Pressure ventilated first E1306E built to Dia 332 in 1949 for the 'Junior Scotsman', the close-up emphasising the solebar fairing which was painted black. At Hull, 1965.

and steel construction.

With the passing of the LNER, existing orders for new construction to existing or modified designs were gradually fulfilled until the large-scale manufacture of the BR standard passenger stock after 1951. These new vehicles were of the all-steel construction the LNER had intended for its postwar standard carriages and a few of the company's features were embodied in the BR stock, such the buckeye couplers and gangways, seat profiles, some interior fittings and the use of anthracite-electric cooking equipment in the first series of catering vehicles. Notably, though, the underframe design, compound-bolster bogies and pattern of lighting equipment were passed over in favour of other Big Four companies' practices.

Production facilities 1923 – 1944
In July 1923, the Locomotive Committee reviewed the LNER's facilities for new construction and reported that the annual capacity for new coaching stock build was 200 at York, 200 at Doncaster and 150 at Dukinfield. No figure was recorded for Stratford although the works was soon involved in the building of standard LNER vehicles. Even with the ample facilities at the LNER's disposal, there were periods of exceptional demand in the late 1920s and late 1930s when there was recourse on a large-scale to outside rolling stock contractors, particularly for suburban stock and general service corridor vehicles. Contractors were necessarily involved after wartime fires affected production at both York and Doncaster.

To improve facilities at York, the main shops were reorganised during 1924 and the old varnishing shop used for new construction. Much new woodworking machinery was also installed. During 1925 Cowlairs shops were equipped for the first time with overhead cranes. From 1928 both Stratford and Dukinfield were organised for the progressive repair of carriages, the main emphasis being on the installation of modern lifting gear and improved reception facilities for stock awaiting attention. This brought notable benefits. At Stratford, for instance, after modernisation the number of vehicles awaiting or under repair was reduced by 50%. Coincidentally, Stratford ceased the construction of new carriages, leaving York, Doncaster and Dukinfield to handle this work, the general division of labour being that Doncaster concentrated on the special stock including the high-speed trains and catering vehicles, York on general service corridor stock and Dukinfield on non-corridor carriages and passenger brake vans. From the mid-1930s there were initiatives to reduce construction costs and use new manufacturing techniques, both York and Doncaster being equipped with arc welding plant for the production of welded underframes.

Until 1936 Heaton (Walker Gate) handled heavy repair work but thereafter this category of work for North Eastern Area stock was concentrated at York, although Walker Gate continued to handle carriage repair work until 1964. With reorganisation and the installation of new traversers among other improvements, York's annual capacity for heavy overhauls was increased to 1,200 vehicles. To accommodate this throughput, forging and stamping work was transferred to Shildon wagon works. After 1939 new construction was discontinued at Dukinfield. This was one result of a report by Edward Thompson dating from March of the same year. Among his recommendations were that heavy repair work at Dukinfield should be transferred to Doncaster as costs at the former GCR works were 'considerably higher', and that general service stock maintenance should continue to be divided between York and Doncaster. However, the latter would lose some of its throughput to its northern neighbour and concentrate on dining and special stock, in preference to York. Stratford should, Thompson recommended, continue to maintain GE section stock, as the shops had been modernised extensively in 1931 and the cost of repair work compared favourably with elsewhere. After October 1936 Stratford took on the maintenance of carriage stock from the former Midland & Great Northern Joint Railway .

In 1939, and before the changes recommended by Thompson, the allocation of carriage repairs at the LNER work was as shown below , Thompson's proposals giving the revised figures shown in brackets. Whether those changes were fully implemented is unknown, given the imminence of war.

	General service passenger carriages	Dining cars,s pecialand high-speed stock	Total
York	3,449 (5,939)	117 (Nil)	3,566 (5,939)
Doncaster	2,490 (1,780)	232 (375)	2,722 (2,155)
Dukinfield	1,780 (Nil)	26 (Nil)	1,806 (Nil)

Both Doncaster and York Works were badly affected by fires, both being accidental and not as the result of enemy action. The fire at Doncaster occurred on 21 December 1940 and destroyed the main carriage building shop and the sawmill, £18,000 worth of stock being destroyed. Before long, work resumed in the shop but on wartime aircraft work. The carriage building shop was reconstructed from 1947 and was ready in 1949, together with accompanying sawmill; in the meantime the paint shop had been used for new construction although it had no overhead cranes. At York the carriage building shop was destroyed by fire in 1944 and its replacement, opened in 1947, was planned for the progressive building of carriages; until it was ready, the paint shop was used for new work. To supplement the two major works, Darlington became involved in some carriage activity during the early postwar years.

In 1946/7 the allocation of carriage repairs to the works was as follows:

Works	Allocation (approx) of coaching stock for repairs
Doncaster	2,484 + 266 Cheshire Lines Committee vehicles
Dukinfield	Light repairs only
Stratford	3,018 + 110 M&GN section

York	3,763
Cowlairs	2,254
Inverurie	No allocation but some heavy repairs carried out.

The former LNER works continued much as before until the publication in 1962 of the Mitchell committee's report on the future of the BR workshops , as a result of which Stratford carriage works closed from the latter part of 1963, with Dukinfield (by postwar days usually referred to as Gorton) and Cowlairs following soon after. Although initially scheduled to remain, inverurie closed in 1969. By 1970, with the formation of British Rail Engineering Ltd, only York of the former LNER works remained as a major coaching stock building centre, a role it retains today under the management of ABB Transportation Ltd.

Methods of building LNER carriages

What follows is primarily based on the procedure for teak-bodied standard stock and is derived from two excellent articles that appeared in the *LNER Magazine*, information supplied by Norman Newsome and from carriage-builders at York Works interviewed in the mid-1960s.

Until about 1926 when York was reorganised and re-equipped for the production of LNER standard stock, each gang in the building shop would work on a single vehicle, assembling all the woodwork and carrying out all fitting. Carriage-building was a craft in those days in that each man was required to be conversant with the complete structure of the carriage. Clearly this method was time-consuming and expensive when it came to major building programmes. After 1926 York moved to sectionalised construction and separate gangs were allocated to partic-ular parts and tasks. Opinion is that this in fact required far more accurate work in order for the independently assem-

Below 'A4' 4–6–2 No 2512 *Silver Fox* on the up 'Flying Scotsman' near Hatfield, the train formed of the 1938 stock for that train with the triplet restaurant car set fourth, fifth and sixth in the train. The effect of the alternate sliding ventilators on the corridor side in the later end-door stock will be noted, the 'Flying Scotsman' sets being marshalled so that the compartment side of the carriages faced east.

bled sections to fit properly.

At this time the underframe shop could lay down five 60 ft or seven 51 ft standard underframes and these would be turned out complete in one and a half to two days. The gangs assembled separate units, then riveted the underframe and fitted the drawgear. After lifting on to the bogies the underframe went forward to the body building shop; the bogie frames and wheels were purchased from outside suppliers. The sawmill was adapted for quantity production to the extent that parts were made to templates on woodworking machines which worked in repetition once they were set up. Teak predominated for these items and comprised 40% of all timber used in the carriage bodies.

Sectionalised construction reduced the timescale from laying the floor of the carriage to its leaving the works from five and a half weeks to two and a half. Doors, partitions, body ends, quarters (body panel sections), seat frames and frame backs were built up by separate gangs. The quarters were partly panelled and fitted with the glass lights before going to the erecting gangs. The floors were built straight on to the underframes and the same gang also dealt with the cant-rails. The erecting gangs received the underframes with the floors fitted and on which the ends, quarters and partitions had already been laid out, each part then being lifted into position for fixing. At the same time, the corridor screens – where applicable – were put in position, having been made in the cabinet shop. The final stage in the building shop was the assembly of the roof and the laying of the electric wiring.

After this, the body and underframe were sent into the cabinet shop for the mouldings, interior doors, droplights and photograph frames to be fitted. The last assembly stage was for the brake shop to receive the vehicle for pipe fitting and heaters, lavatory plumbing and vestibules to be added. After a sojourn in the paint shop for as long as three weeks, the carriage was returned to the cabinet shop for the interior fittings to be finished and items such as the upholstered seats, linoleum and door handles to be added. in all its glory, and after inspection, the completed vehicle was sent on a test run. This sequence of construction was current at York in 1928.

But improvements on this system were possible and in 1931, under the direction of A.H. Peppercorn, what was called progressive building was introduced. The earlier principles of sectionalised construction were extended to the manufacture of the body assembly, roof building and door hanging. Production was reorganised into 'stations', at each of which there was a gang of men undertaking a single function, the carriage being moved along the running road to the different 'stations' until ready for varnishing. Seven 60 ft carriages could be accommodated on the building road as it was called, and there were seven 'stations'. At each 'station', platforms were provided at working height to replace the old method of working from trestles and planks. Here something of the influence of mass production in the motor car industry can be seen and the result for the LNER was that production time was reduced by as much as 30% on the previous system. Before the underframe was moved into the building shop it was fitted out with brake gear, heating pipes and electrical equipment.

The seven stages of construction comprised:
1. Underframe from brake shop. Floor framing put on.
2. Fitting of complete ends – panelled, moulded and part-varnished. Quarters, cant-rails, partitions, bottom-quarters added. Some interior fittings put in place.
3. Roof irons, roof sticks, end sloping sections of the roof made up on a jig. Roof boarded, screwed and painted to receive covering. Lavatory tanks and suspension gear for vestibules put in place.
4. Roof canvas fitted, along with roof fittings. Complete corridor screens installed. Lavatory boarded. Wiring, interior ceilings and partitions into position, having been received in finished state.
5. Outer doors – interchangeable – received complete and hung in position. interior door runs put in place. Lavatory completed, together with steam heating fittings in the compartments. Vestibule face-plates fitted.
6. Body given one coat of varnish. Electric light fittings and ventilators installed. Compartment photographs fitted.
7. Communication cord fitted. Body given final coat of varnish. Upholstered seats in place.

Much the same procedures applied for the construction of standard stock until the appearance of the last teak-bodied vehicles. There were changes such as the simplification of interior finish from the late 1920s and various modifications to the specification of standard stock from 1934 which reduced construction costs. This seems to have preceded the move to all-welded underframes from 1934. The steel-panelled stock was not materially different in the methods of assembly.

With the postwar stock some changes were made with the full introduction of progressive building, both York and Doncaster having new building shops as a result of the wartime fires at both works. Extensive use was made of jigs, with the bodyside quarters built on a jig and dropped into position on the bottomside. Even in these years there were detailed differences in the building practices at Doncaster and York. But the major change came with the large-scale construction of the all-steel BR standard stock which was constructed at Doncaster and York Works after 1951.

Production of LNER coaching stock 1923 – 1944

Year	Built by LNER		Built by contractors	
	A	B	A	B
1923	203	110	–	–
1924	247	171	–	–
1925	248	387	353	–
1926	174	41	139	–
1927	201	108	206	8
1928	201	270	23	26
1929	217	344	118	–
1930	202	298	56	–
1931	110	107	33	–
1932	53	12	–	–
1933	81	94	40	–
1934	246	109	24	–
1935	339	17	308	–
1936	354	341	304	–
1937	309	218	235	–
1938	327	263	384	446
1939	286	856	96	554
1940	179	34	–	–
1941	74	32	–	–
1942	56	5	–	–
1943	25	32	–	–
1944	–	6	–	–
TOTALS	4,132	3,855	2,319	1,034

Notes   A – Passenger carrying vehicles including kitchen cars and electric multiple-units
        B – Other coaching stock

CHAPTER 3
HOW LNER CARRIAGES CAME TO BE BUILT

WHATEVER the stature of the chief mechanical engineer, the decision to construct particular types of locomotives or rolling stock was not his responsibility. It was usually as a result of the recommendations by one or more committee dominated by traffic or commercial officers and approved by the main board of directors. in the case of the LNER, it is instructive to see that the chief mechanical engineer was not always present or represented at some of the meetings when major decisions were reached regarding the provision of new rolling stock. Nonetheless, given Gresley's close liaison with the other chief officers of the company, it is unlikely that he was ever unaware of items with particular implications for the work of his department.

The Superintendents and Passenger Managers

In the previous chapter the work of the Superintendents' and Passenger Managers' Committee was mentioned. This committee was convened before Grouping and its first meeting took place on 14 July 1921, attended by representatives from the Eastern group of companies. At the meeting of 21 November 1922, the representatives sent their proposals for the carriages they wished to see completed in 1923 and, so the minutes record, 'urged that the special attention of the general managers should be called to the necessity for a thorough renovation of the East Coast Joint Stock which has been allowed to get into such a bad state that strong complaints are being received from the travelling public'. This indeed set the tone for the majority of succeeding annual building programmes as the financial affairs of the LNER were often such that the new construction was limited to the renewal of the East Coast stock and little else. With Viscount Grey in the chair, the February 1923 meeting of the Traffic Committee recommended to the Board a Carriage Building Programme for the twelve months from 1 April 1923. This provided for the building of stock costed at £545,893 and identified the construction of two twin sleeping cars and six single sleeping cars for the East Coast stock, together with the repair of the underframes and bogie bolsters of 28 clerestory carriages.

In addition to the annual building programme for new coaching stock, hereafter referred to as the Carriage Building Programme or CBP, the SPMs were concerned with much of the day-to-day policy matters regarding the operation of passenger services, including timetabling and the use, deployment and rebuilding of carriage stock. Their deliberations during 1923 were concerned with the establishment of standards for the newly formed LNER and its passenger stock, not least the exterior finish of the carriages, their numbering and control. There was also the matter of interior fittings such as window blinds, seat reservation plates, wash-basins and window ventilators. But the role of the SPMs was clearly apparent at their meeting on 13 November 1923 when they made recommendations about the dimensions of the standard stock and, meeting a fortnight later, developed their theme by putting forward proposals for new stock to be included in the 1924 CBP and the braking systems to be fitted to these vehicles; at this stage of course the LNER had air and vacuum braking in use on more than one section.

The specification of new designs

At their 30 November 1923 meeting, the SPMs signed the drawings for seven of the standard LNER designs of vestibuled and non-vestibuled stock: open first, corridor first, corridor composite, corridor third, non-vestibuled first, n-v third and n-v composite. The SPMs specified the type of vehicles required. If a new design was required, a diagram was produced by the CME's office, having been before the CME for comment, and then it would be approved in correspondence with the SPMs. They tended to refer to the original designs they knew well so that in

Below The booster-fitted 'C1' 4–4–2 No 4419 heads a down express north of Wood Green in 1931. The leading vehicle of its train is a Dia 23 or 115 vestibule third, followed by an ex GNR vehicle. Alongside is 'N2' 0–6–2T No 4744 on a train for New Barnet. Of particular interest on the Hertford loop flyover is what seems to be an excursion set, consisting of clerestory dining car No 42996 and two all-steel open thirds to Dia 28, one identifiable as No 42464, the visible lining out disguising its non-teak body.

Bottom The 1923 CBP included vehicles to pre-Grouping designs such as this open third to NE Dia 155, No 2945 built in 1924. It is seen as a departmental work study office DE 320716 in 1973, before acquisition for preservation.

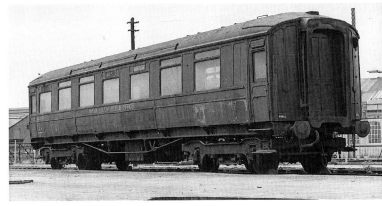

later years they were specifying stock to 1923 standard diagram numbers when in fact a more recent diagram had been produced already incorporating detail differences to the design! The SPMs specified the number of compartments or van space required in particular vehicles that were proposed for construction in a CBP. If there was no suitable existing design, then the CME would prepare a new diagram. Because stock was often specified for a particular service, often as a one for one replacement, there were frequently very small batches completed in a year to a particular diagram, something that was certainly the case with composite and brake composite carriages for through workings.

The SPM meetings were attended by the Superintendents and Managers from the Areas and the chair was taken for a year at a time by one of their number. There were also meetings of the SPMs' representatives who might meet to consider a specific issue or to review a regular procedure such as the annual renovation of East Coast stock vehicles. The main meetings were also attended, as appropriate, by a representative from the CME's office or by a representative of the Hotels Department. Norman Newsome recalls: 'It was a happy and efficient arrangement. Everyone was brought into the discussions, even if they were not at the meeting'. Keeping a close watch over the working of the SPMs' committee was the chief general manager who would advise the chairman of the issues he would like them to consider, as well as commenting on recommendations set out in the minutes of their meetings. in this way, the LNER dealt with its passenger train service and stock matters and provided for new rolling stock.

The preparation of the building programmes
The actual procedure for the annual CBP was instigated by the CME in that he produced a programme for the withdrawal of stock in the coming year, usually on the basis of the renewals of passenger vehicles after 40 years and other coaching stock after 33 years. The withdrawal programme included a calculation of the number of seats (in the withdrawn vehicles) to be 'lost' as a result of the condemnation of the old vehicles, together with the CME's proposals for new stock. A comprehensive statement was then completed by the SPMs which set out the requirements for the building of new stock in the following year, running from 1 April to 31 March the following year; from 1934 the CBP was altered to the calendar year, starting on 1 January. in fact, the Depression had seen the CBP for 1931/2 extended to 15 months, then to 21 months – to 31 December 1932 – and the limited 1933 CBP begin on 1 January.

The statement prepared for the forthcoming CBP comprised a set of forms which detailed the overall programme, the total number of seats in LNER carriages at the conclusion of the CBP and comparing this with the total in 1913, the particulars of the types of vehicle being sought, the justification for building the new stock, details of the East Coast stock released for transfer to the Areas and a statement on passenger traffic figures. Having worked from the CME's breaking up programme, a sub-committee of the SPM committee prepared the CBP which went for consideration at a special SPM meeting at which the CME was present or represented. Then the final recommendation went to the chief general manager (CGM). The CGM then reported on the CBP to the joint meeting of the Locomotive and Traffic Committee, chaired for much of the LNER's existence by the Chairman of the Board of Directors, William Whitelaw. The CBP was then approved or otherwise amended, or referred to another committee if there were questions of finance. The justification for new stock was usually on the lines that existing vehicles were no longer suitable – or

compared unfavourably with LMS stock – or that traffic was being lost for want of particular types of vehicle, or that there were opportunities for new business.

The calculation as to the number of seats available – and indeed number of carriages – at the end of the CBP meant that the principle behind new building was to match seats for seats and perhaps was used as an argument to gain more carriages. From the early 1930s, as the closure of rural branch line proceeded, it was realised that the need for fewer carriages corresponded with a reduction in the overall total of seats. However, as the breaking up programmes continued through the worst years of the Depression, there was concern at a net loss in the number of seats. To those who might argue that the number of seats was no indication of the effective utilisation of carriage stock, the SPMs pointed out that from the mid-1930s passenger traffic was increasing both in volume and in the revenue generated. However, the calculation in terms of seats led to a situation in the mid-1930s when the SPMs wanted more vehicles than seemed necessary at first sight as higher capacity non-vestibuled stock was being replaced usually by vestibuled vehicles. Their concern was whether enough seats – and therefore carriages – would be available for the start of the summer timetable each year but this was hardly a way of improving the utilisation of carriages. By 1939 that seems to have become clear to the LNER's senior management as Wedgwood commented to the SPMs in the March of that year that the central control of freight stock had been in being for some years with marked success and he felt that more intensive use should be possible with the central distribution of coaching stock. This central control office with a rolling stock controller was delayed in its introduction by the outbreak of World War 2 but was in operation at York by 1942. From this all-line control of coaching stock came the complete renumbering of vehicles from 1943. Effectively these changes reduced the importance of the SPMs' committee as far as the control of and specification of new carriages was concerned.

The Carriage Building Programmes 1923–1948
What was proposed as a CBP by the SPM Committee what not necessarily what came to be built although the changes made to their proposals were not always clear. Some of the discrepancies between what was recommended to the Board and what was actually constructed are difficult to explain while there were many instances of vehicles on the previous year's programme not being completed until the next year. What now follows is a brief overview of the CBPs, the intention being to place the construction of both standard and special stock into perspective. Full details of the vehicles will be found in the Appendix.

1923/4 CBP

This represented the summation of the constituent companies' proposals for new construction in 1923 and the completion of their outstanding orders for 1922, except that three batches of standard NER design non-corridor carriages were built for the Southern Scottish Area. There were no carriages to LNER standard designs in the programme.

1924/5 CBP

As presented by the CGM to the Joint Meeting of the Locomotive and Traffic Committee held on 13 December 1923 this comprised 767 vehicles at a total cost of £1.76 million, including a supplementary programme constituting 21 triplets for the GN section and 28 quintuplets for the GE section. This was approved with the exception of the GN suburban stock which was deferred, on the grounds that electrification of the GN suburban lines was being considered. The CBP's main features included the first standard LNER designs, not least over 100 vehicles to

re-equip the East Coast sets. Other priorities were for the Newcastle–South Wales set, the Continental boat train sets, and a number of NER-design carriages for the Southern Scottish Area and for the GE section.

1925/6 CBP

This was similarly significant, comprising 521 vehicles and relied on outside contractors for the major part of its completion. The programme included a large number of non-vestibuled carriages for the London suburban services and North Eastern and Southern Scottish Areas as well as vestibuled stock for most of the Areas and for the replacement of the Continental boat trains. in due course it was amended to substitute bogie vans for some of the six-wheeled vehicles originally proposed. By June 1925 101 vehicles were deferred, the majority of these being vans and horseboxes but also including 13 East Coast carriages. The CGM recommended the reductions 'in view of the present financial situation and falling traffic receipts'. This had doubtless influenced the decision later in the year by the LNER directors that 'they could not pledge themselves to adopt the proposal for the electrification of the GN section suburban lines.'

1926/7 CBP

As approved by the JLT Committee in January 1926, this provided for the building of 545 vehicles, nearly 50% to be ordered from contractors and including a large number of suburban articulated trains and non-vestibuled carriages. It was noted that the Hotels Department was considering the comparative costs of gas and electric cooking for restaurant cars. By July 1926, the industrial disruption of that year influenced the transfer of 145 vehicles to the

Below Newly outshopped GN section quadart set No 86, probably at Stratford in the early 1960s when the overhead electrification warning plates began to be applied. Nearest the camera is Dia 72 brake second (formerly brake third) E86312E, dating from 1927. The renewal of the inner suburban stock for the GN and GE sections absorbed much of the LNER's available investment in the 1920s.

Above 'D49/1' 4–4–0 No 2755 *Berkshire* on a Southern Scottish Area express c 1930. Its train comprises a set of standard LNER Gresley vehicles. The Southern Scottish Area received a number of sets for the Edinburgh–Glasgow service and other principal services from the late 1920s.

1927/8 CBP, principally vestibuled stock and 12 sets of quadruplets.

1927/8 CBP

This took in some but not all the deferred vestibuled vehicles from the 1926/7 programme and also included three triplet restaurant car sets for the East Coast and for the GN in its total of 259 coaching stock vehicles. Not least it included the provision of charging facilities at a number of locations for restaurant cars with electric cooking equipment.

1928/9 CBP

Principally concerned with the building of quadruplet and quintuplet sets for the GN and GE sections but also including 100 vestibuled carriages, seven restaurant cars with electric cooking and two triplet restaurant car sets for the East Coast. Cost of programme included 50% of the cost of 50 Sentinel steam railcars and all the cost of eight trailers. Further electric charging points for catering cars.

A memo from the CGM was submitted to the JLTC regarding the condition of rolling stock on the GE section and, in arguing that main line trains 'should be made more attractive' in view of road competition, proposed that 30 vestibuled carriages should be built by contractors for Liverpool Street–Cromer expresses in advance of stock in the agreed programme, with electric charging plant installed at Cromer. Proposals recommended to the Board on February 1928.

With the decision by the LNER, LMS and GWR to run 'as an experiment' third-class sleeping cars from September 1928, sixteen of the 48 corridor thirds in the 1928/9 CBP were approved for construction as convertible third-class sleepers. Twelve further third-class sleepers approved in advance of the 1929/30 CBP.

1929/30 CBP

This comprised 279 passenger vehicles for the replacement of 405 withdrawn and 32 vans and milk tanks. included were sixteen non-vestibuled twins, ten suburban quad sets and four quint sets. The programme included 50% of the cost of 31 Sentinel railcars as well as the 12 third-class sleeping cars already approved. These and the succeeding third-class sleeping cars were charged to capital account.

1930/1 CBP

As approved, this comprised 280 carriages to replace 369 condemned. Of the new build no less than 108 were

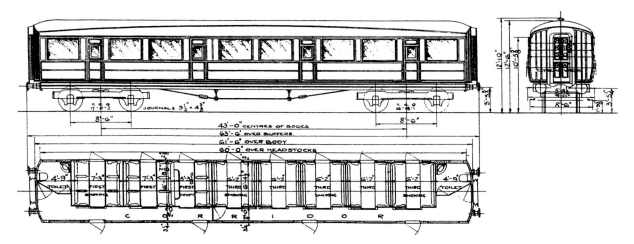

Above LNER Diagram Book: vestibule composite to Dia 137, built from 1930–40, showing the five third-class compartments, two first-class compartments and a first-class coupé. Later vehicles had intermediate armrests.

vestibuled thirds and 53 vestibuled brake thirds. The programme did not include suburban stock as it was said that this was influenced by current proposals to electrify the GN and GE suburban services.

The majority of the vestibuled carriages were for the East Coast, to replace the two sets used for the 'Flying Scotsman'; the GE section, principally on the Norwich service; the GN section, to provide a new set for the 5.45 pm Kings Cross–Leeds/Bradford; for the North Eastern Area, to make up the Leeds–Glasgow express and associated workings, to increase the proportion of vestibuled carriages in the North Eastern Area allocation and to reduce the use of non-vestibuled stock on reliefs to main line services and, for the Southern Scottish Area, to be used between Edinburgh and Glasgow, and York–Edinburgh–Perth, the latter to alternate with a new North Eastern Area set. The new East Coast sets would see the transfer of some of the 1924/5 thirds to the GC and

GN sections, indicating how the LNER 'cascaded' stock from the Anglo-Scottish trains to front-line service elsewhere.

By February 1930 the CGM reported to the Traffic Committee that 'it may be some time' before a decision was made on the question of electrifying the GN and GE suburban lines and so the replacement of old stock must be considered. As a result, the breaking up of GNR and GER four-wheelers was deferred, new construction being limited to two trains of quintuplets for the Enfield line of the GE section.

The programme was not completed within 1930 as at the end of the year there remained 180 vehicles still outstanding, as well as three from the 1929 CBP. This balance was taken forward into the 1931/2 CBP whose currency was extended to 30 June 1932 in order to keep the charge to revenue within the average annual figure in recent years.

1931/2 CBP

As originally drafted by the SPMs this proposed the construction of over 400 vehicles and was intended to provide new vestibuled sets for Liverpool–Hull, Newcastle–Bournemouth, Cleethorpes and Leicester–Manchester, Harwich–Liverpool and GE Cambridge and Clacton line expresses; the 4 pm Kings Cross–Newcastle and for Newcastle–Liverpool; Newcastle–South Wales; Edinburgh–Glasgow and Aberdeen and Edinburgh–St Pancras. Also contemplated were two quad sets for the GE Hertford line; twins to work Kings Cross–Doncaster slow trains and a number of twins

Below TPO sorting van No 2156 to Dia 164 (later 70291) under construction at York Works during 1933 when carriage building had resumed in earnest after the suspension during 1932. Note that panelling of some of the framing in position had commenced. The construction of modern TPOs was agreed with the Post Office during 1932; at that time the 1929 vans were the only post World War 1 TPOs in LNER stock.

to cover GN local services in Lincolnshire. It was also suggested that existing six-wheeled stock in the Northern Scottish area should be made up into six articulated triplets.

This CBP did not materialise in the form at first proposed by the SPMs, later being modified by the committee including the provision of ten first and 22 third end-door corridor thirds for the East Coast sets 'in view of the improved stock which the LMS is using in important services', the displaced vehicles being allocated to Areas in place of new build. Reductions were made before a revised CBP was considered at the Joint LTC meeting of 8 January 1931 which approved the fifteen-month programme mentioned above. This took in the vehicles outstanding from the earlier CBPs and was reduced to a total of 271 carriages and 41 brake vans. The programme included the first 66 ft 6 in first-class and third-class sleeping cars and also the composite twin-sleepers.

In May 1931 the 1931/2 programme was extended to the end of December. It was again reviewed in June 1932 when, as an economy measure, new building to the value of some £271,250 was cancelled. Worse was to follow in August 1932 when, in order to save expenditure, all carriage building was suspended. in early October 1932, of the 249 carriages and passenger brake vans outstanding or sanctioned since 1 January, only 43 had been completed to early September. What remained under construction at the end of 1932 was carried forward to the 1933 CBP.

1933 CBP

Because of the suspension of the extended 1931/2 CBP, the SPMs were told that there was no point in drawing up a 1933 CBP at the usual time. At the start of 1933 a CBP was approved by the Joint LTC on the basis mentioned above – that the outstanding orders should be completed from the previous CBP. The programme's expenditure was capped at £600,000 and comprised 218 vehicles, all ordinary carriages or vans with the exception of three catering cars. in addition, it was agreed to build five trains of Tourist stock, in part replacement of GNR four-wheelers that had been used for excursions. During the suspension of building the condemnation of old stock had continued so that the stock of vehicles declined from 14,100 in 1924 to 12,800 at the end of 1932.

A limited number of vehicles were renewed outside of the CBPs such as the three carriages – corridor brake third, corridor brake composite and restaurant first – built in 1931/2 for the Southern Scottish Area in replacement of stock lost in the Carlisle accident of 3 January 1931, also the third and two corridor composites built for the GE section in 1933 to replace GER corridor vehicles fire-damaged at Stratford in July 1931, the cost of building being charged to the LNER's Fire insurance Fund. From 1932, a number of buffet car conversions from former GNR, NER, GER and GN/NE open thirds were approved by the Traffic Committee.

In each of the years 1933 to 1938 inclusive, the Traffic Committee approved and the Locomotive Committee confirmed the conversion of carriages as camping coaches.

1934 CBP

The reduction in the coaching stock fleet was felt during the summer of 1933 as traffic began to make a slow recovery from the Depression. It was 'essential that some new building be urgently undertaken in order to cater satisfactorily for the traffic offering even at the 1933 level' said the CGM in a memo to the Joint LTC when that committee came to consider the 1934 CBP. One or two other oddments were picked up such as vehicles part-completed under the 1931/2 CBP but set aside and the seven TPO vans authorised in June 1932; in the case of the latter the LNER's share of the cost was not included until

Above NER 'A2' 4–6–2 No 2403 *City of Durham* on an up principal East Coast express, possibly the afternoon 'Scotsman', near Eryholme in 1929. A triplet restaurant car set makes up the third, fourth and fifth vehicles in the train while further down is an all-steel van.

the 1934 CBP.

With the suspension of new construction accompanied by the continuing condemnation of stock, a backlog had built up and the so the first draft 1934 CBP produced by the SPMs was accordingly extensive. The CGM commented as follows: 'The cost of the carriages totals £2 million in the scheme before you whereas in the prosperous year of 1929 we actually spent only £715,000... the largest since amalgamation. I am afraid the Committee cannot profitably discuss a programme which is going to cost more than £750,000'.

So the SPMs had to draw in their horns and a £750,000 CBP was sent forward with the following assumptions: new stock for East Coast, two Tourist train sets for the North Eastern Area, new stock for Areas only where there were no suitable vehicles for transfer from the East Coast such as for new sets for Cromer and Clacton express sets, 14 new catering vehicles, four first-class sleeping cars and articulated stock for GN outer suburban services. Even this was at first only partly authorised through the Joint LTC but a way out was found with a proposal by Gresley that savings could be made on construction costs.

But the improvement in the company's revenue position meant that better days lay ahead. On 13 February 1934, Wedgwood chaired a meeting of LNER officers at Kings Cross with the aim of stimulating further increased business with the following precept: 'Each succeeding year should show some improvement in the matter of passenger train facilities'. He made it clear that he was prepared to consider expenditure to renovate and retrim existing stock, that intermediate armrests should be fitted in vehicles on Kings Cross–Aberdeen services without delay and that the building of new restaurant cars in the 1934 CBP should be brought forward.

1935 CBP

The first draft from the SPMs was for a programme costed at £1.93 million but the chief accountant of the LNER said that the building programme must be revised to £700,000. The CGM appreciated the problem and warned the Joint LTC that a supplementary building programme might be necessary. At the same time the CME was told to retain vehicles otherwise scheduled for condemnation if they were out of date rather than in poor condition.

There was no doubt that some of the carriage stock of the LNER was in dire need of renewal. A special meeting was held in the Board room at Kings Cross on 6

Above 'A3' 4–6–2 No 2504 *Sandwich* passes Harringay with a down express in the late 1930s. The train consists of at least three portions, one of which was the leading vestibuled brake composite, a number of which were built for the GN section in the late 1930s.

November 1934 with Gresley as chairman. This was to consider the replacement of all four and six-wheeled stock by the end of 1936 except for 'third-rate branch lines, miners' and workmen's trains'. On completion of the 1934 breaking up programme there would still be 247 four-wheeled and 2,632 six-wheeled carriages.

Taking the Areas and sections in turn, the position was as follows:

North Eastern Area: No four- or six-wheeled stock. Some 600 non-vestibuled carriages were available for transfer to other Areas, for replacement by new vestibuled stock.
GE section: Four-wheeled stock being broken up. Some 130 six-wheeled carriages in booked workings, 250 bogie vestibuled carriages required to replace loose stock and 500 non-vestibuled carriages needed.
GC section: After the 1934 breaking up programme was complete, there would still be 588 six-wheeled carriages of which 276 would be in booked workings. Would require 180 non-vestibuled carriages for set workings and 180 loose.
GN section: There would be 527 six-wheeled carriages left after the 1934 breaking up programme and the section would need 320 bogie carriages in their place.
Southern Scottish Area: Of the 272 six-wheelers, 78 were in booked workings. Would in replacement require 50 non-vestibuled bogies for sets and 80 vestibuled and 60 non-vestibuled carriages loose.
Northern Scottish Area: The fleet included 301 six-wheelers and 24 four-wheelers, of which 112 six-wheelers and 23 four-wheelers were still oil-lit. Would need 82 non-vestibuled carriages.

In January 1935 the CGM reported that the Board of Directors had agreed that a supplementary programme of rolling stock replacement – locomotives, carriages and wagons – should be prepared. This, taken with the 1935 programme already authorised, should cover the two years 1935 and 1936, carriages being allotted a third of the £6 million programme. The priorities included catering vehi-

cles, 45 East Coast vehicles including corridor firsts, thirds and sleeping cars, a Tourist train set for the Southern Scottish Area, open thirds, sleeping cars, corridor thirds and four train sets for the Ilford service. Some 40% in value of the building programme was put out to contractors.

In April 1935 the CBP was altered to provide for the 'Silver Jubilee' set by reducing the Areas' allocation by four carriages and that for East Coast replacement stock by four.

The CGM reported to the Traffic Committee in June 1935 that the LNER officers had considered dieselisation for the operation of the Newcastle–South Shields service but had concluded that electrification promised better. If the work was carried out coincident with the renewal of the North Tyneside electric stock, and the 1920 stock from the north side reconditioned to work the new electrification, worthwhile cost savings would be achieved.

In October 1935, as instructed by the Board, William Whitelaw chaired a special committee set up to consider schemes that might be eligible for government funding. One outcome was a programme for 172 additional passenger carriages and the conversion of 593 gas-lit carriages under 25 years old to electric lighting. The new stock included six 14-coach train sets for Newcastle and East Coast services together with thirteen additional carriages, five of which were sleeper firsts. The total included 75 other vehicles, some for excursion traffic and others to make up new train sets for the Kings Cross–Scarborough workings, in replacement of North Eastern Area stock transferred to the GE and to form a set of modern carriages for the Edinburgh–Aberdeen service. The justification to government was that passenger traffic was increasing and that the renewal expenditure of the LNER was well below that of the LMS and GWR. As part of the conditions for the government assistance schemes, some £500,000 worth of orders under the additional programme and the already authorised 1935/6 CBP were put out to contractors.

1937 CBP
A programme costed at £1.5 million and proposing the construction of 596 vehicles, with the result that by the end of the year the total number of carriages was +10 on the previous year. Notable features: the four high-speed sets: for the 'Coronation', 'West Riding' and one spare; for the 'Norwich high-speed train'; 15 buffet cars – to

Diagram 167; ten five-coach sets for the Marylebone suburban services; 96 vestibuled carriages for GE section main line and cross-country trains; 100 vestibuled carriages for the GN section; 94 vestibuled carriages for the North Eastern Area; twelve restaurant cars or buffet-restaurant cars for the GE section, North Eastern and Southern Scottish Areas.

1938 CBP
The SPMs pointed to the 'substantial increase in passenger train mileage, passenger carried and revenue in the last four years', in so doing offering the following evidence:

Year	Passenger train mileage	No of passengers	Revenue	Vehicles
1933	100	100	100	100
1934	103.3	102.1	103.1	99.5
1935	105.5	104.8	106.0	99.0
1936	107.8	107.0	109.9	99.1

In the first 32 weeks of 1937 the number of passengers increased by 6.7% over the same period in 1936 and receipts were up by 7.3%.

Above A Middlesbrough–Newcastle semi-fast train near Norton on Tees in September 1947, headed by 'V3' 2–6–2T No 7690. The leading vehicle is a NER non-vestibule carriage but otherwise the train comprises standard Gresley vestibuled stock(with roof-boards) introduced on this service with the 1937 CBP.

The programme proposed included: two train sets for the 'Flying Scotsman' as part of a 105-vehicle build for the East Coast; four five-coach sets for the Marylebone suburban services; 79 lavatory thirds for the GE section for local services but also summer use on cheap fare trains to the coast; teak-bodied excursion stock for the GN and GC sections; nine sets of articulated stock for the Darlington–Saltburn service; non-vestibuled stock, a set of tourist stock and two catering vehicles for party traffic for the Southern Scottish Area.

CGM advised that subsequent to the SPMs' proposals consideration had been given to a new train for the 'Hook

Below Restaurant pantry car E1898E at Doncaster with a BR RU vehicle in August 1963, the former near its demise despite its good condition, having been shopped earlier that month. By then it was classified as a SO, formerly RSP and RTP, and was put into service during 1943 as an open first.

Above included in the 1948 CBP was the first of the 'interlocking berth' layout third-class sleeping cars, No 1348 (Dia 347, built 1947). This shows one cabin, with two berths, the berths in the adjoining cabins being underneath the berths in this view.

Below The down 'Flying Scotsman' near Eryholme in August 1949 headed by 'A4' 4–6–2 No 60013 *Dominion of New Zealand*. The engine is in the BR blue livery and the carriages in simulated teak. This shows how smart a train of the postwar stock could look, particularly the prestige East Coast vehicles with fairings over the solebars. Close examination of the photograph reveals that there are a couple of Gresley vehicles in the formation.

Continental' so its £39,000 cost must be accommodated by a reduction in other stock by 13 carriages, mostly ordinary vestibuled designs but also an unclassed restaurant car for the Southern Scottish Area. Also a new corridor third was to be provided for the 'Silver Jubilee'. As amended this programme was approved by the Joint LTC.

In this programme the Traffic Committee approved the provision of shoulder-lights in 107 corridor thirds being built by Birmingham RCW. Additional electric charging points were to be provided on the GE section for restaurant cars.

1939 CBP

Although only 414 carriages were in this programme to replace 692 being condemned, with vehicles still to be delivered under previous programmes the total number of seats available for the summer 1939 traffic would be in excess of the previous year. in going out to tender, the LNER found that contractors' prices were 'substantially in excess' of the company's workshops so the CBP was trimmed to a total of 400 vehicles – the number of carriages that could be built by the works.

Principal features were: four five-coach suburban sets for the Manchester district; ten five-coach train sets including articulated twins for Hull–Leicester/Sheffield workings; 58 vestibuled carriages for the GE section to 61 ft 6 in Diagrams and 52 vestibuled carriages for Southern Scottish express services.

Proposed by the SPMs but not included in the programme as approved were a number of side-corridor vehicles for the GN and GC sections in replacement for six-wheeled stock used on excursions to the East Coast resorts and intended to be built without intermediate armrests in the compartments, as well as two excursion stock trains for the North Eastern Area.

Of the vehicles actually built, the requirements of the GN section provides an instance of the SPMs specifying limited numbers of carriages for particular services, in this case brake thirds, brake firsts and brake composites for through carriages on the following workings from Kings Cross: 10.10 Harrogate and Hull – BCK + BTK; 1.30 Hull – BCK + BTK; 1.40 – Scarborough, Bridlington and Harrogate – 2 BFK, 2 BCK, 2 BTK; 5.45 Hull – BCK + CK; 5.50 Harrogate – BFK + BTK and 7.15 Hull – BFK + CK + BTK.

In November 1938 the LNER Board approved the Liverpool Street/Fenchurch Street– Shenfield electrification and the construction of 92 electric multiple-units. At the same time the Board approved the Manchester–Sheffield/Wath electrification and the ordering of eight multiple-units to the same design as those for the Shenfield scheme, contracts being placed at the same time. These contracts were suspended in September 1939, the CME authorising the contractors to proceed with the contracts in February 1947.

During 1939, the Traffic Committee approved a number of conversions of existing stock to form push-pull sets on branch lines in the GE and GC sections and the Southern Scottish and Northern Scottish areas.

Nine of the pantry thirds in this programme were not completed and were held at Doncaster until agreement in 1943 that they should be turned out as open firsts.

1940 CBP

This was limited to a programme costed at £397,250, 155 vehicles being built to replace 568 due to be withdrawn during 1940, the Joint LTC recording that 'Under present conditions the expenditure of a larger sum on carriage construction cannot be justified. The programme will enable the company's carriage shops to be kept employed and the new vehicles should maintain the stock to the strength needed for reduced train services.' As approved it included 41 East Coast carriages, six five-coach sets with articulated twins for GC section semi-fast trains; two similar sets for the GN section for use on GN main line and Joint line services and eleven vestibuled carriages for Southern Scottish Waverley Route trains and Aberdeen–Inverness workings.

Carriage construction in the war years

The 1940 CBP was reviewed in June 1940 and priority assigned to vehicles to be completed under the programme, these being listed as: bogie brake vans; articulated sets for the GN and GC sections; corridor thirds; corridor brake thirds; corridor firsts.

Some vehicles in the 1939 and 1940 CBPs were completed over the period 1941–43, the position being reviewed by the Emergency Board meeting on 25 June 1942. This noted that 'slow progress' had been made with the 1939/40 CBPs which was hardly surprising seeing that Doncaster Works had suffered a major fire, that the shops had a considerable amount of war work and that materials were in short supply! The CGM said that output of new carriages was restricted to one weekly but that it was intended to complete the two programmes subject to the following changes: 1939 CBP – one brake composite to be built as a passenger brake van; 1940 CBP – one first, one composite, six brake composites and seventeen thirds to be built as passenger brake vans; two semi-open firsts to be built as firsts. There were also three vehicles built as replacements for those lost to enemy action: two bogie vans and a non-vestibuled composite.

1944 CBP

By the end of 1943, the 1939 and 1940 CBPs as amended had been completed with the exception of the four firsts and seven composites. A CBP for 1944 was approved by the Emergency Board at its meeting in May 1944 because, to quote, 'A small amount of building was now necessary to meet serious shortages'. The LNER had lost 815 vehicles to traffic between the end of the 1938 CBP and the end of 1943 while about 2,500 carriages overdue for withdrawal had been retained and 268 were recorded by the Finance Committee as having been lost through enemy action during the war years.

The 1944 CBP included the seven corridor composites outstanding from the 1940 CBP. These were built as firsts to the 63 ft postwar design on Diagram 332 in 1946, the remainder being classified as new build and these were also to the postwar steel-panelled style for vestibuled stock: six composites to Diagram 328 in 1946/7; 33 thirds to Diagram 329 in 1946/7; fifteen open thirds on Diagram 330 in 1946/7; ten brake thirds on Diagram 331 in 1946 and, lastly, 50 bogie brake vans with deal panelling to Diagram 327 in 1945/6.

1946 CBP

There was no 1945 CBP but the five-year programme approved in October 1945 provided for the building of 773 vehicles, 427 four and six-wheeled and 719 bogie carriages being scheduled for withdrawal.

Of the new construction, 593 were to be vestibuled and 180 non-vestibuled, 300 of the total to be built by the LNER and 473 by contractors, the principal orders being for 263 corridor thirds placed with Birmingham RCW and 100 non-vestibuled lavatory composites with Cravens. included in the total were the sets for the 'Flying Scotsman'. 'Junior Scotsman' and midday Edinburgh trains. Vehicles to the programme approved in October 1945 were built between 1947 and 1949. The situation is a little confusing in that the overall programme lasted for five years but other orders were later added to the annual programmes and some of the 1945 programme was curtailed or modified with the onset of nationalisation. There was approval for a 1947 CBP in October 1946 and the Joint LTC approved the construction of the six sixteen-berth sleeper thirds at its April 1947 meeting for inclusion in the 1948 CBP. There were subsequent programme years up to and including 1952, the programme for the last year being delayed because of a shortage of steel. The last vehicles to a LNER pattern design were the 1953 conversions of Ilford stock as non-vestibuled carriages for the Tilbury line. These were neither covered by a CBP nor by a LNER series order number.

CHAPTER 4
THE GRESLEY LNER STANDARD CARRIAGE FROM 1923

Evolution of designs
PASSENGER rolling stock for the newly formed LNER was largely determined by the most pressing renewals which were for the prestige East Coast main line sets and the London area suburban sets. The last major building programme for East Coast stock had been between 1907–9. The condition of the London area suburban stock left a lot to be desired, particularly on the GE section, and dictated immediate and large-scale replacements. As soon as possible after Grouping, design work went ahead on new general service stock.

When it came to standards for the new stock it was clear that policy decisions would be governed by GNR design practice established at Doncaster and in particular the features embodied in the ECJS vehicles built after 1911. 'Standard' is a relative term when looking back at vehicles that were fashioned partly from wood and were largely craftsmen-built and also when the works involved had differing ideas on how to do things. So the standards were a little variable when it came to best practice and from time to time the CME's department or the traffic people discovered to their displeasure that works or outside contractors had gone their own way on detail such as chroming door handles for general service stock when they should have been brass or not fitting the required inside handles to doors in brake compartments, to take two examples.

The main decisions from the design angle concerned overall and internal dimensions, materials to be used and standard of finish. These were set out in the specifications. Over and above were the requirements of the operating departments, as represented by the superintendents and passenger managers whose involvement with designs and specifications has already been covered. These were influenced to no small extent by the preferred practices of the Areas, derived in turn from the pre-Grouping companies. Carriages continued to be built at the various workshops to

Below Vestibuled brake third (by now brake second) E16525 to Dia 178, built 1940 as No 57456. This view shows the rigid trussing of the later Gresley standard vehicles, the double doors to the van compartment and the lights under the cantrail.

orders placed by the constituent companies while progress was made during the spring of 1923 towards drawing up the principles behind the new standard stock which would govern individual designs. The most important of such principles involved the standardisation of braking systems, dimensions, gangways and couplings.

Setting the standards
Correspondence from the CME's Kings Cross office in June 1923 put the following standards to A.C. Stamer, the assistant CME, at Darlington:

Compartments:
First-class compartments to be 7 ft 6 in in length instead of 7 ft 3 in as previously. (This was the dimension between the partitions.)
Third-class to be 6 ft 3 in instead of 6 ft 2 in.

With these dimensions fixed body designs were to prepared for 52 ft (later altered to 51 ft) and 60 ft underframes, the size of the lavatories being dependent on the space left over. The result was to produce dimensions over body end mouldings of 51 ft 1½ in and 61 ft 6 in respectively. The ten types of standard carriage mentioned at this stage were:

Vestibuled	*Non-vestibuled*
Composite	Third
First	Composite
Third	Brake Third
Brake First	Brake Composite
Brake Third	
Brake Composite	

The instructions from Kings Cross continued:
Body design:
All windows to have square corners.
Stamer objected to this and stated the preference of the NER for radiussed corners to windows.
Width over body mouldings:
To be 8 ft 6 in.

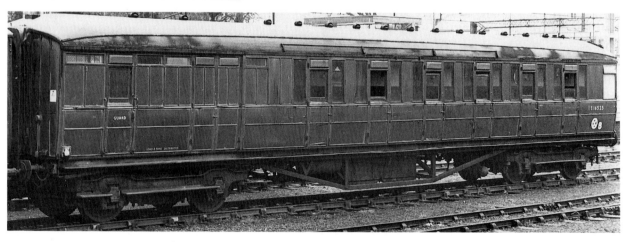

In this case Kings Cross agreed with Stamer that this dimension should be fixed at 8 ft 9 in, giving a width of 9 ft over the bodyside handles, the portion of the carriage body at the brake end of brake vehicles being recessed and measuring 8 ft 6 in wide. The unrestricted use of 61 ft 6 in by 9 ft 3 in vehicles over the North Eastern and Southern Scottish Areas was not possible until alterations were made to various structures after 1928. in that year, a maximum body width of 9 ft 3 in over the handles was approved by the Traffic Committee for restaurant and sleeping cars only, provided that entrance doors were recessed into the body.

The general details began to be set out. At a meeting held at Kings Cross in August 1923 regarding rolling stock policy, with O.V.S. Bulleid as chairman, the Darlington drawing office was instructed that all brake carriages and full brakes were to have the familiar toplights at cant-rail level. Other points clarified at the time were that the guard's duckets on brake vehicles should be of a faceted design and that there would not be continuous stepboards on vehicles. That said, most brake vehicles appeared without duckets up to 1928 when an instruction went out that they were to be fitted in future on all new brake vehicles. Another decision was that all first-class seating was to be three a side. It was decided to dispense with the toplights used in the GNR Gresley carriages and to fit hit and miss ventilators above the door droplights.

So the process went on until by December 1923 the various standard carriage types and their dimensions were established as follows:

On 60 ft underframes:

Vestibuled	First	Brake Composite	Full Brake
	Open First	Third	
	Brake First	Brake Third	
	Composite	Open Third	

There was also a design agreed for a non-vestibuled full brake, a type never built in practice.

On 51 ft underframes:

Non-vestibuled	Firs	Third
	Composite	Brake Third
	Brake Composite	*Full Brake

*There was also a vestibuled Full Brake built for the GE section

The designs had been presented to the December 1923 meeting which finalised the standard designs, subject to the drawings being signed by the superintendents and passenger managers.

There was also the question of stock for the GE section.

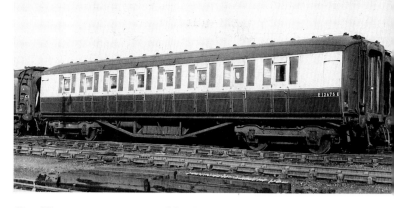

Above The most numerous type of Gresley vestibuled carriage-a Dia 115 third. By this stage, No 56033 of 1938 was running as corridor second E12675E for BR in carmine and cream livery. The inability of Gresley vehicles to accommodate the usual top band of carmine under the cantrail is obvious from this photograph.

General service 60 ft stock was not acceptable to the GE section operators, 'on account of the limited length of Liverpool Street platforms', as the records have it. The implications of this are dealt with in Chapter 8.

Daunting problems in the way of standardisation concerned the choices to be made as regards the gangway type and as between air and vacuum brakes. The Locomotive Committee meting of April 1923 saw the chief general manager propose that Pullman type gangways should be made standard for the LNER as the majority of GNR and ECJS vehicles were fitted with this type. The Traffic Committee recommended that the policy of individual companies should be continued for the present, except in the case of complete new trains, for which Pullman type gangways were the standard. Work was needed to evolve satisfactory gangway adaptors to enable carriage fitted with different types of gangway to be coupled together satisfactorily. A series of evaluation tests was held in 1923/4 to establish compatibility between the stock of LNER constituents and with the British Standard gangways fitted to GWR and LMS vehicles. It was at first decided to adopt the GER's variety of British Standard gangway for LNER vehicles requiring this type but after tests early in 1924 this was changed to the NER pattern gangway, with that company's swivelling gangway adaptor. BS gangways were required for LNER vehicles working on such services as Aberdeen–Inverness or Newcastle–Liverpool when they might be coupled to LMS stock.

A meeting of the Traffic Committee held on 22 February

Below LNER Diagram Book: vestibule composite to Dia 6. This was the original 9 ft extreme width version. The 9 ft 3 in example was Dia 130. Note the representation of the adjustable trussing.

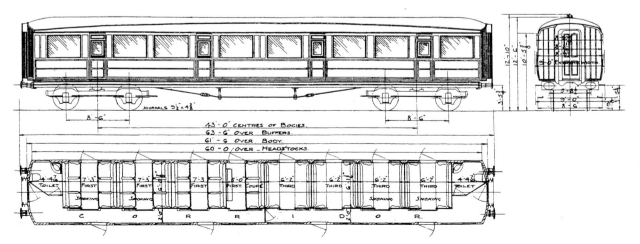

Above An end view of a standard Gresley vestibule vehicle showing the characteristic buffers and full height of the gangway and vestibule door. The cast metal plate giving details of dimensions is to the left of the gangway.

1923 set out the policy on braking systems to be adopted for new stock as: GN section and Southern Scottish Areas – vacuum; GC section – vacuum, except for carriage trucks which were to be dual; GE section, dual, except for suburban sets which were to be air only as well as non-vestibuled stock ordered from contractors; North Eastern Area and Northern Scottish Area, dual fitted. However, some new stock for both these Areas was vacuum fitted only. All new stock was to be fitted with electric lighting and steam heating.

In March 1928 Bulleid chaired a meeting at Kings Cross which resulted in the following programme for the unification of braking systems: North Eastern Area, loose air braked stock first to be converted to dual braking, then to vacuum only. Set trains were to be converted to vacuum; GE section, conversion of air braked stock to vacuum where this was required to work with vacuum fitted stock. Suburban sets were to remain air braked; Scottish Areas, air braked stock to be converted to vacuum as soon as possible. All common user stock was to be dealt with on a line basis.

In March 1928 there were 964 loose air braked carriages in stock and all were to be converted between October 1928 and July 1929. New stock to be built during 1928 was to be fitted with dual braking, where appropriate. Apart from GE section suburban set trains, the last new vehicles with air braking were some carriages built in 1924 to a NER design for the GE section and some four-wheeled parcels vans for the GE section and Northern Scottish Area in 1929/30. On the GE section Westinghouse air braked stock survived in some sets working on the Southend line until electrification and until 1960 or so on Enfield, Chingford and North Woolwich services.

Underframes and running gear

The underframes for the LNER standard stock followed the pattern set in GNR days and with the two standard lengths,

60 ft for vestibuled stock (except in the case of the GE section) with buckeye couplers and 51 ft for non-vestibuled stock with screw couplings, again with the exception of the GE section and its vestibuled stock with buckeye couplers on 51 ft underframes. The buffers of the 60 ft underframe measured 1 ft 9 in from headstocks to buffer face, with the buffers in the extended position, for the 51 ft type that dimension was 1 ft 10 in.

The underframes had bar trussing. It was decided that York Works would build all new steel underframes, as well as assembling bogies for those vehicles built at Doncaster. in 1927 the all-steel passenger brake vans built on Dia 45 by Cammell-Laird were interesting as the underframe trussing was eliminated. At about the same time, Newsome records that there was a proposal to use a single casting for the underframe end of a vehicle with buckeye couplers, the casting extending from the bolster cross-members to the headstock, the intention being to produce an underframe capable of withstanding a higher end-loading in a collision. Welding technology helped to achieve much the same result for less cost and weight within a few years. The development of a 65 ft underframe in 1930/1 led to the general adoption of angle trussing for the shorter underframes as well, in place of the bar sections and turn-buckle adjustment.

But thought continued to be given to new developments, such as with the 'Alpax' carriage and its use of aluminium, for which an aluminium underframe had been contemplated. This would have been a notable innovation but the carriage was completed with a conventional steel underframe. Bulleid's interest in welding technology has been mentioned in the various books on his engineering career and he was responsible on the LNER for the adoption of all-welded underframes. in December 1932 the first welded wagon underframe had been produced and the next year York experimented with welded underframes for standard carriages. These proved to be more rigid that those of riveted construction and did not settle when the bodywork was in position. The first carriage so constructed was an open third on Dia 186, No 21308 built in February 1934. This resulted in a gradual change to welded underframes, made practical by the improvements in welding technology during the 1930s. One benefit was a saving in weight: the Dia 186 open thirds with all-welded underframes were 1 ton lighter than those with riveted frames.

There is little to say about underframe construction of the postwar stock but had all-steel stock materialised for general service there would no doubt have been development in this respect. in the evolution of the BR standard stock an examination was made of the underframe designs of the Big Four companies and there was criticism of the LNER design that stresses were not uniformly distributed, some members carrying very heavy loads. The maximum end load which the LNER pattern underframe withstood on test was 120 tons, compared with 200 tons for the BR design while the underframe itself was heavier than the LMS design.

Bogies

Bogie designs were standardised in 1923, principally on the compound bolster Gresley Spencer Moulton bogie with pressed steel side frames and bolsters and cast iron centre and side castings. Variants to this design were introduced over the years. From 1929 the main crossbars in the heavy type standard 8 ft and 8 ft 6 in bogies were made thicker. This followed the inclusion of strengthening angles from 1927, a response to an incidence of cracking at the bottom flange of the crossbar.

The compound bolster bogie was expensive to manufacture and in 1927 thought was given to the design of a simplified version of the Heavy Type. The set of swing links carrying the inner bolster was eliminated, the bolster instead being carried in a steel casting supported on the outer bolster springs. But side control was found to be inferior on

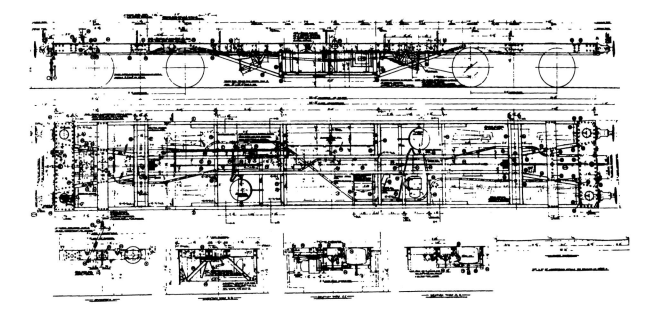

test and this and the similar Light Type produced in 1930, both manufactured by Metro-Cammell, were not built in quantity. The 10 ft wheelbase bogie was produced as a replacement for the articulation bogies used under the 'Silver Jubilee' restaurant car triplet. Components in the original bogies had begun to crack as they had clearly been carrying loads greater than they were designed for. The 8 ft 6 in bogies under the other carriages in this set were also strengthened.

The single bolster all-welded design was built at York and used for some of the postwar vestibuled carriages and, in a similar form, for the Shenfield electric multiple-units. The Tyneside electric units had 8 ft wheelbase compound bolster bogies throughout. Generally speaking, the articulation bogies differed only from the others in having stronger laminated springs. in his quest for good vehicle riding, despite general satisfaction with the standard designs, Gresley considered the use of rubber suspension using rubber balls sandwiched in cups, one set of these on the underframe, the other on the bogie. A prototype was made but the idea was dropped.

None of the standard bogie types was fitted with roller bearing axleboxes in LNER days although these were used for the compound bolster bogies adopted for some electric multiple units built for BR in the 1960, and from 1957 for the bogies fitted to the 'Coronation' twin firsts and one or two other LNER carriages included in the 'Talisman' sets. Newsome records that in LNER days the use of roller bearing axleboxes was considered from time to time but not adopted on grounds of cost and the fact that the number of hot boxes on the LNER's coaching stock seldom exceeded

Above The standard 51 ft underframe, again with rigid trussing. This also shows the buffing gear for the screw coupled non-vestibuled stock.

two a month before 1939. Some of the Tyneside electric units had Hoffman bearings on the motor bogies.

Body construction

A building specification for standard vestibuled stock dated 1930 may be taken as typical of practice in the earlier years of the LNER:

All body framing, best quality Moulmein or Rangoon teak with the exception of: the cross-bearers – oak; cant-rails – pitch-pine; roof boards – red deal; stepboards – pine and roofsticks – steel bars, rolled channel section. Restaurant and kitchen cars differed only in that teak was used for the cant-rails.

The body framing was fitted together with tenons and mortises bound with iron and steel knees, the body panelling – $3/8$ in thick – was secured by copper pins and each panel was fastened with glued softwood blocks. Half-round wooden beading or mouldings were arranged to give square-cornered panels on the body sides. The roof boards were covered with raw roofing canvas once they had been painted, then filled with putty and a layer of thick white lead and boiled oil was applied using a brush. The canvas was nailed down on top of this and left for fourteen days. As to the interior, the corridor partition, doors, panels and mouldings were of teak covered with $1/4$ in millboard. Hardboard or

Below A heavy type 8 ft 6 in compound bolster bogie.

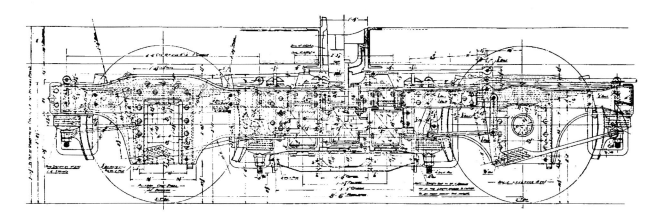

LNER bogie designs

Standard types

Duty	Wheelbase	Pivot Weight	Journals*	Drawing No/Notes
Bogie brake vans – up to 35 tons gross weight – 1914	8 ft	12 tons	9½" + 4⅜"	1776N inside solebars
Passenger carriages – not exceeding 35 tons weight – 1914 Light Type	8 ft 6 in	12 tons	8" + 4"	1367N
Vehicles with a tare weight over 35 tons or articulated stock, also used 'Coronation' sets – 1921 Heavy Type	8 ft 6 in	18 tons	10" + 5"	3378N
Heavy Type for GE section suburban stock – 1921	8 ft	18 tons	10" + 5"	6405N

Other designs

Duty	Wheelbase	Pivot Weight	Journals*	Drawing No/Notes
Alternative Heavy Type – 1927 single bolster	8 ft built	18½ tons	10" + 5"	44841 Met-Cam
Alternative Light Type – 1930 single bolster	8 ft built	12½ tons	9½" + 4⅜"	6776N Met-Cam
'Silver Jubilee' replacement	10 ft	24 tons	10" + 5"	11829N
Single bolster all-welded – 1942	8 ft Outside frames	14 tons	9½" + 4½"	15448N

* The larger journals had a higher tin content in the white metal when used for main line stock

millboard was used for the lavatory panelling (earlier first-class lavatories had vitrolite panels) above the lower match-boarded teak, the latter also being used in the compartments to waist height. in later vehicles, to reduce costs, there was more use of millboard, described by the carriage restorers of the LNER(SVR) Fund 'as a close relative of cardboard', and of blockboard, for partitions and tables. The vestibuled carriages with end-door access were much more satisfactory in terms of construction as the body framing members were continuous and as a result were stronger.

Steel panelling on teak body framing was used increasingly from 1935, first being used for general service sets for the GN section and for the 'Silver Jubilee'. The 16 SWG steel panels were screwed to the teak framing, but construction was otherwise similar to the teak-panelled carriages. Such composite vehicles were in the minority before Gresley's death but in postwar days they became the standard. The Gresley period steel panelled stock had square corners to the windows. Double glazing was first applied in 1935 with the 'Silver Jubilee' set, the carriages having two sheets of ¼ in plate glass with ¼ in space between. The other high-speed, 'Flying Scotsman' and 'Hook Continental' sets of 1938 had similar double windows.

Less common in the 1930s was the use of plywood and aluminium in carriage construction, the former being used for the 'Tourist' stock and the latter in the experimental 'Alpax' carriage. All-steel construction had been considered by Gresley as long ago as 1914 but apart from the open thirds and full brakes built by contractors in 1927/8 there was no challenge to the traditional wooden bodied carriage until after 1945.

Dimensions, body design features, heating and lighting

The standard vestibuled carriages were characterised by their teak panelled bodywork, roof sloping down at each end and bowed body ends. Pullman type gangways, buckeye couplers and retractable buffers were fitted to all, except for a limited number of carriages used on through workings in trains of LMS stock, as a result of which they had British Standard gangways.

Standard dimensions

Length of underframe	60 ft 0 in
Width over body mouldings	61 ft 6 in
Distance between bogie centres	43 ft 0 in

Width over body mouldings
8 ft 9 in only until 1928,
then 9 ft for sleeping and restaurant cars with recessed doors and for end door carriages from 1930.
Width overall, 9 ft, 9 ft 3 in respectively

Seating

Three a side for first-class compartments, four a side for third-class from 1923. Hinged armrests and headrests introduced for new first-class carriages after November 1928. From 1930 some East Coast vehicles were two a side first-class, three a side third-class. Three a side third-class with armrests introduced for selected services 1932–4, thereafter generally. Older vehicles converted to three a side after 1936.

Open thirds were designed to sit two to the larger seat in the Dia 27 series vehicles and one on the other side when used as dining cars, otherwise three one side, one the other.

Bucket seats, first introduced with the Tourist stock, were fitted to the teak-bodied Tourist Open Thirds and Brake Opens on Dias 186/196/216/217 but such seats were unpopular with passengers. They began to be replaced in early postwar days by conventional seats. This may have been encouraged by the official accident report into a train fire in April 1941, the seats being a contributory cause in that there was a space between the seats and the body sides which was something of a dust-trap. Schoolboys travelling in a down East Coast train had been flicking lighted matches at each other, one of the matches seeming to have lodged in one of the dust-traps in the open third in which they were travelling. An initial fire was soon out of control, unhappily resulting in the deaths of six boys, their carriage and the adjoining one being burnt to the frames. The seat design was not in itself blamed although the accident report suggested that the Rexine seat-back covering encouraged the spread of flame.

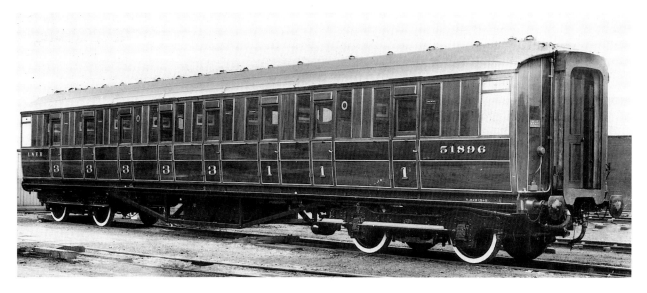

Lighting

Train lighting equipment was supplied by Vickers or J. Stone & Co and was interchangeable. Through lighting control was introduced from the 1929 CBP, with the exception of vehicles built for the North Eastern Area, but all had through lighting control from 1933. Four shoulder or reading lights per compartment in first-class from 1934, in third-class from 1938, this being accompanied by the provision of larger dynamos in the lighting equipment.

Standard fittings per compartment	From Apr 1930	From 1939 CBP
First-class vestibuled	Two + 30W bulbs	One 15W in roof, 4 + 15W shoulder- lights
First-class non-vestibuled	One + 15W 2 + 30W	As above
Third-class vestibuled	2 + 30W	As above
Third-class non-vestibuled	2 + 30W	As above

Heating

This was not always a strong point in standard stock. From 1927, after public complaints of inadequate heating, improved heaters were fitted in compartments and from 1930 larger diameter pipes were used in restaurant cars. in 1945 pressure steam heating replaced the previous adherence to pressureless supply. One weakness of the underseat heaters was the temperamental thermostat.

Gresley appreciated the limitations of steam heating and

Above Vestibule composite No 51896 to Dia 137, built at York in 1938 but photographed at Dukinfield where the photographer's preference for three-quarter views generally resulted in more useful records for posterity! The Smoking labels were a rectangle, the non-smoking ones the 'doughnut' design. The clear photograph also shows the effect of the lining out on the beading.

went so far as experimenting with electric heating – in steam hauled stock! – before introducing pressure ventilation. He first mentioned the trials with electric heating during a lecture he presented to the debating society at York in 1928. The carriage featuring in the trials was vestibuled composite No 1063, Dia 7, which was fitted with electric heaters in the compartments and electric water heaters in the lavatories. It proved difficult to maintain heating without the provision of heavy battery equipments. interest in electric heating led to the development of pressure ventilation, initially from 1930 with the Thermotank system with fans, filters and heating unit in a cupboard next to the lavatory, such equipment being used in the 'super firsts' Dias 147/156 and first-class sleeping cars. From the main unit air was circulated through trunking running above the corridor ceiling, with ducts into each compartment. No steam heating was provided in these vehicles as first operated but it was soon found that steam heating was also required to heat the carriage sufficiently before the train departed.

In 1934 Gresley informed a meeting of the SPMs that he was 'making tests with a new system of heating to overcome the difficulty in the rear vehicles of long trains'. The set

Below LNER Diagram Book: vestibuled open third to Dia 186, the plan view showing a fair representation of the original bucket type seats.

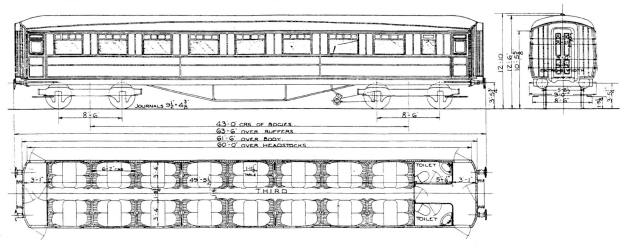

chosen was that working the prestigious 8.15 am Newcastle–Kings Cross and 5.30 pm return. Stone's fully automatic pressure ventilation system was adopted. Fresh, filtered air, drawn through ducts mounted on the underframe, entered the compartments at near floor level, being heated to a given temperature in cold weather, the thermostat being placed in the corridor. The equipment containing the air filters, heater, fan and motor and master thermostat for 'winter' or 'summer' working was mounted on the underframe, the power supply coming from the train lighting equipment. The carriages were pre-heated half an hour before departure, with the pressure ventilation equipment starting automatically when the steam heating was applied through the train. The vehicles in the Newcastle set were corridor third No 168, Dia 115; open third No 175, Dia 27A; corridor first No 1138, Dia 173; semi-open first No 1139, Dia 172 and restaurant triplet set Nos 16441–3. Dias 12–14. Similar equipment was used for the 'Silver Jubilee' and after 1935 in a developed form for the high-speed and other prestige trains.

By World War 2 there were 35 carriages with Thermotank pressure ventilation and 71 with the Stone's system. There was concern in 1941 that, in the case of an enemy poison gas attack, trains including vehicles with pressure ventilation would present a hazard as the underframe fans might draw in contaminated air to the interiors. By removing the fuses from the fan motor circuits the vehicles could be made safe but then they would be without heating. So a programme was begun to fit the Stone's PV carriages with steam heating, the fan circuit fuses being removed at the same time. Some of the Stone's pressure ventilation equipment was not restored as it was considered too expensive to make it serviceable again.

Standard vestibuled carriage interiors
Much of the interior panelling of standard vestibuled Gresley carriages before the mid-1930s was teak, variously stained, varnished and polished. The interior furnishings as used in ECJS vehicles were adopted as the LNER standard in mid-1923. During 1926 a passenger, a Mr Lupton, complained about the type and style of LNER carriage interiors and his remarks resulted in experimental furnishings being considered; Mr Lupton's Complaint became a long-running item on the agenda at the SPMs' meetings. Three vestibuled thirds were turned out with experimental improvements and in due course these were incorporated in standard carriages, in particular new, lighter coloured upholstery from 1928, a reduction in polished wood surfaces in compartments and their replacement by white paint, a simplification from 1927 in the design of light fittings, window blind boxes and mouldings as well as improved flooring, increased knee-space in compartments from 1932 and improved light fittings and the use of teak paint on interior metalwork in place of polished metal finishes.

Stock for the East Coast was usually to a higher specification or else included small touches such as vestibule mats or cushions and hassocks in the first-class not to be found in the standard stock built for the Areas.

In 1930 the standard specification for interior finishes was as follows: first-class compartments, teak panelling darkened and French polished , third-class, teak left in its natural colour bodied up with polish and given one coat of varnish. This remained more or less the same through the 1930s except that corridor partitions and doors were simplified in design and panelled in plywood and more of the surfaces in the compartments were covered in Rexine. The remainder of the interior painting included the use of white enamel for the compartment panelling above the luggage racks, ceilings finished in flat white paint, brake compartments finished in light stone on the sides and ends, with a white ceiling.

Painted surfaces in the compartments and saloons were increasingly replaced by Rexine from the early 1930s when four first-class sleeping cars appeared after overhaul with the extensive use of this material in the berth compartments. The new material, a type of leathercloth comprising a cloth fabric coated with nitrocellulose, was preferred to painted finishes because it resisted scuffing better. in time its condition deteriorated and it was then painted and became less appealing. Rexine was used to a major extent after about 1935. Usual colour schemes were ivory Rexine for ceilings in the first-class, cream in the third-class, dove-grey for the wall covering in the first-class compartments and brown in the third-class. Peach coloured Rexine was used in the immediate prewar period, the colour having taken Gresley's eye when used in the 1938 'Flying Scotsman' sets. Stock for special purposes had some fairly hectic colour schemes using Rexine and these are referred to in the appropriate sections.

Although Rexine was so popular with the LNER, it presented a fire hazard. A serious fire was caused at the Smethwick Works of Birmingham Railway Carriage & Wagon in December 1936 when the solvent used to clean up Rexine in newly built stock caught fire. Several corridor thirds to Dia 115 then being built were burnt out and had to be replaced at BRCW's expense. in 1949 Rexine was recognised by BR as unsatisfactory in view of the fire risk it presented but it took a serious train fire before its real dangers were appreciated. That incident was the destruction at Huntingdon in 1951 of one of the high-speed train twins and the fire was made worse by the nitrocellulose coating of the Rexine and also sponge rubber used as part of the floor covering. The inspecting Officer's report included the recommendation that 'the sooner nitrocellulose cloth is removed from carriages, the better'. One consequence was that Rexine was stripped from the waist level downwards on a number of vehicles and fireproof skirtings fitted..

Until 1932, the standard upholstery materials were first-class, blue cloth, third-class, fawn rep, except for suburban stock where crimson and black pile was used. First-class restaurant car seating was upholstered in leather, third-class in moquette. The lighter styles instigated by Mr Lupton's Complaint were being used as well but from 1932 Gresley instructed that the standard upholstery materials must be replaced by the following range: first-class, except end-door firsts, floral moquette; third-class, with intermediate armrests, 'special' brown moquette, without armrests, ordinary brown moquette; composite and third-class sleeping cars, blue moquette in the third-class. Second-class upholstery was generally blue and brown in colour. Armrests were trimmed in morocco leather. Materials for use in restaurant cars and end-door firsts, not to mention special stock, was to be referred to Gresley for approval and could vary considerably from standard. A velvet material, usually with an Art Deco pattern, was used for the first-class upholstery in the late 1930s. The teak bodied Tourist third opens were upholstered in Art Deco patterns chiefly in orange and brown colours.

Standard metal fittings in carriages, as agreed in November 1923, were brass or stainless steel in the first-class and dark oxidised brass in the third-class. Later such fittings in the third-class were often painted brown cellulose. Hat pegs were fitted in first-class compartments. Door handles and corridor window rails were polished brass, except for restaurant firsts, sleeping cars and corridor firsts for which chrome plating was used. Suburban stock had inside door handles and these were also fitted to Outer Suburban stock from the 1939 CBP. From late 1941 net rails were made of steel and corridor and lavatory window rails from timber. Most other fittings became mild steel at this stage.

Liveries and finishes – including references to other than standard carriages

Teak panelled stock

During 1923 the future standards for LNER passenger carriages were evolved by the chief mechanical engineer's departments at Kings Cross, Doncaster and Darlington and it was decided that all general service stock would be of teak construction on all-steel underframes. The traditional finish of such vehicles for the GNR and ECJS was to varnish and polish all external and internal panelling, and similar methods were continued under the LNER following the directors' inspection at Marylebone station of constituents' rolling stock before their February 1923 meeting. Varnished teak, and what is described in the records as 'artificial teak', were the finishes on display. The other choice would have been painted mahogany but as three of the constituents used variations on crimson lake as their carriage livery it was felt that if a similar colour was adopted it would lead to confusion with LMS stock. The SPMs had no doubt of their preference, their chairman of the time going on record as saying that 'as there was no material difference in cost there was no objection to the superintendents' preference for varnished teak instead of painted mahogany'. Their contribution was also to recommend that the class of compartments should be indicated by figures in the bottom panel (of the doors) and, regrettably, that no coat of arms should be shown on carriages. Pre-Grouping stock continued to appear in old liveries until paint stocks were used up.

As Newsome pointed out in discussion following presentation of his paper in 1948 as a teak exterior finish was the LNER's standard finish it was necessary to use either teak itself or an imitation. Imitation was necessary for the steel panelled stock built in immediate prewar days and before nationalisation, as soon to be described. As the varnished finish relied on the natural textures and colourings of the teak, despite careful matching of the panels each carriage varied in appearance. Successive coats of varnish changed the overall colouring and the varnish itself faded or mellowed with age. Teak panelled stock normally went for shopping every three years to receive a fresh coat of varnish. in the course of time older vehicles assumed a darker colour with the process of successive varnishing and staining in everyday service. Bad cases of panel staining and watermarks were treated by bleaching the affected area with oxalic acid. Elderly carriages, badly disfigured by staining, were sometimes outshopped in a teak paint finish.

Bodyside varnishing, lining out and transfers

A standard procedure for varnishing teak-panelled stock was based on the methods in use at the works and agreed at a meeting held at Kings Cross on 14 August 1923 and chaired by Bulleid. The process of applying the finish in stages was as follows:

1. One coat of gold size.
2. One coat of preparing varnish.
3. As 2, rubbed in while wet.
4. Stopping up, then sandpapered.
5. One coat of preparing varnish rubbed in while wet.
6. One coat of preparing varnish.
7. When surface hard, faced down with pumice and water.
8. Lining out, primrose two coats, fine line red.
9. Varnish transfer panels.
10. Putty and touch up cornice, hinges etc.
11–14. two coats of preparing varnish, two coats finishing varnish.
15. Flat down with pumice dust and water.
16/17. Two coats of finishing varnish.
18. Exterior touched up.

After such painstaking industry surely no vehicle could fail to be protected adequately nor appear resplendent! It makes a contrast with today's two-pack paint finishes, particularly when contemplating the 1925 requirement that 'in painting and varnishing not more than one coat per day must be applied which must be quite dry before another coat, and at least one day must be allowed between each coat of finishing varnish'. On this basis the complete varnishing process must have required about 20 days. There were attempts to spray finish the varnish but this was not a success.

All vestibuled stock was lined on bodyside and bodyend mouldings and upright casings with a $\frac{3}{8}$ in primrose line edged both sides with a $\frac{1}{16}$ in red line – stage 8 in the above procedure. in practice widths varied with $\frac{1}{4}$ in primrose and/or $\frac{1}{8}$ in red lines. The terminations of these lines had a small arrow-like head which in later days, at least, was a transfer. The lining out was done with a long-haired pencil brush held between the finger and thumb and placed on the centre of the moulding. No other aid was employed. Non-vestibuled stock was subject to the same varnishing process except that lining out was in primrose only on the mouldings. Articulated suburban sets were devoid of any lining and indeed lining out was officially abandoned for all stock

Below Open brake third to Dia 196 as BR E16629E in May 1964 when such vehicles were becoming rare. It was originally No 43554 of 1938. No 16629 was in a set used for the memorable Gresley Society special from Kings Cross–Darlington, the gangway shield being a BR reinforced plastic version.

from November 1941. The ends of non-vestibuled carriages were painted plain black after October 1925.

These traditional methods were used during the life of the LNER but there were changes with the composition of paints and varnishes during the 1930s. Synthetic materials displaced natural ingredients which had been mixed in the paintshop. Cellulose lacquer interior finishes were used from the late 1920s but its flammability was to be demonstrated in the serious train fire at Penmanshiel in June 1949 although in this case the contractor-built postwar carriage should not have had cellulose lacquer. Such finishes were then stripped from all LNER design stock.

Lettering and numbering

Letters and numbers were gold leaf transfers with each letter or numeral shaded to the left and below in red, pink and white and backshaded to the right and below in black and brown.

The letters (LNER) and carriage stock number were 4 in high and 5 in over the gold in width. Until 1928 the 'LNER' was placed, to quote, 'as near the centre as practicable on the waist panel on both sides of the body'. After that date the 'LNER' was moved to the furthest left position on each side of the body. in all cases, from July 1925 the vehicle number was positioned on the waist panel at the opposite right-hand end of the body to the 'LNER'. The suffix lettering to the running number, discontinued from April 1925, was $2^{1}/_{2}$ in by 3 in. Guard's compartments were lettered 'Guard' in transfer letters $2^{3}/_{8}$ in by 3 in over the gold on the waist panel of the doors on both sides of the body. Carriages in the Cheshire Lines Committee fleet received standard type transfers with 'CLC' in place of the 'LNER'. One feature of the body ends was a plate giving details of length over headstocks, width over body, maximum width over projections and weight. Before 1934 the plate also gave the height of centre from rail and the number of seats. The LNER standard telegraphic codes were not painted on vehicle ends – in white – until at least 1942.

Class designations (1,2,3) were numerals 7 in high over the gold (9 in over the shading) to the same elaborate shading as letters and numerals and were placed on the lower panels of the doors. Special vehicles were designated 'Restaurant Car' or 'Sleeping Car' with lettering of the same size as the class numerals. The title 'Sleeping Carriage' was officially discontinued after September 1925.

The figure '3' denoting third-class accommodation was abolished from July 1940, the '2' designation ending with the abolition of that class in the London suburban area from 1938 and the withdrawal of the Continental boat trains on the outbreak of World War 2. From November 1940 a transfer figure '1' was applied to the windows of first-class compartments. Other wartime changes included the abbreviation of 'LNER' on the body sides to 'NE' and this lasted until January 1946, after which the 'LNER' and running number were moved inwards on the bodyside. in the 1947–8 period a number of carriages appeared with the running number in sans-serif characters, before and after nationalisation.

Internal designations were as follows. Non-vestibuled stock had 7 in class numerals on the lower inside door panels in black-shaded primrose transfers. The running number and class designation were 1 in black-shaded gold transfers affixed to door garnish rails. The running number was written in 4 in black numerals on the body end of the brake compartments or full brake, but this was discontinued after 1935. 'Toilet' was a transfer in white-shaded black script on the appropriate door. There was a variety of ivorine notices placed in LNER carriages instructing or admonishing passengers, as well as red transfer panels informing likewise.

Labels for windows denoting 'Smoking' in blue were introduced in 1925. A 'Smoking Prohibited' label began to be applied from 1930, replaced by a red triangular label the following year. in 1933 a profitable contract was concluded with Imperial Tobacco for 'Smoking' labels to appear in windows. On expiry of the contract in 1942 it was decided that only 'No Smoking' labels should be displayed on carriage windows.

Imitation teak finishes and other liveries

Although varnished teak carriages made up a significant proportion of the LNER's fleet, there were also other wooden bodied vehicles which previously had been painted. These were accordingly finished in an imitation teak finish, referred to from time to time as 'mock teak'. As agreed in 1923 the painting process for a previously painted carriage comprised the following:

1. Wash down.
2. Burn off paint.
3. Prime, one coat teak ground paint.
4. Stop up.
5. Face stopping.
6. One coat teak ground paint.
7. Grain.
8. First varnish.
9. Over-grain.
10. Second varnish.
11. Transfers applied, lining out.
12. Two coats finishing varnish.

The teak ground paint was peculiar to this process and was almost buff in colour and not less than 80% zinc oxide. Graining and shading was painted on with raw sienna and vandyke brown water colours. This was feather grained. After varnishing – stage 8 – this combination of colours was used for over-graining. The purpose of this elaborate process was to give depth to the finish and simulate the cross-graining present in natural wood.

As steel-panelled carriages appeared from the mid-1930s they were similarly painted in this simulated teak 'livery'. The method of achieving the finish was much the same as described above although the steel panels had first to be treated with a special primer, then lead coloured paint was applied before the first coat of teak ground paint. Whatever the merits of this idea the results were so skillfully executed in earlier prewar days, at least, that unless closely examined it was difficult to tell that the bodywork was not varnished teak. Quite apart from imitating the grain and texture of the wood, the outlines and shading from traditional mouldings were also reproduced. Sample panels that were still on hand at York Works in the 1960s were most convincing. But it was an expensive finish as a grade 1 painter had to be employed to achieve satisfactory results. Necessarily, a less exacting process was used in time and the ground colour and some of the graining was even spray-painted. The first stock so treated were those twins for the Darlington–Saltburn service built in 1938/9. The NER Tyneside electric units were painted in imitation teak finishes before 1937, as were the earlier LNER steam railcars. After World War 2 the new steel-panelled stock was grained and stipple-finished but mouldings and lining out were omitted. The exterior appearance of these vehicles was not always very convincing, one strange feature being that the sides were painted as if the steel panelling in fact constituted a mosaic of teak panels.

As mentioned above, elderly teak panelled was painted in teak paint if it was considered to be beyond varnishing and this applied to nearly all pre-Grouping stock not of teak construction after the 1930s. It was an unattractive finish and continued to be applied at York Works and elsewhere until 1952. The teak paint was similar in shade to BS 490 'Beech Brown' and was made up from zinc oxide and

linseed oil. The York variant was slightly lighter to the paint used by Doncaster. The passenger brake vans with horizontal deal boarding built in 1946 to Dia 327 were turned out in teak paint overall. Miners and workmen's stock was painted brown-red oxide with white lettering and numerals. in the 1930s and 1940s departmental stock was painted Oxford blue with white block lettering.

All special stock liveries are detailed in the appropriate chapter dealing with the stock. Generally speaking, and apart from the high-speed sets which anyway were in store, after 1942 those carriages with non-standard liveries becoming due for repainting were outshopped in the teak finish.

Roofs

Nearly all vehicles had deal-boarded roofs with canvas covering. The roof was painted two or three coats of white lead paint and the cornices remained in teak finish. After November 1941 roofs were painted in bauxite, some later in grey, to a shade similar to that used in BR days.

Underframes and running gear

Carriage solebars, headstocks, buffer shanks and sleeves were painted in teak paint and varnished. Wheel centres were also in the same colour. Solebar nuts, at least in earlier days, were picked out in green. The teak paint has been referred to above. The pine stepboards were painted black. The underframes, bogies, drawgear, brakework and buffer heads were black. Wheel rims and axles were painted white. Wartime finishes standardised in November 1941 dictated that the whole underframe, bogies, wheels and axles were to be painted black lacquer.

Exposed internal chains and indication discs of the passenger communication cord system were painted red and the bodyend boxes were black. Underframe lettering was picked out in white.

Destination and similar boards

Introduced from 1927, the roof-mounted destination

Above 'J72' 0–6–0T No 68722 shunting at York in June 1958. The first vehicle is brake second E16037E (Dia 37A, built 1936 and formerly 24051). This was a five-compartment type, with one set of doors to the van.

boards had black characters 4 in high on a white ground, the original block lettering changing to Gill Sans after 1935. Small boards for through carriage workings were in the same style but with 2 in or 2½ lettering. They were not used universally but were to be found on some Outer Suburban trains. Some inner Suburban trains carried similar boards but many sets had roller blind indicators. in postwar days the carriage identification plates were placed in the small destination brackets fixed to the cornice and were painted standard LNER dark-blue, with white characters.

As nationalisation took effect, Doncaster and York worked out some alternative liveries and of the chocolate and cream and plum and spilt milk, the latter was used to a limited extent during 1948. From March 1949 the carmine and cream livery became the BR standard and the former 'West Riding limited' vehicles were the first to be outshopped in this scheme by Doncaster. There were some variations in the styles used particularly as regards lettering and numerals and one characteristic feature of the Gresley teak bodied stock in this livery was the absence of the carmine band just under the cant-rail which was otherwise part of this livery scheme. in general, the teak panelled stock literally took the carmine and cream and later maroon BR liveries very badly. The panelling had to be primed with gold size to prevent condensation from coming out through the panels. Some LNER design carriages and full brakes survived to be painted in the blue and grey or all-blue styles from 1966, notably a number of Dia 167 buffet cars, the former buffet lounge cars from the postwar 'Flying Scotsman' sets, a few postwar sleeping cars and a fair collection of bogie brake vans and the six-wheel vans to Dia 358.

CHAPTER 5
GRESLEY VESTIBULED 61 ft 6 in
TEAK STOCK FOR GENERAL SERVICE

HAVING produced a range of standard designs for types of vestibuled carriages in 1923, the LNER continued to build to many of these Diagrams for most of the period during which HNG was Chief Mechanical Engineer. As the requirement for new types lay with the superintendents and passenger managers of the Areas and sections, if they were happy to remain with an existing Diagram then it continued to be specified; as it was, the SPMs often referred to a particular type using a Diagram number that had been superseded. The general principles of ordering were to keep the East Coast sets as up to date as possible and then attend to the principal trains of the various Areas or sections, usually on the basis of one for one, seat for seat replacements. This last objective explains why there are often very small numbers of carriages ordered on some Diagrams, particularly first-class vehicles. In addition, the one for one principle resulted in the need for a full range of composites and brake composites, with varying proportions of first and third-class accommodation and van space.

When the LNER began to recover from the depths of the Depression it built a number of sets of carriages for particular services such as Midlands to North West in the GC section, Newcastle–Carlisle in the North Eastern Area and Edinburgh–Glasgow in the Southern Scottish Area. The big replenishment Programmes of 1935/6, 1937 and so on resulted in relatively large numbers of carriages being ordered to the Diagrams for corridor thirds, corridor brake thirds and open thirds. More carriages were built for special and excursion traffic than would be imagined on today's railway and the total included open firsts as well as the ubiquitous Diagram 186 open thirds.

So to the Diagrams where the two main changes arose firstly from the change in the permitted maximum width from 9 ft to 9 ft 3 in in 1928, thereby explaining the production in or around this year of new Diagrams for practically all types of standard carriage, and the introduction from 1930 of the end door stock. This description covers those vehicles with access to the carriage through end vestibules only and dispensing with the old convention of an outside door to each compartment. As with the restaurant cars built from 1928 the extreme width over the body mouldings of the end door vehicles was 9 ft 3 in, and this was only permissible because the end doors were recessed, the width over the door mouldings being 9 ft. At first, these vehicles were for East Coast service only but in due course there was a full range of Diagrams, the end door stock being built for the principal services and the side door counterparts for general service. Effectively, the first end door vehicles were the third-class sleeping cars of 1928 to Dia 95 which similarly had no compartment side doors. By the mid/late 1930s vestibuled carriages were replacing non-vestibuled stock on semi-fast and cross-country trains, particularly in the North Eastern Area which had a historically low proportion of vestibuled carriages in its fleet.

What follows is a summary of all the Diagrams of 61 ft 6 in vestibuled stock built for general service between 1923 and 1942. Not included in this chapter are the 1937 'East Anglian', 1938 'Flying Scotsman' and 'Hook Continental'

Below Brake second E16288E (Dia 114, built 1937 and formerly 24330). This was the most common four-compartment type. In generally good condition when seen on a Baldock–King's Cross train in July 1963 – close examination reveals minor patching of the main teak panels.

stock or the 52 ft 6 in vestibuled general service stock built for the GE section.

LNER standard vestibuled carriage types and Diagrams

Type	Dia	Width	Compartments	Seats	First Built	Last Built
Open first	3	9' 3"	2 saloons	42	1925	–
(FO)	4	9' 0"	2 saloons	42	1925	–
	218	9' 3"	2 saloons	28	1936	–
	262	9' 3"	2 saloons	42	1936	1940
Semi-open first (Semi-FO)	5	9' 3"	1 saloon, 4 compts	42	1928	1931
	173	9' 3"	1 saloon, 4 compts	42	1933	–
	219	9' 3"	1 saloon, 4 compts	42	1936	1938

Dias 3 'Continental'/4 had seven seating bays and were similar except for the different body widths, the windows having shallow ventilators with glass louvres. Dia 218, a one-off for the 'Hook Continental', and Dia 262 were simply merely updated versions of the earlier examples, with deeper ventilators to the windows.

The semi-open firsts all provided the same accommodation, with four side-corridor compartments and a saloon seating eighteen. These carriages normally adjoined a restaurant car in a set specified for particular trains such as the 5.45 pm Kings Cross–Hull/Leeds and the Leeds–Glasgow express. Dia 219 had the corridor on the other side of the carriage to the earlier Dias and was without outside doors to the compartment.

Above End door composite GE18416E (Dia 296, built 1939 and formerly 1860). This shows the compartment side, as compared to No 1531 (page 46). The deep ventilators were a feature of the late 1930s' vehicles. At Cambridge in May 1964.

Type	Dia	Width	Compartments	Seats	First Built	Last Built
Corridor first (FK)	1	9' 3"	7	42	1925	1939
	2	9' 0"	7	42	1926	1927
	139	9' 3"	6 End doors	36	1930	–
	147	9' 3"	6 End doors	24*	1931	–
	156	9' 3"	6 End doors	24*	1932	–
	172	9' 3"	6 End doors	36	1933	1940

★ Later 36 seats.

Dias 1/2 were similar, except for the body widths. Dia 1 lasted throughout the Gresley period as the standard general purpose first corridor although earliest examples were for 'Continental' sets only.

Dias 139/147/156 were the first end door Gresley designs, officially referred to as the 'super firsts', and were for the principal East Coast sets. Full details are given of their features in Chapter 7. Dia 172 was built for East Coast stock and the Southern Scottish Area only, the latter specifying them for main line sets such as Edinburgh–Aberdeen.

Below LNER Diagram Book: semi-open first to Dia 5. This type was specified for workings where dining accommodation was required, these vehicles being marshalled next to a restaurant car.

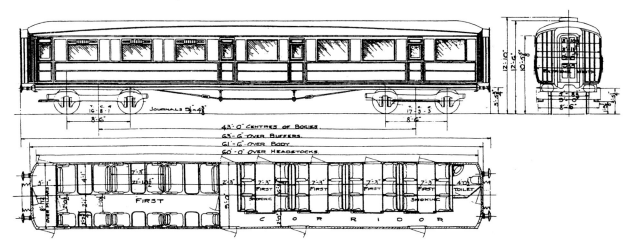

Type	Dia	Width	Compart-ments	Seats	First Built	Last Built
Open	22★	9' 3"	2 saloons	48	1925	–
third/	27	9' 0"	3 saloons	48	1925	1927
open	27A	9' 3"	2 saloons	64	1927	1935
second	27C	9' 3"	2 saloons	48	1936	1937
(TO)/	150	9' 3"	2 saloons	64	1931	–
(SO)★	225	9' 3"	2 saloons	46		
	CLC 82	9' 3"	2 saloons	56	1937	–
Tourist	186	9' 3"	1 saloon	64	1934	1938
open third (TTO)	302	9' 3"	1 saloon	64	1939	–

★ open second

Dia 22 was for the 'Continental' sets of 1925 and were built at Stratford. In keeping with the practice of the time these dining vehicles were without lavatories. With the arrival of new vehicles for the 'Hook Continental' in 1936, two of Dia 22 were each rebuilt with one lavatory, so reducing the seating to 46, were altered to Dia 225 and transferred to the North Eastern Area. The other pair remained on Dia 22 but became third-class in 1942.

Open thirds in the Dia 27 series were generally intended to work with an adjoining restaurant car, to provide meal service, except for East Coast and GN section workings for which pantry thirds were preferred. Dia 27 vehicles were also allocated to Areas for party traffic. The seating was arranged to give 48 places when used for dining and 64 in general traffic, with 3 + 1 seating across. Dia 27 had shallow ventilators with glass louvres. Dia 27A covered vehicles for 'Continental' sets and these were designated second-class, see Chapter 8. GE section Dia 27 series carriages worked in pairs with restaurant kitchen cars and were lettered Restaurant Car; as were some in other areas but by no means all. The GE section Dia 27s were subject to a somewhat confusing renumbering in order to bring them all into the 61xx series.

No 22314, Dia 27A of 1930, was converted to a buffet car in 1934 on Diagram 185 and worked on the 12 noon Newcastle–York and 6.15 pm return. Dia 150, although nominally 64-seaters, were used on the 5.45 pm Kings Cross–Hull/Leeds for dining. This design had luggage shelves at one end and one lavatory only. One oddity was the open third built for the CLC to Gresley design by Cravens in 1937 as CLC No 700, numbered after

Below LNER Diagram Book: open third to Dia 27. The idea was that the larger seats could seat three a side for normal purposes but two a side when the vehicle was used for meal service. Some were designated as restaurant cars and lettered appropriately, others were used for excursion work.

Nationalisation as M999M.

One of the most numerous single designs of Gresley standard carriage were the Dia 186 open thirds, of which 410 or so were built from 1934–8. The classification 'Tourist Third Opens' denoted their primary use for excursion and party traffic in train sets with Dia 191 or 196 brake open thirds and the majority had bucket seats as built. They were also intended for work on main line reliefs and for holiday trains. In terms of duties it is difficult to draw a clear demarcation between these teak liveried vehicles and the sets of green and cream liveried Tourist stock but the former were more likely to be used on timetabled services. Several were appropriated for ambulance trains during World War 2 but returned to service postwar. Many Dia 186 carriages were converted from 1946 onwards with the standard high-backed type of seats which were fitted as new to those on Order 959 and on Dia 302. Interiors of the TTOs comprised one saloon, the two vestibules and two lavatories at one end. Oval mirrors were placed vertically on interior body walls between seating bays. Extinguished by 1965, one late use of a set of these carriages was on the Gresley Society's 'London and North Eastern Flier' of 2 May 1964 from Kings Cross to Darlington, formed BSO 16623, TSOs 13447/53, 13524/9/31/13604, former buffet lounge car 1852 and BSO 16629. Several Dia 186 vehicles have survived for preservation as a result of their conversion during the 1950s/60s for inclusion in BR/ Ministry of Transport emergency control trains.

No 13369 (Dia 186) was the prototype cafeteria car authorised by the Railway Executive and its conversion was completed by Eastleigh Works at the end of February 1952. It was the first of 65 such conversions from a variety of pre-nationalisation carriages drawn from all Big Four origins and including several former GNR dining cars. The layout of the cafeteria cars comprised a small kitchen, a self-service/bar counter and seating accommodation. As modified, No 13369 had tip-up seating for 48 passengers taking refreshments and an interior repanelled in laminated plastics.

Type	Dia	Width	Compart-ments	Seats	First Built	Last Built
Third/	21★	9' 3"	8	48	1925	–
Second	23	9' 0"	{8	48	1924	–
(TK)/			{8	64	1926	1927
(SK)★	24	9' 0"	7 + Locker	48	1926	–
	115	9' 3"	8	64	1928	1939
	155	9' 3"	7 End doors	42	1932	1938
	298	9' 3"	7 End doors	42	1938	1941

★ Second-class

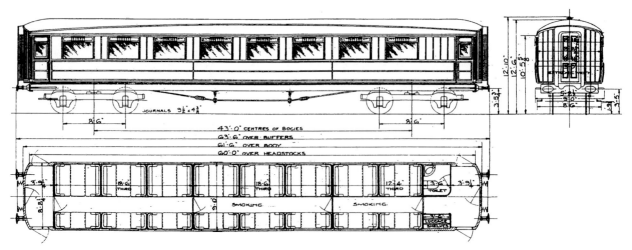

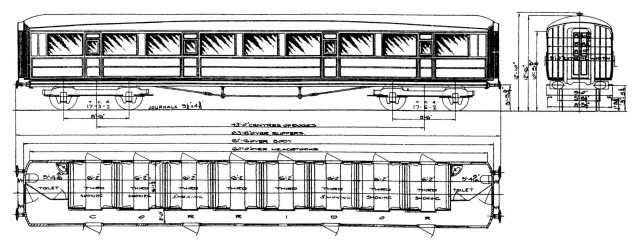

These were the most numerous type of standard LNER carriage built, numbering some 900, of side door and end door types.

Construction began in late 1923 at York on the first batch of thirds to Dia 23, most of which went to form the 'Flying Scotsman' and other East Coast sets, but of the early post-Grouping allocation the North Eastern and Northern Scottish Areas and Great Central section received examples. Dia 23 vehicles had eight compartments, two lavatories and four corridor side doors and were of 9 ft width. Indeed they were very similar to the basic ECJS vestibuled third. The four Dia 23 thirds, two Dia 7 composites and three bogie vans to Dia 43, built in 1925/6 for the Northern Scottish Area, were transferred to the Southern Scottish Area in 1928 as a result of difficulties when working with BS gangwayed LMS vehicles in Aberdeen–Inverness workings. They were also vacuum only when the other NSA stock was air or dual fitted.

Dia 21 was built for the GE section 'Continental' sets, three at Stratford in 1925 and two in 1936. Whether transferred or remaining on the GE section they were redesignated Dia 115 – all were 9 ft 3 in wide – and became thirds.

The 1000 series thirds in East Coast stock were, with the 'A1' Pacifics, the pride of the newly formed LNER and some remained in the principal EC sets or as spares until 1935/6, thereafter being transferred to the Areas. Exceptions were the so called Toilet Thirds Nos 1007/12 (Dia 23A), described in Chapter 8. These remained in the 'Flying Scotsman' sets until the arrival of the new stock in 1938. Dia 24 comprised the locker third version for East Coast use, the three vehicles to this diagram later being transferred to the Northern Scottish Area.

There were some 520 Dia 115 thirds, almost identical externally to Dia 23, but of 9 ft 3 in width. The design remained current until 1939, the later vehicles incorpo-

Above LNER Diagram Book: third to Dia 23, to 9 ft extreme width. Earlier examples seated 48, then four a side seating was the norm, as in this drawing, but later intermediate armrests were fitted to some vehicles so that they were designated for 48 seats. Unlike the practice of the other Big Four companies after Grouping, the LNER vestibule thirds had only four, not eight corridor side doors.

rating some of the detail changes in finish mentioned in Chapter 4. Large number were built for the Areas under the 1935/6, 1937 and 1938 CBPs, many of these being formed into into sets for cross-country workings. Effectively, Dia 115 had declined in status once the end door designs were being specified for principal services, the older design replacing non-vestibuled stock in many cases, particularly in the North Eastern Area. Until 1964 these carriages were in general use but few survived beyond the end of that year.

Dia 155 was introduced from 1932, initially for East Coast sets, but after 1934 some 160 were built for allocation to the Areas; these also received some of the earlier East Coast Dia 155 allocation displaced by the new build under the Government Assistance Works authorised in 1936. The earliest examples had drop-type windows to the compartments. The updated diagram was 298, some of which were redesignated firsts after the start of World War 2. Five had BS gangways and buckeye adaptors for working with LMS stock on Edinburgh–Inverness trains, along with composites and brake thirds to Dias 296/7.

Below LNER Diagram Book: end door third to Dia 155, indicating clearly how the absence of intermediate bodyside doors permitted the use of longer and therefore stronger longitudinal body framing. The early examples had adjustable trussing. Fifty-six seats without intermediate armrests, 42 with. The compartment side had shallow, drop type windows, later sealed.

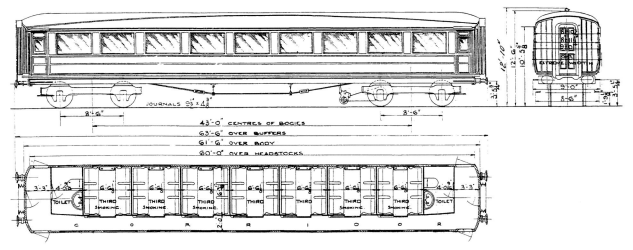

Type	Dia	Width	Compartments	Seats	First Built	Last Built
Composite (CK)	6	9' 0"	3½ 1st, 4 3rd	21/32	1926	1929
	6A	9' 0"	3 1st, 4 2nd	21/32	1926	–
	7	9' 0"	2½ 1st, 5 3rd	15/40*	1924	1926
	8	9' 0"	2½ 1st, 4 3rd + Locker	15/32*	1924	1926
	116	9' 3"	2½ 1st, 4 3rd + Locker	15/32	1928	1929
	130	9' 3"	3½ 1st, 4 3rd	21/32	1930	1940
	137	9' 3"	2½ 1st, 5 3rd	15/40*	1930	1940
	211	9' 3"	3 1st, 4 3rd End doors	18/24	1936	1938
	296	9' 3"	3 1st, 4 3rd End doors	18/24	1939	–

* Some later with intermediate armrests and seating reduced by eight.

One consequence of adhering to a standard dimension for underframes and compartments was a 'left over' space which in most of these composites became a first-class coupé measuring just over 5 ft 3 in between partitions and seating three passengers. Dia 6A was for 'Continental' sets

Below End door composite No 1531 (Dia 211, built 1936 and a war loss).

Bottom LNER Diagram Book: locker composite to Dia 8, among the early post Grouping vehicles for the East Coast stock. This was basically Dia 7, with the locker compartment in place of one third-class compartment, but the layout of windows and panelling on the corridor side was different.

and later became Dia 6 with the withdrawal of second-class. Dia 116/130/137 were the 9 ft width versions of the earlier diagrams, Dia 130 being the usual accompaniment to Dia 115 in sets.

The end door composites were built for the East Coast and Southern Scottish Area only.

Type	Dia	Width	Compartments	Seats	First Built	Last Built
Brake first (BFK)	29	9' 3"	5	30	1927	–
	30	9' 0"	3	18	1925	–
	136	9' 3"	3	18	1928	–
	142	9' 3"	4	24	1930	1938
	149	9' 3"	4	24	1931	1939
	221	9' 3"	3 End doors	18	1936	–
	263	9' 3"	5 End doors	30	1938	–
	300	9' 3"	3	18	1939	–

A good example of a type built for use in specific train sets only. The brake first was particularly favoured by the GN section which specified the lion's share of those built. Good examples of uses were the 5.45 pm from Kings Cross and Leeds–Glasgow (again!) and the Dia 300 examples were intended for the 1.40 pm Kings Cross–Harrogate, 5.50 pm Harrogate and 7.15 pm Hull to replace GNR vehicles. At different times Nos 4204/6 saw use on the 'Northern Belle'. Nos 24487–9 on Dia 149 had BS gangways and Nos 4165/6 on the same diagram were in ambulance trains.

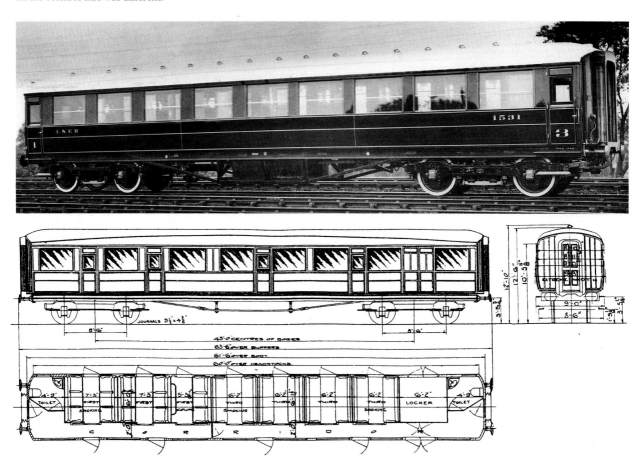

Above A smart looking set of carriages forms a down Cambridge line express headed by 'B1' 4–6–0 No 61283, approaching Bethnal Green in 1959. The Gresley vehicles certainly looked better in the BR maroon livery. The leading example is a brake second, then a second, a composite and next a Dia 167 buffet car.

Type	Dia	Width	Compart-ments	Seats	First Built	Last Built
Brake	135	9' 3"	1 saloon	32	1930	–
third open	191	9' 3"	1 saloon	32	1935	–
(BTO)	196	9' 3"	1 saloon	48	1935	1938
	303	9' 3"	1 saloon	48	1939	–
	326	9' 3"	1 saloon	32	–	–

Dia 135 were ordered with some Dia 27A open thirds for use on excursions and for party traffic – they were intended to seat 24 if used for dining – and indeed all the brake open thirds on the above four diagrams were similarly employed. Bucket seats as fitted prewar were gradually replaced during BR days. Dia 196 was the principal design and vehicles to this diagram ran with Dia 186 open thirds in sets. Dia 303 had the conventional armchair type seats as built, as did Nos 3115/50 to Dia 196. Dia 326 covered the conversion of one Dia 196 vehicle – No 57706 – with the loss of two seating bays and a resultant larger brake compartment.

Below Brake third No 22202 (Dia 40, built 1926 and later 16140). This was a three-compartment type, the van having two pairs of double doors. To 9 ft extreme width.

Type	Dia	Width	Compart-ments	Seats	First Built	Last Built
Brake	35*	9' 3"	4	24	1925	–
third/	36	9' 0"	6	48	1926	–
brake	37	9' 3"	5	40	1927	–
second	37A	9' 3"	5	40+	1929	1940
(BTK)/	38	9' 3"	4	32	1925	–
(BSK)*	39	9' 0"	4	32	1926	–
	40	9' 0"	3	24	1924	1926
	40A	9' 3"	3	24	1928	1934
	114	9' 3"	4	32+	1929	1939
	174	9' 3"	3	24	1933	1939
	178	9' 3"	6	36	1933	1940
	212	9' 3"	4 End door	24	1936	1937
	297	9' 3"	4 End door	24	1939	1940
	301	9' 3"	3 End door	18	1939	1942
	324	9' 0"	4	24	–	–

* brake second + Some later with intermediate armrests, seating reduced to 24.

The earliest examples did not have guard's duckets – Dias 36/37/38/39/40, nor did Nos 1262–4 of Dia 40A. All had the recessed bodywork for the length of the brake compartment ahead of the double doors nearest the passenger compartments. Some fifteen or so carriages to Dia 37A and sixteen of Dia 114 were converted for overseas ambulance trains in World War 2.

The principal types were Dias 114/174/178, of which the first listed was the most numerous and effectively the counterpart of the Dia 115 thirds. Two of Dia 114 for the

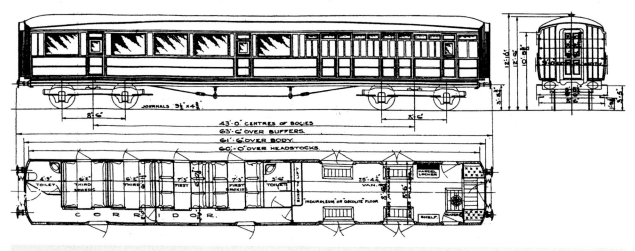

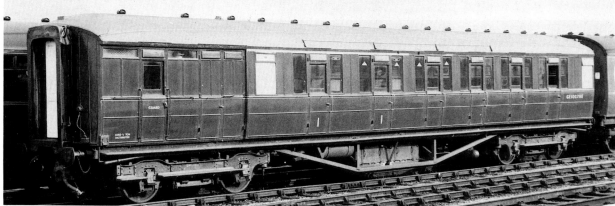

North Eastern Area had BS gangways to work with LMS stock. The three-compartment design, as Dia 174, was specified for services with significant postal traffic. All but a handful of these carriages on all diagrams were withdrawn by 1965.

Only two configurations of end door brake thirds were built, Dia 301 including some of the last Gresley teak carriages to be constructed, in 1942. Vehicles to Dias 297/301 were the last non-special Gresley carriages to remain in service, a number surviving into 1965 and the last into 1968.

Dia 324 was produced in 1943 to cover the conversion of Dia 34 brake composites to brake thirds.

Top LNER Diagram Book: brake composite to Dia 34. This was the 2 + 2 version in terms of classes and to 9 ft extreme width. During World War 2 a number were altered to brake thirds and remained as such.

Above One that got away! Dia 175 brake composite GE 10078E, at Cambridge in May 1964. This had been shopped the previous year when the yellow stripe to denote first-class accommodation had been applied. This was to be one of the very few ordinary Gresley vehicles to be sold for preservation from BR service and is now in safe hands on the Severn Valley Railway.

Some to Dia 34 were redesignated brake thirds in 1943 to Dia 324, seating 24. The most numerous design was Dia 175, of which 70 or so were built, and they were used mainly by the Areas for through carriages such as Harrogate–Southport (with BS gangways), Leeds–Whitby, Kings Cross–Horncastle and cross-country workings including Newcastle–Southampton and Newcastle–Sheffield. One notable survivor into preservation is No 24068 (10078) outshopped at York in 1963 and then stored there – after a period in traffic – from 1964 until purchased in 1969.

Dia 314 was the only end door design of brake composite.

Type	Dia	Width	Compart-ments	Seats	First Built	Last Built
Brake	31	9' 0"	2 1st, 4 3rd	12/32	1926	–
composite	32	9' 3"	2 1st. 3 3rd	12/24+	1927	1930
(BCK)	33	9' 0"	2 1st, 3 3rd	12/24+	1926	–
	34	9' 0"	2 1st, 2 3rd	12/16+	1924	1926
	127	9' 3"	2 1st, 2 3rd	12/16+	1929	1937
	134	9' 3"	2 1st, 4 3rd	12/32	1930	1932
	143	9' 3"	2 1st, 3 3rd	12/24	1930	1940
	175	9' 3"	2 1st, 3 3rd	12/18	1933	1940
	314	9' 3"	2 1st. 3 3rd End door	12/18	1941	–
	316	9' 3"	3 1st, 3 3rd	18/18	1940	–

+ Some later with intermediate armrests, third-class seating reduced accordingly.

CHAPTER 6
GRESLEY NON-VESTIBULED TEAK-BODIED STOCK

DURING 1923 the standards for non-vestibuled stock were drawn up and the following dimensions agreed:

Length of body over mouldings	51 ft 1½ in
Length of underframe	51 ft 0 in
Between bogie centres	35 ft 0 in
Width over body panels	8 ft 9 in
Width overall	9 ft 0 in

Compartment partition to partition dimensions were maintained as closely as possible to 7 ft 3 in for the first-class and 6 ft 2 in for the third-class. The major exceptions were the GN/GE sections' articulated suburban trains and the Ilford stock of 1935 with compartments of just 5 ft 3½ in between partitions. After 1927 new diagrams were issued with the overall body width increased to 9 ft 3 in. Van compartments up to 17 ft long had one pair of doors each side, those over 17 ft having two pairs of doors, with a guard's door in addition in each case. The guard's seat and hand brake were normally at the far end. End windows were fitted in non-vestibuled brake vehicles. In general, the specifications

Below A Waverley-bound local train threads Princes Street Gardens, Edinburgh in 1938 behind 'V1' 2–6–2T No 2910, its train comprising Gresley non-vestibuled stock and two NBR vehicles, Nos 3 and 6 in the formation. The two brakes are the four-compartment version, the other Gresley vehicles being lavatory composites – Dias 49 or 50. The small white painted destination boards can be seen at cantrail level on the brake vehicles.

adopted in 1923 were maintained until the last teak-panelled non-articulated non-vestibuled carriages were built in 1938. From that date new construction was to steel-panelled designs.

The principal changes over the years affected the interior finish and standard of lighting, details of which are featured in Chapter 4. Until the mid-1930s interior panelling was initially varnished and polished teak, then veneered block-board for the partitions and Rexine for the side walls, with teak frames for mirrors and system maps, advertisements or pictures above the seat backs. The familiar black and crimson pile upholstery, to take the third-class as the example, was relieved by compartment side armrests trimmed in leathercloth and with blinds of the same material, or Rexine, usually in brown. The increasing use of Rexine for compartment interior finishes perpetuated largely similar colour scheme such as the ivory ceiling and brown side walls to be found in the Dia 204 seconds in the Ilford sets, offset by blue and brown moquette. In all fairness, the interiors of the teak bodied non-vestibuled stock are best described as adequate – but a lot better than their later steel panelled counterparts.

The LNER maintained second-class on the GN/GE sections' suburban services until withdrawal with effect from 1 January 1938. After 6 October 1941 first-class accommodation was discontinued on local services originating within the London area.

In the period immediately following Grouping the LNER

NON-VESTIBULED STOCK – list of types and Diagram numbers

TABLE 6A

Type	Diagram 51' 1½" body unless shown/width	Width	Compartments	Seats	First Built	Last Built
First	46	60' 0½", by 9' 3"	8	64	1924	–
(F)	47	9' 0"	7	56	1925	1926
	48	9' 3"	7	56	1927	1934

TABLE 6B

Type	Diagram 51' 1½" body unless shown/width	Width	Compartments	Seats	First Built	Last Built
Second	55	9' 3"	8	80	1927	–
(S)	204	54' 1½", by 9' 3"	10	120	1935	–

embarked on the general replacement of all types of coaching stock in a manner that it was unable to sustain after the late 1920s, given the prevailing restrictions on expenditure. The priority was for complete trains to re-equip the GN and GE London suburban services but non-vestibuled stock was also built in quantity for the North Eastern and Southern Scottish Areas, a large proportion being ordered from contractors, and this replaced four and six-wheeled stock. The numbers of non-vestibuled carriages, other than in articulated twins, declined from the early 1930s, largely because their construction came well down the list in terms of priorities when the rather frugal building programmes of that time were being conjured up and also in view of the decision to use the steam railcars for local and branch services.

From the 1930/1 CBP there were transfers of non-vestibuled stock, principally from the North Eastern Area where they were displaced by vestibuled carriages. Some were 'transferred' to the Cheshire Lines Committee although their removal from LNER stock was effectively a sale. In the period up to the outbreak of World War 2 around 120 thirds and brake thirds of LNER standard non-vestibuled stock, not to mention pre-Grouping vehicles, were transferred from the North Eastern Area to the Southern Scottish and Northern Scottish Areas and to the Great Eastern section. Some of the transfers went to make up complete sets, others to make an inroad into the ranks of

Below First/second composite No 63891 (Dia 215, built 1936, later 88148). This was a one-off for GE section outer suburban services. This Dukinfield photograph shows that antimacassars were fitted to the first-class seats.

four and six wheeled stock, of which the LNER had more than its fair share. At its November 1928 the Locomotive and Traffic Joint Committee had discussed public complaints regarding carriages in Wrexham, Chesterfield and Sheffield local workings. These still had flat-flame gas lights and one conclusion was that those between 25 and 35 years old should be fitted with incandescent gas lighting as they were unlikely to be withdrawn in under ten years. This indicates something of the problem, made worse by the absence of replacements during the 1932/3 'freeze' on most new construction. When Gresley chaired the meeting at Kings Cross during 1934 referred to in Chapter 3 the objective was that by the end of 1936 all four and six wheeled stock would be eliminated, on everything but the backwoods services. The Areas' representatives attending that meeting identified around 1,700 vehicles, 90% of these being non-vestibuled, as required for the replacement of four and six wheeled stock. The North Eastern Area was able to offer some 2,000 non-vestibuled bogie carriages for transfer and a proportion of these, supplemented by new construction, went some way to cutting down the ranks of the ancients. Of the transfers, the GE section received Dia 56 thirds under the 1935/6 CBP to replace air braked four and six wheeled stock, particularly on the Felixstowe branch.

Those teak non-vestibuled and non-articulated carriages built after the early 1930s were mainly for semi-fast services. The exception was the construction under the 1935/6 CBPs of eight trains, with spares, of 54 ft underframe air-braked vehicles for the Liverpool Street–Ilford service, catering for all three classes of passengers. Each train was made up of two sets formed: BT + T + S + C/ C + S + T + BT. The

NON-VESTIBULED STOCK – list of types and Diagram numbers (continued)

TABLE 6C

Type	Diagram	Length •/Width	Compartments	Seats	First Built	Last Built
Third	56	9' 0"	8	80	1925	1926
(T)	57	9' 3"	8	80	1927	1930
	58	56' 0½", by 9' 3"	9	108	1924	–
	203	54' 1½", by 9' 3"	10	120	1935	–

TABLE 6D

Type	Diagram	Length ★/Width	Compartments	Seats	First Built	Last Built
Composite	51	9' 3"	4/3	32/30	1927	1937
(C)	110•	9' 3"	4/3	32/30	1929	1937
	188	Former Dia 47 F– 9' 0"	4/3	32/30	–	–
	189	Former Dia 48 F	4/3	32/30	–	–
	205•	54' 1½", by 9' 3"	4/5	40/60	1935	–
	215•	9' 3"	2/6	20/60	1936	–
	283	Former Dia 46 F	4/4	32/48	–	–
	306	Former Dia 48 F	6/1	48/12	–	–

• First/second composites, later first/third on the same diagrams.

TABLE 6E

Type	Diagram	Length★/Width	Compartments	Seats	First Built	Last Built
Composite	49	9' 0"	3/4	19/33	1925	1926
(Lavatory)	50	9' 3"	3/4	19/33	1927	1935
(CL)	244	9' 3"	2/5	13/41	1936	–

TABLE 6F

Type	Diagram	Length★/Width	Compartments	Seats	First Built	Last Built
Brake Third	59	9' 3"	6	72	1924	–
(BT)	60	9' 3"	6	60	1928	–
	61	9' 3"	5	50	1927	1928
	62	9' 0"	5	50	1925	–
	63	9' 0"	5	50	1926	–
	64	9' 0"	4	40	1926	–
	65	9' 3"	4	40	1926	1931
	66	9' 0"	3	30	1926	–
	117	9' 3"	5	50	1930	–
	119	9' 3"	3	30	1928	1930
	128	9' 3"	4	40	1930	1931
	133	9' 3"	6	60	1928	–
	202	54' 1½", by 9' 3"	7	84	1935	–
	246	9' 3"	6	60	1938	–
	254	Former Dia 63	5	50	–	–
	317	Former Dia 65	4	40	–	–
	320	Former Dia 64	4	40	–	–

TABLE 6G

Type	Diagram	Width	Compartments	Seats	First Built	Last Built
Brake	52	9' 3"	2/3	16/30	1927	–
Composite	53	9' 3"	2/2	16/20	1927	–
(BC)	54	9' 0"	2/2	16/20	1926	–
	118	9' 3"	2/4	16/40	1930	–
	318	9' 3"	2/4	16/40		–

★ In the above tables, all vehicles have 51' 1½"bodies, unless otherwise shown.

51

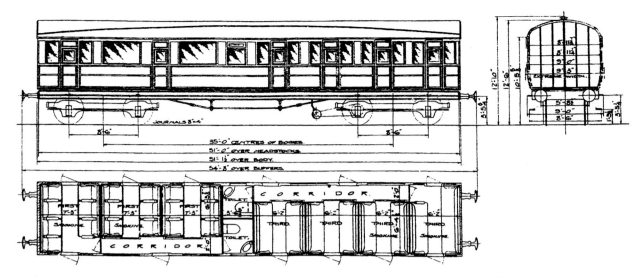

Above LNER Diagram Book: lavatory composite to Dia 50, revealing the neat layout of this useful type, to be perpetuated in Dias 299 and 338.

underframe length was chosen to ensure uniformity with GER-design stock and to suit platform and siding lengths and GER pattern bogies were fitted. The displaced GER sets were transferred to the North Woolwich line services to replace 60 four wheeled vehicles. The 1935 Ilford stock was originally intended to be included in the 184 steam carriages scheduled for conversion into trailers to run with new compartment electric motor coaches for the Shenfield electrification. With the decision to build all-new saloon type multiple-units for this service the Ilford sets were redundant once electrification was completed in 1949. Some vehicles had been lost to enemy action but the displaced survivors, together with GER-design sets, rotted away in open store at Stratford until 24 were used to provide underframes for new stock for the London, Tilbury & Southend line in 1953. Thirty-five others formed the basis of motor car vans built in the mid-1950s and numbered 71000–34 in the LNER van stock series.

LNER non-vestibuled, non-articulated teak bodied stock from 1923

Dia 46 was non-standard, built at Dukinfield for GC section use; these employed underframes from GCR vehicles returned after use in ambulance trains. No 51856 remained on Dia 46 but became all-third, but the other three were altered to composites to Dia 283. One of Dia 47 was altered to a composite to Dia 188 and seven of Dia 47 to composites on Dia 189. (see table 6A)

Below Brake second E86033E (Dia 62, built 1925 as 10339B, later 3594). Note the destination board brackets and the excellent condition of this 30-year old vehicle. With five compartments there was room for just one pair of double doors to the van.

Dia 48 vehicles built for the GE section were used typically in main line stopping train sets or for Liverpool Street–Royal Albert Docks boat trains. (see table 6A)

Dia 55 vehicles were later altered to Dia 57. Dia 204 was Ilford stock and became all-third on the same diagram number (see table 6B).

Dias 56/57 (table 6C) were among the most numerous non-vestibuled carriages, some 360 being built, principally by contractors. The majority of those built for the North Eastern Area were transferred to other Areas and sections from the 1930/1 CBP and up until 1938 while four on Dia 57 went to the CLC. Those transferred to the Southern Scottish Area were used to form sets working between Helensburgh and Glasgow and Edinburgh and Dundee and for the Singer works trains. Dia 57 Nos 773/4 were fitted to work in push-pull trains. Dia 58 employed underframes from GCR vehicles returned after ambulance train use. Dia 203 was Ilford stock (see table 6C).

Dia 51 was the main type of composite, see Table 6D, used by the Southern Scottish Area and the GE section, the latter also using Dia 110, the first/second composite version, this subsequently transferring to Dia 51. GE section Dia 51 carriages later had the intermediate armrests removed which increased the first-class seating in each carriage to 40. Dia 205 was Ilford stock and Dia 215 was a one-off for the GE section. The other diagrams covered former firsts downgraded to composites with the decline of first-class season ticket-holders.

Listed in Table 6E, the semi-corridor lavatory composite – to give it its full name – was intended for longer distance journeys and to that end all compartments had access to lavatories, reached by side corridor. There were long windows along the corridor sides, the first-class corridor being on one side and the third-class corridor on the opposite side. Dia 50 Nos 32443 and 63265 were later fitted for push-pull working. Nos 63898–900 on Dia 244 were originally dual-fitted.

The varying van space available in the various types of brake third (table 6F) usually reflected the amount of parcels and postal business on the workings they covered. Dia 62 had the guard's position next to the first compartment. Earlier examples did not have windows at the van end and from 1932 a ducket was provided on the right-hand side of the van. Dia 65 vehicles built for the GE section had 8 ft wheelbase bogies, were 8 ft 11⅛ in over the cornices and the vans were labelled to carry three tons. There were a number of transfers of Dia 64/65 vehicles from the North Eastern Area to the Northern Scottish Area and GE sections. Dia 63 Nos 62543–6 were converted in 1936 for push-pull working and received large windows in the brake end, a driver's compartment and the necessary operating gear. They were classified as Ordinary Brake Third Driving Carriage and ran

Right Push-pull train on the Epping–Ongar line, propelled by a GER 2–4–2T and seen in early BR days. This shows well the driving cab created in the Dia 64 or 65 brake third, working as a set with a Dia 56 or 57 third. The narrower width of the brake compartment is apparent in this view.

with ex-GER trailers to provide two-car sets. Dia 317 was a 1940 conversion of Dia 65 Nos 3233/7572 as OBTDCs while Dia 320 was the 1942 conversion of No 7572 on Dia 64.

Push-pull working was introduced by the LNER for a number of local services from 1933 in order to reduce operating costs by dispensing with guards. At first, use was made of pre-Grouping vehicles to provide push-pull sets but in due course LNER standard carriages were converted although the numbers involved were relatively small. The process of conversion to push-pull working was stepped up from 1939 to include services such as to Audley End–Bartlow, Ongar–Epping, Buntingford–St Margarets, Craigendoran–Arrochar and the St Combs branch. The last but one named resisted dieselisation until 1959.

Vehicles from Dias 60, 128 and 133 were transferred to the CLC in 1930 and 1932. Dia 202 was Ilford stock with very limited van space.

All brake composite vehicles to the four diagrams (table 6G) were built for the Southern Scottish Area. Dia 318 was the push-pull conversion of Nos 32533/4 in 1940.

With widespread dieselisation and electrification from the mid-1950s withdrawals of the teak non-vestibuled carriages began in earnest, the fate of the Ilford stock having been referred to already. All but a very few had succumbed by 1964 or so but among those non-vestibuled carriages still in service in early 1962 were some of the thirds of 1927/8 vintage.

Articulated teak bodied non-vestibuled twins (table 6H)

These followed the pattern introduced at the end of the GNR's existence with the articulated twins to GNR Dias 218QQ and 218RR which were used for Outer Suburban and Cambridge line trains from Kings Cross. Similar twins, but with 51 ft bodies, were introduced in 1929/30 for Kings Cross Outer Suburban services and were similar in general outline to the GNR designs but with typical Gresley LNER features. Four composite twins on Dias 124/6, two built in 1929 for the GN section and two in 1930 for the GC section, were later altered to Dia 242. Dia 242 new construction covered composite twins completed in 1937/8 for the GC section and the Southern Scottish Area. Dia 105 was also used for the brake third of the GE section quadruplets built in 1929.

Despite the appearance of steel-panelled designs the traditional teak bodied vehicles were built to two body lengths for the re-equipment of the Marylebone suburban services, beginning in 1935. In all, there were 84 twins built between 1935–1938. The earliest build were used to make up three trains of four twins and the 1937/8 vehicles used in fourteen five-car sets. With the concentration of all GW/GC Joint line services on Marylebone soon after Nationalisation the sets were made up to six vehicles using two twins and an additional third and brake third.

During 1936/7 39 twins to Dia 210 were built for the GN

section for use on stopping services on the GN main line, in Lincolnshire and in the Nottingham area. In 1937 twelve twins were built to Gresley LNER design by Cravens for the Cheshire Lines Committee and after nationalisation were numbered in the LNER series as 60101–24, at least one twin being lettered M601xx/xxM. Dieselisation and the transfer of former LNER lines in the Nottingham area to the London Midland Region resulted in the withdrawal of all the above articulated stock in the early 1960s.

GN and GE quadruplet and quintuplet sets

GN section quadruplets

Quadruplet sets were included in the GNR's 1922 building programme and four sets were completed in the first year of Grouping, described as GNR Dias 467A, 467B and 478, the first two diagrams being for the quad brake third sets, the last for the quad composite brake sets (first, second and third-class). GNR 467B covered vehicles known by the LNER Diagrams 72B/73/74/75 and 478, 68B/69/70/71. Of those completions during 1923, Nos 48121–4, to Dia 467B or 72B–75, had windows full height to the cant-rail and hit and miss ventilators above the door droplights but retained the GNR type duckets, as did Nos 48141–4/51–4 on Dias 68B–71. While the 8 ft bogie was fitted to three sets, Nos 48141–4 had the 8 ft 6 in heavy type. There was also an increase in weight as compared to the GNR quads, partly as a result of their electric lighting, from 71 tons 12 cwt for Dia 467A to 76 tons 14 cwt for 467B while Dia 478 were heavier at 80 tons 8 cwt, but still providing a remarkably good payload/weight ratio!

The 1923 CBP included eight sets of each type to make up eight trains which were completed at Doncaster in 1924. The underframes were designed so that they could take motor bogies in the case of electrification, with the result that weight was increased further to 83 tons in the case of

Below Twin third brake Nos 52512 (the third – Dia 105) and 52511 (the brake third – Dia 125), built at Doncaster in 1930 and later Nos 86796/7.

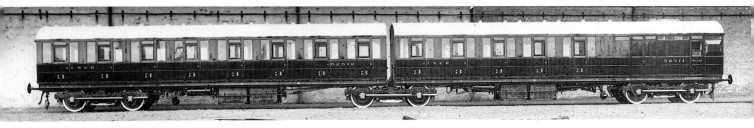

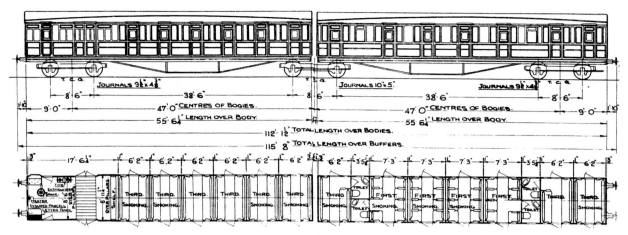

Above LNER Diagram Book: twin brake composite to Dia 214, as built for the Marylebone suburban services. Note the limited van and guard's space.

the quad brake third sets. These sets retained the GNR type duckets and were mounted on the heavy type 8 ft 6 in bogie. It was then decided that these bogies were an unnecessary expense for suburban duties and the 8 ft variety was used from 1925. At this stage it is worth mentioning that the

LNER regarded the London suburban sets for the GN and GE sections apart from the other non-vestibuled stock and they were referred to as the 'suburban trains'; in today's parlance perhaps they would be regarded as high density stock. There were a number of ways in which they were treated differently such as the reduced partition to partition compartment dimensions and finish, notably the lack of lining out and in the choice of upholstery materials.

There were no quadruplets in the 1924 CBP: those origi-

TABLE 6H

Type	Diagram 51' 1½" body unless shown/width	Width	Compartments	Seats	First Built	Last Built
Twin third						
{ Third	105		8	80	1929	1940
{ Third	106		8	80	1929	1940
Twin composite						
{Lav compo	123		3/4	23/39	1929	1930
{ Third	124		8	80	1929	1930
{ Third	124		8	80	1929	1930
(First	126		7	56	1929	1930
{ First	242		7	56	1937	1938
{ Third	242		8	80	1937	1938
{ First	274		7	56	1939	–
{ Third	274		4/3	32/30	1939	–
Twin third brake						
{Third	105		8	80	1929	1930
{Brake third	125		5	50	1929	1930
{Brake third	273		5	50	1939	–
{Third	273		8	80	1939	–
{Brake third	278		4	40	1939	–
{Third	278		8	80	1939	–
Twin brake composite						
{Brake third	107		4	40	1929	1930
{Lav compo	108		3/4	23/39	1929	1930
{Composite	210}	55' 6¾"	2/5	14/48	1935	1937
{Brake third	210}		6	60	1935	1937
{Brake third	213}	55' 6¾"	5	50	1936	1937
{Composite	213}		3/4	22/38	1936	1937
{Brake third	214}	55' 6¾"	6	60	1936	1938
{Composite	214}		4/3	30/28	1936	1938
{First	272}	55' 6¾"	7	56	1939	–
{Brake third	272}		5	50	1939	
CLC twins						
{Brake third	CLC 83}		4	40	1937	–
{Third	CLC 83}		8	80	1937	
{Third	CLC 84}		8	40	1937	–
{Lav compo	CLC 84}		3/4	20/34	1937	

nally proposed were deferred while the London Suburban Traffic Committee was considering the electrification of the GN suburban section. But orders for quads were included in the 1925 CBP in advance of the LNER directors' decision in September 1925 'not to pledge themselves to adopt the proposal for the electrification of the GN section suburban lines'. To relieve pressure on the company's workshops orders were placed with contractors for the building of six further trains in the 1925/6 CBP. But in the year of the General Strike new construction was deferred and the four further trains delivered by Midland Carriage & Wagon Co during 1927 had been deferred from the previous CBP. At this date each train cost £17,000 and in their 40 or so years of life this sum had been written down well before then, leaving the LNER's successors the problem of re-equipping with modern stock in place of fully depreciated equipment. Two trains were built in 1928 and four trains in September 1929. In late 1929, the possible electrification of the GN and/or the GE suburban services was again being considered and it was recognised that, if neither scheme was

progressed, more quadruplets would be required. Five sets were included in the 1931/2 CBP but were cancelled during 1932. The grand total of all GNR/LNER quadruplets built was 97 sets.

One familiar feature of the quads was the illuminated destination box at the brake end. These were not fitted as new but as the result of a suggestion from the chief general manager and, after approval by the Joint Locomotive and Traffic Committee in January 1928, 82 GE section and 40 GN section quads/quints were equipped. The 1929 sets

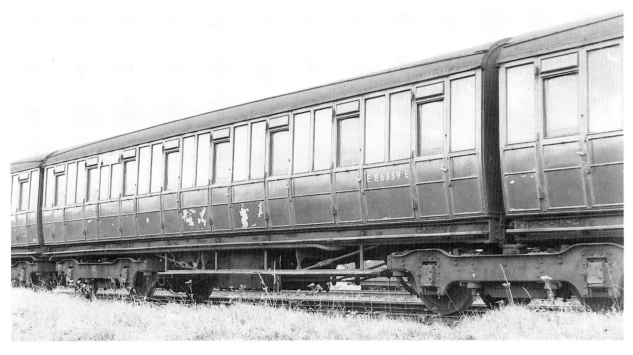

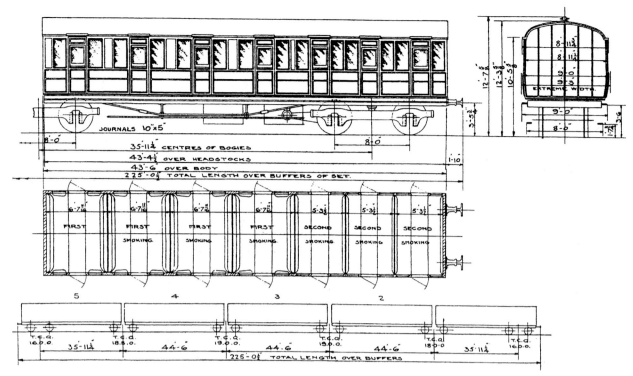

Above LNER Diagram Book: GE section suburban quintuplet first/second composite to Dia 81, later all-third. This also illustrates the length of the quintuplet set. In 1923, the first proposal was to build 54 ft vehicles for the Enfield/Chingford lines.

appeared with the destination boxes as new.

Until 1940 there few changes to the routine of the GN suburban services. In 1936, two sets, Nos 73 and 93, were fitted with Westinghouse quick service brake valves and, in the course of tests were whisked up to 90 mph behind an 'A4' Pacific. After the New Works Programme electrification to High Barnet was inaugurated in 1940 a number of sets were displaced but any excess was absorbed by their use on additional war workers' trains in various parts of the country. Several vehicles were damaged as a result of enemy action. Four trains were transferred to the Marylebone suburban services between 1949 and 1951. With the withdrawal of first-class accommodation from October 1941 stations north of Potters Bar were without first-class facilities and, after complaints from commuters, set No 85 – vehicles 86196–9 – was overhauled at Stratford in 1954 and the first-class accommodation restored. This set worked on the 5.58 pm Kings Cross–Welwyn Garden City which was accordingly dubbed the 'Pottersbarbarian'!

Diesel multiple-units were introduced on the inner

Below One of Stratford Works' photographs, showing a quintuplet brake third, No 10607E, its original 1925 number, later given a GE section number.

suburban services from 1959 and withdrawals of the quadruplets began. By this time they were given minor facelifts with the use of laminated plastic panelling to brighten the partitions and more cheerful paintwork. But by 1964/5 the Eastern Region was conscious that they were overdue for replacement, despite their ability to clear crowds of waiting commuters from platforms more quickly than their successors, and BR standard non-vestibuled stock was transferred from other Regions to effect their retirement. Among the last survivors were those dating back to 1924 and their last workings in the London area occurred in April 1966. Their demise saw the end of locomotive hauled articulated stock in Britain.

Each train of quadruplets was formed by two sets of four carriages, one brake third set and one brake composite set, as follows: BS + S + C + C/ T + T + T + BT, the former comprising vehicles to Dias 68–71, the latter to Dias 72–75. There were detail differences between the sets built over the period, best summarised as:

1923/4 sets Dias 68B/69–71/ 72B–75
 Height over ventilators, 12 ft 7⅞ in; 8 ft 6 in compound bolster bogies; body of brake vehicles with provision for an extra compartment at brake end; GNR style duckets.
1925–8 sets Dias 68–71/ 72–75
 Height over ventilators, 12 ft 7⅞ in; 8 ft single bolster bogies; arranged for conversion to electric stock; no duckets.

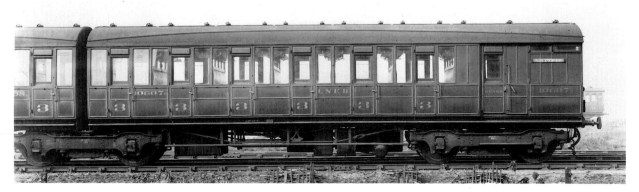

1929 sets   Dias 68A–71A/ 72A–75A
   Height over ventilators, 12 ft 8⅝ in; 8 ft 6 in single
   bolster bogies; not designed for conversion to electric units; no duckets.

At various times bogie types were changed on a few sets so
that those which by rights should have had 8 ft bogies had
received the 8 ft 6 in compound bolster type

GE section quintuplets
H.A.V. Bulleid records that his father examined the GER
suburban stock after Grouping and reported to Gresley
that 'they are falling apart... most of the body frames are
rotting away...' The trains were operating on the most
intensively timetabled steam worked suburban service,
from Liverpool Street to Enfield and Chingford, and their
utilisation was high. Twenty-nine replacement trains of
quintuplet stock were included in the 1924/5 main and
supplementary CBPs at a cost of £452,600, representing
nearly 26% in value of the LNER's total expenditure on
new carriages for that year. All vehicles were delivered
during 1925 by the six outside contractors concerned.
Given the regular overloading of the trains-twenty passengers to each compartment were frequent – the vehicles
were mounted on the 8 ft 6 in compound bolster bogies.
Even though allowances had been made for such loadings
the underframes were observed to bow under the weight of
the passengers and the doors became difficult to open. As
a result, the carriage underframes had to be stiffened and
the bogie springs strengthened. Outwardly the quintuplets
followed many of the features of the GN section quadruplets although the end windows in the brake compartments were larger. Internal compartment dimensions were
almost similar to the GN quads. Each ten-coach train of
two quintuplets could convey 872 passengers and probably that meant 1,500 full and standing passengers at the
peak periods.
   The 1926/7 CBP included four sets of quintuplets but
their completion was deferred in July 1926 to the 1927/8
CBP, 'in view of present circumstances', namely the
effects of the General Strike. Eight more sets followed in
the 1928/9 CBP, built by Clayton Wagon, and four more
the following year, 1929/30, built by Metro-Cammell.
This gave a total of 37 trains and enabled the Enfield line
to be operated entirely with bogie, steam heated stock. All
the quintuplets were fitted with Westinghouse air brakes as
a result of the policy decision of 1928 that all GE section
suburban stock should continue to be air braked only. The
equipment and generally smart working by the locomotive
crews resulted in brisk running on these trains that went
some way to rival modern electric units. Later units had
some variations in body design and were mounted on the 8
ft bogies.
   Apart from the Enfield and Chingford lines, the quintuplets also covered workings to Palace Gates, to Hertford
East and to Stratford and elsewhere on evening excursions
and during World War 2. Unlike the quad sets on the GN
section, the quintuplets were diagrammed to work as
single five-car units such on trains to Palace Gates and, in
later days, on the Enfield line. One set was lost during the
war and new bodies were built for war damaged vehicles in
two other sets.
   In their latter days the quintuplets became a particular
target in the campaign of public criticism of the steam
worked services out of Liverpool Street and, in outward
appearance at least, this was justifiable given the grimy
state of the carriage exteriors which changed their nomi-

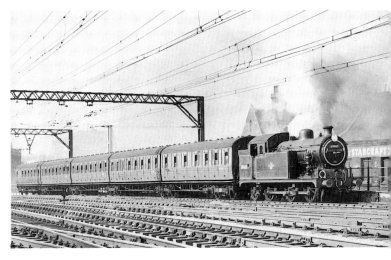

Above The quintuplets were used as single units on GE section
suburban workings, such as on this Enfield Town train
approaching Bethnal Green in the late 1950s behind 'N7' 0–6–2T
No 69665. The extra width of the former first-class compartments
in the leading vehicle will be noted.

nally maroon livery to something like a dirty teak colour.
From the railwaymen's point of view they did their work
nobly until electrification of the north east London
suburban services came in late November 1960. One or
two quintuplets lasted a little longer on the Palace Gates to
North Woolwich service.

The train formations were originally:

BT + T + C(2nd/3rd) + S +C(1st/2nd)/ C(1st/2nd) + S +
   C(2nd/3rd) + T + BT
   From 1938 1st/3rd only, all 3rd from October 1941.
   1925 vehicles Dias 76–80, later sets Dias 81–85.
Brake thirds Dias 80/85, thirds Dias 79/84, comp-
   osites(2nd/3rd) Dias 78/83, seconds Dias 77/82,
composites(1st/2nd) Dias 76/81.
   The later brakes had different side and end panels and
the guard's seat at the end. All the later vehicles were
slightly lower overall, as well as having the 8 ft bogies.

GE section quadruplets
The fourteen GE section quadruplet sets, built at York in
1929, were sometimes overlooked and differed considerably from the GN section trains. Two carriages in each
quadruplet were on standard 51 ft underframes – the
brakes shared the diagram with the GN section articulated
twins – and the stock was intended to work singly or in
pairs on the outer suburban Liverpool Street–Hertford
East line. The sets, numbered 151–164, continued to
operate on this service until electrification in November
1960 although postwar LNER design stock appeared after
displacement from the Southend line. The brakes were
intended to handle parcels and postal traffic and two sets
of doors were provided to the brake compartment, the sets
being regarded as secondary passenger rather than
suburban stock and built to main line standards with
compartment partition to partition dimensions of 7 ft 6 in
in the first-class and 6 ft–6 ft 2 in for the second and third-
class. Vehicles 61800/62804 were rebuilt, the first as a
result of a mishap at Ware in 1940, the latter damaged by
enemy action.

CHAPTER 7
EAST COAST STOCK
FROM 1923–39

AFTER Grouping the LNER decided to continue with a separate allocation of carriages and vans for East Coast services, taking in the former ECJS and GN/NE stock. This was logical in that the services on which they ran had always been operated as a separate entity and with Grouping three LNER areas would be involved: Southern, North Eastern and Southern Scottish; four, if one takes the Northern Scottish Area into account for the through carriages beyond Aberdeen. As before, when stock was displaced from East Coast use, if not condemned it was transferred to the Areas. The East Coast stock remained as a separate fleet until after nationalisation and even into the 1960s new BR vehicles were branded 'East Coast'. Of one thing there was no doubt, the East Coast carriages constituted the elite of the LNER coaching stock and the provision of new vehicles was a priority above all else.

New innovations such as the end door carriages appeared first in East Coast services, special services were provided only on East Coast trains and the stock allocated had extras not to be found on less exalted vehicles. The East Coast service was always strongly influenced by the start of the summer timetable which usually saw the introduction of new stock. During January the existing sets were taken into works – Doncaster or York, depending on the works responsible for individual vehicles – for lifting, washing and, if necessary, for alterations to be carried out. The carriages were returned to Hornsey for correct marshalling, the sets returning to traffic during late March or early April. The sets for the relief or 'Junior Scotsman' were allocated first to the 'Flying Scotsman', to be replaced by fresh stock in early

Below 'A3' 4–6–2 No 2577 *Night Hawk* on the down 'Flying Scotsman' near Darlington in the early 1930s. Leading the train is an all-steel Dia 45 full brake.

July. Similar attention was given to the sleeping cars. The emphasis was, to quote a typical instruction from the SPMs, that 'carriages working in important workings should be in first-class condition for the summer'. The 'important workings' so far as daytime trains were concerned were the down and up 'Flying Scotsman' and their summer reliefs – these four trains usually referred to by LNER officials as the '10 o'clocks' – and the 1.15 pm Kings Cross–Edinburgh and the 1.45 pm from Edinburgh (the precise times varied over the years). Later the high-speed trains would be added to the list. One little touch worth mentioning is that the 'Flying Scotsman' sets were turned in 1930 so that tourists would benefit from the compartments being on the east side of the train, the better to see the East Coast 'sights' such as Peterborough Cathedral. York Minster, Durham Cathedral, the castles in Northumberland and Holy Island and the coastline north of Berwick; the sets then in use for the afternoon 'Scotsman' were similarly turned in 1938.

The innovations for East Coast stock included not only the end door carriages but the hairdressing saloons and cocktail bars in the 'Flying Scotsman', the sale of newspapers, magazines and postcards on this train, the wireless service on the afternoon Scotsmen, the provision of ladies' retiring rooms (each with an attendant) and the presence of train attendants and travelling cleaners on East Coast trains. The train attendants answered questions on LNER services and provided stationery, sent telegrams and posted letters. Some if not most of these facilities lost money but the official reasoning was that they were important for public relations and contributed to the overall image of a first-class service. The LNER's calculations in that respect usually took into account what was happening with the principal LMS Anglo-Scottish trains. Some of the innovations are less well-known, such as the provision from 1934–6 of a

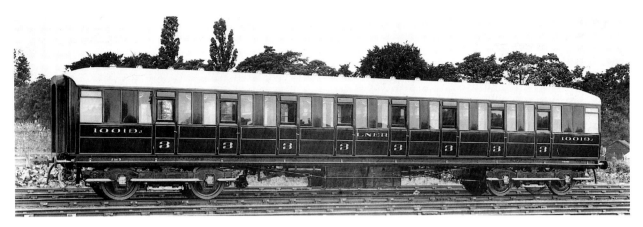

Above Dia 23 third No 10019J, built 1924, later 1000, then 4462 and finally 12039. This vehicle displays the original layout of the lettering and numbering, with the numbers at each end and the 'LNER' in the centre. The solebar is branded 'J Set 3'.

Dictaphone secretarial service on the 8.15 am Newcastle–Kings Cross, this being regarded as an East Coast crack train and it was made up of vehicles in the East Coast allocation.

Then there were the features special to East Coast stock. These included the provision of hassocks from 1924 and, later, cushions in first-class compartments, roller towels in lavatories from 1925, fibre mats and corridor carpeting in the 'super firsts', in both the 'Flying Scotsman' and 'Silver Jubilee' stock and the distinction of eschewing advertising in the first-class compartments of East Coast stock. Criticism from the public of East Coast trains was dealt with most carefully and when Lady Irvine complained in 1934 at the lack of armrests in third-class stock the consequence was the fitting of armrests without delay in carriages working to/from Aberdeen. The more general adoption of armrests in third-class carriages soon followed.

New stock after Grouping

By Grouping the 1914 'Flying Scotsman' sets were due for replacement and the East Coast stock was generally in need of renewal. Accordingly, the construction of four new trains of standard stock was approved under the 1924 CBP in December 1923, including five restaurant car triplets with electric cooking equipment. In addition, charging apparatus for the cooking equipment was to be installed at Hornsey and Craigentinny, Edinburgh. Work proceeded apace on the new stock, the urgency being such that when the directors ordered that overtime must be discontinued early in 1924 the only exception was construction of the East Coast stock at Doncaster and York. Even so, for once the sets were not ready for the summer timetable and entered service on the 'Flying Scotsman' and afternoon Scotsmen from 1 October 1924; initially at least, the sets retained earlier brake thirds and bogie vans. The new vehicles in the sets were thirds to Dia 23 – with armrests and seating 48, composites to Dia 7 and locker composites to Dia 8. These were numbered in the short-lived 100xx series, the first set of catering vehicles being initially and inexplicably 6431–3, then 16431–3; the other triplets seem to have been 16441–3 etc from the start. Brake thirds to Dia 40 and bogie brakes to Dia 43 were available later, while further thirds were delivered for East Coast sets in 1925/6, as well as locker thirds on Dia 24 in 1926. The firsts used were among the last of the pre-Grouping examples, built in 1922. The vehicles in the six premier East Coast sets were diagrammed to work on the down and up 'Flying Scotsman', the down and up relief 'Flying Scotsman' and the 1.15 pm from Kings Cross and 1.45 pm from Edinburgh Waverley, the sets being numbered 1–6 respectively and the vehicles concerned being marked J Set 1–6 – as appropriate – on their solebars.

The restaurant car triplets built at Doncaster were the first articulated catering vehicles for East Coast service and the first of many with electric cooking equipment. The triplet comprised a first-class restaurant car with two saloons, a full kitchen car and a third-class car, also with two saloons, smoking and non-smoking. The internal panelling was in mahogany, with brass fittings and with green hide upholstery in the first-class and teak panels and standard moquette in the third-class. Rubber flooring was applied to restaurant cars Nos 16471/3 but was not found satisfactory and was covered by carpets in the first-class after 1928. Mechanical refrigeration was fitted as new to the second and third of the triplet kitchen cars and all such were similarly equipped during 1927.

The 'non-stops', the Louis XVI restaurant cars and the hairdressing saloons

From mid-1927 preparations were under way for the introduction the following year of non-stop running between Kings Cross and Edinburgh. In view of the agreement between the East and West Coast companies not to run day trains between London and Edinburgh or Glasgow with a journey time of less than $8\frac{1}{4}$ hours, with the introduction of the 'non-stops' competition was focussed on the on-board facilities. The usual wintertime renovation of the stock took place early in 1928, ready for the inauguration of the non-stop 'Flying Scotsman' on 1 May 1928; in subsequent prewar years the 'non-stops' did not commence running until late June or early July. The work on sets Nos 1/2 also included fitting some of the carriages with larger lavatory water tanks, the retrimming of all compartments with the new floral upholstery in the first-class, fawn rep in the third-class, the provision of headrests for first-class compartment seating and lampshades fitted to electric lights in compartments and corridors. However, these two sets were replaced as from 9 July 1928 by fresh Nos 1/2 sets, formed of stock dating from 1924 – and two 1922 firsts – but graced with the new triplet restaurant cars, Nos 16481–3 and 16491–3 respectively. The bogie brakes for East Coast sets after 1928 were the all-steel type to Dia 45. Vehicles from the earlier 1/2 sets were held as spares or for strengthening while the 1924 restaurant triplets were used to replace the 1914 'Flying Scotsman' kitchen and restaurant cars in sets Nos 3/4, employed on the relief 'Flying Scotsmen'. In addition to the set trains, there were some 40 carriages – and vans as well – held as replacement or strengthening vehicles.

The new triplet restaurant cars were to 9 ft 3 in width. The two sets for the 'Flying Scotsman' to Dias 12A/13/14 featured an entirely fresh approach to interior design, the result of Gresley commissioning his friend Sir Charles Allom of Allom & Co to evolve a scheme similar to that in first-class restaurants on terra firma. The decor and furnishings in the first-class car were in the style of Louis XVI. The cornice line was taken up higher than normal and the ceiling decoration was incorporated in an overall scheme which featured pilasters between the seating bays and dispensed with polished woodwork in favour of painted finishes, those in the first-class being soft blue and stone. The lighting was concealed behind translucent and decorated pelmets and the seating was in loose armchairs. The interior was made to seem more spacious by the exclusion of net racks and instead there was a cupboard for coats and hats. The third-class car was more conventional, featuring a less exuberant decor scheme but still in an eighteenth century mode. The seating in this car was in fixed, high backed seats, there were shaded lights in the ceiling and the colour scheme was green and stone. The LNER's press handouts for the new vehicles expressed the hope that public enthusiasm might result in their style being extended to other restaurant cars in time. Wedgwood was enthusiastic about the 1928 triplets, but his feelings was not shared by the more conservative SPMs who criticised the movable seats and lack of net racks. In the summer of 1928 the triplet off the 'Flying Scotsman' worked through to Aberdeen on the 6.15 pm from Edinburgh, returning the next day on the 9.50 am from Aberdeen and then the 1.50 pm Edinburgh–Kings Cross. North of Aberdeen, so the SPMs claimed, the effect of the loose first-class chairs was to unseat passengers on some of the curving stretches of line. The lack of net racks was also a subject for complaint. The result was that the Allom styled triplets were soon confined to working from Kings Cross to Edinburgh or Glasgow only and Southern Scottish cars were reinstated on the Edinburgh–Aberdeen working connecting with the 'Flying Scotsman'. Hooks for hats and coats were fitted in the first-class cars and longitudinal net racks in the third-class. The other triplet built for the East Coast in 1928 had a conventional interior in the first-class car.

Another innovation in the 'non-stops' had been the hair-dressing saloon and ladies retiring room incorporated in two Dia 23 thirds – Nos 1007/12 – which were reclassified Dia 23A. The facilities were available to first and third-class passengers alike and the converted vehicles were introduced during the summer of 1928, probably in concert with the new triplets. The East Coast inspector of the time had recommended such a innovation in 1926 but the SPMs had turned it down firmly, so possibly the initiative in 1928 was taken by Wedgwood and Gresley. As originally arranged, there was a ladies' retiring room with dressing table, armchair and full-length mirror, formed from an end compartment and leading into a lavatory, reduced in size from the original. The next compartment – and part of the third – were converted to a hairdressing saloon, with chair, washbasin and showcase. The remainder of the third

compartment became a coupé compartment serving as a waiting room. The side doors were made fast, panelling replaced the exterior space between the saloon and the waiting room and the quarterlights received obscured glass. In addition, an extra roof water tank was provided. The original hairdressers were not employed by the LNER and complaints from the public of extortionate charges soon led to the Hotels Department taking over the service. For the summer service in 1932 Nos 1007/12 were further modified with the two compartments at the other end of the carriage stripped and replaced by a cocktail bar serving drinks only and with bar stools and chairs. These vehicles were introduced into the 'non-stops' from 18 July 1932 and in not abstracting from restaurant car receipts were reckoned to justify their conversion. From the 'Northern Belle' cruise train starting on 18 August 1933 one of what seem officially to have been called, somewhat quaintly, the 'Toilet Thirds', was included in the set for the cruise train each summer until and including 1939. When so engaged its replacement in the 'Flying Scotsman' was GNR saloon No 4397 which was fitted with a cocktail bar in 1934. From 1934 the cocktail bars in Nos 1007/12 were redesignated as buffets and both vehicles remained in the 'Flying Scotsman' sets until the arrival of the new stock in 1938. For the next year they remained in East Coast stock, deputising for the 1938 buffet lounge cars, until the SPMs recommended the conversion of No 1012 as a full length buffet lounge car and the reversion of No 1007 to an ordinary third. The war intervened to frustrate this plan and sometime during the duration both were converted to full thirds on Dia 23.

Early in 1929 it was decided to build new vestibuled firsts for the East Coast to the end door pattern and these were included in the 1930/1 CBP, along with other new stock to provide sets for the '10 o'clocks', the afternoon 'Scotsmen' and new vestibuled firsts for the 8.15 am Newcastle–Kings Cross and 5.30 pm return. The three other triplet restaurant cars were already available so that all six East Coast sets were now covered. The ordinary stock delivered in 1930/1 included brake thirds to Dia 114, thirds to Dia 115 and composites to Dia 137 but the 1931/2 CBP was revised in the autumn of 1930. 'In view of improved stock that the LMS is using in important services it is decided that 22 thirds and 10 firsts should be built with end doors and wide side lights for our main line services', according to the minutes of the SPM meeting and so fewer thirds were built for the Areas to compensate and 1924 and later East Coast vehicles transferred instead.

The 'super firsts' and other end door stock
The first end door carriages to enter service on the East Coast were firsts Nos 1132/3 (Dia 139) allocated to the 'Flying Scotsman' sets in August 1930. These and their successors, Nos 1131/4–9 of Dias 172/147/156/172, were known as the 'super firsts' in their earlier days. The

Below LNER Diagram Book: Dia 23A was for the so-called Toilet Thirds, Nos 1007/12. This shows the diagram after it was decided in 1934 that the cocktail bar should be redesignated as a buffet. When used on the 'Northern Belle' the non-smoking compartment became an office.

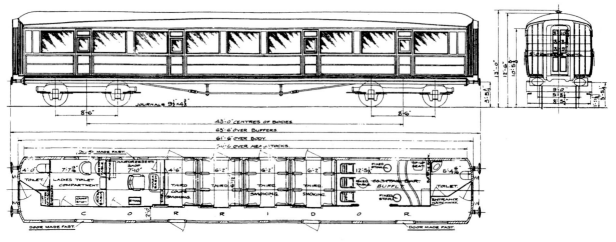

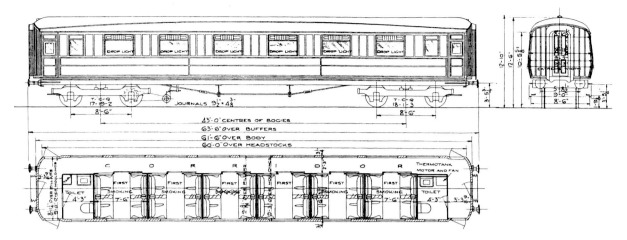

compartment windows were large, of the drop type and featured Vita glass, louvred glass ventilators, as well as curtains with pelmets. The interior panelling in the compartments had a shaded, painted finish, pale blue in the smoking compartments and rose pink in the non-smokers. The moquette was continued up to waist height on the window side and there were footstools in the compartments, carpeting in the corridor and a number of other improvements. Some were appreciated, others not. As built Nos 1132/3 had seating in each compartment for six in loose armchairs but passengers' complaints were such that within a couple of months the two carriages were converted to fixed two a side seating to match recent LMS firsts. The next 'super firsts', to Dia 147, were four a side as built in 1931. Their innovation was Thermotank pressure ventilation and an absence of conventional underseat heating, a feature that soon led to complaints and rectification as the pressure ventilation did not warm up the compartment sufficiently at the start of the journey. From the 1932 CBP end door firsts for the East Coast stock had heating in the corridor. The drop type windows in the 'super firsts' were fixed and deeper louvre ventilators fitted as from July 1936.

There was no doubt that the end door firsts represented a significant breakthrough on a number of counts and the LNER senior management was justifiably proud of them. Nos 1134 (as 11064) and 1136 were destroyed in the Goswick accident of 1947.

The third-class end door carriages entered service in the East Coast sets from late 1932. More followed in 1934/5, along with Dia 115 thirds.

Radio and records on-board trains

From November 1930 the LNER experimented with radio reception on ordinary service trains and fitted a receiving set in the brake compartment of the Leeds GNR quintuplet set. The set was tuned into the 5XX radio station and turned up for selected programmes, passengers listening to the programmes on headphones. This service on the 10.10 am Kings Cross–Leeds and 5.30 pm return was discontinued in 1933 but in the aftermath of its introduction the LNER had so became enthusiastic about the novelty of radio reception on trains that a major programme of equipping train sets was discussed in 1931. Yet the only extension of the facility came in April 1932 when East Coast sets Nos 5/6 for the afternoon 'Scotsmen' were fitted out with the necessary radio receiving apparatus and wiring to work on the then 1.20 pm Kings Cross–Edinburgh and 2.5 pm return. As with some of the other LNER innovations it was seen as primarily a publicity and advertising gambit. The Gramophone Company – HMV – was entirely responsible for the installation in one set and the LNER, working with the GEC company, for the other. Preliminary work dealt with the problem of combating interference caused by the electrical equipment – principally the lighting dynamos – on

Above LNER Diagram Book: 'Super first' to Dia 147, showing the two a side seating crudely marked up on this diagram to three a side as from 1943. The drop windows are also indicated. The body profile on these earlier end door carriages was different with a width over the mouldings of 9 ft 2 in, instead of 9 ft.

the carriages. The receiving set was located in the brake compartment of the brake third in each set, in a tiny office for the DJ up against the partition of the passenger compartment nearest the brake. The set comprised two three-valve receivers and there was also a record player for programme continuity and for musical interludes and this had an automatic record changer. Leads ran from the main cable to output sockets fixed above the seat backs in compartments, or to a central socket above pairs of seats in the restaurant cars. Power supply was obtained from the lighting batteries. Passengers paid 1/- (5p) for the hire of headphones which had volume control and lads on board the train tuned the receiver and handed out the headphones to passengers . The following carriages were fitted up with the necessary equipment:

Locker CK Nos 121/1294, TK Nos 1320–3, Triplet RCs 16501–3/ 11–3, FK Nos 1132/3, BTK Nos 1263/4. TK No 1043 and FKs Nos 1134/5 were initially the spares.

When sets 5/6 received new vehicles during 1934 the equipment and fittings were transferred from the earlier thirds to TKs Nos 1313–5/27–9. At the time, the record choice included a repertoire by Paul Robeson, selections from *The Mikado* and *The Merry Widow*, popular songs of the day and, one hopes inappropriately, *Your Tiny Hand is Frozen*. Patronage of the on-board entertainment was never very encouraging but all concerned with its operation were reluctant to dispense with the service. As more end-door vehicles were delivered for East Coast sets sets 5/6 were exceptional in retaining earlier pattern stock and, late in 1935, the SPM Committee recommended the withdrawal of the facility which ceased with the old year; the wiring was retained in the vehicles so fitted for some time longer.

The 'Northern Belle' cruising train

In February 1932 the SPM committee discussed the idea of cruising by train, involving a set of carriages with self-contained facilities on board – effectively a hotel on wheels – travelling over parts of the LNER network and aiming to attract the well-off tourist. By April that year plans were well-advanced and the cost of the cruise was set at £20 per person. The first train departed from Kings Cross for a week's tour on 16 June 1933 and its itinerary took in Edinburgh, Aberdeen, Balloch, for a cruise on Loch Lomond, Mallaig and return, over the Border Counties line to Humshaugh for a visit to the Roman wall, Penrith for a coach trip around part of the Lake District, Saltburn,

CRUISES OF "THE NORTHERN BELLE"

LEAVING
KING'S CROSS
STATION, LONDON,
FRIDAY EVENINGS,
MAY 29th, JUNE 12th
and JUNE 19th,
1936

L·N·E·R

Above Brochure cover for the 'Northern Belle', 1936 season.

Scarborough and York, finally returning to London. Motor coach tours were included in the cost of the cruise. With the successful operation of the first train the next was scheduled for 18 August. For this GNR saloon No 46 was fitted out with a lounge and writing room and one of the Toilet Thirds was added to the formation, 'a necessity for the cruise', said the SPMs. For the future it was decided to run three or four cruises between Whitsun and the start of the summer timetable.

The 1934 tours were made slightly less frenetic for the travellers and excluded the east coast English resorts. The train formation in 1934 was as follows:

BFK 4206 – train staff; SLT 1344 – train staff accommodation; RK 42183; FOs 1220/1 – as dining cars; Toilet Third 1007 – which included an office and 'smoking rooms'; Saloon 46 – writing room and lounge; SLFs 1317, 1156(with shower), 1318, 1319, 1157(with shower), 1261 and BG 171, the last for luggage and with lockable hanging wardrobes for passengers' clothes. The train weight was 507 tons. Spare vehicles were held at various locations and comprised FO 21509, RK 42182 and an SLF.

Much the same pattern applied for the 'Northern Belles' run in 1935 but for 1936 the three tours run omitted the English stopovers and tours and concentrated on Braemar, Inverness, a tour of the Trossachs by road coach, a cruise on Loch Lomond, Fort William, Mallaig, a tour to Oban and a day in Edinburgh before return to Kings Cross. There are distinct similarities with the present day 'Royal Scotsman' itineraries! A staff of 27 male and female looked after the well-being of 60 passengers. The 'Northern Belle' required careful planning and operation as well as the agreement of the LMS for its trip to Inverness and then down the

Highland main line to Perth. Norman Newsome remembers: 'It was another of the stunts! There was a great commotion every time the "Northern Belle" was run. Vehicles had to be put through shops in advance. Also we had to arrange for suitable locations for battery charging.' The use of a kitchen car with gas rather than electric cooking equipment avoided the need to restrict stopovers to locations with charging equipment. At times during the tour the day and night portions were run separately, so that while one was carrying the passengers the other was en route for servicing. The 1936 cruises had produced the best commercial results so far and so much the same arrangements applied for the next three summers' 'Northern Belles', the last operated being the tour starting on 23 June 1939. That last summer's formation comprised BFK 4204; SLT 1342; RK 42182; FOs 1220/1; Toilet Third 1007; Saloon 46 – all these made up the day portion; SLFs 1165, 1317, 1166, 1318, 1167, 1319 and BG 171 comprised the night portion.

The 'Northern Belle' was not so much an East Coast service as an LNER speciality but it has been included in this chapter as it epitomises much of what the company did best and because East Coast stock vehicles were used. Readers will have noticed that the train's formation made use of stock from Areas' allocations as well. A more downmarket cruise train was run for boy scouts in each summer from 1935 to 1939.

The 'Silver Jubilee'

Sir Ralph Wedgwood established the formula for the LNER streamline trains and in so doing launched the principle of the modern express trains epitomised by the InterCity 125 and 225 services. The LNER had considered using a diesel unit of German inspiration to operate a projected Newcastle to Kings Cross service for businessmen. Gresley reported to the LNER Board in June 1934 on his visit to Germany to inspect the 'Flying Hamburger'. In that same month the LNER Board called for an investigation into the running of 'high-speed units' and one outcome was the famous test run of 5 March 1935 using 'A3' Pacific No 2750 *Papyrus* between Kings Cross and Newcastle and return. This indicated that a steam worked service would not only equal but better the performance likely with a diesel unit. The success of this trial saw Wedgwood set down a specification of what was to become the 'Silver Jubilee' and he even suggested the name in his memo dated 28 March 1935 to the Traffic Committee. What was proposed was a Newcastle to Kings Cross and return service on weekdays only with a journey time of four hours in each direction, to commence on 1 October 1935 and worked by a streamline Pacific. His memo detailed the formation of the seven-coach train as it was to materialise, describing it as 'of special design, offering the least wind resistance, but no additional cost will be involved as the stock will be built in part of the Programme for 1935/6 already sanctioned by the directors'. Later Wedgwood proposed that 'the whole of the arrangements shall be reviewed after they have been tried for an experimental period'. That was to prove unnecessary caution as the 'Silver Jubilee' was a commercial and technical triumph from the start. The Traffic Committee meeting of 28 March 1935, chaired by Sir Murrough Wilson, duly recommended that the CGM's proposals be adopted and work started at once on the new project. The new set was to be regarded as East Coast stock but rather than reduce the East Coast's new build in the 1935/6 CBP accordingly, the Areas had to give up four vehicles to keep the total within the agreed budget.

The 'Silver Jubilee' was timed to leave Newcastle at 10 am, returning from Kings Cross at 5.30 pm. In both directions meals were to be served principally to businessmen and the limited load train necessarily had a high proportion of heavy catering vehicles. So it was perhaps no surprise that articulation featured as the solution, with one triplet and

two twin sets. The result was to produce a more stable and easier rolling train although the 'Silver Jubilee' was also known for its rough riding at times. Supplementary fares were charged per seat, 5/- (25p) in the first-class and 3/- (15p) in the third-class.

Construction was not authorised until 29 March 1935 and Doncaster Works was responsible for building the set. Time was at such a premium that the craftsmen carriage builders commenced planning the bodywork components from chalk markings sketched out on the shopfloor before the complete drawings were issued. The carriage body frames were of conventional teak construction with $\frac{1}{16}$ in steel panels for the sides and ends. The fairings covering underframe equipment extended between the bogies to within 10 in of the rails and were fabricated from lead coated iron sheeting. The space between each articulated body was covered from solebar level and round over the roof by rubber sheeting. Sound reduction to a level of 60 decibels was achieved by the extensive use of insulating material in all resonant spaces. Apart from the Stone's pressure ventilation system which reduced the need for opening windows, there was double glazing throughout using $\frac{1}{4}$ in plate glass with a $\frac{1}{4}$ in space in-between.

The external finish chosen was arguably one of the most attractive of any train. The steel body panels were covered in silver-grey Rexine of a specially thick grade. Attractive stainless-steel trim was applied, together with Gill Sans characters in the same material for the 'LNER' and all numerals. The roofs were sprayed in aluminium paint over a white lead base, with the title 'The Silver Jubilee' in 4 in high lettering fixed to the carriage roofs over a dark-blue background. Carriage identification plates – A–F, as originally formed – had Gill Sans characters also 4 in in height. The underframe fairings and bogie frames were painted lead-grey while wheels and axleboxes were black. The vestibule end covers were painted silver grey with 'The Silver Jubilee' in dark blue letters. Despite careful cleaning, within six months the Rexine on the exteriors became stained and the set went to Doncaster Works to be resprayed silver, something that was repeated at regular intervals. In due course the panels were stripped of Rexine for examination and corrosion was found to have taken place as moisture had

Above The 'Northern Belle' near Potters Bar on 24 June 1938 headed by 'A3' 4–6–2 No 2598 *Blenheim*. The leading vehicle is brake first No 4204 (Dia 29), then Sleeper third No 1342, the sleeping quarters for the train staff, and next the 1914 kitchen car No 42182.

percolated through the material.

The Stone's pressure ventilation equipment used for the set was a development of that fitted the previous year to carriages forming the 8.15 am Newcastle–Kings Cross and 5.30 pm return. The first-class accommodation was at the Kings Cross end, the leading vehicles being twin corridor first/ semi-open first Nos 1581/2. The five compartments in No 1581 seated two a side and there were three similar compartments in No 1582 adjoining. The latter's saloon initially seated 18 passengers in 2 + 1 fixed seating but this was changed during 1936 when the three bays were furnished instead with twelve loose armchairs, four to a bay, from the adjoining restaurant first No 1583. In turn, this received the fixed seating from 1582 and extra partitions were added in this vehicle, the idea behind the change being to increase first-class seating as opposed to dining places; by claiming half the accommodation in restaurant third No 1585 32 seats were added to the total for ordinary seating purposes in the third-class. These changes also marked a stage towards the principle of 'meals at all seats' as adopted for the 'Coronation'.

The interior decor was dignified and kept relatively simple with a blue colour scheme in the first-class and green in the third-class. In the compartments the walls and ceilings were covered in Rexine of the appropriate shades. There was blue rep upholstery with Art Deco patterns in the first-class, foam rubber padded headrests, four loose blue silk cushions to each compartment and footstools. The lighting comprised one central strip lamp and a candle-type strip lamp in each compartment corner. All metal fittings were chromium plated. A Flaman type speed indicator was a feature of the brake compartment in No 1581 and was driven off the axles.

The triplet restaurant car set comprised first-class car No 1583, kitchen car No 1584 (with the usual all-electric equipment) and third-class car No 1585. As already described, the layout of No 1583 was changed in 1936. The interior panelling in this vehicle was in figured maple and the upholstery was to the blue trellis pattern. There was a table lamp to each table, with strip lights of the type already mentioned, fixed to the cornice above each side window. The third-class car had quartered Burma teak panelling with 2 + 1 seating, upholstered in shades of green to an Art Deco pattern. Unshaded light bulbs provided the illumination, one of the few poor design features in an otherwise exemplary train. The kitchen car had the customary all-electric cooking equipment.

As built there were just two third-class vehicles, third No 1586 and brake third No 1587, each of side-corridor layout and with seating for 72 passengers. This total was increased in 1936 with half the seating in No 1585 claimed for non-dining passengers, as required. The finish of the third-class compartments was less luxurious than in the firsts, with two standard ceiling lamps and green upholstery. Third-class accommodation was increased by 35 seats in February 1938 with the building of another vehicle, a full third numbered 1587. This was inserted between the existing third and third brake to create a triplet, these vehicles being renumbered to suit. The new third was just 45 ft 11 in long over the body panels and had one lavatory and six compartments, the one nearest the brake end having five seats only as a recess was provided to increase space in the vestibule. The other vehicles were 56 ft 2½ in over the end panels, with the exception of the shorter length kitchen car. One feature of Nos 1581/2 and 1586/7 was that the corridors were arranged on different sides of the bodies, no doubt to allow the passenger a clearer walk though the train.

Below Interior of a first-class compartment in the 'Silver Jubilee'. The colour scheme was in tones of blue. Note the candle type corner light, silk cushions and footstools.

As originally constructed the 'Silver Jubilee' carriages had the heavy type 8 ft 6 in bogie throughout. After each journey the train was carefully inspected and before long it became apparent that the articulation bogies were showing signs of fatigue and a number of bogie springs had fractured. As a result, a new 10 ft wheelbase bogie was designed in September 1937, capable of carrying 24 tons on the pivot and with 10 in by 5 in journals. This design was used to replace the articulation bogies in the train. Early journeys on the 'Silver Jubilee' had been marked by alarming lurches to the carriage bodies, caused as the springs of the bogies which controlled lateral movement were suddenly compressed. To dampen this effect, rubber blocks were inserted between bogie blocks and side stops but the riding of the set was generally agreed to be lively. When first put into traffic in 1935 the 'Silver Jubilee' had brake power equivalent to 100% of the tare weight, in place of the 80% figure for normal stock. It was soon found that this had the effect of making the wheels pick up on wet rails and the brake power was reduced to 90%.

In these and other ways the 'Silver Jubilee' and the other LNER high-speed trains demonstrated the challenges offered by continuous high-speed running which was not simply a matter of raising intermediate speeds. Operating costs for the stock were higher in view of the greater wear on running and brake gear which necessitated more frequent renewals. Between entry into service and October 1937 the 'Silver Jubilee' set covered no less than 277,370 miles, of which 162,030 were reckoned to be at 75 mph yet only one hot-box was recorded. It says much for the design and maintenance of the 'Silver Jubilee' vehicles that it was possible to maintain booked workings without the use of a spare set until 1937 although a 1924 restaurant car triplet was nominally held as spare for the train. The spare high-speed set No 105 was used for three weeks during October

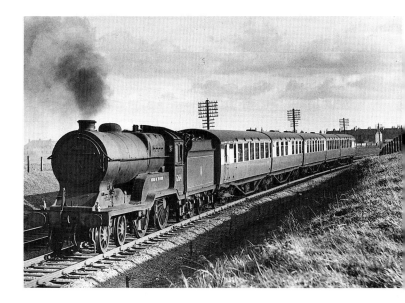

1937, presumably during the fitting of the new articulation bogies, and for four weeks in February/March 1938 when the eighth vehicle was added to the 'Jubilee' set. For booked maintenance the set went to Doncaster Works during public holidays when the train was not scheduled to run. With the arrival of the 1937 high-speed sets the 'Silver Jubilee' was referred to as set No 101.

The 'Silver Jubilee' ran for the last time, in both directions, on 31 August 1939 and the set of carriages then went for storage. From time to time the set was exercised to prevent parts from seizing up. By the end of World War 2 set No 101 was in store at Doncaster and from mid-1946 consideration was given to the reintroduction of all the high-speed stock. The problems raised by the SPMs as preluding the early use of these prestige vehicles is described below but the 'Silver Jubilee' set was different in layout from the remainder and it was recognised that it must remain as an independent unit. However, the introduction in 1948 of the 'Tees-Tyne Pullman' removed the chance of using it complete on a premier East Coast service. Early that year the twin first and triplet third were dispatched to the Scottish Region and before long were used together for the summer only 'Fife Coast Express' between Glasgow Queen Street and St Andrews. During the winter the train was unnamed and ran to Leven only. Despite such secondary work the carriages were well-maintained and the stainless steel trim was kept unpainted but the underframe fairings were removed. Dieselisation displaced the stock from the Fife coast workings but it continued to find employment in the Scottish Region until withdrawn in late 1962. That August the twin first brake was recorded as working between Manchester and Newcastle, returning to Glasgow, on what was possibly one of its final workings and almost certainly its last acquaintance with the East Coast main line. Sadly, there was no reprieve for preservation.

The restaurant car triplet returned to Newcastle–Kings Cross services from mid 1948 and was normally used in the 8.0 am up and 5.35 pm down workings until new BR catering vehicles saw its displacement from booked duties in 1960/1. It remained in store at Manors station until sent for scrapping at Tyne Dock in 1963.

More stock for the East Coast

By earlier standards the LNER embarked on a profligate expansion of the East Coast stock in the late 1930s, in response to increasing traffic. Fifty-two additional vehicles, including sleeping cars, were included in the original 1935 CBP and of these 24 were end door thirds and nine, Dia 115 thirds. But the availability of funds under the government assistance for development works saw additional proposals for six sets each of fourteen vehicles for East Coast stock, with thirteen spares including five sleeper firsts. These additional carriages were intended for summer and holiday period traffic on the East Coast and allocation at other times to the Areas, the idea being to avoid the use of Areas' stock for strengthening East Coast services. Each train was made up of: BTK+ nine TKs + TO + RF + CK + BCK; the end door vehicles involved were mostly built by contractors and the new build was identified by their 16xx series numbers. There was discord when it was found too late to change the order for the open thirds to pantry thirds, a type preferred for East Coast services. Some of the 97 additional vehicles were used in East Coast Nos 1–6 sets which were granted new stock in 1934/5, 1936, 1937 and, in

the case of the 'Flying Scotsman', again in 1938. Twenty-nine further standard carriages were included in the 1937 CBP, along with the new 'Scotsman' sets. A remarkable re-equipment had been affected but, given the number of elderly vehicles on front-line duties in 1935, it was entirely justified.

The 'Coronation' sets

When the 'Silver Jubilee' started running the LNER said that depending on public reaction further high-speed trains would be introduced. By the middle of 1936 there was no doubt that the 'Silver Jubilee' had proved itself commercially and its considerable contribution to the prestige of the LNER was very gratifying. The 'Silver Jubilee' had been instrumental in boosting Newcastle to London traffic by 12% since the train had started running and had 'acted as a stimulus to traffic', said Wedgwood in a memo to the Joint Locomotive and Traffic Committee in October 1936. He proposed two new services, one between Bradford, Leeds and London, to start in the autumn of 1937 and the other between Edinburgh and London which he suggested would be called the 'Coronation' and begin in the summer 1937 timetable. In fact, there had been planning from the spring of 1936 for a high-speed Kings Cross–Edinburgh–Aberdeen train to a nine-hour overall timing but the idea of an extension to/from Aberdeen was abandoned that October. As part of the 1937 CBP, 27 vehicles were included to make up two sets for the Edinburgh high-speed service as well as one

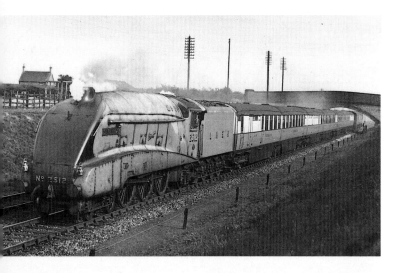

Top The down 'Coronation' near Claypole behind 'A4' 4–6–2 No 2512 *Silver Fox*.

Above The construction of one of the 'Coronation' twin open firsts (Dia 229) at Doncaster Works, showing the skirting in place, as well as the stainless steel trim.

spare set for this, the Leeds train and the 'Silver Jubilee'. The initial planning was for eight-coach trains only, but in the event 26 vehicles were built at Doncaster, including the two observation cars which were ordered after the rest of the vehicles.

Newsome records that originally the 'Coronation' sets were to have followed the 'Silver Jubilee' so far as internal design was concerned. By January 1937 it was decided that all eight carriages to make up each set would be of open layout, with all seats reservable and, by the provision of two kitchen cars in each set, with the ability to serve all passengers with meals at their seats. To the objection that open stock was less popular on long runs, the answer was to divide the interiors of the carriages with partitions: each seating bay was enclosed in the first-class, every second bay in the third-class. To Norman Newsome who was closely involved with the design of the stock, 'there was nothing to beat the "Coronation"... it was designed with a specific purpose in mind-feed the passengers at their seats and give them a comfortable ride.' As in the case of the 'Silver Jubilee' supplementary fares were charged and all seats – except those in the observation car – were reservable.

In construction the carriages were similar to the 'Silver Jubilee' stock in having teak framed, steel panelled bodies but were carried on welded underframes. The bodies were to the 56 ft 2 ½ in length of some of the vehicles in the earlier

set. The train was arranged in four twin sets: third brake/third (Dia 231), third/kitchen third (Dia 230), twin first (Dia 229) and kitchen third/third brake (Dia 228). Then there were the two beaver tail observation cars to Dia 232 for use with the pair of sets working on the 'Coronation'. The principal change to construction as compared to the 'Silver Jubilee' involved the provision of comprehensive sound insulation, with asbestos acoustic blankets lining the roof spaces and bodysides and sprayed asbestos on steel sheeting on the underside of the bodies to absorb noise from the running gear. Sponge rubber was laid under the carpets and hair felt between the floorboards. Double glazing was fitted and sliding ventilators but these were kept closed in normal conditions.

The interior decor of the carriages merited special attention and Acton Surgey Ltd was commissioned to design a scheme that made full use of Rexine for internal surfaces. Most internal trim was in anodised aluminium fret with aluminium architraves to the first-class partitions. The parcel racks throughout the train were of aluminium as heavy luggage was intended to be left in the luggage lockers in the entrance lobbies. The integrated design concept extended to the table linen, glassware, crockery and silverware which were all to a distinctive pattern.

In the third-class the seating was arranged 2 + 1 on each side of the centre gangway. The upholstery was of uncut fawn moquette with green carpets while the Rexine wall coverings were in stone for the upper panels and shagreen for the lower portions. Detail was picked out in scarlet. In each bay there were tables with hinged leaves. The first-class featured sumptuously upholstered swivelling armchairs, one to each side of the gangway, and for meal service the armchairs were intended to face the tables at 45 degrees; to allow passengers to move easily the glass topped tables were cut away on the gangway side. The light fittings in the first-class were to an elaborate Art Deco fretted pattern, supplemented by light fittings in the parcel racks. There were two decor schemes in the first-class accommodation. One was in tones of green, with the chairs trimmed with scarlet braid and the carpet with a scarlet trellis pattern. The other scheme featured dark green Rexine for the lower internal panels and cream above, with the Rexine and doors studded with silver nails. The lavatories represented a noticeable improvement over existing stock with water sealed bowls in coloured porcelain, an immersion heater for use when steam heating was absent during the summer and a full-length mirror.

Stone's pressure ventilation and heating equipment was fitted, designed to change the air in each saloon every three minutes. In the third-class the air was discharged under the seats, in the first-class at floor level in front of the partitions; stale air was extracted through openings in the light fittings, to be passed along trunking in the roof for discharge at the roof ends. Although there was no trouble with air circulation in the third-class it was a different matter in the first-class where there were sharp draughts at times and the air discharge nozzles had to be sited elsewhere. Although the temperature within the train was always higher than outside, by the end of a run on the 'Coronation' it was noticeably warmer in the rear vehicles, a phenomenon without apparent explanation.

At the tail of the 'Coronation' was the observation saloon. The roof boards of this vehicle were shaped to form an end that curved downwards while the body sides tapered inwards. The complex shape thus created made the use of curved glass panels impossible so acrylic sheets were used to good effect for the rear observation windows. The view from the rear was limited to all but the passengers in the end swivelling armchairs, of which there were sixteen in all and a supplement of 1/- (5p) was charged for a hour's occupation of each armchair. At the train end of the car there was a compartment for letter mail and also for luggage. The shape

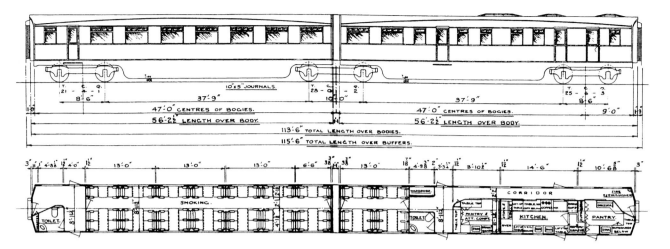

Above LNER Diagram Book: the twin restaurant open third to Dia 230.

of the observation car was cleverly designed as a complement to the matching shape of the 'A4' Pacific at the front of the train. Eddy currents were absent from the rear of the train when it was in motion and the windows were kept clear of the traffic dirt normally deposited on vehicles. The idea of running observation cars on the 'Flying Scotsman' had been considered in 1929 but rejected on grounds of adding unnecessary weight to the train. It was certainly a luxury in operating terms and of course the cars had to be turned at the end of each journey. The cars were taken off in winter, as from 7 March 1938 when the Newcastle stop was introduced and thereafter from the start of the winter timetable; this gave the locomotive and crew a margin for time recovery which was often needed in bad weather. During the summer the lights were dimmed in the car after dark.

Fashions change: at the time of the first edition of this book Art Deco design was not highly regarded and the interior decor of the 'Coronation' seemed mannered and a little fussy. Nowadays it is fair to say that a re-appraisal has brought admiration of the effects created by Acton Surgey and general regret that it is no longer possible to sample such handsome vehicles. In the words of the original LNER press briefing: ' the decoration... belongs to no period or style in art... it is quite original'. In contrast to the interior, the finish of the carriage exteriors has always been admired, with the clever use of colour combinations and the excellent trim and lettering details. As with the 'Silver Jubilee' the exterior was air-smoothed, with fairings covering the sole-bars, underframes and rubber shrouds in place between adjoining vehicles. For the celebration of King George VI's coronation various paint shades were sponsored by the British Colour Council. Two of these, Marlborough blue and Garter blue, were chosen for the external paintwork of the 'Coronation' vehicles. The darker shade was used for the lower body panels, the lighter colour above, the two colours being continued around the body ends. The window frames, exterior mouldings and fittings were in stainless steel and the Gill Sans lettering 'Coronation' (6 in high) and numbering (4 in) high were also in this material. The roofs were spray-painted in aluminium while the underframe fairings, bogies and wheels were black. The carriage identification letters were 12 in high Gill Sans.

The first working of the 'Coronation' was on 5 July 1937 and great care was always taken with the running of the train and with its maintenance. The introduction of the 'Coronation' was accompanied by a number of improvements in carriage cleaning, inspection and maintenance facilities at Hornsey and at Craigentinny, as well as the employment of over twenty extra staff at both depots. Although this indicated the need for special facilities for the high-speed trains there is little doubt that improvements were needed in any case, given the increase in the number of East Coast stock generally. After arrival of the up train at

Kings Cross at 10.30 pm the stock proceeded to Hornsey for inspection by a carriage and wagon examiner until 2 am or so. Fitters worked until 6 am if necessary to rectify any defects. The cleaning of the stock started at 6 am and lasted no less than eight hours. The carriage exteriors were hand-cleaned, washed down with a solution of soap flakes and water and finally leathered and polished. Small wonder that when contemplating the introduction of high-speed trains in the grim postwar days the operations quailed at the idea of the resources needed to maintain the stock properly. Yet the high-speed trains earned profits for the LNER, none more so than the 'Coronation' which in one month in July 1938 made a profit of 13/8 (69p) per loaded train-mile, marginally more than the 'Silver Jubilee'.

The operation of the 'Coronation' and the other services made a major contribution to the operation of high-speed passenger trains. In their search for continual improvements the Gresley team appreciated that the existing vacuum braking had its limitations in that the application of brakes at the rear of the train was slow and, in the case of sudden braking retardation, could be both violent and cause snatching. From 1935 experiments had been carried out with quadruplet suburban sets in which Westinghouse quick

Below The interior of the observation cars with some fine Art Deco effects.

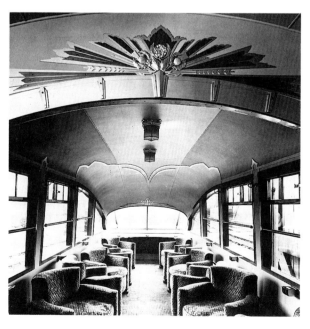

service valves were fitted. The results were encouraging and the 1937 'East Anglian' set was so fitted from new. In due course, 'Coronation' set No 103 was similarly equipped, together with automatic slack-adjusters, and the set was used for *Mallard's* record breaking run on 3 July 1938. All the high-speed sets were fitted in due course.

The third set built under the 1937 CBP was the spare for all three high-speed trains and did not carry lettering for a particular working although finished otherwise in the style of the 'Coronation' sets both externally and internally. When working a high-speed service destination boards were carried appropriate to that working and it was also used on special trains, such as for the launching of a ship on Tyneside.

The 'Coronation' last ran on Thursday, 31 August 1939 and the rolling stock was stored although, from time to time, it was given an airing to ensure that the running gear did not seize up. The position with the four sets from the 'Coronation' and the 'West Riding Limited' was as follows:

102 – 'Coronation'	Brake Third/Third-Kitchen(Twin) 1711/1712; Open First/Open First(Twin) 1713/1714; Third/Third Kitchen(Twin) 1715/1716; Third/Brake Third (Twin) 1717/1718; Observation Car 1719. Stored Ballater
103 – 'Coronation' Same formation as No 102	1721/1722;1723/1724; 1725*/1726*;1727*/1728; 1729. Stored Doncaster *Vehicles damaged by fire
104 – 'West Riding' Same formation as No 102(observation car excepted)	45801/45802; 45811/45812;45821/45822; 45831/45832. Later Nos 9166/9167; 11115/11116; 9168/9169; 16719/20. Stored Copley Hill
105 – Spare set Same formation as No 102(observation car excepted)	1731/1732;1733/1734; 1735/1736;1737/1738. Stored Ballater

The fire that occurred at Doncaster Works on 21 December 1940 was responsible for the damage to three of the vehicles in Set 103; the brake third, although undamaged,was unusable because it was articulated to the adjoining burnt carriage.

The LNER's development programme was publicised in *Forward the LNER* , distributed in 1946. The high-speed trains received specific mention and, naming the 'Silver Jubilee', 'Coronation' and 'West Riding Limited', *Forward the LNER's* comments were that 'these trains will require track in first-class condition for their high speeds'. It went on to say:'seating capacity in these trains is strictly limited and their re-introduction must wait awhile. But they will return just as soon as possible and, no doubt, be more popular than ever'.

Such intentions were backed by practical work as a high-speed test run was undertaken in May 1946 between Kings Cross and Edinburgh and back using 'A4' Pacific No 2512 *Silver Fox*. This demonstrated what was possible but not in the way of day-to-day running at the time.

Behind the scenes the practicability of restoring the high-

speed trains to everyday service was the subject of discussion between the chief general manager, Sir Charles Newton, and the SPM Committee. The minutes of that Committee are available but not all the supporting correspondence. This is a pity as on 12 January 1946 we find the CGM writing to the SPM Chairman, Mr Rutter, as follows:'in your report (*not available*) of 19 January 1945, you made proposals with proviso that Pullman services should not be restored before the Company's own high-speed trains are reinstated... a proviso with which I heartily agree.'

In the event, it was decided from the summer timetable to hire 29 Pullman cars for use in normal service 'in the interest of being able to resume supplement services', in the words of the CGM who saw scope in running the Pullmans singly in East Coast trains as non-supplement refreshment vehicles. This was not necessarily a contradiction from what he had earlier said as the Pullmans were being used thus as stop-gaps, in view of the rolling stock shortage on the LNER.

In April and May, the CGM was expressing his concern that the SPM Committee had made no reference to the possible employment of the high-speed sets, even at slower speeds, in the winter 1946/7 timetable. In response, the SPM Chairman said that the committee members appreciated the prestige value of the stock even though it could not be run at high speeds. However, the high-speed sets had limited seating and the East Coast trains of the time had to be high-capacity. To obtain even a couple of sets to comply with this aim, nearly all 42 vehicles of the high-speed stock would have to be employed and the work to make them available for traffic would delay the refurbishment of ordinary stock. Newton agreed with this reasoning and the matter was left until the end of 1946.

A report on the status of the stock was written in November 1946. As the 'Silver Jubilee' set was non-standard, it was disregarded and in the report the Committee looked at pooling the 28 vehicles available from Sets 102, 104 and 105. From these, they showed that it was not possible to form more than two trains of more than ten carriages, except by including two kitchens or two brakes in each set. The third-class accommodation was regarded as totally inadequate. They did consider making up one train of fourteen vehicles which, had it materialised, would have made an impressive sight.

The Committee's conclusion was that as operation at prewar train speeds was impracticable, the only option available was to use the stock at lower speeds, but then it would be found wanting on grounds of inflexibility and reduced seating capacity as compared with standard stock. So they were unable to justify its restoration in favour of tackling the backlog of overhauls to other vestibuled vehicles.

In the summer of 1947, and seemingly just before his retirement, Newton again informed the SPMs that he would like to see the restoration of high-speed stock to a service between Kings Cross and Newcastle or to Edinburgh and he asked the committee to review the position of the sets still languishing in store. A report was produced for consideration at the SPM Committee meeting of 26 August 1947. The remit for those preparing the report was to look at the use of the stock less for high-speed journeys than for business travellers seeking comfortable and reserved seat accommodation. The chief mechanical engineer informed them that one of the sets could be made ready for traffic within a few weeks and that all the sets, including the damaged No 103, could be turned out 'within three to four months'.

Vehicles from the 'Coronation' sets made their reappearance in 1948. They were used principally on East Coast workings but also appeared north of Edinburgh, on the 'Master Cutler' and on less exalted trains such as between Manchester and Cleethorpes. The underframe skirting was removed in due course, as well as the solebar fairings from some of the twins. The 'West Riding' had begun running in

May 1949 with high-speed stock from the prewar 'West Riding Limited' but twin sets from the other sets made their appearance and on 14 July 1951 this had tragic consequences. Nos 1738/1737 were standing-in for 16719/16720 when they caught fire near Huntingdon and were burned out. The cause of fire was a real fluke. A live coal from the locomotive hauling the train had bounced up from the track and become lodged in a hole cut in the floor of No 1737. A number of passengers were injured in vacating the pair of carriages, some seriously. The Railway Executive was criticised in the Inspecting Officer's report on several grounds. These carriages had nitrocellulose coating on the Rexine decorative interior finishes although this substance's contribution to an earlier train fire on the West Coast main line had been identified. Also, the exit doors were at the outer ends only of the articulated twin which meant that passenger evacuation in an emergency was very difficult. There were criticisms, too, that the passenger communication chain was accessible at one end of the twin only. As a result of the inquiry report, the stock was modified with an additional side door provided in each twin body but not all were in fact converted. To that extent, the earlier reservations on the part of the SPMs at the use of the stock in normal service trains were justified, but for different reasons than they could have foreseen.

The remaining service life of the stock was fortunately without incident and two twin-firsts, Nos 1723/4 and 1733/4, ran a considerable mileage in the 'Talisman' sets on Kings Cross–Edinburgh workings until 1963/4 and had been fitted with roller bearing axleboxes in 1957. The third of the twin firsts, Nos 1713/4, was normally spare for the other two. From that point of view, fair use was made of the high-speed stock in postwar years but it always seems disappointing that it was never used in full set formation. The two observation or beaver-tail cars lasted longer and, in modified condition, continued in use on the West Highland line until the end of the summer 1967 season. The original ends were modified, to be replaced by a angled profile in order to improve viewing. Both vehicles have survived for preservation, the only examples of the LNER's high-speed stock to have done so. The restaurant car twins were withdrawn by the end of 1962 and the other twins survived into 1963/4.

What a pity that the other 'Coronation' vehicles were disposed of! There would have been no finer sight in the Great Hall of the National Railway Museum than *Mallard* coupled to the ex-NER dynamometer car and one of the brake third twins from the 'Coronation' sets. Not only would this have provided an appropriate representation of that record breaking run in 1938 but served to commemorate the fine achievement that these prewar carriages undoubtedly were.

Below Twin open first E1713/4E (Dia 229), regarded as the spare for the 'Talisman' sets but not fitted with roller bearing axleboxes. At Bounds Green in April 1962.

Above Observation car E1719E at Mallaig when in use from Fort William. The less attractive restyling of the 'tail' nonetheless improved viewing. As rebuilt, the interior featured 28 1950s style armchairs, some taking up the space of the former mails compartment.

The 'West Riding Limited' – and the high-speed service that never was

This, the third high-speed train, is perhaps less well-known than its companions and the set of eight carriages – four twins – was almost identical to those for the 'Coronation', there being some differences in the decor scheme and aluminium fretwork and trim. In the first-class there was blue and brown stippled Rexine above the waist and silver below. The moquette and carpets were blue. But the third-class decor was very similar to that in the 'Coronation' sets. The external livery was the same as the other sets, with the exception of being lettered 'West Riding Limited' and its numbering within the GN section series. This set was not in the East Coast allocation but it seems convenient to include it in this chapter. As with the other high-speed trains a supplementary charge was made. The 'West Riding Limited' began running between Bradford, Leeds and Kings Cross on 27 September 1937 and its subsequent operation was uneventful until, like the other trains, it made its last run on 31 August 1939 and the set of carriages was stored.

Three of the twins were the first carriages to be repainted at Doncaster in BR carmine and cream livery and during May 1949 were put into service on the 'West Riding', as the 7.50 am from Leeds–Kings Cross and 3.45 pm return had just been named. The twins used were: Nos 16719/16720, 11115/11116 and 9168/9169, the last serving as the catering vehicles in the set which had postwar LNER-design vehicles as well. They continued on these duties until the late 1950s

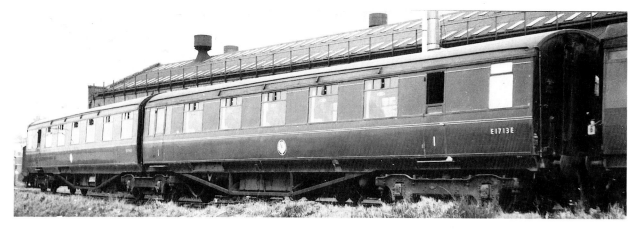

Above Twin brake first E1727/8E at York in August 1963 on a summer Saturdays train. The fairings over the solebars have been removed and there is no additional door cut into the innermost seating bay on 1727 (nearest).

Below A third-class compartment of the 1938 'Flying Scotsman', stock. The seat backs were shaped but Gresley said that a straight top should be retained for standard carriages. Bakelite picture and mirror frames and shoulder-light mouldings.

and the restaurant twins lasted until 1962.

One proposal for a high-speed service which never came to fruition was that for Hull–Liverpool which was considered by the SPMs in June 1935. Four-coach trains, including catering facilities, would have been used and the routeing would have been via Doncaster and Sheffield. High-speed in this instance was a relative term but it shows that the operation of tightly timed steam worked trains was also contemplated on other sections of the LNER.

The 'Flying Scotsman' sets of 1938

Although new stock had been allocated to the 'Flying

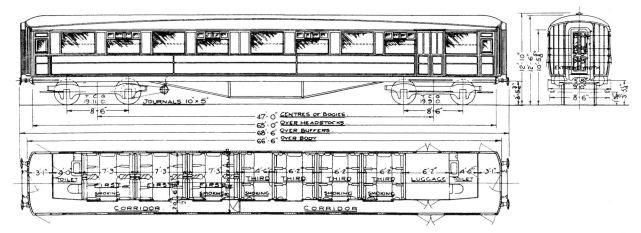

Scotsman' through the mid 1930s, 30 vehicles to a higher specification were included in the 1938 CBP which was approved in October 1937. Two thirteen-coach formations were made up for the winter timetable. During the summer the train comprised thirteen carriages for Edinburgh and Aberdeen during the time that the relief or Junior Scotsman was rum. Heavier loads often featured. The booked formation of the winter train was:

BTK (Dia 261) + CK (Dia 259) for Glasgow; locker CK (Dia 251) for Perth; two TKs (Dia 256), buffet lounge car (Dia 258), triplet RC (Dia 255) and FK (Dia 257) all for Edinburgh; locker CK (Dia 251), TK (Dia 256) and BG for Aberdeen.

These were standard outline teak bodied, end door carriages. Dias 251 and 258 were to 66 ft 6 in length, the rest 61 ft 6 in and all were to diagrams unique to these sets. The 30 carriages were equipped with Stone's pressure ventilation and heating and had double glazed windows. One noticeable feature was the provision of alternate windows with sliding ventilators on the corridor side, the decision having been taken in late 1937 that end door vehicles suffered from inadequate ventilation in the corridors. The first-class compartments seated two a side, sponge rubber headrests being a special feature, along with loose, scatter cushions. The peach coloured Rexine wall covering was set off by blue/fawn upholstery in the smoking compartments and red/fawn for non-smoking. In both first and third class there were reading lamps, largely made up from plastic components. The third-class compartments also had the peach coloured Rexine and fawn and brown upholstery. The seat backs had shaped tops, a small feature that improved appearances no end.

The triplet restaurant car sets were similar in many respects to the earlier examples of 1924 and 1928 but the individual vehicles were slightly longer, the kitchen cars having all-electric equipment. Acton Surgey were commissioned to produce a special interior scheme for the restaurant cars and the result was to divide the saloon by aluminium framed partitions fitted with clear acrylic panels, in order to provide some privacy for passengers, at the same time allowing the stewards to have a clear view down the car. A blue and silver decor scheme was chosen. The seating was well-cushioned, upholstered in powder blue and blending in with the two-tone blue Rexine wall coverings, offset by a rose coloured carpet. In the third-class car, the Rexine wall coverings were cream for the upper surfaces and shagreen below, trimmed in red, and there was fawn upholstery. In 1957 both triplets were fitted out with a cocktail 'standing' bar in the first-class car for use on the 'Northumbrian' and other Kings Cross–Newcastle trains. By the late summer of 1961 both sets were displaced from such workings and eventually were sent for breaking up in 1963.

Above LNER Diagram Book: locker composite to Dia 251, a 66 ft 6 in vehicle. Originally with two a side seating, altered to three a side in 1943. Nos 1740–8 did not have pressure ventilation and the lavatories had the washbasins placed transversely, a feature which incurred Gresley's displeasure and which was corrected for the later vehicles.

In replacement of the Toilet Thirds there came buffet lounge cars, to the 66 ft 6 in length, for the two train sets. At one end was a pantry equipped with a range of modern appliances such as a grill, coffee machine, toaster and ice cream cabinet. The saloon, seating twenty, was partitioned off by a glass panelled screen to provide a corridor for passing passengers. At the other end of the car was a ladies' retiring room. The hairdressing saloon, never profitable in the earlier cars, was noticeable by its absence. Interior finishes in the new cars were in green and silver for one car and rose pink in the other. In their first six months of service

Below The interior of one of the buffet lounge cars for the 1938 'Flying Scotsman', with the internal corridor to the right in the photograph. Mirrors were placed at the end of the saloon and between the windows to create the impression of greater space.

Above Buffet lounge car E1852E, as rebuilt in 1959 and as running in the Gresley Society special from Kings Cross–Darlington in May 1964.

the buffet lounge cars increased receipts by 50%, as compared with the Toilet Thirds, and were regarded as a success although they seem to have diverted some business from the restaurant cars. The two cars were rebuilt as conventional buffet cars with propane gas equipment in 1959 and one survived until 1965 when it was purchased for preservation by the Gresley Society.

The new 'Flying Scotsman' stock was demonstrated to the press in a way that typified the best of the LNER's public relations. Guests and press party entrained at Kings Cross on 30 June 1938 not into the pristine vehicles but into a set of Howlden six-wheelers hauled by Stirling 4–2–2 No 1 which took them to Stevenage. There was waiting 'A4' Pacific No 4498 *Sir Nigel Gresley* at the head of one of the new sets for a trip to Grantham and back. These sets and the 'Hook Continental' train were the final flowering of the Gresley teak bodied stock and were fine vehicles which had no more than two brief summers before the outbreak of war. Some attempt was then made to avoid dispersal of the stock

and early in 1940 the eight thirds were redesignated as first-class. Two of the 30 vehicles were lost as a result of enemy action and others were fitted with steam heating from 1941 onwards. In postwar days the 'Flying Scotsman' stock continued to receive some preferential treatment but from the late 1950s was dispersed to secondary duties until withdrawn in the 1962/3 period.

New stock for East Coast sets Nos 3–6 was delivered during 1939, including 66 ft 6 in end door locker composites Nos 1838/9 (Dia 279) which went into service on the afternoon Scotsmen, as well as end door thirds and composites to Dias 298 and 296 and brake composites to the earlier Dia 175.

From 1946, stock to the postwar design began to appear in East Coast sets and their story and that of the 'Flying Scotsman' is told in Chapter 12.

Below The 'Flying Scotsman' in 1939 with 'A4' 4–6–2 No 4484 *Falcon* at its head. The train consists largely of the latest stock, including the restaurant car triplet but it looks as if the buffet lounge car has been replaced by one of the Toilet Thirds; there was a complaint about the unreliability of Nos 1852/3 in their early days.

CHAPTER 8
GE SECTION SPECIAL VESTIBULED STOCK

THE Great Eastern section of the Southern Area earns a chapter to itself because of the vestibuled sets built for the Continental boat trains between Liverpool Street and Harwich Parkeston Quay, the two sets ordered in something of a hurry for Liverpool Street–Cromer expresses in 1929, the 'East Anglian' set of 1937 and the unique 52 ft 6 in vestibuled stock for general service.

Continental sets 1925–36

Replacement of the twenty-year old GER set for the Hook of Holland boat train was regarded as a priority by the newly formed LNER and the proposals for new sets of vestibuled carriages for this train and the Antwerp service were largely finalised in December 1923 and included in the 1924/5 CBP. In 1924 the Hook train left Liverpool Street at 8.30 pm, followed ten minutes later by that for the Antwerp sailing; this service had been restored in 1921. The provision of new stock for the Continental boat trains was regarded as secondary only to the premier East Coast sets in importance.

It was decided by the SPMs that the twenty new vehicles for the two trains should have vacuum brakes only, whereas the remaining GE section stock, other than on the suburban services, was to be dual fitted. The twenty vehicles were to standard 61 ft 6 in design, with Pullman type gangways, and all were built at Stratford Works. As they were intended for the GE section only they were built to the 9 ft 3 in width not then permitted for general service stock. First and second-class accommodation was provided on the boat trains in order to match the Continental railways' corresponding classes. The second-class in the boat sets seated three a side. The Antwerp boat train went on to Harwich Town and so the brake third in the set was for passengers not making use of the boat sailings.

The sets were originally to be made up as follows:

Hook service	Antwerp service
Brake second (Dia 35)	Brake third (Dia 38)
Second (Dia 21)	Second (Dia 21)
Second (Dia 21)	Open second (Dia 22)
Open second (Dia 22)	Restaurant second*
Restaurant second*	Restaurant/ kitchen first (Dia 10A)
Restaurant/kitchen first (Dia 10A)	Restaurant first *
Restaurant first*	Open first (Dia 3)
Open first (Dia 3)	First (Dia 1)
First (Dia 1)	Full brake (Dia 43)
First (Dia 1)	
Two Pullman cars	
One or two full brakes (Dia 43)	

* See text below

There was clearly some debate about the amount of dining accommodation to be provided on the train because there had been a change to both formations before the proposals were (almost) finalised in December 1923 and, by

all indications, a change back to the original idea by the time the orders were placed. Those vehicles marked with asterisks were altered, the restaurant firsts materialising as firsts to Dia 3 and the restaurant seconds as Dia 22 open seconds, two of these being lettered as restaurant cars – Nos 695/6. Probably someone with a practical mind looked at the cost of providing two extra designs – the restaurant firsts and seconds in the December 1923 proposals were of a type never built – and at the extravagant amount of dining accommodation being proposed, Pullman cars included, and scaled things down. A 66 ft 6 in restaurant/kitchen car was shown in the proposals, this length having been considered as a standard for LNER catering vehicles in 1923, but in the end the new boat train cars were to the customary 61 ft 6 in length; vehicles to the greater length were built for East Coast service in the 1930s.

Although the vehicles in the sets were to standard layouts and outlines they were given a high standard of finish. The first-class compartment carriages had lights under the cornice rather than bulbs fitted in the ceiling with two side-bracket lights in addition and were upholstered in maroon leather(smoking) or blue cloth (nonsmoking). The second-class had green upholstery. In the first-class dining cars there were shaded table-lamps, mahogany panelling and green leather upholstery. One small touch that seems in keeping with the ambience of the train was a warmed cupboard for cigars in the restaurant/kitchen car which had gas cooking equipment. The first runs with the new stock were on 30 March 1925, this inaugural working with the Hook set comprising eleven LNER vehicles and two Pullman cars with a train weight of 441 tons; this made a testing proposition for the 'B12' 4-6-0

Below The 'Flushing Continental' on the last lap of its journey to Parkeston Quay comes round the curve to Manningtree East Junction and the driver of 'B17' 4-6-0 No 2822 *Alnwick Castle* opens up for the climb to Mistley. There are three Pullman cars, three 61 ft 6 in carriages and two vans, not all the Continental boat trains being as heavy as the 'Hook Continental'.

and its crew on the 82-minute timing from Liverpool Street to Parkeston Quay.

Under the 1928/9 CBP three restaurant/ kitchen cars were built to Dia 10B for use on the Continental boat trains but there was little change to the Continental sets for ten years or so, although during the early 1930s falling traffic saw the combination of the Hook and Antwerp trains. A new set for the Hook/Antwerp service was contemplated in the 1934 CBP but excised in October 1934, only to reappear in reduced form in the 1935/6 CBP, along with three new restaurant/ kitchen firsts to Dia 144, with electric cooking equipment. As gas equipped cars were required in the North Eastern Area and Gresley was reluctant to build new vehicles with gas cooking, the two 1925 Dia 10A and one of the 1929 Dia 10B cars were transferred from the GE section.

The new vehicles for the Hook/Antwerp train were included in a formation that began running from 3 March 1936 and has been often referred to as a completely new set. It comprised Dia 115 seconds, Dia 27B open seconds, newly built, and the most notable vehicles which were Dia 218 open first No 689, used for dining and with movable armchairs, and Dia 219 semi-open first No 6468, with one saloon for eighteen passengers and four compartments. These last two carriages were up to East Coast standards and each featured a grey-blue colour scheme and electric water heating in the lavatories. After a couple of years this set was transferred to the cover the Antwerp train which once more ran separately from what was now known as the 'Hook Continental'. During the late 1930s Pullman cars replaced LNER restaurant cars in the Antwerp train. There was some disgruntlement at the failure to provide a top-rate set for the 'Hook Continental' and Wedgwood reminded the SPMs that in preparing the building programmes 'there should be regard for building Continental trains at frequent intervals. These should be dealt with on the same basis as East Coast services.' That was certainly to be the case for the 1938 'Hook Continental' set which is described below.

General service 52 ft 6 in stock

When the standards for the 61 ft 6 in stock were being established towards the end of 1923 it was accepted that shorter vehicles would be needed for the GE section. At the SPM meeting in November 1923 the GE section was excluded from the rule of vestibuled stock on 60 ft underframes because 'of certain difficulties in connection with the length of stock generally for the section.' This related particularly to Liverpool Street station and the length of its

platforms which meant that with the number of through carriages on most principal trains a shorter vehicle than the 61 ft 6 in standard was required, otherwise trains would have been too long for the platforms. Where there were standard and unchanging formations such as with the boat trains then the longer vehicles were used. There is also the matter of the Areas' independence in specifying rolling stock and with the Southern Area headquarters at Liverpool Street the GE section's wishes were unlikely to be disregarded in the interests of standardisation.

The earliest vestibuled carriages to be ordered for the section were to North Eastern design under the 1923 CBP and at 53 ft 6 in over the end panels were near the former GER 54 ft standard. The types ordered were thirds, brake thirds and composites and they were delivered in 1924/5, all with dual braking. One curiosity was the rebuilding at Stratford in 1924 of two former ambulance cars converted from GER 54 ft stock as open thirds with dual braking for the North Eastern Area. As converted, they followed all the design features of GER open stock. Presumably because they were nominally of post Grouping construction they were allotted an LNER series diagram number – 26. They retained their North Eastern Area numbers 23801/2 under the 1943 renumbering scheme.

By 1926 the first 52 ft 6 in designs for vestibuled carriages were available see table, page 75 and the first examples, thirds to Dia 25 and brake thirds to Dia 42, were completed that year at Stratford Works. All new carriage construction ceased at this works from the end of that year. Until late 1930 only 76 standard 52 ft 6 in carriages were built for the GE section. With the principal demand for the Continental trains met by 61 ft 6 in vehicles in sets the rest of the GE section's requirements were regarded as of low priority, a matter only rectified by the 1929 Cromer sets mentioned below. In general, the shorter vehicles had one less compartment per carriage as compared with the 61 ft 6 in counterparts and slightly smaller lavatories. All other details followed the practices adopted for the 61 ft 6 in standard vehicles. Orders from 1936 for 52 ft 6 in vehicles were intended to replace ex-GER vehicles in main line sets but production of the shorter carriages ceased in 1938. Thereafter all new GE section vestibuled stock was to the full length. Certain types for which there was a 61 ft 6 in design were not specified in the 52 ft 6 in version nor were there any end vestibule examples or catering vehicles.

Under the 1943 renumbering the 52 ft 6 in vehicles were initially allotted blocks of numbers in the main 1xxxx series but in the event they retained their original numbers in the series 6452–6991 and 60500–63994. In later days they roamed all over the BR network and lasted as long as their full length compatriots.

Below LNER Diagram Book: 52 ft 6 in composite to Dia 9, this type being built for the GE section from 1927–38.

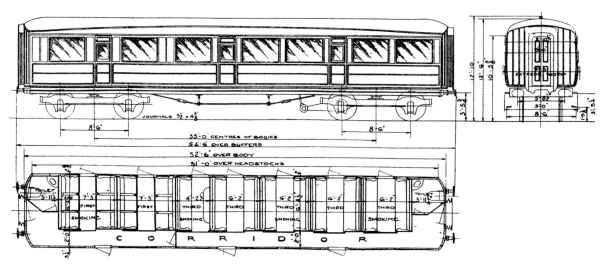

TABLE 9A

Type	Diagram	Compartments	Seats	First Built	Last Built
Open first	197	2 saloons (5½ bays)	33	1935	–
First	140	6	36	1929	1938
Second	141A*	7	56	1930	–
Open third	182	2 saloons (6½ bays)	39	1934	1935
	216=	1 saloon	52	1936	–
Third	25	7	56	1926	–
	141	7	56	1929	1938
Composite	9	2 1st, 4½ 3rd	12/27+	1927	1938
Open Brake third	217=	1	24	1936	–
Brake third	41	3	24	1927	1929
	42	3	24	1926	–
	146	3	24+	1930	1938

* Later thirds to Dia 141
+ Later examples intermediate armrests and three a side seating in thirds
= Bucket seats

The 1929 Cromer sets

Although the 1928/9 CBP was approved in January 1928, a month later the Joint Locomotive and Traffic Committee received a report from Wedgwood on the GE section passenger stock which pointed out that of the 2,600 main line carriages, 1,482 were six-wheeled and that every available vehicle was in use in summer. More to the point perhaps he commented that 'in view of intensive road competition for long-distance traffic it was more than ever necessary to make main line services more attractive.' His proposal was that 30 new vestibuled carriages should be built and that charging points for the electric cooking equipment of the restaurant cars should be installed at Cromer. The new vehicles would be to standard 52 ft 6 in and 61 ft 6 in designs, with vacuum brakes only. The estimated cost of £ 96,110 for the 30 carriages and the charging plant was based on the assumption that the

Below LNER Diagram Book: 52 ft 6 in open third to Dia 182...

Bottom ... and the York Works photo of Dia 182 No 61883, alongside Poppleton Road. This shows the other side to that on the diagram. Just visible are the oval mirrors in the saloons, placed between the windows.

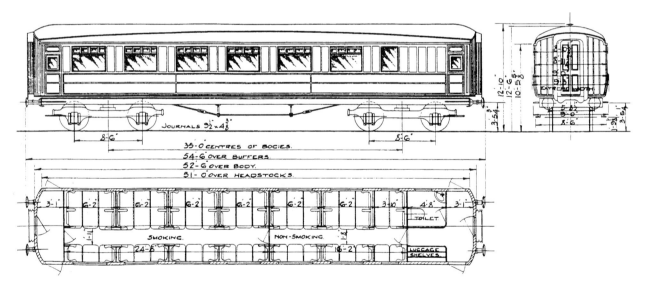

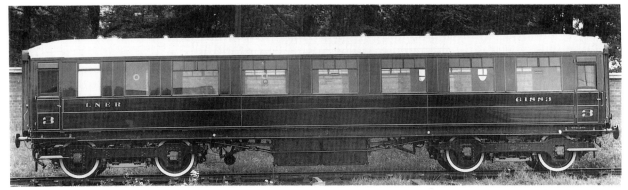

Interiors of the 'East Anglian' stock: *Above* the open first displaying Acton Surgey's effective decor scheme. Several features common to the East Coast high-speed trains are present. *Below* the open third is much plainer but still pleasing.

LNER workshops would built the stock. Although Wedgwood's proposals were recommended to the Board by the committee, the construction of the two sets of carriages plus spares for replacements and strengthening was put out to tender in May 1928. The order went to Metropolitan Carriage Wagon and Finance Co for eight third brakes to Dia 41, eight thirds to Dia 141, eight composites to Dia 9, two firsts to Dia 140 – all 52 ft 6 in vehicles – and two 61 ft 6 in open thirds (to Dia 27A and lettered as restaurant cars) and two restaurant/kitchen firsts (to Dia 10C).

Some useful publicity was gained by the introduction of the new sets on the Liverpool Street–Norwich–Cromer services with the summer 1929 timetable. Their introduction came at a time when deficiencies on the GE section were being rectified on the motive power front, too, with the building of ten additional 'B12' 4–6–0s in 1928 and the appearance of the first 'B17' 4–6–0s. The interior furnishings of the new stock followed standard practice. Given the urgency of ordering this was not surprising, but the restaurant cars with their dated brass fittings, mahogany panelling and green buffalo hide upholstery could have been ordered at any time over the previous twenty years.

The 1937 'East Anglian' set

The construction of a new set of carriages for the Liverpool Street–Norwich service was approved in November 1936 for inclusion in the 1937 CBP, along with the stock for the 'Coronation' and the 'West Riding Limited', although as late as February 1937 details of the formation and seating had not been finalised. From the beginning the 'East Anglian' was referred to as a high-speed train which it was in style, if not in journey time. Wedgwood said that it was 'not practicable to run a service in less than 2 hours 15 minutes' over the distance of 115 miles but the timing for the first few months was 5 minutes slower. While the late C.J. Allen was always rather scathing about the schedule of the 'East Anglian', the fact is that the 'B17s' were only able to maintain the timings at the cost of high coal consumption and the train was the least profitable of the LNER high-speed trains. A journey time very little better than the best existing train was the reason for not making this a supplementary fare service, according to Wedgwood's report to the JLT Committee.

The six carriages built at York for the 'East Anglian' were 61 ft 6 in in length, teak panelled and all of open layout, so allowing meals to be served to all seats. The set was formed brake third (Dia 240), restaurant/kitchen first (Dia 236), first (Dia 237), third (Dia 239), restaurant/kitchen third (Dia 238) and brake third (Dia 240). The restaurant cars had all-electric cooking equipment. The original fully open interior layout does not seem to have proved very satisfactory as the Dia 237 first and the brake thirds were given additional partitions in 1938; the former as converted then had three single bay sections rather like those in the 'Coronation' firsts and one 24-seater saloon. In due course, the restaurant first was converted to third-class and altered to Dia 264. The armchair type seats in first and third-class were neat in appearance and the overall style of the train was attractive, less fussy perhaps in detail than the East Coast high-speed sets. To ease passenger movement into and out of seats the tables had hinged leaves. The interior decor was the work of Acton Surgey and featured combinations of aluminium trim and Rexine wall coverings, stone and green predominating in the first-class and stone and shagreen in the third-class. The upholstery in the first-class was deep rose and gold with a mulberry carpet and in the third-class, uncut fawn moquette with a green carpet. The light fittings and parcel racks were chromium plated.

After the withdrawal of the 'East Anglian' at the

outbreak of World War 2, the stock remained in general service. Following overhaul the six carriages were restored as a complete set to the 'East Anglian' when it was reintroduced as from 7 October 1946, although as traffic had increased the train normally consisted of eight vehicles. At a later date restaurant/kitchen third No 9185 (Dia 264) was earmarked for the 'East Anglian' which continued to feature its 1937 stock into the 1950s. At least the semi-open first was still extant during 1963.

The 1938 'Hook Continental' set
In October 1937, after the initial approval of the 1938 CBP, it was decided to build a set of ten carriages for the 'Hook Continental' with the result that thirteen vehicles already in the programme were cancelled to compensate for the £39,000 cost of the new stock. One suspects that there had been some discreet lobbying of the chief general manager behind the scenes to include the set in the building programme but, whatever the circumstances, the result was that the new carriages were fully to the standards set by the design and layout of the 'Coronation'.

Above 'B1' 4–6–0 No 61040 leaves Norwich Thorpe at the head of the 'East Anglian' in May 1951. Most of the prewar vehicles seem to be present, by now in the BR carmine and cream livery.

Stone's pressure ventilation and heating as well as double glazing were fitted to all vehicles, other than the restaurant/kitchen cars and brake second.

Apart from three vehicles – the brake second, second and the semi-open first – the rest of the set was of centre gangway layout throughout and, with the two restaurant/kitchen cars, meals could be served to all seats. This facility was valuable for the 'Hook Continental' in view of the limited time available to serve breakfast in the up direction and dinner in the down direction. It was intended to cater for a maximum of 234 covers. Both kitchens had all-electric cooking equipment. The set normally comprised twelve vehicles, formed as follows:

Brake second (Dia 285), vestibule second (Dia 288),

Below LNER Diagram Book: 'Hook Continental' semi-open first to Dia 290, a one-off.

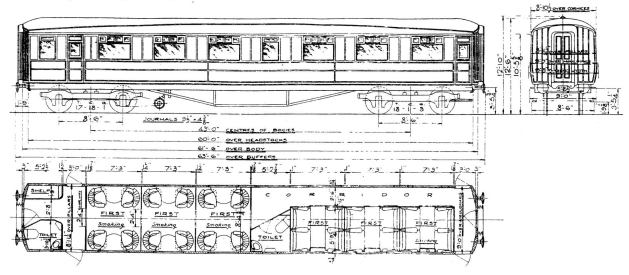

Above 'Hook Continental' open first to Dia 289, formerly 6486 and latterly GE 11135E. Here it is awaiting its final journey following internal use at York Works. It had been in the middle of an overhaul which seems to have been aborted. It is still lettered 'H' from its place in the boat train set.

second (Dia 287), restaurant/kitchen second (Dia 286), second (Dia 287), second (Dia 287), first (Dia 289), restaurant/kitchen first (Dia 291), first (Dia 289), semi-open first (Dia 290), two Pullman buffet cars normally *Irene* and *Fortuna* and usually one or two full brakes.

The vestibule second was to the end door pattern. The semi-open first comprised three seating bays with four armchairs to each, in 'Coronation' style, and three side-corridor compartments with two a side seating. The compartments resembled those in the 'Silver Jubilee' for style, with strip lights to each corner of the compartment and Jacobean tapestry upholstery. There was a lavatory at one end and another amidships. Once again, this splendid vehicle ought by rights to have survived, as a reminder of what boat trains could aspire to! The brake second to Dia 285 was of end door pattern. In addition, there was a brake

second to Dia 292 which was a curiosity in that although allocated to a new diagram it was a standard Dia 114 brake third altered to second-class for the new train and apparently was retained as a spare.

The open firsts – and the open section in the Dia 290 vehicle – were very similar to those in the 'Coronation' and 'West Riding' sets with the interior divided by partitions, large swivelling armchairs and cutaway tables. Similarly, all interior trim was of anodised aluminium, as were the partition architraves, but the parcel racks and some other fittings were chromium plated. The colour scheme was light green Rexine above the waist line and a darker shade below. The upholstery was green and fawn, with dark maroon carpets. The second-class saloons likewise resembled those in the 'Coronation', with six seats to each bay and similar tables. The Rexine finishes were shagreen for the lower panels and cream above, including the ceilings. The upholstery was fawn and the carpets, green. The two Dia 289 open firsts were not identical: No 6485 was marked for smoking and had one lavatory, No 6486 was non-smoking with two lavatories.

With the outbreak of World War 2 the first-class stock was placed in store but the open seconds and end door second were kept in traffic and designated first-class. In common with the other vehicles with Stone's pressure ventilation and heating steam radiators were fitted in 1941/2. Newsome remarks that when the first-class stock was refurbished following storage the chromium plated fittings had become tarnished and discoloured whereas the anodised aluminium had retained its looks. As soon after the war as November 1945 the 'Hook Continental' began running again, the train formation remaining very similar to that in prewar days although all second-class accommodation was now third-class, at least until 1956. The demand for third-class seating was met by running a second train, as a relief in winter and regularly scheduled in the summer. A public address system which made use of pre-recorded tapes in three languages was installed throughout the set in 1952. The stock was given an internal refurbishment during the early 1960s and. in 1961, one of the open seconds, No 13685, was given aluminium framed windows in BR style at Stratford Works. The 1938 stock was still regarded as prestigious until the end which came with the 1963/4 winter timetable. Dia 289 first No 11135 was in York Works for attention during 1964 but work was suspended and, after a period serving as a works canteen, it was sent for scrap.

The sight of this train, 'Britannia' at its head, on the Harwich branch was awe-inspiring and one not easily forgotten.

Below 'East Anglian' open first E11117E (Dia 237, formerly 6483) still looked in reasonable shape when photographed at York in August 1962.

CHAPTER 9
GRESLEY CATERING VEHICLES

ONE of the Gresley specialities was the development of electric cooking equipment for use in restaurant cars. This had its roots in the situation just before and during World War 1 when several bad train fires occurred as a result of accidents, and had been intensified by burning gas. By 1914 most new carriages had electric lighting, at any rate for main line use, and we have already seen how the GNR had moved away from oil-gas soon after Gresley had come to Doncaster. The other option was to produce fireproof rolling stock and retain gas lighting. In the case of restaurant cars, as long as gas fired ovens were used then the vehicles containing them had to be made fireproof. Obvious examples are the all-steel kitchen cars in the 1914 'Flying Scotsman' sets and the massive all-steel restaurant cars built by Cravens for the North British Railway after World War 1. The penalties were weight and problems with corrosion. The NBR cars were quoted in the Inspecting Officer's report into the Castlecary accident of 1937 as being withdrawn on the grounds of the deterioration of the steel panelling and excessive maintenance costs.

Meanwhile Gresley, true to form, had moved one step ahead by introducing all-electric equipment in the 1921 Leeds quintuplet set. This relied on ground points, main batteries and axle-driven generators to provide current as required while stationary and on the move. So there was little doubt that electric equipments would feature in the new catering vehicles for the LNER, at any rate once there had been investment in charging points at stations and carriage depots. Their cost was offset by the progressive elimination of oil gas plants, still necessary for gas-lit stock. But much was done to rid the LNER of gas-lit vehicles, even if by 1935/6 there were still over 2,000 of them. For most of the principal services all-electric restaurant cars were steadily introduced through the 1920s and 1930s, as the accompanying table demonstrates by way of the installation of charging points.

After Grouping, the first restaurant cars with electric cooking equipments were the triplet sets for the 'Flying Scotsman' and other East Coast trains, the decision to

adopt this system following a successful trial in 1923. The choice was for a more expensive installation but one that was freer from fire risk, ensured a lower temperature in the kitchen and an end to gassy smells while power was also available for refrigerated storage of foodstuffs. Two Stone's dynamos rated at 7.2 kW were normally mounted on the underframe to provide power, belt-driven from one of the axles and supplemented by batteries. But the crews had to be skilled in avoiding overloading of the equipment and to judge when to begin cooking entrées and other items requiring heavy use of current. By 1926 there was no doubt that all-electric kitchens were regarded by the

Above The interior of restaurant pantry car No 1226 (Built 1934, Dia 151, later No 9098). This shows the smoking saloon, looking towards the lavatory.

Installation of charging points for all-electric restaurant cars			
London Hornsey	upgraded 1937	London Marylebone	approved 1927
London Holloway	upgraded 1930	Manchester Ardwick/	
London Kings Cross	pre 1923	London Road/Central	approved 1927
		Sheffield Victoria	approved 1928
London Liverpool Street/		Bradford Laisterdyke	approved 1928/upgraded 1930
Stratford	approved 1928	Parkeston Quay	approved 1928
Cromer	approved 1928	Clacton	approved 1935
Ely/Hunstanton/Norwich	approved 1935		
Leeds GN	pre 1923	Starbeck	approved 1931
Leeds New/Waterloo Sdgs	approved 1930	Newcastle	approved 1928
Hull	approved 1935	Heaton	approved 1928
Scarborough	approved 1936		
Edinburgh Waverley	upgraded 1934	Aberdeen	upgraded 1928
Edinburgh Craigentinny	upgraded 1937	Aberdeen Joint station	approved 1935
Glasgow Queen Street	approved 1928	Fort William/Mallaig	approved 1935

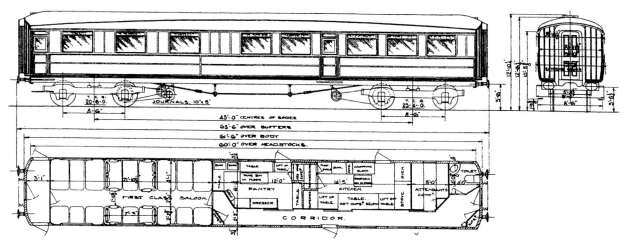

Above LNER Diagram Book: restaurant kitchen car (first-class) to Dia 10C. These were to 9 ft 3 in width and had electric cooking equipment.

LNER as practicable and reliable, the comparison in operating costs having been examined thoroughly.

For the earlier types of LNER restaurant cars, other than East Coast stock, gas cooking had been specified but in July 1926 the SPMs conducted a major review of the policies to be followed on catering vehicles and effectively established guidelines that applied until the late 1930s. In 1926 there were only a handful of post Grouping cars in service: the East Coast triplets and vehicles on Dias 10/10A/15/16. With immediate effect and with the recommendation of the Hotels Department which managed train catering, it was decided to standardise on three types of vehicle – see table below.

The SPMs set down other principles: new cars should have an attendants' compartment; there was no need for kitchen cars (other than in the triplet sets) and that all new restaurant cars for the East Coast and Kings Cross–Leeds trains should have electric cooking equipment. From the 1926/7 CBP all new restaurant cars had electric equipment, conditional on the concomitant installation of charging points.

Broadly speaking these principles held good until 1939. In practice, there were rather more of the Diagram 16 type cars than seemed to be contemplated in 1926, in time there was a composite restaurant car design and a full kitchen car was specified in the late 1930s, for party and excursion work. One type not foreseen in 1926 was the buffet car which came to be built from the mid-1930s.

The next major development was in November 1928 when the Traffic Committee recommended the adoption of a 9 ft 3 in width for all future restaurant and sleeping cars. This was to allow more room in the saloons and the change was possible once structural alterations had been made at a number of locations, principally Newcastle Central and Penmanshiel and Ipswich Tunnels. The greater width was only acceptable provided that the exterior doors of the vehicles were recessed. The heavy type compound bolster bogie used for restaurant cars was expensive to build and maintain. Around 1927 Gresley decided to experiment with a modified single bolster version. There were two versions of this new bogie, one suitable for a 12 ton load on the pivot and the other for 18 tons and they were supplied by Metro-Cammell, being referred to as 'Metro' type in LNER documents. These bogies were fitted as new to restaurant cars built in 1931 and 1933, the heavy type version under the kitchen end, and the light type under the saloon end. Some were used for existing vehicles. But Gresley did not regard them as successful and no more were ordered. From then onwards the compound bolster bogies were unchallenged, the heavy type being used for restaurant cars and the light type for buffet cars.

From 1932 buffet cars were placed in service and initially these were conversions of existing vehicles, of GNR, NER, GN/NE Joint and GER origins, all originally open thirds. The earliest conversions of GNR open thirds, the 1932 prototypes apart, had much the same layout with a kitchen, bar counter and saloon seating 21–24 passengers. The interior decor made much use of Rexine and chrome. From 1933 new buffet cars were built, either for inclusion in the Tourist train sets or, in the case of the ubiquitous Dia 167 cars, for general service duties, usually on semi-fast services and those subject to competition from road services.

Standard types of restaurant cars agreed by SPMs at July 1926 metting		
First-class restaurant/kitchen car	Current Diagram 10	With kitchen and pantry
		To work with open thirds and pantry thirds
Third-class restaurant car	Current Diagram 15	Pantry only
		To supplement the pantry in an adjoining restaurant/kitchen car, an arrangement preferred to one large pantry
Triplet restaurant car set	Current Diagrams 12/13/14	For important services with heavy and regular restaurant work – 'Flying Scotsman' and afternoon Scotsmen, as well as the 8 am Newcastle–Kings Cross and 5.30 pm return
For further consideration it was proposed that there would be two other types:		
Third-class restaurant/kitchen car	Current Diagram 16	With kitchen and pantry
		To be used with an open first on booked trains and for third-class parties.
Composite restaurant/kitchen car	No current Diagram	With kitchen and pantry
		Only able to serve a limited number of meals.

Above Restaurant kitchen car (first-class) to Dia 144, No 51776, built 1931 and later 9070. Glass louvred ventilators to the saloon windows.

Right Burner, oven and exhaust outlet for an anthracite-electric cooking equipment, as fitted to a number of immediately prewar cars and all the postwar cars.

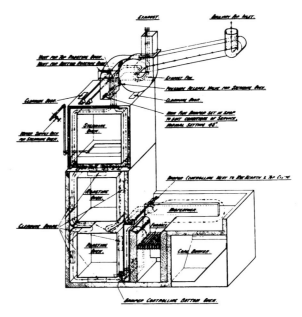

The earliest buffet cars had gas cooking equipment, but from 1935 the Dia 167 buffet cars went all-electric. When the North Eastern Area required gas fitted kitchen cars for excursion work in 1933, Gresley made it clear that he was anxious not to build new gas cars and instead former GNR restaurant cars were extensively converted to full kitchen cars. The all-electric cars could not be used for through excursions to destinations outside LNER territory, one reason why the North Eastern Area wanted gas cars but the Area's operators also needed vehicles capable of serving large numbers of meals to excursionists and this was probably beyond the capacity of an all-electric kitchen.

Gresley informed Wedgwood in 1935 that it was not possible to have a self-contained electric car, independent of mains charging points, but that he was looking at oil-fired ovens on the lines of those used on ships. Self-contained cars were needed on scheduled cross-country trains as well as for excursion work. Experiments were carried out with J. Stone & Co during 1937 to evolve a satisfactory self-contained installation, employing a solid-fuel range to supplement the electric equipment. The anthracite-fired range heated water and the main roasting and steaming ovens. As a result, underframe equipment was restricted to two 10 kW generators and a 180V battery. These were sufficient to supply current for the grills, hot cupboard, sink, refrigerator and fish fryer now that the main demands for power were met by the solid-fuel range. Adequate draught for combustion was ensured by electric fans in the exhaust trunking. The procedure for lighting the stove was that it was laid with paper, firewood and anthracite only. Once it was lit, a draught fan switch was turned on full until, after 45 minutes, the ovens had reached the required temperature and then the fan was reduced to half-speed; the heat in the ovens being controlled by the use of the two dampers. Anthracite consumption was between 30–40 lbs daily. From 1938 onwards a number of restaurant cars and one kitchen car were built with anthracite-electric kitchen equipment.

Louvre ventilators were used for the windows in the saloons of first-class restaurant cars and sliding ventilators for those in third-class cars until the early 1930s, thereafter ventilators only. From 1936 the kitchens of all new restaurant cars and kitchen cars were vented by 40 W exhaust fans. Seating was often a source of discussion. From 1925 Wedgwood instructed that all new restaurant firsts must be upholstered in green leather and that existing cars with moquette should be retrimmed, despite the disapproval of the SPMs who were not enamoured of leather seating! Second and third class cars were upholstered in the material chosen by their owning Area. But Wedgwood was less successful in his attempt during 1934 to persuade the SPMs to accept the idea of loose chairs in restaurant cars

Below Restaurant kitchen car (first-class) to Dia 11, SC9021E, built 1929 and formerly No 31868. It was still largely intact at Eastfield depot when seen in April 1964, in use as a mess room although withdrawn from traffic in 1961. It lasted until 1968 as DE 321067.

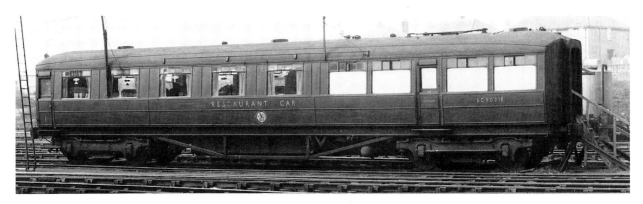

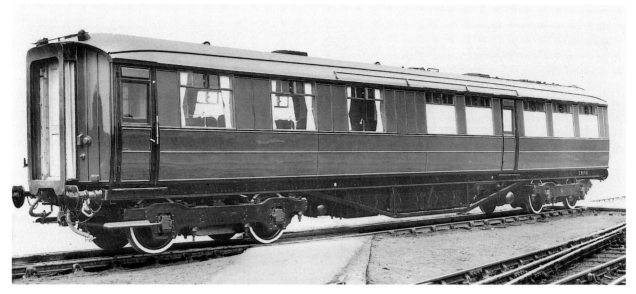

Above Restaurant kitchen car (first-class) to Dia 264 (originally Dia 236), E9171E, built 1937 and formerly No 678. As appropriated for royal train use and painted in claret livery, at Doncaster Works in 1954. It remained in the list of the royal train vehicles in 1961 but its subsequent fate is unknown.

and they made it clear that fixed seating should be the rule except for the 'Flying Scotsman' although the 1938 stock had fixed seating. After unsatisfactory experiments with rubber flooring, cork lino with a centre strip of parquet lino was the standard adopted for restaurant cars in 1926, but a year later all new first-class cars were given fitted carpets, third-class saloons having carpet down the centre aisle only. From 1925, bell communication was provided in all restaurant cars as well as open firsts and thirds used for dining. Clocks went out of fashion in dining cars from December 1924, back into fashion briefly in 1937 but were then dispensed with on grounds of inaccuracy.

Below, left Restaurant kitchen car (first-class) to Dia 264, E9170E, built in 1937 and formerly No 677. This started life as a first-class car for the 'East Anglian' set but then became third-class, reverting to first-class. In poor condition when seen in 1962.

Right Restaurant kitchen car (second-class) to Dia 267, E9190E, built 1938 and formerly No 24286. This was one of the early anthracite-electric cars. When photographed in 1962 it was a spare car at York.

Below, right The kitchen of gas-equipment third-class car No 42791, as built (Dia 241, later No 9175). This was the last batch of gas cars.

Catering vehicles 1923–1939 by type

In the tables which follow, A – attendants' compartment; K – kitchen; L – lavatory for staff; P – pantry

Diagram	Seating		Features	Bogies	Built
All cars 9 ft 3 in width except where shown * which were 9 ft only					
Restaurant/kitchen first-class cars (RF) , some (RU)					
Gas cooking equipment					
10*	1 saloon, 18 seats		PKAL	Heavy	1925/6
10A	1 saloon, 18 seats		PKAL	Heavy	1925
10B	1 saloon, 18 seats		PKAL	Heavy/ Light	1929

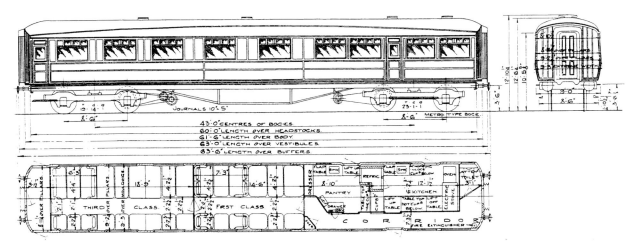

Above LNER Diagram Book: composite restaurant kitchen car to Dia 187.

Dia 10A cars were for the 1925 'Continental' sets and were transferred to the North Eastern Area, along with Dia 10B No 678, under the 1934 CBP, replaced by new Dia 144 cars in 1935. No 678 was then used as an unclassed car, painted cream and green for use with the Tourist stock. Dia 10B No 679 was transferred to the Southern Scottish Area in 1939. Dia 10B had the entrance lobby and saloon reduced in size compared to Dia 10/10A as well as a larger kitchen.

Diagram	Seating	Features	Bogies	Built
Electric cooking equipment				
10C	1 saloon, 18 seats	PKAL	Heavy	1928/9
11	2 saloons, 30 seats	PKL	Heavy	1929–34
144	1 saloon, 18 seats	PKAL	Heavy	1931–36
236	1 saloon, 18 seats	PKAL	Heavy	1937/8
291	1 saloon, 12 seats	LPKP	Heavy	1938

Dia 10C: No 6119/20 were the Cromer service cars, later 651/2; Dia 11: Nos 42782/3/43041 were classified RU – either class, Nos 31922/3/4/6/35, 42783, 43041 were converted for ambulance trains, Nos 31926/42783, 43041 being employed overseas. Of these, most were restored to their former state soon after the end of the war but those on the Continent did not return until the early 1950s and were then converted to the cafeteria cars mentioned at the end of this chapter. Dia 144: Metro bogie fitted at one end on some, several converted to propane gas cooking and generally modernised by BR, so outliving the remainder of the prewar restaurant cars, as described below. 1935-built cars had a different colour scheme of mahogany panelling, blue and rose painted ceilings and blue and rose upholstery. Dia 236: No 677 for the 'East Anglian', later redesignated third-class on Dia 264. No 658, similarly changed to Dia 264, also No 678 which was the first anthracite-electric car. No 678 at first ran between Liverpool Street and Norwich in January 1938, then on the Harwich–Liverpool train with its associated Liverpool–Hull and return journeys. Later it was allocated to the royal train. Dia 291: 'Hook Continental'.

Diagram	Seating	Features	Bogies	Built
Restaurant/kitchen either class car (RU)				
Anthracite-electric equipment				
267	2 saloons, 24 seats	PKAL	Heavy	1938

Three cars built for the Southern Scottish Area, with armrests to the seats. One for the North Eastern Area for cross-country services and without armrests, almost identical to the car on Dia 268 for this Area.

Diagram	Seating	Features	Bogies	Built
Restaurant/kitchen third-class cars (RT),				
Dia 286 originally second-class (RS)				
Gas cooking equipment				
16*	2 saloons, 24 seats	PKAL	Heavy	1925
241	2 saloons, 24 seats	PKAL	Heavy	1937
Electric cooking equipment				
145	1 saloon, 18 seats	PKAL	Heavy	1930
238	1 saloon, 24 seats	PKAL	Heavy	1937
264	1 saloon, 18 seats	PKAL	conversions from Dia 236	
Anthracite-electric				
268	2 saloons, 24 seats	PKAL	Heavy	1938
286	1 saloon, 18 seats	PKP	Heavy	1938
Also lavatory for diners				

All cars 9 ft 3 in width
except where shown * which were 9 ft only

Dia 16: Shallow window ventilators; Nos 1225 and 52040 were both in ambulance trains during World War 2 and in 1953 were converted at York as kitchen buffet cars (RKB) with a buffet counter and a kitchen serving meals to an adjoining vehicle. The first-named became M1225E, the other car was by then E9064E. Dia 145: No 22650 only, built for the Leeds–Glasgow service in 1930 and working with semi-open first No 21254 (Dia 5) and open third (as dining car) No 22660. By running Leeds–Glasgow and return each day the set covered 555 miles during which all meals were served from breakfast to dinner, probably one of the most intensive workings of its kind at the time. Dia 238: 'East Anglian'. Dia 241: intended for additional ordinary services and party trains. Dia 268: Newcastle–Bournemouth, as built. Dia 286: 'Hook Continental'.

Diagram	Seating	Features	Bogies	Built
Restaurant/kitchen composite (RC)				
187	1 saloon 1st, 12 seats 1 saloon 3rd, 18 seats	PKL	Heavy	1934–36
266	As above	PKL	Heavy	1938
Anthracite-electric				
All cars 9 ft 3 in width				

A type used only by the Scottish Areas. Dia 187: The three in the 1934 build were in replacement of older cars and used between Edinburgh and Aberdeen and Edinburgh and Newcastle. Of the four Southern Scottish Area cars built in 1935/6, one was used in a set with other

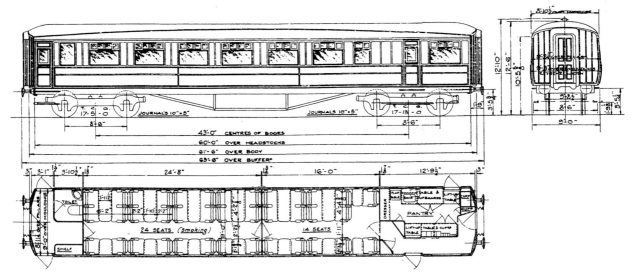

Above LNER Diagram Book: restaurant pantry car to Dia 321, the diagram as first issued in 1942 designating these as open firsts. Note the details given of the capacity of the water tanks which indicated the intended use of these vehicles, to relieve the adjoining restaurant car, rather than just providing extra dining capacity.

new stock between Edinburgh and Aberdeen, the others on the Glasgow–Fort William/Mallaig trains, electric charging points being installed at the last named places for their operation. Three former GNR Sheffield stock cars were displaced from the West Highland services and were transferred away, two being converted to kitchen cars. The Northern Scottish car was to work in the 8.5 am Aberdeen–Inverness and 1 pm return, again with new stock, and a charging point was installed at Aberdeen Joint station. Nos 9160–2 received propane gas cooking equipment in 1961. Dia 266: Replacements for pre-Grouping cars.

Diagram	Seating	Features	Bogies	Built
Restaurant pantry third (RTP)				
15	2 saloons, 39 seats	P	Light	1925
112	2 saloons, 39 seats	P	Light	1929
151	2 saloons, 39 seats	P	Heavy	1931–38
321	2 saloons, 38 seats	P	Light	1942/3

A lavatory was provided for diners in the lobby.
All cars 9 ft 3 in width

A type preferred for East Coast stock and the GN section where other Areas might use Dia 27 open thirds. The pantry contained a sink, tables and cupboards and a

water boiler, supplied by a cold water tank in the roof. A good example of use was shown in 1933 with the 5.45 pm Kings Cross–Leeds/Hull with TO No 4175 (Dia 150), RTP No 42784 (Dia 151), RF No 42787 (Dia 144) and Semi FO No 4100 (Dia 5), indicating the anticipated demand for meals on a principal service, a level of provision that declined rapidly in postwar days. Nos 9094–9103 (Dia 151) altered in 1960 with a service point at the pantry end. Dia 321: Ordered in 1939 but not completed until 1942/3 and then put into traffic as firsts with the pantry sealed up. These vehicles had an electric water boiler and pre-heat tank (see table below).

The 1924 triplets were used on the 'Flying Scotsman', the afternoon Scotsmen and the 8 am Newcastle–Kings Cross and 5.30 pm return. The 1928 sets included the White Allom decorated vehicles for the 'Flying Scotsman', sets 16481–3/91–3. With their arrival the two displaced triplets went to the relief 'Flying Scotsman'. Thereafter there were six in regular use between Kings Cross and Scotland and two to cover for winter renovation and for repairs. The other set, invariably 16441–3, was on the Newcastle service, the others also appearing on trains such as the 'Norseman'. The 1928 order included a GN section set to work the 7.50 am Leeds–Kings Cross and 1.30 pm return. Steam heating was fitted to the pressure ventilated cars c 1942. By postwar days the triplets were short of duties, the 1938 sets by then being used between Newcastle and Kings Cross, principally on the 'Northumbrian' for which duty the first-class car of each set was fitted out with a cocktail bar and the seating reduced to 24. The 1924 sets were condemned from 1959/60 and all were out of traffic by the summer of 1961. The inner bogies on four sets were of the Metro heavy type.

Diagram	Seating	Features	Bogies	Built	Notes
Articulated triplets (RTS) Formed first + kitchen car + third					
12*	2 saloons, 36 1sts	–	Heavy	1924	
13*	–	LAP 3rd classK P 1st cl	Heavy	1924/8	
14*	2 saloons, 42 3rds	–	Heavy	1924	
12A	2 saloons, 36 1sts	–	Heavy	1928	White Allom cars
12B	2 saloons, 36 1sts	–	Heavy	1928	
14A	2 saloons, 42 3rds	–	Heavy	1928	
255	[2 saloons, 36 1sts	–	Heavy	1938	First-class car
	[–	LAPKP	Heavy	1938	Kitchen car
	[2 saloons, 42 3rds	–	Heavy	1938	Third-class car Dia 255 with pressure ventilation and heating

All cars 9 ft 3 in width except where shown * which were 9 ft only

Diagram	Features		Bogies	Built	Notes
Kitchen cars (RK)					
226	Larder, PKPAL		Heavy	1937	
293	Larder, PKPAL		Heavy	1939	Anthracite-electric

All cars 9 ft 3 in width

These were built for guaranteed excursion and party work, Dia 226 with gas cylinders on the underframe. All windows were obscured. Dia 226 cars intact until 1963, the last, No 9164, surviving until 1965.

Diagram	Seating	Features	Bogies	Built	Notes
Restaurant buffet car (RB)					
167	1 saloon, 24 seats	Kitchen and counter	Light	1933–7	Gas before 1935, rest electric
168	saloon, 24 seats	Kitchen and counter	Light	1933/4	Tourist stock
185	1 saloon, 24 seats	Kitchen and counter	Light	–	Conversion
258	1 saloon, 20 seats	Pantry and counter also ladies retiring room	Heavy	1938	Pressure ventilation and heating
275	1 saloon, 12 seats 1 saloon, 18 seats	Kitchen and counter	Heavy	1939	

All cars 9 ft 3 in width

Dia 185 was the conversion in 1934 from a Dia 27A open third. Dia 167 was the most numerous type and was employed for a variety of uses. The kitchen included water tanks and a refrigerator and the counter a coffee machine or Still's boiler and a cash register. In 1933 there was an investigation of all passenger trains where restaurant cars might be replaced by buffet cars or where catering services might be provided for the first time using a buffet car. The first Dia 167 car went to the Southern Scottish Area and was used between Fort William and Glasgow. It was the only example to have a gas stove. Nos 21608–11 were used in Newcastle–Carlisle and Leeds–Hull sets, Nos 24079–82 excursions and reliefs, Nos 24275–8 five Newcastle–Middlesbrough, two Leeds–Scarborough; No 43138 for reliefs and excursions; No 51769 Manchester–Cleethorpes; No 641–4/9/50 two for Liverpool Street–Cambridge fast trains, 648 Yarmouth–Liverpool Street. Meals and drinks served in these cars were at reduced prices as compared to restaurant cars. The Dia 167 cars proved to be long-lived, several being modernised from 1958 and fitted with propane gas equipment. Dia 168: Tourist stock buffet cars, described in Chapter 11, but with an interior almost identical to Dia 167.

Dia 258: the 'Flying Scotsman' buffet lounge cars, described in Chapter 7. Dia 275: These were a hybrid between a buffet and a restaurant car and were ordered under the 1937 CBP but not delivered until 1939, Dukinfield building the structure, the fitting out being

completed by Doncaster. They were ordered for the York–Swindon train that conveyed the through carriages from Aberdeen to Penzance and replaced the 1919 GNR articulated tea-car twins. In Dia 275 the kitchen was at one end, next came the counter, then a section for buffet passengers with eighteen tip-up seats, finally a dining section with twelve seats at tables with lamps. The saloons were divided by acrylic screens in aluminium framing. With the outbreak of World War 2 the two cars were used between Leeds and Newcastle. No 9195 was modernised in 1961 and fitted with propane gas equipment.

Just before the start of war in September 1939 Wedgwood was very critical about the layout of the standard buffet cars and asked for an existing car to be rebuilt to a layout similar to the GWR Quick Lunch Bar Cars Nos 9631/2. No 43135, a conversion from a former GN/NE vehicle, was chosen but apart from putting in a half-partition to screen the buffet counter little else was done.

Catering services and vehicles after 1939 … and the Pullman agreement
Despite the withdrawal of most restaurant car services in 1939 a number were restored before long as buffet services only so that, by 1941, there were 91 such workings compared to 42 in 1939. There were also some new trains, run largely for forces traffic, such as Colchester–York and Ashford–Newcastle. Full restaurant car service began to be restored to the day East Coast trains from 1 October 1945.

In prewar days, fifty-eight Pullman cars had been employed on scheduled and special services on the LNER. Of the total, fourteen were used on the 'Queen of Scots', nine on the 'Yorkshire Pullman', nine on Continental boat trains, four as restaurant cars on express services in the Southern Scottish Area, and the rest for special duties or as spares. The agreement with the Pullman Car Co inherited by the LNER from the GER ran from 17 December 1919

Below LNER Diagram Book: buffet car to Dia 167, in original form although the vehicle depicted represents the first completed in 1933, with gas cooking.

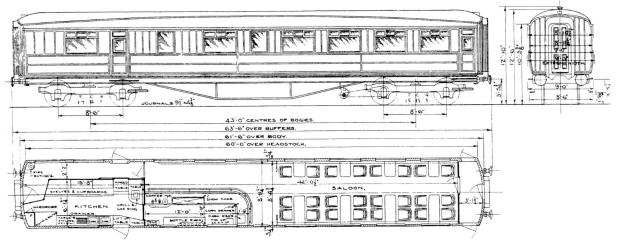

and terminated on the last day of 1938. The terms for a new agreement discussed with Pullman included the replacement of six old cars by seven new vehicles for the 'Queen of Scots' and 'Yorkshire Pullman' and that a fresh ten-year agreement would begin with the delivery of the modern stock. A formal agreement was never concluded but from 1940 the LNER (and Southern Railway) compensated the PCC for the loss of net receipts due to the withdrawal of services. This is relevant to the next development which saw the wartime use of Pullman cars by the LNER, as a way of making some contribution to the compensation paid to PCC. Thirty cars were used from 1942–6, as open firsts, open thirds and brake thirds, painted in brown livery and numbered in a series 468–498. After overhaul, 29 Pullman cars were used from May 1946, in Pullman livery but with the titles obscured, up until the resumption of the first supplementary fare service, the 'Yorkshire Pullman', in November 1946.

Gresley catering vehicles in BR days

The postwar LNER-design catering vehicles are described in Chapter 12 but the teak bodied and pre Grouping stock enjoyed an extended life for the main part, in view of the slowness in introducing BR standard designs, the earliest examples of which were far from popular. Of the Eastern/North Eastern Regions' catering vehicle allocation in 1950 more than 51 were over 30 years old. The major

Below and bottom Restaurant buffet car No 24287: the exterior, when new and the uninspiring interior showing the dining section which was at the other end to the kitchen. This car survived to be preserved, in its form as converted by BR to a full buffet car.

concern at the time was the replacement of oil-gas and Calor gas by propane gas in restaurant, buffet and sleeping cars and this got under way from 1955, all but the oldest cars being converted by 1961. The oil-gas for propane programme did not include the all-electric and anthracite-electric cars and in 1955 it was decided that these would not be converted. Eventually a five-year replacement programme comprising 430 new catering vehicles was authorised in 1957, with the aim of replacing all those of pre 1939 construction.

Despite a general decision by British Railways not to convert all-electric cars whose running costs and reliability were causing concern, a limited programme of conversions to propane equipment began from 1958. First, five restaurant/kitchen cars to Dia 144 (E9075–8E) working between Liverpool Street and Cromer were dealt with and modernised internally with laminated plastic panelling. Then the conversion of six East Coast cars to Dia 144 was authorised in April 1959, E1668–72E and E9084E, their estimated life being twelve years. In fact they were withdrawn more quickly with the general cut-backs of the catering vehicle fleet. The last regular turn of an ex-LNER RF on the East Coast route was on the 1962 'Elizabethan', using No 1671. No 9077 was a late survivor working in the 'Hook Continental' until March 1966 and it remained as a spare until condemned in 1970.

There was considerable criticism of the state of many of the LNER buffet cars during the 1950s. One memorable official comment concerned a Tourist stock Dia 168 car described as 'bleak and repellent... one felt one's stomach muscles tightening... there was an electric blue dado to the ceiling, olive green walls and bog green curtains.' As a

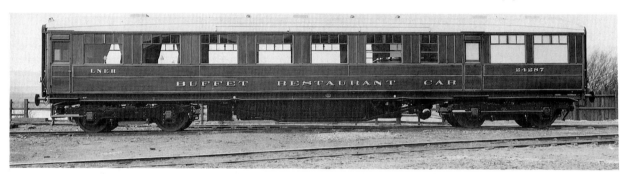

result, some were modernised before a general improvement programme began with twelve buffet cars approved for conversion in October 1958 and six in June 1959, the work being carried out at Doncaster and York Works. Those dealt with included Dia 167 cars Nos 9115/8/9/22–5/8/9/31/2/4/5, Dia 168 Tourist stock cars Nos 9138/9/46/9, the Dia 258 buffet lounge cars Nos 1852/3, Dia 275 car No 9195 and postwar buffet lounge cars Nos 1705/6. Some of the conversion styles were fairly lurid with laminated plastics deployed in bright yellows and reds although others were more restrained. The quality of work was not particularly good as the preservationists now caring for a number of these cars have found to their cost. The Dia 167 cars now roamed far and wide, some such as 9117/24/7/34 on Waterloo–Southampton boat trains, 9135 on the Western Region. The 'wooden walls', as they were called, also had regular diagrams on the Eastern Region, such as the Kings Cross–Cleethorpes, Liverpool Street–Lowestoft and Kings Cross–Cambridge buffet expresses. They were at work into the 1970s, Nos 9115/28/31/2/5 being in traffic into 1974. Dia 275 car No

Above Restaurant kitchen car (first-class) to Dia 144, E9075E, built 1935 and formerly No 655. This was one of the cars modernised with propane gas cooking equipment, plastic panelled interior and loose chairs for seating. Here it is in use in 1962 for a special party and attached to a Newcastle–Kings Cross express.

9195 had put in some work on the Harwich Parkeston Quay–Manchester train until withdrawn in 1973. The last Dia 167 car in BR traffic was W9135E, withdrawn in late 1977 as the last wooden bodied passenger vehicle in service with British Rail. It was acquired for the National Collection and restored for the Centenary of Train Catering celebrations in 1979.

The LNER catering vehicles remaining in their original form continued in traffic until 1961/2 but there was then a massive slaughter. In part this was due to the completion of the five-year re-equipment of the catering vehicle fleet

Below The grand survivor, buffet car W9135E (Dia 167, built 1937 and formerly No 650) on a West Country special to the Spalding bulb fields in May 1975.

Above Restaurant cafeteria car S9211E, in Southern Region green livery and condemned at Eardley sidings in March 1963. The picture shows the hybrid appearance of these vehicles, with several Eastleigh features and steel panelling. This had been a Dia 95 third-class sleeping car before its wartime overseas service in an ambulance train.

but it was also a consequence of cut-backs in rolling stock instigated at the onset of the Beeching era. All but very few of the un-modernised LNER catering cars were withdrawn before 1962 was out.

The restaurant cafeteria cars (RCAF)

The final LNER outline catering vehicles did not appear on LNER diagrams but were numbered within the LNER number series as 9209–14. These were conversions from vehicles appropriated for overseas ambulance trains but not repatriated until about 1953, their conversion to what the British Transport Hotels & Catering Services termed as Type D or RCAF cafeteria cars being authorised in the June of that year. Type D denoted that they featured a self-service cafeteria and a kitchen designed to serve full meals to a dining section within the car and to an adjoining vehicle. The kitchen was equipped to prepare meals from deep frozen food supplied by J. Lyons & Co.

The nine vehicles comprised six former third-class sleeping cars to Dia 95 and three Dia 11 restaurant/kitchen firsts. The design work on these conversions was the responsibility of the Southern Region at Eastleigh Works where the extensive and relatively costly conversions were carried out. The eighteen-seat restaurant section was at one end, a kitchen in the centre and a cafeteria serving snacks at the other. As rebuilt they were a curious mixture of styles, still unmistakably 'Gresley' in

outline but with a different arrangement of windows, some Southern features and steel-panelled exteriors. The interior surfaces were mainly laminated plastics and the seats upholstered in hide. Their weight as remodelled was 35 tons. The first to be completed went into service on Midland Division expresses from July 1954 but their tenure of these duties was relatively short-lived. Most spent the rest of their time on excursion work, one exception being S9213E which could be seen on the Margate–Birkenhead train during 1960. Withdrawals took place from 1962.

Below Table d'hôte prices 1937/8

RESTAURANT CAR CHARGES

1st CLASS BREAKFAST – Table d'hôte Menus . 3/6

3rd „   „   „   „   „ 3/6

    Curtailed Meal.. 2/6

1st CLASS LUNCHEON – Table d'hôte Menus ... 3/6

3rd „   „   „   „   „ 3/6

    Curtailed Meal.. 2/6

1st CLASS DINNER – Table d'hôte Menus 5/-

3rd „   „   „   „   „ 4/6

    Curtailed Meal... 3/6

For children travelling with half-fare tickets, half-price only is charged for breakfast, luncheon or dinner, with a minimum charge of 1/9

CHAPTER 10
GRESLEY SLEEPING CARS

DEVELOPMENTS in the interior design and facilities of East Coast sleeping cars typify the attention to detail and technical innovations characteristic of the Gresley team. These were illustrated by a range of developments extending from Bulleid's special coat-hanger to the evolution of a satisfactory ventilation and heating system. Articulation was particularly satisfactory for sleeping cars with their normally low passenger/weight ratio. The 1926 twin first cars weighed 63¼ tons compared with 74¾ tons for two separate firsts carrying the same twenty passengers. Bulleid's decision in 1920 to simplify interior decor set the standard for the neat and functional treatment of accommodation in East Coast sleeping cars.

The early post-Grouping cars
The first of the modern 60 ft underframe sleeping cars comprised the six to EC Dia 64B built at York in 1923, and generally very similar to the 55 ft cars produced in 1906/7. These and the two twins of the same year, Nos 198J/9J and 200J/1J, were replacements for clerestory vehicles and were seen as essential in reducing the average age of the East Coast sleeping car fleet and competing more effectively with the West Coast. The twins were to EC Dia 68. The prototype was No 181/181A, built in 1922. This design had twenty berths, sixteen of which could form double berths with the adjacent berth. There was one lavatory and one attendant's compartment. The overall length of the twin was 113 ft 6 in, and the total weight 61 tons 17 cwt.

No 181/181A (later Nos 1181/2) had introduced a simpler interior finish to sleeping cars. The corridors were panelled in natural teak, while the sleeping berths had plain mahogany panelling to waist height and, above that, white enamel.

At the same time, some of the older cars were repaired and generally spruced up. The new cars in the fleet, including those to Dia 20, allowed for the introduction of new services such as Aberdeen–Penzance which started running just before Grouping and Kings Cross–Aberdeen–Inverness. The first of these proved something of a nine-day wonder and lasted for only a year, being withdrawn from 12 May 1924. Fifteen of the 61 ft 6 in ten-berth cars to Dia 17 were built between 1924 and 1927. No 10196J was exhibited at the 1925 Wembley Exhibition with *Flying Scotsman*. Nos 1317–9 to this diagram, built in 1927, were the first sleeping cars to have electric water heating so that passengers were not deprived of hot water during the summer when steam heating was unavailable.

Another new type of this period was the composite sleeping car to Dia 20, ten of which were completed in 1925/6. As yet there was no third-class sleeping accommodation but these cars had two third-class compartments arranged to provide eight places for recumbent passengers at night and sixteen seats by day. There were also six first-class convertible berths, two lavatories, an attendant's compartment and a locker compartment. Three of these cars were equipped with dual braking for the Kings Cross–Lossiemouth service, the others working over the West Highland line. After the introduction of third-class sleeping accommodation in 1928 the third-class compartments in the Dia 20 cars were changed to give two-tier berths for eight sleepers in all. Six of this type were taken for ambulance trains during World War 2. They were restored to traffic afterwards but did not survive long in BR days.

Five twin first sleeping cars were built between 1924 and 1926 to Dia 18/19 in further modernisation of the fleet and these were largely similar to the 1922 cars, Nos 181/181A. At the time it was considered that there was insufficient all the year demand for more than a few of the twin cars, except on the Newcastle service. No 1204 of 1204/5 gained a footnote in history with the conversion of one berth in 1930 to provide a shower compartment, the first on a British train. A charge of 1/- (5p) was made for its use.

These sleeping cars of the mid and late 1920s were standard teak bodied vehicles with glass louvred ventilators to the outer windows of the berths. Their interiors followed the style of the 1922 twin cars, with plain polished woodwork and white enamel paintwork. Bulleid's clothes hanger dated from 1927 when he was asked by the SPMs to design one superior to the LMS pattern and so allow a gentleman to hang up his trousers once his jacket was on the hanger.

Third-class sleeping cars
The demand for sleeping accommodation grew rapidly during the 1920s but so far third-class passengers had to put up with rudimentary facilities. The commercial managers watched the situation carefully, their calculation being that the improvement and development of third-

Below Twin first-class sleeping car Nos 198J/199J (Dia EC68, later Nos 1198/9). Until 1925 such vehicles were lettered Sleeping Carriage.

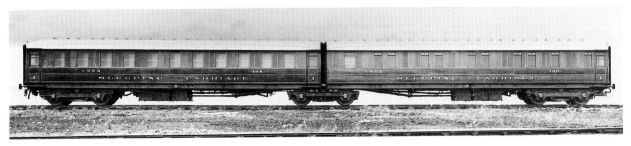

Above Composite sleeping car No 1091 (Dia 20, originally 10208J and 1710 in the 1943 numbering scheme). Photograph dated 1929, No 1091 having been converted to lying down accommodation in the third-class.

class accommodation might abstract from the lucrative first-class business while they were also reluctant to make a move without agreement with the LMS to prevent a free for all in sleeping car traffic. The SPMs first discussed the matter in 1923, concluding that 'no commercial case can be made for third-class sleepers... unable to recommend their introduction unless pressure of public opinion demands action'.

At last in May 1928 it was agreed to build sixteen convertible third-class sleeping cars: allowing for ten in service and the rest spare; in fact, ten cars were already under construction at the time the expenditure was sanctioned! They were regarded as an additional travelling

Above Non-convertible third-class sleeper as E1338E, (Dia 148) at the end of its days in 1963.

Below LNER Diagram Book: convertible sleeping car to Dia 95, 28 'berths' for night use, 56 seats in daytime.

facility and their cost was charged to Capital Account. Built to Dia 95 they had seven compartments and a separate washroom and lavatory at each end. The compartments each contained four berths, the upper ones folding back during the daytime, hence their description as convertible. A pillow and rug were provided for each passenger and a charge of 7/- (35p) was made for journeys between England and Scotland and 6/- for those within England. The initiative resulted from the joint agreement of the LNER, LMS and GWR to introduce third-class sleeping cars 'as an experiment' from 24 September 1928 but only on those trains already having first-class sleeping accommodation. The inaugural services from Kings Cross with these facilities were the 7.30 pm, with one car for Aberdeen and one for Inverness, and one car on each of the 10.25 pm to Glasgow and 9.45 pm return; 10.35 pm to Edinburgh and 10.50 pm return and 10.45 pm to Newcastle and return. From 28 October, a car was run on Sundays at 8.50 pm from Dundee but there was no return working.

Public reaction was such that in November 1928 Wedgwood asked for approval to build twelve additional cars in anticipation of traffic during the summer 1929 timetable and in advance of the 1929/30 CBP. These were to Dia 109 and differed from the earlier cars in having the entrance doors slightly recessed, thereby allowing the width over the body mouldings to be increased by 2¼ in. Seven more cars were added to the order in a matter of weeks, as well as agreement to convert the third-class accommodation in the Dia 20 composite cars to the same standard; the latter were used on the Kings Cross–Inverness services via Carr Bridge and via Forres and between Kings Cross and Perth. Ten more Dia 109 cars were included in the 1930/1 CBP. Of the fleet of 45 convertible third-class cars, thirteen were used for ambulance trains during World War 2 and one other was lost to enemy action. Six of those from the overseas ambulance trains were not returned to this country until 1953 and were then used as the basis for the cafeteria cars described in Chapter 9.

The 1930/1 CBP included ten third-class sleeping cars

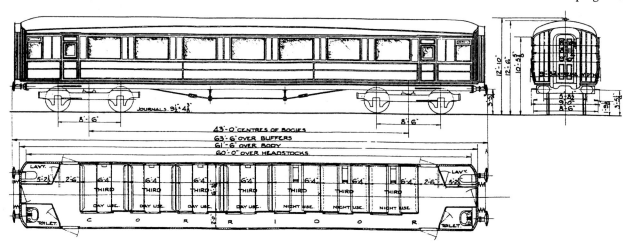

that introduced a better standard of accommodation, with proper mattresses but without full bed linen. These cars, to Dia 148, were built on a new design of 65 ft underframe with angle trussing and their facilities comprised eight 6 ft 4 in compartments, arranged for 32 fixed berths, and a separate washroom and wc at each end. Dia 148 were referred to as 'non-convertible'. Interior fittings were generally improved, with heating in the corridors, a reading lamp to each berth, mirrors on the partition doors, better insulation and drinking water taps in the washrooms. These cars also had the heavy type bogies, in place of the light type used for the previous third-class cars. As they were not convertible for daytime use they were labelled 'Sleeping Car'. The ten vehicles to Dia 148 were introduced on the 7.30 pm Aberdeen, 10.25 pm, to/from Dundee only, 10.35 pm Edinburgh and 10.45 pm Newcastle trains.

The prestige first-class cars

Improvements were made in the design of first-class sleeping cars. The most important advance was with the development of a full ventilation and heating system of the Thermotank pattern, first fitted to Dia 17 car No 1261. The heating equipment with fans were placed in a unit next to the lavatory. Warmed and cool air passed along separate plywood ducts above the corridor ceiling. Branch ducts led into each cabin and a nozzle above the head of the berth could be adjusted to provide warm, cool or blended air. In 1929 electric water heaters had been fitted to two Dia 17 cars, as noted above.

All these new developments were included in four ten-berth first-class cars built in 1930 on Dia 138. Gresley engaged consultants for the interior decor of these cars. Two were finished to Waring & Gillow's scheme, two to White Allom's, the latter being the less attractive, somewhat in the style of the Louis XVI restaurant cars with heavy mouldings and bluish green walls relieved with biscuit coloured mouldings. Dark blue Persian carpeting completed the picture. Waring's decor consisted of highly glossed painted surfaces, in shades of blue applied with a stippled effect. All other furnishings were also in blue. The painted surfaces soon suffered from scuffing and scratching, one result being that at their first overhaul Rexine was used to cover the painted surfaces, this material more easily

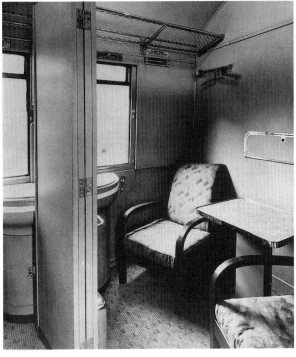

Above right and right An official montage showing the combined berth/sitting room in a Dia 157 car.

Below LNER Diagram Book: first-class sleeping car to Dia 157. Note the shower compartment; the details of the underframe water raising equipment are omitted from the diagram. The Thermotank equipment was above the WC compartment. From 1943, most were temporarily converted with two-tier berths in each end compartment. Compartments 5/6 could be converted to form a berth/sitting room.

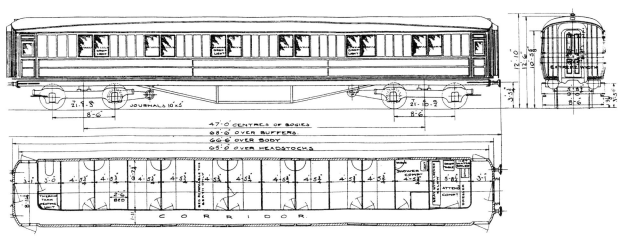

Above First-class sleeping car E1211E (Dia 157, built 1935), in BR blue and grey livery at King's Cross in September 1968. It was withdrawn in 1972 as the last wooden bodied sleeping car in service on BR.

resisting marks and able to be washed down using industrial cleaners. These new interior styles had their critics and they wrote in strong terms to the LNER but the brighter image was here to stay and continued with variations in all pre 1939 sleeping cars. There were no complaints though about the more comfortable mattresses.

The 65 ft underframe was used for the first time for first-class cars Nos 1156/7 to Dia 157 which entered service in August 1932 between Kings Cross and Fort William. They embodied all the improvements of the Dia 138 cars and their extra length enabled a shower cubicle to be included, in addition to ten berths. There was always some disappointment on the part of the LNER's managers at the low usage of the showers, a civilised but expensive facility. A 100-gallon water tank was mounted on the underframe and Stone's pumping apparatus was needed to deliver water to the shower, all of which added to the complexity of the cars when it came to maintenance. Rexine wall coverings in these cars were in shaded tones of cream and blue. The two centre berths were designed to be converted to a sitting room and bedroom for the use of VIP passengers. Eight more cars on this diagram were built in 1934/5.

Below Dia 227 car No 1676 was rebuilt with a steel panelled body, with not unpleasing results. Seen here in BR carmine and cream livery in a 1954 Doncaster photograph.

The LNER took especial care with these vehicles which were finished to a high specification. Although economies had been made in the construction of the floors for ordinary carriages, the sleeper firsts were exempted from such cost cutting. As in the case of the East Coast day stock there was a winter renovation programme for sleeping cars so that they would be in tip-top condition for the start of the summer timetable. Their duties included allocation to the 'Northern Belle' for which the shower bath cars were held to be essential. The Dia 157 cars were certainly long-lived and their interiors were modernised in BR days; No 1211 was in service until 1972, having lasted late enough to be repainted in the blue and grey livery.

Ordered at a time when there was a marked increase in first-class sleeping car travel on the East Coast route, the other prewar first-class sleeping cars were on Dia 227. They were very similar to the Dia 157 vehicles except that they had steam heating in addition to pressure ventilation, to overcome the complaints from passengers that cars with this equipment alone were not always warm enough at the start of a journey. There were some variations in the body panelling, as compared with the previous Dia 157 design.

During 1944 No 1592 was rebuilt at Doncaster Works for use by General Eisenhower as his personal carriage, code – named Bayonet, in the SHAEF train which was otherwise formed of GWR vehicles. The exterior was entirely armour-plated and shutters were fitted to the windows, resulting in a tare weight of 51 tons. Six of the berths were replaced by a conference room and Eisenhower's personal sleeping and dressing room. The conference room was equipped with a desk, table and

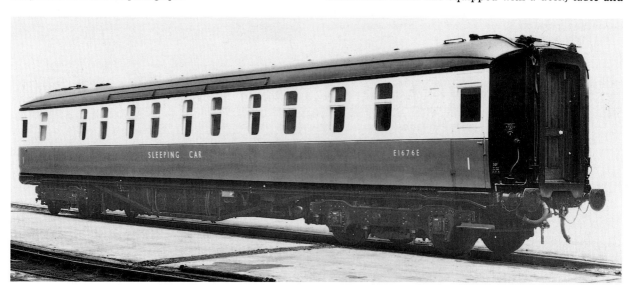

chairs. In April 1945 Eisenhower wrote to Sir Ronald Matthews expressing his thanks for 'such fine work on the new Bayonet, concluding that 'the whole-hearted cooperation of the British railways will stand out as one of the finest examples of Anglo-Americanism'. In postwar days No 1592 was rebuilt to its former state as a sleeping car and survived in service until 1966 after which it and No 1591 were restored at Doncaster, the former to something of its appearance as the Bayonet car, having been purchased for preservation by the National Railroad Museum at Green Bay, Wisconsin, USA. No 1676 suffered wartime damage and was rebuilt with a steel-panelled body to the same outline as the teak panelled original. The other one-off was No 1677 which received six-wheeled bogies with Timken roller bearings in 1949. Nos 1593, 1673/6/7 were in service on the East Coast sleeping car trains until 1966–8, usually as spares.

Other Gresley sleeping cars

Dia 223 covered three composite cars built in 1937, also on the 65 ft underframe. The layout included two lavatories, a locker compartment, three four-berth third-class compartments, five first-class berths, an attendant's compartment and a first-class lavatory. The pressure ventilation and heating system was available for the whole car. The object of this type was to avoid using a SLF + SLT combination to certain destinations when traffic was lighter, such as on the Perth and Fort William services.

Two composite articulated twins to Dia 161/162 were built in 1932, one vehicle first-class with nine berths and pressure ventilation and the other third-class with seven four-berth compartments without pressure ventilation. They were very similar to the twin sleeping cars of 1923 or 1926, but of 9 ft 3 in width. Following withdrawal in 1961, a section from No 1186, a third-class car, was retained for preservation and one compartment restored to original condition. The exterior was carefully stripped of its BR livery, cleaned and revarnished and, in the opinion of the Doncaster paintshop personnel acquainted with the 1930s, represented as nearly as possible the finish and tone characteristic of newly built teak panelled carriages. This important item is in the National Collection at the National Railway Museum.

The last of the prewar sleeping cars was an odd man out, not only on account of its features but as the only LNER sleeper not built for East Coast service. Under the arrangements for replacing stock used on the former Midland & North British Joint service between St Pancras and Edinburgh, the LNER was initially required to provide two sleeping cars. First intentions were to contribute a first-class car to Midland Railway design, allotted to the company on the disbandment of the joint stock in 1928, and a non-convertible third-class car from East Coast stock. It was then agreed that the LMS would purchase the ex M&NB first-class sleeper on the understanding that the LNER for its part would provide a sleeper composite for the working! As a result a new vehicle on Dia 160 was custom-built for the service and constructed at Doncaster during 1932. There were three four-berth third-class compartments and six first-class cabins, with attendant's compartment. Pressure ventilation served the first-class only from a Thermotank unit next to the first-class lavatory which had an electric water heater. The third-class had its own washroom and wc. This car, No 32322, was allocated to the Southern Scottish Area which until 1939 provided stock for the night service between Edinburgh and St Pancras and return, with through carriages to/from Aberdeen, and for the midday trains between St Pancras and Edinburgh. No 32322 was considered a non-conformist by East Coast standards but was allocated to East Coast stock as No 1100 after World War 2.

The LNER sleeping car fleet in prewar days

In 1935 the LNER's sleeping car fleet comprised 47 first-class, fourteen composite and 55 third-class cars, the last named including 45 convertibles and ten non-convertibles. York maintained the third-class cars and Doncaster the others. As an illustration of their usage, a typical scheduled midweek employment of sleeping cars in the down direction on the East Coast route for the summer of 1935 was as follows:

7.25 pm 'Highlandman' – SLT Dia 95 + SLF Dia 17 for Inverness via Carr Bridge; SLC Dia 20 for Inverness via Forres. Fort William portion of 7.25 pm – SLF EC Dia 64B + SLT Dia 95

7.40 pm 'Aberdonian' – SLC Dia 20 for Lossiemouth; two SLTs Dia 95, twin SLC Dias 161/162 Nos 1183/4, SLT Dia 148 for Aberdeen.

10.25 pm 'Night Scotsman' – Two SLTs Dia 95 and SLF Dia 157 No 1156 for Glasgow; SLC Dia 20 for Perth; SLF Dia 17 for Dundee; SLT Dia 148 for Aberdeen.

10.35 pm to Edinburgh – SLT Dia 95, SLT Dia 148, twin SLF EC Dia 68 , SLT Dia 148 for Edinburgh; SLF Dia EC 64B for North Berwick.

10.45 pm to Newcastle – SLT Dia 95, twin SLF EC Dia 68, SLT Dia 148.

1.05 am to Edinburgh – SLC Dia 20 for Darlington; SLF EC Dia 64B for Newcastle; SLF Dia 17, SLT Dia 95 for Edinburgh and intermediate stations north of Newcastle.

Below Extract from the winter 1937/8 timetable.

SLEEPING CAR TRAINS
FIRST AND THIRD CLASS
BETWEEN LONDON (King's Cross) and SCOTLAND
27th SEPTEMBER, 1937 to 1st MAY, 1938

NOTES

B —Commencing 13th October calls at Dunbar 11.50 p.m. when required to take up passengers for King's Cross. Passengers require to be at the station at least 10 minutes before train is due.
C —Until 31st October inclusive leaves Aberdeen 7.35, Montrose 8.36, Arbroath 8.59 and Dundee 9.30 p.m.
D —Not after 31st October.
F—Restaurant Car King's Cross to York.
H—Restaurant Car Newcastle to Edinburgh.
J—Calls at Dunbar 11.55 p.m. (11.50 p.m. on Sundays) when required to take up passengers for King's Cross. Passengers require to be at the station at least 10 minutes before train is due.

K—Runs from King's Cross until 17th October inclusive.
L—Runs from Nairn, Forres and Grantown-on-Spey until 2nd October inclusive.
M—Commences 13th October.
N—Runs from Lossiemouth and Elgin until 23rd October inclusive.
SO—Saturdays only.
SX—Saturdays excepted.
U—Runs from King's Cross until 22nd October inclusive.
Y—Not after 12th October.

PASSENGERS ARRIVING LONDON (KING'S CROSS) IN SLEEPING CARS MAY REMAIN IN THE CARS UNTIL 8.0 A.M.

SUPPLEMENTARY CHARGES FOR SLEEPING BERTHS	First Class	Third Class
Between any two Stations in England	15/9 per berth	6/6 per berth
Between any two Stations in Scotland (including Berwick)	15/9 per berth	6/6 per berth
Between any Station in England and any Station in Scotland (including Berwick)	21/- per berth	7/6 per berth

CHAPTER 11
STEEL, ALUMINIUM
AND PLYWOOD

The all-steel stock of 1927/8

AS we have seen Gresley proposed the construction of an all-steel carriage in 1914 but it was not until 1927, once the immediate post-Grouping requirements for new stock had been met, that the first all-steel vehicles appeared. None of the company's own works was equipped to build all-steel stock and so orders were placed with outside contractors. There were two types of vehicle: a 64-seat open third, of similar layout to the teak bodied Dia 27, and a passenger brake van conforming to the standard 61 ft 6 in design on Dia 43.

Twenty-two open thirds on Dia 28 were constructed under the 1927/8 CBP by the Metropolitan Carriage Wagon & Finance Co, Saltley. They were of 61 ft 6 in length with end vestibules, three saloons with 2 + 2 seating and one lavatory. The bodies had the same tumblehome sides as the teak panelled stock but there were variations to the body profile such that the vehicles were not suitable for running generally over the Southern Railway although permitted between Basingstoke and Portsmouth or Bournemouth after 1935. The external appearance was also different, with radiussed corners to the windows. A simulated teak finish was applied.

The 34 all-steel bogie brake vans to Dia 45 were built by Cammell-Laird & Co Ltd of Nottingham during 1927/8 and followed the design of their teak bodied counterparts in general appearance and layout except that they had no underframe trussing. A number were allocated when new to the principal East Coast sets and remained on top-link duties until 1937.

Gresley's comments on these all-steel vehicles came in his paper entitled 'Recent developments in railway carriage stock', presented in late 1928 to the Federation of Railway Lecture and Debating Societies. He pointed to British railways' persistence with the provision of compartment doors to carriages and that this did not favour all-steel construction because long steel sections could not be used for the bodysides. Specifically referring to the 1927/8 LNER vehicles, his comments were that timber was increasing in price and that the railway wished to assist the steel industry which was one of its most important freight customers. He noted that all-steel stock could now be made less noisy, that it would have a longer life than carriages of teak bodied construction and that it was very suitable for the application of cellulose paints. To their disadvantage, the all-steel carriages were more expensive and were heavier. The open thirds of 1927/8 cost £3,950 as against £2,700 for their teak counterparts, and were over 1½ tons heavier; the full brakes weighed two tons more than the teak examples. In his report on the Castlecary accident of 1937, the inspecting officer conducting the inquiry commented on the case for all-steel carriages and, no doubt drawing on evidence supplied by the LNER, noted that the all-steel vehicles built in 1927/8 'proved to be… more expensive and involved higher maintenance'. The 1927/8 stock lasted well. Newsome recorded that when one of the full brakes went into the works during 1947 for collision damage to be repaired, the unpainted inner surfaces of the body panelling were relatively corrosion-free although the end body panels had corroded. It was found that the lower panels of the doors needed replacement from time to time.

The 'Alpax' carriage – 1933

Aluminium had been little used for railway rolling stock up until the 1930s, apart from some electric multiple-units built for the Lancashire & Yorkshire Railway. In 1932, Gresley wrote to Wedgwood as follows: 'I have prepared a design for a carriage on a new principle. Sides of Alpax castings (Alpax was a proprietary name) would be bolted to a steel framework. The roof comprises Duralumin sheets on Alpax carlines. The doors are Alpax castings.' Weight was reduced by two tons compared with a teak bodied vehicle. Gresley continued: 'A vehicle constructed on this principle will be materially stronger than one constructed in the ordinary way with a teak body.' The vehicle chosen was one of a pair of non-vestibuled lavatory composites authorised in the 1931/2 CBP for the GE section. Gresley said that the cost of the experimental vehicle, No 65000 on Dia 163, would be 'not greatly in excess of the budgeted £2,000'.

H.A.V. Bulleid writing of Gresley in his book *Master Builders of Steam* suggests that the idea of the Alpax carriage was put forward by the suppliers who had successfully sold to the LNER smaller castings such as for brake hose fittings. Gresley used a standard 51 ft underframe for this vehicle, all the drawings for which were produced by Norman Newsome. The side body panels were cast flat and then bent on a jig to the correct radius before being bolted to the body frame and to the compartment partitions. The doors were cast to the usual profile. Alpax roof stringers were used in place of teak and most of the interior fittings were of aluminium. No 65000 went into service on the GE Cambridge line.

Below All-steel open third No 42463 (Dia 28, built Metropolitan CW & Finance, 1927 and later 12223). The windows were slightly recessed.

The Tourist stock 1933–39

At the most dismal period of its fortunes the LNER decided to build excursion trains to compete for day-trip traffic beginning to be captured by motor coach operators. The decision was taken in January 1933 at a time when construction work under the 1932 CBP had been suspended. The initiative seems to have come from Gresley who proposed the idea of the excursion stock late in 1932. The cost of the new vehicles was covered by considering them as part-replacements of 36 sets of old GNR close-coupled four-wheel suburban stock which had been used for excursion workings and were written off at this time. The initial order of what became known as the Tourist stock covered five twelve-coach trains for the GN section at a total cost of £150,000.

Each train comprised two open brake thirds, four twin open thirds and two buffet cars. With the need to economise on construction costs a number of interesting innovations were made. It was decided to avoid the use of shaped and pre-formed components where possible in order to save timber and so the roof ends did not slope down to the ends and the ends themselves were flat rather than bow-ended. Savings in cost were also made by reducing the number of bodyside pillars. The most revolutionary change came with the use of plywood body panelling screwed to the teak body framing. Plywood had been used for flying-boats for some time and the aircraft manufacturer, Saunders-Roe, supplied the LNER with ¼ in three-ply sheets, these being used in as large sheets as possible and with scarf jointing for adjacent panels, the joins being sealed with adhesive. The doors were built up with plywood backed by copper sheeting. The main hazard was delamination, likely to be caused by water seepage between the joints. To reduce this problem, the lower body panels extended below the bottom-sides to allow rain-drops to clear and the windows were fitted in square-cornered die-cast aluminium frames well bedded-in with white lead. This last precaution was a great success compared with the square-cornered windows of steel-panelled carriages which suffered bad corrosion at the corners. Service experience saw later batches of Tourist stock with the body panels so arranged that the wood grain was horizontal.

The brake vehicles (Dia 169) were on 60 ft underframes and were built by Doncaster, the 60 ft buffet cars (Dia 168) at York and the twin thirds (Dia 171), whose bodies were 52 ft ¹⁄₁₆ in, by outside contractors. The twins had the light type bogie at the outer ends and heavy type articulation bogies. The interiors were built up with 1 in ply partitions and with thinner plywood for all saloon panelling, covered with Rexine. The interiors were open saloons, the expanse being broken amidships by deep fairings running from floor to ceiling. There were parcel racks along the interiors of the bodies above the windows and oval mirrors between the windows and on the end partitions. The seating was provided in bucket seats made up with ash frames, with plywood backs and sponge rubber roll-round tops covered in leather. Newsome says that it was Bulleid's idea that motor-car type seats should be used and that the design was worked out with the manufacturers. These seats may have been adequate for shorter journeys but provoked complaints on longer runs because there was no support for passengers' necks or heads.

Above Interior of Tourist stock buffet car.

The buffet cars were intended to serve light refreshments only and had gas cylinders, a small grill, gas-ring, beverage boilers and a refrigerator. The layout was identical to the Dia 167 teak bodied buffet cars and comprised a streamlined counter at one end, fixed tables and loose chromium-plated chairs. The lighting consisted of unshaded bulbs throughout the train, supplemented by side bracket lamps. Stone's pressure ventilation was fitted to brake No 43509 in one of the GN section sets and to the twin thirds and brake vehicles in the first North Eastern Area set. All these received steam heating during World War 2. The interior decor of the Tourist stock was calculated to match the contemporary Art Deco styles in cinemas and restaurants and used Rexine extensively for the interior finishes. Each train had a variety of colour schemes. The brake vehicles had dark blue Rexine below the waistline, silver blue to the ceiling and ivory ceilings. The twins had either a dark brown (lower) and light brown (upper) scheme or dark green (lower) and stippled grey (upper), both varieties with cream ceilings. There were two decor schemes for the buffet cars, either blue and silver grey or stippled blue and gold.

The exterior finish similarly was a match for the contemporary road coaches and represented a complete break from previous practice. The Tourist stock was painted cream enamel above the waist and locomotive green below. The lettering and numbering was of the same style for standard stock but of an

Below Twin open thirds Nos 45192 (left-hand) and 45191 of the Tourist stock (Dia 171, built Metro-Cammell, 1933 and later Nos 13181/80). Painted letters 'L' and 'K' on bodies.

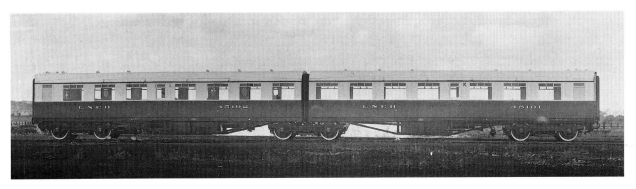

Above Tourist stock brake No 31865 (Dia 308, built 1939 and later 16846). This was a steel panelled vehicle with high backed seats, outshopped by York in November 1939 and with grey painted roof. Note the deeper ventilators compared with previous Tourist stock.

elongated pattern, 5 in deep over the gold and 7½ in over the shading. No class numerals were carried. The roofs were painted white, inner body ends black and the outer ends of the brake carriages were cream and green. All underframes and running gear were painted black, the wheel centres were painted 'teak' and the wheel rims white. Each carriage in a train was lettered and the identification letter – A, B, C etc – was painted in 12 in black Gill Sans characters on a white panel to the right-hand of the outer door. The earlier sets had the train set number painted on the outer body ends. From 1942 onwards, vehicles in need of repainting were supposed to be turned out in teak paint.

The first of the five GN section sets was displayed to the press and public at Kings Cross on 28 July 1933 and used the next day on an excursion to Blackpool from stations in Lincolnshire. The provision of two buffet cars in the early sets was intended to speed service in a full twelve-car train but it was expected that trains might also run in six-car sections. The total seating capacity of the full train was 552, and with 48 seats in the buffet cars.

The first Tourist stock sets proved popular and the 1934 CBP included two twelve-car sets for the North Eastern Area. These, to Dias 179/180 and 168, differed in that the brake vehicles had more space for beer storage and four less seats. In addition, the joints between the upper and lower body panels were covered with aluminium mouldings. The 1935/6 CBP included two trains for the Southern Scottish Area, deferred from the 1934 CBP, and spare vehicles for the North Eastern Area, four brakes and a buffet car. These spares were to allow half-sets to be made up. In all, the North Eastern Area had 32 Tourist stock vehicles, including three green and cream painted catering cars of differing origins: kitchen car No 21484, formerly a GCR restaurant car; Dia 10B restaurant car No 21474 classified RU, transferred from the GE section in July 1934 and formerly No 678; restaurant car No 21487, classified RU, to NER Dia 170 .

The SPMs reviewed experience with the Tourist stock early in 1938, following complaints from the LNER Board that the distinctive livery of the Tourist stock necessitated more expensive cleaning. The evidence was that the exteriors needed a soap wash after every second trip to maintain their smart appearance. In their review the SPMs were generally in favour of the Tourist stock, commenting that although the two-tone livery helped to attract passengers' interest 'the popularity of the vehicles was due to their modern interior equipment'. But they were not favourably disposed towards the bucket seats and the North Eastern Area's representative held that the organisers of guaranteed excursions objected to the provision of the stock on overnight trains as the seats were uncomfortable. Two trains of green and cream painted stock for such workings were

included in the 1939 CBP: these were to have been to Dias 27C and 240 and, at the same time, four Tourist stock TTOs were ordered. A Board decision in October 1938 resulted in the 1939 CBP being reduced to the capacity of the LNER's workshops and with this came cancellation of these vehicles.

The Tourist stock was operated only by the GN section and the North Eastern and Southern Scottish Areas, the other sections and Areas relying on teak bodied stock, also with bucket seats. The final Tourist train set was built at York during late 1939 for the Southern Scottish Area; it had been intended that outside contractors would be used but York was able to build more cheaply. This train, of four twin thirds to Dia 307 and two brakes to Dia 308, had various differences, including steel body panelling, welded underframes and deeper ventilators to the windows. High-backed seats were fitted and, as the vehicles were completed after the outbreak of war, the roofs were painted dark grey.

After several years' service the condition of the plywood exterior panelling varied. Some vehicles had deteriorated so badly that steel panelling was substituted while others were in a perfectly sound state. Most surviving until 1962/3 were steel panelled although buffet cars Nos 9140 (withdrawn December 1964) and 9147 (withdrawn 1963) were plywood panelled until the end. In postwar days the buffet cars generally worked separately from the other carriages which in any case were more often in general service. Nos 9144/50 were in use on the Liverpool Street–Clacton interval services in 1960 and others appeared in the Cambridge Buffet Expresses. By then the rather cheerless interiors of the buffet cars had earlier given cause for complaint. An official BR report spoke of them as 'truly very bad indeed'. Some were modernised with new laminated plastic panelling and propane gas cooking equipment, as part of the programme authorised from 1958, examples including E9138/9/46/9E. No 9139 was to be seen as late as 1963/4 in the formation of the 7.50 am Newcastle–Kings Cross as a self-service buffet car in addition to the restaurant car set. The last two Tourist buffet cars were withdrawn from London Midland Region stock in 1967.

Steel-panelled stock 1935–43
Teak rose in price during the 1930s, with the result that steel-panelled stock began to be built from 1935, and although this may be seen as cheaper than teak it is interesting that three of the high-speed trains had steel panelled vehicles. The most obvious candidate for replacement was the body panelling and the structural timbers generally remained teak. In 1935 vestibuled stock for secondary services and non-vestibuled sets for the Kings Cross outer suburban workings, mostly articulated twins, were constructed, together with passenger brake vans for general use, and all these had the simulated teak finish. The windows had square corners, the general appearance following the Alpax carriage built in 1933. But no more steel-panelled carriages were built, apart from the high-speed stock, until 1938 when the first of a series of articulated sets for local and secondary service were constructed. No general service

vestibuled stock was built with steel panelling in Gresley's time as CME.

The steel-panelled stock seemed to be a little austere in interior finish but otherwise was little different to the teak bodied vehicles. One reason for this impression is that a number of economies were brought in with the 1939 CBP, thereby coinciding with the building of most of the steel panelled carriages. One characteristic feature of their appearance was the use of fixed glass fanlights above the door droplights, apparently because the usual hit and miss ventilators were difficult to fit. At least, this was the case until May 1939 when it was agreed by the CME that hit and miss ventilators would be fitted to the doors of all new non-vestibuled stock. From the 1939 CBP the steel body panels were welded to adjacent panels rather than the previous practice whereby the joints between the panels were butted up and filled with jointing paste to provide a smooth overall finish.

Vestibuled stock 1935–42

The 1931/2 CBP had originally included a number of articulated twins to form trains for secondary services on the GN section, particularly for the main line, East Lincs line and other routes in Lincolnshire. These were 'lost' with the curtailment of the programme during 1932 but were put forward by the SPMs in the 1934 CBP as ten articulated train sets to be diagrammed for Peterborough–Cleethorpes, Kings Cross–Doncaster–Leeds and Kings Cross–Cambridge services. In justification of part of

Above A down semi-fast at Belle Isle behind No 4472 *Flying Scotsman*, its train consisting of (at least) a five-car steel panelled set of vehicles to Dias 190/194/195. The lighting shows the effect of the flush panelled bodies and the recessed van section of the brake third.

the request it was said that 'vehicles in the Peterborough–Grimsby services have been for some time the subject of complaint'. In the event only eight train sets were built, each formed BTK + TK,CK, TK + BTK. One feature of interest was the use of welded underframes. Under the 1943 renumbering the short composites were treated in the same manner as the GE section 52 ft 6 in vehicles and retained their GN section numbers. In postwar years the stock remained at work on the East Lincs and main line services until displaced by diesel multiple units, after which it was formed in relief sets.

The 1939 CBP included ten sets for the GC section made up of five carriages, BTK + TK, CK, TK + BTK, from vehicles built to Dias 304/5. The brake third twins were very similar to the 1935 GN section examples but the composites were to the 61 ft 6 in length and similar in layout to the teak bodied Dia 130 composites. The ten five-car sets were intended for Hull–Leicester, Hull–Sheffield and other cross-country workings in the section. These sets were built in 1939/40 and were followed by six others for the GC section in the 1940 CBP, for cross-country trains routed via Manchester and Sheffield; there were also two five-car sets allocated to the GN section for

Steel – panelled vestibuled stock 1935-42 – list of types and Diagram numbers

Type	Diagram	Dimensions 9' 3" body width	Compartments	Seats	Built
Composite (CK)	190	52' 6"	4 1st, 2 3rd	24/12	1935
Brake third twin					
Third	194	51'11¾"	7	42	1935
Brake third	195	51'11¾"	4	24	1935
Composite	305	61' 6"	3½ 1st, 4 3rd	21/24	1939/42
Brake third twin	304				
(Brake third)		52' 0"	4	24	1939/42
(Third)		52' 0"	7	42	1939/42

Steel-panelled non-vestibuled and articulated stock 1935-43 – list of types and Diagram numbers

TABLE 11A

Type/Diagram	Dimensions 9' 3" body width	Compartments	Seats	Built
Brake composite twins				
{Brake third 192}	55' 6¼"	5	50	1935
{Composite 193}	55' 6¼"	3/4	22/38	1935
Brake third twins Dia 247				
(Third)	51' 1½"	8	80	1938
(Brake third)	51' 1½"	4	40	1938
Twin composites Dia 248				
(First)	51' 1½"	7	56	1938
(Third)	51' 1½"	8	80	1938
Twin firsts Dia 249				
(First)	51' 1½"	7	56	1938
(First)	51' 1½"	7	56	1938
Twin brake thirds Dia 250				
(Third)	51' 1½"	8	80	1938
(Brake third)	51' 1½"	5	50	1938
Twin composites Dia 253				
(First)	51' 1½"	7	56	1938
(Composite)	51' 1½"	4 1st, 3 3rd	32/30	1938
Also, non-articulated firsts to Dia 252:				
First	51' 1½"	7	56	1938

TABLE 11B

Type/Diagram	Dimensions	Compartments	Seats	Built
Twin brake thirds Dia 269				
(Brake third)	55' 6¼"	4	40	1938/9
(Lavatory Third)	55' 6¼"	8	74	1938/9
Twin thirds Dia 270				
(Third)	55' 6¼"	9	90	1938/9
(Third)	55' 6¼"	9	90	1938/9
Twin composites Dia 271				
(Lavatory Composite)	55' 6¼"	2 1st, 6 3rd	16/54	1938/9
(Lavatory Composite)	55' 6¼"	2 1st, 6 3rd	13/57	1938/9

TABLE 11C

Type/Diagram	Dimensions	Compartments	Seats	Built
Twin composite Dia 309				
(Third)	51' 1½"	8	80	1940
(Lavatory Composite)	51' 1½"	3 1st, 4 3rd	23/39	1940
Twin brake composite Dia 310				
(Brake third)	51' 1½"	5	50	1941
(Lavatory composite)	51' 1½"	3 1st, 4 3rd	23/39	1941
Twin brake third Dia 312				
(Brake third)	51' 1½"	6	60	1940/43
(Third)	51' 1½"	8	80	1940/43
Twin brake composite Dia 313				
(Brake third)	55' 6¼"	6	60	1940
(Lavatory composite)	55' 6¼"	2 1st, 5 3rd	14/48	1940
Twin brake composite Dia 322				
(Brake third)	55' 6¼"	6	60	1943
(Lavatory composite)	55' 6¼"	4 1st, 3 3rd	25/25	1943

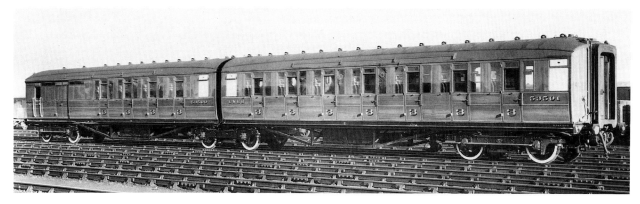

workings on the GN main line and GN/GE Joint line. The GC section sets continued to work Retford–Manchester, Manchester–Cleethorpes and Leicester–Sheffield–Manchester into the 1950s, although usually with a postwar or BR Standard composite in place of the Dia 305 vehicle. Displaced by diesel units, their remaining life was spent on relief main line duties.

Non-vestibuled stock 1935–43
Articulated stock
The Dia 192/193 vehicles were ordered under the 1935/6 CBP for the Kings Cross outer suburban services. (see table 11A)

The 51 ft 1½in vehicles (table 11A) were ordered under the 1937 CBP to provide sets for the Edinburgh and Glasgow suburban services and were built by R.Y. Pickering & Co; additional teak bodied sets for these services specified in the 1938 CBP were constructed at Dukinfield, and are described in Chapter 7.

A report to the Locomotive Committee in 1933 had shown that time was lost on the Darlington–Saltburn service as a result of trains having to draw up twice at stations and that it would be sensible to have uniform train sets. The 1938 CBP included 72 articulated carriages to Dias 269–271 to form nine eight-coach sets for the half-hourly frequency Darlington–Saltburn service, replacing some vehicles which dated from 1896. The trains were formed: Dia 269 twin + Dia 271 twin + Dia 270 twin + Dia 269 twin. The first-class compartments had reading lights. The stock was built by Birmingham RCW and Metro-Cammell and delivery was not complete until 1939. Soon after entry into service large quantities of oil were reported as being lost from the axleboxes and a palliative was found but wartime traffic did not reveal fully a problem resulting from the long distance – 47 ft – between the bogie centres of this stock. Holiday traffic during the summer of 1944 showed the problem more dramatically as the underframes and bodies were observed to be deflecting under load. It was decided that the bodies should be stiffened and new underframe trussing provided, the necessary modifications being authorised by the Board in May 1945.

The stock (see table 11B) continued on the Darlington–Saltburn service until dieselisation in 1957, after which a number of twins migrated to the London Tilbury and Southend line until electrification of that line in 1962.

Dias 309/13 (table 11C) were ordered under the 1939 CBP

Above Steel panelled articulated and vestibuled brake third twin No 53501(third, nearest) and 53500 (brake third). The photograph's quality emphasises the skill with which the painters simulated the appearance of varnished teak. The twin carries the shopping date of late August 1939.

to form an eight-coach train for the Kings Cross outer suburban services. The composites to Dia 309 had lavatory accommodation for adjacent compartments only, those on Dia 313 having four lavatories to serve four compartments of both classes.

Dia 310 twins (table 11C) were also ordered under the 1939 CBP to form three-car sets, with a brake third, for service in the Nottingham area and the West Riding where they replaced the earliest articulated sets converted from GNR six-wheelers.

Vehicles on Dia 312 (table 11C) were originally to comprise six trains made up of two twins and a composite to Dia 311 (see below) for Manchester suburban services but only four sets were delivered. Several of the Dia 312 twins finished their working lives on the LT & S.

The twins on Dia 322 (table 11C) for the GN section were ordered under the 1940 CBP but not delivered until 1943 and were intended to form train sets working between Kings Cross and Cambridge, to replace GNR vehicles. The two twins on this diagram for the North Eastern Area were for use between Scarborough and Hull. The composite in Dia 322 was semi-corridor, with four first-class and two third-class side-corridor compartments and all compartments with access to lavatories.

Non-articulated stock
These were rather a mixed bunch and served a variety of purposes. No less than 118 non-vestibuled carriages were ordered under the 1938 CBP for the GE section where they were to make inroads into the stock of four and six-wheeled GER stock. All were 51 ft ½in vehicles, except for the 54 ft 1½ in lavatory thirds, and were intended to be made up into sets with carriages transferred from the North Eastern Area to provide complete train sets for services between Liverpool Street and Southend and on the Cambridge line. The intention

Below LNER Diagram Book: steel panelled non-vestibule twin brake third to Dia 269 for the Darlington–Saltburn service. The interiors were somewhat cheerless!

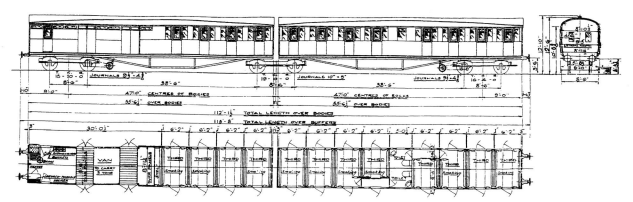

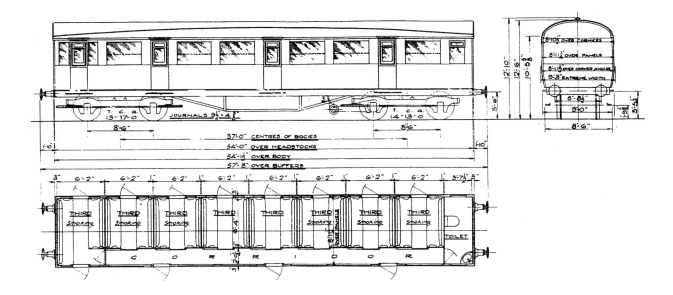

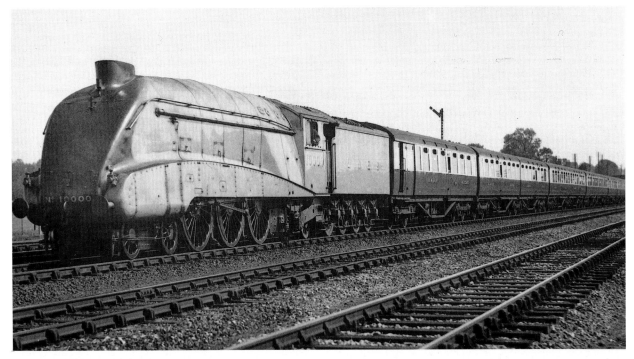

Top LNER Diagram Book: steel panelled non-vestibule lavatory third to Dia 265 for GE section services.

Above The unique 'W1' 4–6–4 No 10000 heads what appeared to be a complete GN section 12-coach set of Tourist stock, said to be forming a relief York express and so illustrating the use of these vehicles in this role.

was that during the summer months they would be used for cheap fare trains to coastal resorts such as Hunstanton, Yarmouth and Clacton; traditionally, suburban sets without lavatories had been used for such duties on the GE section, necessitating comfort stops en route! The vehicles were deliv-ered in 1938/9 and comprised 79 eight-compartment, side-corridor lavatory thirds to Dia 265, 24 non-corridor thirds to Dia 276, ten four-compartment brake thirds to Dia 294 and five lavatory composites to Dia 299, the last named being of similar layout to the teak bodied Dia 50.

Many of the steel-panelled vehicles ordered in 1939 were new versions of the old staple types of Dias 50, 57 and 65, their equivalents being Dias 299, 294 and 276. The North Eastern Area's 1939 requirement included enough vehicles to make up complete 'C' Link sets for use in the Hull, Leeds, York and Scarborough districts but the order was not completed until 1941 and reduced in quantity. Five Dia 299 vehicles delivered in 1943 were replacements for those lost to enemy action.

CHAPTER 12
POST-WAR STOCK

THE post-war LNER carriages were a compromise and if they lacked a certain something it was not their fault for they were creatures of their time, less a reflection on the abilities of the company than of prevailing circumstances that dictated their specification.

Planning for the future...

In common with the other Big Four companies the LNER began to look at its prospects after the war at a time when Britain's circumstances were anything but good. Under the chairmanship of O.H. Corble, the LNER Postwar Development Committee was set up in January 1942 but did not report until September 1943. Its report was mainly concerned with the infrastructure of the railway and in particular with electrification, the proposals including the electrification of the GN main line and the provision of multiple units, the Shenfield stock being the standard pattern for the GE and GN suburban routes. All that was said about main line stock in the committee's report was that its 'design must keep pace with modern ideas of comfort; restaurant and sleeping car services will require to be extended wherever a satisfactory demand exists or can be created'.

As noted in Chapter 3, during the war the Carriage Building Programmes had come to an end with that for 1940, vehicles ordered under the programme being completed as late as 1943. In May 1944 the LNER Emergency Board of Directors received a memo from the CGM setting out the scale of the problem that faced the company in terms of vehicles retained in traffic although overdue for withdrawal – some 2,500 – and deferred withdrawal generally, the result being to indicate a postwar carriage building programme totalling some 4,000–4,500 vehicles. In the meantime it was necessary to proceed with a limited amount of new construction. This comprised some 121 carriages and vans, seven of the former being deferred from the 1940 CBP.

A three-year building programme was approved by the Board in November 1944 and provided for the building of 4,600 carriages and vans. Most of the work on the postwar

building programme was contained in a memo dated November 1944 from Newton to the Emergency Board and this set out the main principles of the stock to be built. As already noted in Chapter 2, Newton commented that further construction of timber bodied stock was not possible because of the shortage of suitable supplies and in the longer-term the LNER would opt for all-steel stock, to be built at Shildon, Faverdale and York or ordered from contractors.

The main characteristics of the new stock would be as follows:

Vestibuled stock, including catering and sleeping vehicles, 60 ft over the headstocks and 9 ft wide, length varying for certain types 'to give better and more comfortable interiors'.

There would be no compartment side doors for stock intended for long-distance journeys but the existing end door design would be replaced as it was said to cause congestion in corridors. Compartment side doors would be provided in vehicles for shorter distances and there would also be open stock. The windows would be 6 in wider and the sills 3 in lower than before. There would be three a side seating in both first-class and third-class, and the design of the seats would be the subject of experimentation and public trial. Interior fittings would be of a 'higher standard' than previously. For most of the LNER's trains, said Newton, there would be a normal exterior outline but the high-speed trains might require special treatment though what that might be was left unsaid, as was the likely livery for the all-steel stock. He said merely that the decision awaited the provision by the CME of specimen colours and finishes. Non-vestibuled stock

Below LNER Diagram Book: vestibule first to Dia 332. The layout of the transverse corridors was to improve detraining, the end door stock having proved unhelpful in discharging wartime crowds. However, the transverse corridors were said to be unpopular with passengers.

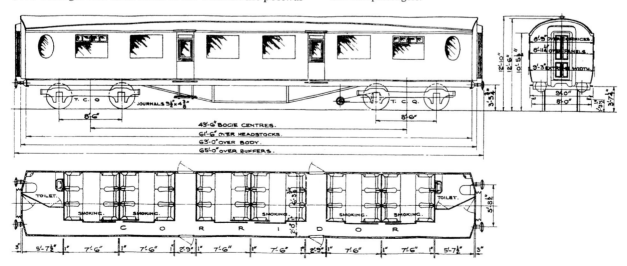

Above Doncaster built the prototype vestibule third, No 1347 (Dia 329), completed in the spring of 1945. It ran on the single-bolster, all-welded bogies.

would be 52 ft 4 in over headstocks.

When it came to the building programme for the 4,600 vehicles, the types being considered included a preponderance of non-vestibuled composites, thirds and brake thirds, with smaller numbers of vestibuled stock but these to include 192 open thirds, 40 restaurant and kitchen cars, seven buffet cars, seven pantry thirds, 55 third-class sleeping cars and two buffet lounge cars. Priority in the programme would be given to six new trains for the main East Coast day trains 'provided we can be assured that this will not involve sacrifice of luxury to austerity'. Next in the list would be vestibuled stock to displace non-vestibuled carriages from regular trains running more than 30 miles without a stop. In 1939 it had been recognised that new third-class non-convertible sleeping cars would be needed, and Newton reiterated this requirement, noting that the displaced Dia 95 and 109 vehicles would be retained for use as ordinary thirds. In the new scheme of things catering vehicles would not be articulated but they would have solid fuel or anthracite electric cooking equipment. New London area suburban stock would not be proposed in view of electrification of the GN lines and the release of stock from the GE section.

There was nothing at which to take exception in Newton's proposals and the departure from teak bodied vehicles, articulation and all-electric cooking equipments in the catering cars was not surprising, for the disadvantages of some of these Gresley specialities had been recognised before the great man died in 1941. There were now two developments. A team of LNER officers travelled to the United States in October 1945 to observe current railway operating and manufacturing practices, their subsequent report strengthening the case for all-steel construction for carriages but drawing attention to the need for new production facilities and the availability of low-alloy steels. Meanwhile the prototype standard carriage had appeared during January 1945 in the shape of vestibule first No 1531.

This, at the time known as the Newton coach, entered service to the accompaniment of a major exercise in public consultation. A brochure entitled *Design for Comfort*, subtitled 'an invitation to passengers of the LNER' was distributed on trains, remarking that the company was now able to plan for the future comfort of passengers and that large orders were shortly to be placed for new rolling stock. Readers of the brochure were invited to ensure that these vehicles 'conform to their own ideas of perfection in travel comfort' and there were twelve questions asking for passengers' preferences as to open or side-corridor stock, seat design, window design, lighting, interior decor and catering on trains. The brochure included illustrations of No 1531, described as 'the new 1945 standard', its features compared with those of a Gresley end door first and attention was drawn to the transverse corridors in No

1531 and its larger windows. Some 17,000 replies were received in response to *Design for Comfort*, a similar exercise incidentally being conducted at about the same time by the Southern Railway.

The next approach by the LNER to its public came in November 1946 with the publication of *Forward the LNER*, already mentioned in Chapter 2. This brochure described the features of No 1531 as representing the new design evolved in 1945, focussing attention on the two transverse passages which divided its interior into three, the advantages being summarised as the reduction both in congestion and of the distance between seat and door. *Forward the LNER* commented that the replies to *Design for Comfort* 'have been very closely studied and many ideas will be incorporated in future designs for rolling stock'. Whether the public's views had much influence in the course of the production of postwar LNER design stock is debatable but as an attempt to employ modern methods of market research it was admirable.

Work continued on the design of all-steel stock, although No 1531 and the prototype vestibule third, No 1347, had teak framed, steel panelled bodies. Drawings for all-steel carriages were in preparation as late as April 1947 but subsequent effort was overtaken by nationalisation a few months later. In the case of passenger rolling stock matters moved quickly for the evolution of new standard vehicles as design work was well in hand as soon as mid-1948 on what became the BR Standard vestibuled stock. We now return to the compromise inherent in the LNER postwar stock that entered service before and after the company ceased to be.

... and the postwar stock that was actually built

The first of the postwar, Newton or Thompson carriages – all titles are relevant – were approved in the 1944 CBP by the Emergency Board at its May 1944 meeting, as described in Chapter 3. Construction took place over the period 1945–47 at Doncaster and York Works, the capabilities of both being affected by the aftermath of the wartime fires. All these vehicles were to the postwar standard pattern with straight ended roofs, bow ends, steel panelling, transverse passages, large square cornered windows and opal glass oval lavatory windows. Some had the welded 8 ft wheelbase bogies.

The November 1945 JLTC meeting saw approval of the plan to condemn 5,500 vehicles over the period from 1946–51, rather than the three-year plan originally forecast, with the construction of the same number of replacements, of which 3,400 would be built by contractors. As part of this plan the 1946 CBP featured 180 non-vestibuled and 593 vestibuled carriages, with no less than 263 vestibuled thirds, 30 brake composites and 180 non-vestibuled carriages to be built by contractors. However, Government control in the shape of the Ministry of War Transport as well as associated trade association committees revised the LNER's agreements with manufacturers for the delivery of vehicles so that this were spread over a longer period. Because of shortages of materials there were

changes to specification. Although the contractors quoted for the supply of the 8 ft wheelbase bogie, the difference in price compared to the compound bolster bogie was £60 per bogie and the latter was preferred.

As an example of the standard of the new vehicles, the standard Dia 329 thirds ordered from Birmingham RCW were built to the following specification: teak body framing, apart from cross and longitudinal floor bearers which were of oak, pitch pine cantrails, deal roof boards and floor boards and 16 SWG mild steel body panelling. The interior woodwork was varnished, the lavatories and corridors were mainly natural varnished teak and there was teak matchboarding on doors. The interior metal fittings were cellulose finished and there were bakelite picture frames and an oval framed mirror in the compartments. Rexine was specified for interior finishes in the earlier batches but the majority of vehicles constructed had plain cream paintwork for the interior surfaces above the seat-backs, those for the prestige East Coast sets having veneered panelling. The exteriors were in simulated teak finish devoid of lining, with a lead-grey painted roof. In

Above Among the earliest of the postwar carriages was a batch of fifteen open thirds built at York to the 1944 CBP. These were very similar internally to the Gresley Dia 186 vehicles. No 13791 here was to Dia 330.

Right Interior view of restaurant kitchen car (first-class) E1217 (Dia 354, built 1950). The effect is disappointingly old-fashioned, with prewar design upholstery on admittedly comfortable seats. The interior panelling appears to be sycamore veneer. Note the light fittings, later to become familiar in BR diesel multiple-units, as well as the chromed parcel racks and ventilator of prewar design. The 'Flying Scotsman' restaurant vehicles of 1948 had prewar light fittings, as used in the high-speed stock.

Below Restaurant kitchen car (first-class) E1657 (Dia 354, built 1949). This shows well how the simulated teak finish had been applied with horizontal graining on the lower panels and vertical graining on the upper panels. Lettering in Gill Sans. Large figure '1' on the saloon windows.

TABLE 12A

Type	Diagram	Length	Compartments	Seats	Built
First	332	63' 0"	6	36	1946/8/9/50
(FK)	334	61' 6"	6	36	1945
	348	63' 0"	5 + Ladies room	30	1947 Flying Scotsman
Open	330	63' 0"	1 saloon	64	1946/7 TTO
Third	337	61' 6"	2 saloons	48	1947 TO
Third	329	63' 0"	7	42	1946–50
(TK)	336	61' 6"	7	42	1946/7
	349	63' 0"	6 + Ladies room	36	1947 Flying Scotsman
Composite (CK)	328	59' 6"	3/3	18/18	1946–50 Some Flying Scotsman
Brake third	331	63' 0"	3	18	1946
(BTK)	343	61' 6"	4	24	1946
	346	63' 0"	4	24	1947–50 Some Flying Scotsman
	376	63' 0"	4	24	–
Brake composite (BCK)	345	63' 0"	2/3	12/18	1947/8/50

short, the finished result was little advance on the standard 1930s Gresley carriage, thereby accounting for the somewhat lacklustre appearance of the run of the mill postwar vehicles, as compared with contemporary GWR, LMS or SR examples.

But if there were delays in vehicles ordered from contractors, there were problems, too, at Doncaster and York. The new trains for the 'Flying Scotsman' and other East Coast services included in the 1946 CBP were under construction at York but work came almost to a halt in October 1947 as a result of the tardy supply of materials and components. So that work could commence on ordinary vehicles, it was decided that the prestige sets should be turned out as soon as possible, in time to go into service by early 1949 at the latest, even if some fittings might be sub-standard and replaced at a later date.

The main difference between the early and late batches of postwar stock came with the introduction from 1949 of radiussed corners to the large bodyside windows, ostensibly to combat corrosion but it also improved the appearance of the vehicles, as did the application of the carmine and cream livery in place of the simulated teak finish. Although the construction of vestibuled general service stock came to an end in 1950, LNER design sleeping cars were built in 1952 and the last all-new non-vestibule carriages were completed in 1953. The same year saw the

appearance of rebuilt stock for the London Tilbury & Southend line with reused underframes, these being included in the LNER series of diagrams.

Vestibuled ordinary stock

The principal diagrams were 332, 329, 328, 346 and 345 (table 12A). A number of these vehicles were built for the prestige East Coast sets and are dealt with below. The 'non-conforming' diagrams included 334 – the prototype 'postwar' carriage, even if completed in wartime – which went into service in the 12.45 pm Kings Cross–Edinburgh from 11 January 1945. It could be readily distinguished by the square half-width windows at each end on the corridor side. When new, the lavatory windows had a teak tinted interlayer, the effect of which was to make them look a dirty yellow. Edward Thompson wrote to the Assistant CME at Doncaster to say that 'the colour of the glass was about the only criticism that the Chairman levelled at the coach…'

The open thirds were non-standard only that few were built. Dia 337 was a single vehicle on a recovered underframe from a Dia 186 open third.

Dia 336 was to a non-standard length and a number of this series had the 8 ft welded bogies.

The composites to Dia 328 were built to this length in the interests of the 'better and more comfortable interior' promised by Newton, namely one without coupé compartments.

Dia 343 comprised two vehicles built on the recovered underframes of prewar brake thirds. Dia 346 Nos 1690/1,

Below York-built Dia 329 vestibule second GE 13886E at Cambridge in 1964, exemplifying the rounded window pattern, with oval windows on the corridor side opposite the lavatories.

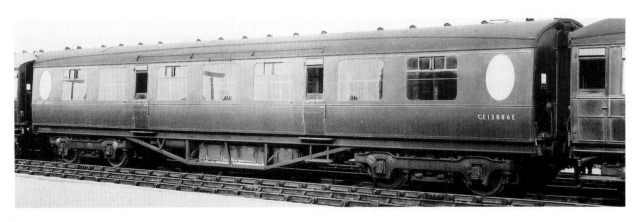

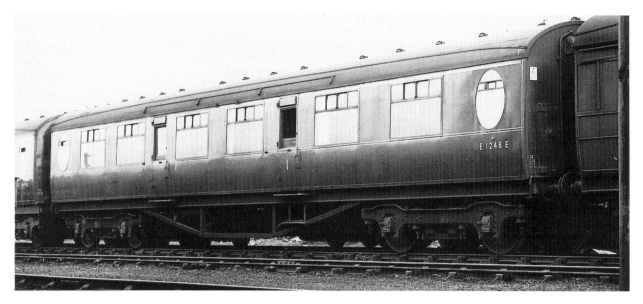

1868/72 had two compartments converted for use as sleeping compartments in 1956. At least Nos 1690/1 were coded SLBSK. Dia 376 resulted from the fitting of security screens inside the van compartments of 38 Dia 346 vehicles in 1956.

Dia 345 No 1148 and Dia 329 No 1498, both built by Birmingham RCW in 1947, achieved notoriety as a result of their destruction in the Penmanshiel Tunnel train fire of 23 June 1949. The fire started in No 1498 and spread rapidly as a result of the nitrocellulose lacquer used on the corridor panelling, the LNER having specified oil-bound paints. Steps were taken to strip the lacquer from all other vehicles although the similar hazard from Rexine was not acted upon until the Huntingdon train fire of July 1951. Other early losses were Dia 336 No 1370 and Dia 329 No 1441, destroyed in the Goswick accident of 26 October 1947.

Catering vehicles (see table 12B)
The types of postwar catering vehicles followed prewar practice as far as layout and accommodation were concerned, as well as in the use of anthracite-electric cooking equipment. With the decision to eschew articulation the prestige East Coast sets had a three-car formation of open first + kitchen car + open third, although the open thirds were also used with RF cars, as were the pantry thirds.

Above Vestibule composite E1248E to Dia 328 was at Kittybrewster in 1966, revealing anti-corrosion strips welded in around its square cornered windows.

'Flying Scotsman', 'Elizabethan' and other East Coast sets
As early as September 1946 the 'Flying Scotsman' had nine of the postwar vehicles in its formation but the sets specified in the 1946 CBP were not ready until 1948, for reasons already mentioned. With the delivery of the kitchen cars the 'Flying Scotsman' sets were made up completely of the new stock from December 1948, an attempt having been made to introduce as many of the new vehicles as possible for the resumption of non-stop running between Kings Cross and Edinburgh on 31 May 1948. With the exception of the buffet lounge cars, the vehicles were to standard diagrams but were specially equipped as well as having fairings over the solebars. These imparted a distinctive look; indeed, the stock made up arguably the most handsome of the early postwar expresses. In addition, all carriages for the 'Flying Scotsman' sets, and some for the 'Junior Scotsman', had double glazing and Stone's pressure ventilation and heating, corridor side windows without ventilators and

Below Vestibule brake third E1942, as built on Dia 346 and in BR plum and spilt milk livery with the number placed centrally and lacking the final 'E'.

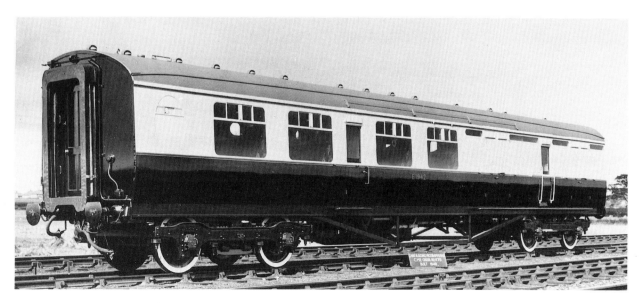

TABLE 12B

Type	Diagram	Compartments/Layout	Built	
Open third (TO)	350	2 saloons, 48 seats	1948/9	Some Flying Scotsman
Open first (FO)	351	2 saloons, 42 seats	1948/9	Some Flying Scotsman
Buffet lounge car (RB)	352	1 saloon, 8 seats	1948	Flying Scotsman
Kitchen car (RK)	353	Kitchen + pantries	1948	Some Flying Scotsman
Restaurant first (RF)	354	1 saloon, 18 seats, PKAL	1948	Some Flying Scotsman Anthracite electric equipment
Third pantry (RTP)	355	1 saloon, 38 seats, P	1949/50	

All 63 ft 0 in length In the table A – attendants' compartment; K – kitchen; L – lavatory for staff; P – pantry

large size journals for the bogies. The roofs were painted white on the prestige set vehicles.

The two 'Flying Scotsman' sets were allocated the following vehicles: third brakes (Dia 346) Nos 1901–4; thirds with ladies retiring rooms (Dia 349), Nos 1608–10; composites (Dia 328) Nos 1195–7/1206; firsts with ladies' retiring room (Dia 348) Nos 1326–8; open thirds, with

Below Kitchen car E1951E (Dia 353) in 1963.

Bottom Vestibule first with ladies' retiring room, E1328E to Dia 348. It is branded East Coast Set No 4 and was seen in the 'Heart of Midlothian' in July 1963, by then the only LNER design vehicle booked to run in the formation.

seats for dining (Dia 350) Nos 1982–4; kitchen cars (Dia 353) Nos 1943–5; open firsts with seats for dining (Dia 351) Nos 1956–8 and the buffet lounge cars (Dia 352) Nos 1705/6.

When it came to the Dia 350/351 cars, the interior finishes were unremarkable and best described as a simplified form of the 1938 'Flying Scotsman', the open firsts having prewar type light fittings. The other carriages in the sets perpetuated some of the features of prewar East Coast stock such as corridor carpets and fibre mats in the vestibules while the extra provision of ladies' retiring rooms was to be welcomed. The buffet lounge cars were unique and their interiors featured a pantry, a long buffet/bar counter, and a small lounge seating eight, screened in the same manner as the 1938 cars. The interior panelling was in figured and matched mahogany, there was a tiled linoleum floor and the light fittings were opaque or concealed. The overall effect was well-executed and dignified but lacked the élan of the various prewar special vehicles. The exteriors were painted in simulated teak and numbered in Gill Sans transfers as E1945 etc. The teak livery was retained until 1952.

From May 1949 the 'Flying Scotsman' retained its intermediate stops and the former relief train now became the summer non-stop working, retimed to leave earlier, named the 'Capitals Limited' and notable for the Dia 344 full brake marshalled at one end. In 1952 a restaurant first replaced the kitchen car and two dining saloons. The ambience and formation of the stock feature in that excellent British Transport Films documentary, the *Elizabethan* which name was bestowed on the 'Capitals Limited' from June 1953. As in prewar days the sets were lifted and attended to each spring and were turned out in first-class condition. For the summer service of 1953 the two 'Elizabethan' sets were formed:

Set A – from south end: BG 11 or 12, FK 1328, RF 1219 or 1598, RTO 1983, TK 1002, TK 1005 or 1600, TK 1609, RB 1706, TK 1516, TK 1001, BCK 1161 or 1142 or 1175

Set B – from south end: BG 10, FK 1327, RF 1216 or 1599, RTO 1984, TK 1606 or 1600, TK 1607, TK 1610, RB 1705, TK 1518, TK 1605 or 1000 or 1604, BCK 1175 or 1161 or 1160.

From then onwards the Aberdeen BCK became a BR Standard vehicle and after the summer 1957 season the buffet lounge cars were omitted and were later to be rebuilt as conventional buffet cars. That apart, the 'Elizabethan' sets remained in much this form until the end of the 1960 season but for the train's final two summers more Standard stock was introduced.

The 'Flying Scotsman' gradually lost the LNER postwar stock from 1953 onwards, the principal change occurring with the 1957 winter timetable when the kitchen and the buffet lounge cars were removed from the formation in order to reduce the train weight and so allow an acceleration of the train's timings. However, the postwar vehicles with ladies retiring rooms remained in the East Coast sets until the 1964/5 winter timetable. SOs Nos 1984/90/4 were allocated to the 'Talisman' sets and received roller bearing axleboxes. From the early 1960s onwards dieselisation accompanied a steady change in East Coast operations, as did the completion of the restaurant car building programme, with the result that the majority of the postwar catering vehicles were condemned by the end of 1962. Kitchen cars Nos 1946/8/51/2 survived until 1966, the last of the LNER-design anthracite electric cooking cars. Other late survivors were SO No 1985 used on Liverpool Street–Norwich expresses and on the East Coast main line during 1967/8 and the two former buffet lounge cars, Nos 1705/6 which, in their rebuilt form with 24-seat saloon and propane gas equipment, lasted in traffic until 1979. They were the last passenger carriages to pre-Nationalisation design in main line use on BR.

The arrival of the postwar stock saw a major reallocation from mid 1948 of prewar stock in the East Coast fleet to what was now the all-line allocation. In turn, some of the earliest postwar vehicles to Dias 328, 331, 332 and 345 were themselves transferred in the early 1950s from East Coast to all-line stock and renumbered. But the postwar stock was also built in quantity for general service on the Eastern and North Eastern Regions, being distinguished in the carriage working books of the time as 'transverse corridor' vehicles. The 'South Yorkshireman' is an example of one train formed with a number of postwar carriages into the mid 1950s. Generally the postwar stock deteriorated in condition markedly once the monetary repair limits were introduced for all coaching stock at the end of 1964. Transfers of postwar stock to other BR Regions took place in the mid 1960s including that of a

Above Restaurant pantry car E1334E (Dia 355, built 1949), condemned in July 1963 having been repainted less than a year before.

number of 1000 series Dia 329 SKs to the London Midland Region while later examples to the same diagram moved from the Scottish Region to the London Midland and Western Regions. By 1967, the majority of the pre 1949 carriages had been condemned and the remainder were mostly extinguished by the end of the year, only a few surviving into 1968.

Below Former 'Flying Scotsman' buffet lounge car E1705E in its rebuilt condition, working in a Cambridge Buffet Express set in 1967.

Bottom The prototype 'interlocking' layout third-class sleeping car No 1348 (Dia 347, built 1947), with the same simulated teak finish as on restaurant car 1657.

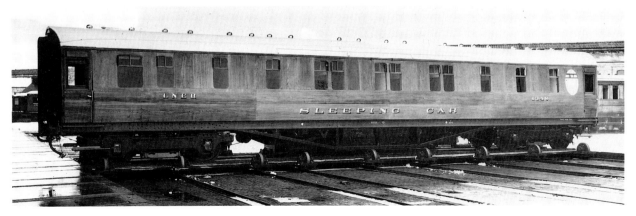

Above Dia 368 sleeping car of the 1760–1764 series, in traffic and in blue and grey livery at Preston in October 1969. Note that the doors are slightly recessed.

Sleeping cars

Type	Diagram	Compartments/Layout	Built
Third (SLTP)	347	4 double berths, eight single	1947–9
First (SLF)	359	11 berths, attendant's compt	1950
Third (SLTTP)	368	11 double-tiered berths, attendant's compt	1952
Third (SLTT)	369	12 double-tiered berths	1952

All 66 ft 6 in length and 9 ft 3 in wide

The third-class sleeping cars with 'lying down' accommodation were not thought appropriate for the postwar era in the view of the SPMs and their belief was that passengers would pay for full bedding, washing facilities in the compartments and the elimination of tiered berths. The result was the production of a novel design with accommodation for sixteen passengers, eight in single berths and the rest in four double compartments; the principle was that no berth should be immediately above another. The standard of accommodation was improved but designed not to be competitive with the first-class cars. The ability to increase third-class sleeping car supplements meant that the cars would earn as much revenue as the first-class cars when fully laden but not as much as the old 32-berth vehicles. The first car was No 1348, built in 1947 although it was not put into service until others were available in 1948 as difficulties were foreseen with just one vehicle in service to the new design alongside older cars with inferior accommodation. The services in these cars included Thermotank pressure ventilation and steam heating. Nos 1348/50 were written off as a result of the Lincoln accident of 1960 which involved an East Coast train diverted because of engineering works but the others continued in service until the winter 1964/5 timetable.

First-class cars to Dia 359 were on traditional lines and had pressure ventilation. Nos 1257/92 were repainted in BR blue and grey livery and the batch survived until 1970. Also conventional in layout were the two diagrams of 1952-built third-class cars, one with attendant's compart-

Non-vestibuled stock – list of types and Diagram numbers

TABLE 12C

Type	Diagram	Length/width	Compartments/Seats	Built
First (F)	341	52' 4"/9' 3"	7/56	1949
Third (T)	339	52' 4"/9' 3"	8/80	1947–52
	372	54' 1½"/8' 11¼"	8/96	rebuilt 1953
Third Open (TO{NG})	375	54' 1½"/8' 11¼"	2 saloons, 80	rebuilt 1953
Composite (CL)	338	52' 4"/9' 3"	3 1st, 4 3rd/ 19/33	1947–5
	370	51' 1½"/8' 11¼"	3 1st, 4 3rd/ 19/33	1952
	374	54' 1½"/8' 11¼"	3 1st, 1 3rd saloon 19/40	rebuilt 1953
Composite (C)	371	52' 4"/9' 3"	3 1st, 4½ 3rd/ 24/44	1953
Brake third (BT)	340	52' 4"/9' 3"	4/40	1948–51
	361	52' 4"/9' 3"	5/50	1951
	373	54' 1½"/8' 11¼"	6/72	rebuilt 1953
Brake composite (BC)	360	52' 4"/9' 3"	2 1st, 4 3rd/ 16/40	1951/2

ment, the other without. These were the first East Coast third-class cars with two berths to all compartments and they entered service from April 1952. All had pressure ventilation. These were also late survivors, three passing to the Western Region in 1967/8 and being repainted in blue and grey livery. The last, No 1767, was withdrawn in late 1970.

Non-vestibuled stock (table 12C)

A 52 ft 2½ in underframe, with screw couplings, was used for the standard non-vestibuled postwar stock. Underframes, running gear and bodywork followed the arrangements of the immediately prewar steel panelled non-vestibuled stock except that the windows, still square cornered, were deeper and the doors had hit and miss ventilators. The interiors were simple but perfectly adequate with painted finishes, enlivened only by the excellent series of LNER framed pen and wash or water-colour studies and oval mirrors. The compartment dimensions were standardised at 7 ft 4 in for first-class and 6 ft 4 in for the third-class.

First to appear during 1947 were the thirds and lavatory composites and these were allocated to GN outer suburban services and Edinburgh local sets. After 1949, new build had radiussed corners to the windows. From 1950/1, the production of non-vestibuled stock was increased and a high proportion of the later batches was allocated to the Scottish Region. Construction continued until 1953, delayed as a result of the steel shortage which saw postponement of the 1952 building programme.

In 1953, the Eastern Region produced reconstructed stock for the London Tilbury & Southend section which had been incorporated into the Region from November 1948. The steel-panelled rebuilds used the underframes,

Above, top and bottom A less usual view – non-vestibule second E82801E (Dia 339, built 1951). At Knebworth, 1963.

Non-vestibule lavatory composite E88412E (Dia 338, built 1948). with square cornered windows. At Knebworth in a King's Cross outer suburban train, 1962.

floors, some of the body framing and electrical equipment of the Ilford stock of 1935/6 which had been made redundant by the Shenfield electrification. The LT & S stock originally made up six, four-car close-coupled sets, these being formed into trains with existing carriages. Each set comprised: brake third, third, open third and lavatory composite, the second and third vehicles having short buffers. The open third and lavatory composite were to a new layout, more akin to electric multiple units such as the Class 310s introduced on the LT & S in the 1980s. The external appearance of the 1953 stock was similar to the standard postwar stock except for the large windows with ventilators which featured in the open thirds and composites while one difference was the non-standard width. The interiors were panelled throughout in laminated plastic panelling.

Dia 375 had two open saloons with two central lavatories. Dia 338 was the modernised form of the semi-corridor composite Dia 50. Dia 370 was a one-off using a recovered underframe. Dia 371 was allocated only to the Scottish Region when new and was unusual in having a third-class coupé compartment. Dia 374 had three first-class compartments with side corridor, two central lavatories and a centre gangwayed third-class saloon. Dia 340 Nos 87245/70 were transferred to the Western Region during 1962 for use on the Tiverton Junction–Hemyock branch to displace a pair of gas-lit ex Barry Railway

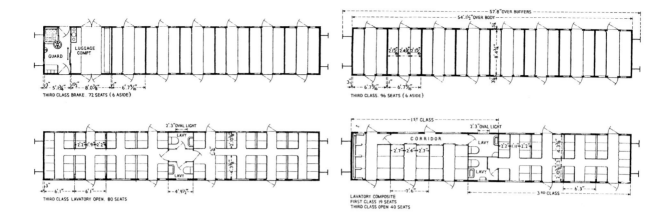

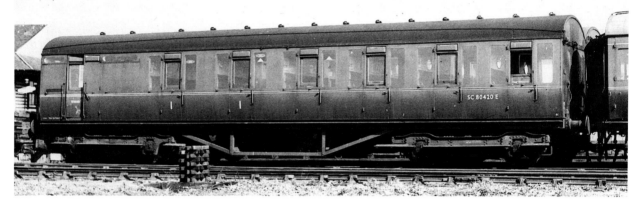

Above, top The layouts of the four vehicle types of the LT & S rebuilt stock of 1953, showing, top to bottom, brake third, open third, third and lavatory composite.

Above Non-vestibule brake composite SC80420E (Dia 360, built 1952). At Thornton Junction, 1966.

carriages. The van of Dia 361 had a single pair of doors each side.

Dieselisation and electrification of the GE lines' suburban services in the 1950s and 1960s saw numerous reallocations although, at the onset of electrification, the LT & S rebuilt stock seems to have been withdrawn en masse. Withdrawals of the general types were heavy from 1962 onwards although there could always be surprises such as Dia 338 non-vestibule composite SC88339E which was turned out at the head of a down Paddington–South Wales relief in late 1965. The electrification of the Glasgow suburban services saw the final extinction of the non-vestibuled stock by early 1967.

Production of LNER design coaching stock 1945–1953

Year	Built by LNER		Built by contractors	
	A	B	A	B
1945	2	49	–	–
1946	67	15	30	–
1947	43	3	223	–
1948	129	11	242	–
1949	195	12	306	–
1950	250	657	47	–
1951	181	14	254	–
1952	32	–	173	–
1953	47	–	–	–
TOTALS	946	761	1,275	–

Notes A – Passenger carrying vehicles including kitchen cars and electric multiple-units
B – Other coaching stock

CHAPTER 13

NON-PASSENGER STOCK, SALOONS AND LNER ROYAL TRAIN

Vestibuled 61 ft 6 in passenger brake vans

ECJS passenger brake van No 126 of 1906 was the proto-type for all pre-1945 vestibuled passenger brake vans. The standard LNER designs were finalised in December 1923 with the 60 ft underframe for general use except on the GE section which opted for the 51 ft underframe. In general, the LNER did not favour non-bogie vans. The bodies of the standard 51 ft and 60 ft vans followed most details of the pre-Grouping ECJS and GNR vans but had neither their guard's duckets – the earlier examples only – nor the roof skylights, instead having toplights under the cantrail. There were three sets of hinged doors and a guard's door on each side and the flooring was of Decolite composition. The GNR design of 8 ft wheelbase bogie was at first used, permitting a maximum payload of eight tons. The single bolster bogie used for suburban stock was then adopted for bogie vans and with 10 in by 5 in journals their payload was increased to ten tons. The various diagrams built for general service up to 1945 are summarised below:

Bodies of 61 ft 6 in length and 9 ft width, Pullman type gangways and buckeye couplers Eight tons payload. Classified BG, or BGP for pigeon traffic.

Dia 43 Standard 1923 design, built 1924–28. Withdrawn by 1967.

Dia 45 All-steel bodies, built by Cammell Laird, 1927/8. See Chapter 12.

Dia 113 As Dia 43 but with guard's ducket on the right-hand side. Built 1929–34. Some with 10 in by 5 in journals and ten tons payload. Withdrawn by 1967.

Dia 198 Steel body panelling, built 1934–7. Ten tons payload. Some still in traffic into the mid-1970s.

Dia 245 Generally as Dia 113 and teak panelled, built 1938–43. Intended for racing pigeon traffic with shelves

Below Dia 198 van E1007E, built 1936, at Stranraer Harbour in 1966. This had retained its East Coast van stock number.

along each side of the interior, but generally used for parcels and mails. Ten tons payload. Some still in traffic into the mid-1970s.

Dia 260 Generally as Dia 113 and with teak or steel panelling but of 8 ft 11½ in width. Built 1938–40. Ducket right-hand side. Ten tons payload. Some still in traffic into the mid-1970s.

Dia 315 Generally as Dia 245 but steel panelled and 8 ft 11½ in width. Built 1940/1. Later shown as Dia 245.

In May 1945 the Emergency Board authorised the provision of partitions in 352 vestibuled brake vans, the first to be fitted with the guard's enclosure being No 70499, inspected by the SPMs in July 1945. A number of vans were also fitted with solid fuel stoves for heating.

A new design (Dia 327) was prepared in 1944 following the lines of what became the postwar passenger carriages, with bowed ends and straight roof ends. All bodyside and end panelling was in deal planking. Some of the last Gresley design vans built later in the war had hardboard body panels in order to economise on the use of teak. Fifty-three were built to Dia 327 in 1945/6 and one or two were still in traffic into the mid 1970s.

The standard postwar bogie van was Dia 344, on a 61 ft 6 in underframe with a steel panelled body of 9 ft 3 in width and with three pairs of doors on each side. The payload was ten tons. Earlier examples had square corners to the toplights, in later vans these were radiussed. Nos 10–19 had fairings over the solebars to match the postwar carriages for the 'Flying Scotsman'. Some of Dia 344 remained in traffic into the mid-1970s.

Other vestibuled vans

The GE section 52 ft 6 in vans – to Dias 111, 154 and 282 – had 9 ft width bodies but otherwise were generally similar to the 61 ft 6 in variety. They ran on GNR type 8 ft wheelbase bogies and their maximum permitted load was eight

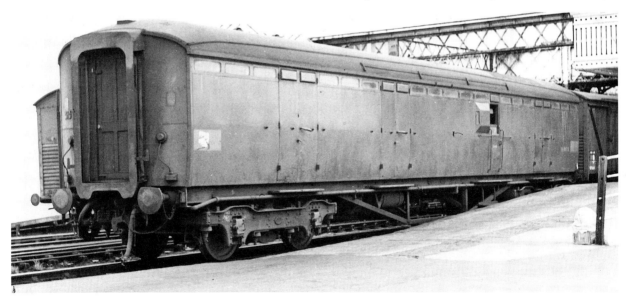

tons.

While the 1935 CBP was being drawn up, and before the agreement to go to a two-year programme for 1935/6, the chief accountant expressed concern at the cost of new construction. As a palliative, it was decided to save money by using the underframes of four condemned sleeping cars and build new bodies generally to the outline of the 61 ft 6 in vehicles. Three of the condemned cars, withdrawn in January 1935, were to EC Dia 74 built in 1910, the conversions as vans on Dia 208 having 56 ft 6 in bodies. The odd man out was the fourth car to Dia 207. This had a 58 ft 6 in body and took the underframe of GN/NE Joint car No 1410, built in 1908. All had heavy type bogies.

Below Dia 129 van E70256E, built 1931, condemned and being shunted at Micheldever, 1967.

Above Dia 344 van E153E, built 1950 but with square cornered toplights. At Thornton Junction, 1966.

Left Deal panelled van to Dia 327, E70606E, built 1945. When seen at Cambridge in 1963 it was in lined out maroon livery although most were unlined.

Non-vestibuled bogie vans

These were based on the design of the standard GNR milk van and used the underframe specified for non-vestibuled carriages. The bodies of the vans, 51 ft 1½ in by 9 ft, had two sets of double doors to each side. All except one of the vans was allocated to the GE section. Those built in 1926/7 had dual brakes.

Dia 67 Standard design of 1923. Built 1926/7. Eight tons permitted load.

Dia 129 For racing pigeon traffic and with shelves for pigeon baskets. Ducket right-hand side. GER type 8 ft wheelbase bogies fitted to some at a later date. Built 1931. One converted as a Post Office tender, page 116.

Dia 284 As Dia 129 but for general use. One converted to Post Office tender, see page 116.

A piece of social and economic history introduces the next vehicles. During 1945 bread rationing was introduced and the LNER bought four ex-Highland Railway bogie vans to convey bread between Glasgow and Perth. Two of these vans became damaged and, as a result, two replacement bread vans (Dia 335) were built at Doncaster in 1946 using the 51 ft underframes of two GE section carriages whose bodies had been destroyed during World War 2. In

their new form the vehicles had flat ended bodies of deal boards, with two sets of doors to each side. The interior was taken up largely by racks which could hold 288 trays of bread. Louvre ventilators were fitted to the bottom quarters of the body. The vans continued in use for parcels traffic.

The redundant ex GER and LNER Ilford stock lay at Stratford unconverted for a number of years. The underframes of some were fitted with new bodies as passenger vehicles for the London Tilbury and Southend section and are described in Chapter 12. Others were rebuilt at Stratford during the mid 1950s as parcels vans and motor car vans, retaining their 54 ft underframes and with new bodies corresponding in outline to their former identity. The ex GER carriages became parcels vans E6001–81E, in the GE van number series, and motor car vans, E71035–99E in the main LNER 1943 series. Former LNER Ilford stock of 1935/6 became motor car vans Nos E71000–34E.

The cinema cars

In addition to the other specialities introduced for passengers, such as hairdressing facilities and wireless on East Coast trains, the LNER was responsible for the first and only cinema cars on British railways. After a demonstration was arranged by Pathé on board the 10.10 am Kings Cross–Leeds, the CGM instructed the SPMs to arrange to provide and equip a van to run a three-month trial early in 1935.

The first cinema car service began on 27 May 1935, the car working in the formation of the 10.10 am to Leeds and

Above One of the types of Covered Carriage Truck produced by the conversion of redundant Liverpool Street–Shenfield stock, classified CCT (E). This was one of the 1935/6 LNER vehicles, now E71005E, at Bristol Temple Meads in 1966 and one of those branded for the car carrier services, for which the end loading doors were vital.

3.15 pm return to Kings Cross. Although cinema shows were seen as a possible replacement for the wireless services, the weight of the afternoon Scotsmen precluded the use of the car on these trains. On Sundays the car was often used on excursions. The agreement with Pathé Equipment Ltd was that the LNER provided a suitably equipped vehicle, as well as an attendant to look after passengers, while Pathé supplied projection equipment, screen, films, tip-up cinema seats and projectionist. The vehicle chosen for conversion was Dia 113 passenger brake van No 4040. This was stripped internally for the conversion and fitted with a floor sloping towards one end to improve viewing, the double pair of doors sealed and sets of accumulators provided to power a generator; this measure was adopted as a supply from the usual vehicle lighting system would not be constant and so vary the speed of the film. The side walls of the van were covered in Rexine but

Below The Dia 325 bread vans do not seem to have been photographed much. Sunlight adds a patterned shadow to E70637 at Glasgow Buchanan Street in 1965. The vehicle is classified 'B Bread'; by that time its original purpose must have been lost on those working with it.

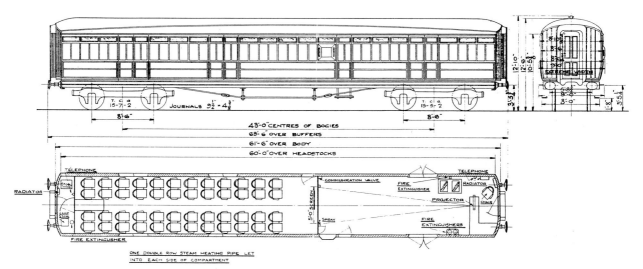

ONE DOUBLE ROW STEAM HEATING PIPE LET
INTO EACH SIDE OF COMPARTMENT

Above LNER Diagram Book: cinema car conversion of Dia 113 van No 4041 to Dia 224.

there was no sound insulation. There were 44 seats in pairs and a central gangway. Because the projector could not be located behind the seats as in a normal cinema, back projection was employed, with the images thrown on to a 5 ft wide ground glass screen. Steam heating radiators were provided for the interior. There was telephone communication between projectionist and attendant. Smoking was allowed and although there were fire extinguishers in the car, it is probably fortunate that they were never put to the test in what was a fairly hazardous environment!

Each film showing lasted an hour and the programme included news items as well as sports and human interest features, two performances being given on each journey. The admission charge was 1/- (5p). It was decided to extend the experiment and by the end of November 1935 No 4040 had run 63,300 miles as a cinema car and programmes had been shown to some 16,000 patrons. Light type bogies were later fitted to try to reduce the noise from the running gear.

The first car was enough of a success to encourage the introduction of a second although another influence was that as the films were prepared in duplicate a second set was available and might as well be used. Another Dia 113

Below Interior of one of the cinema cars, probably No 4041.

van, No 4041, was approved for conversion in November 1935 and this featured improvements learned from experience with the first car. The interior was generally the same although the initial seating capacity was 52, later reduced to 48. The main improvement concerned the power supply, two 48 volt batteries being mounted on the underframe, so arranged that one was fully charged for running the projector while the second was connected to the dynamo. The interior was made more attractive and the heating more effective as steam pipes ran along the side walls of the van. A suitable cinema interior was created with gold and blue trappings and a rose coloured carpet. Light type 8 ft 6 in bogies were fitted from the start. No 4041 went into service on 2 March 1936 working on the 9 am Leeds–Glasgow and 4 pm return, to and from Edinburgh only. As with the earlier car No 4041 was used from time to time on excursions. Initially patronage was encouraging but gradually it declined with the result that No 4041 was transferred south and from 3 May 1937 ran in the formation of the 1.13 pm Doncaster–Kings Cross and 7.15 pm return. The original agreement with Pathé was extended after 1935 but the cars were withdrawn from service following their journeys on 25 September 1938 and in December 1942 reverted to their identities as passenger brake vans. This was a little surprising as they might have proved useful as mobile instruction units during the war. It was left to the airlines and road coaches to develop video presentations to travellers.

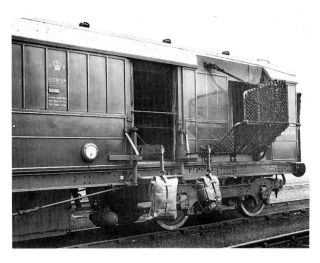

Above left Collection net and mail pouch brackets demonstrated on Dia 131 TPO van No 2260 (later No 6130 and then 70277 under the 1943 numbering scheme).

Above right TPO van E70290E in BR service in the late 1960s, the collection net having been removed.

Right The Doncaster photograph of the TPO van to Dia 342, built in 1946 and at this stage numbered 30281, for the LMS/LNER joint Newcastle–Bristol service, on which it began work as 70640.

As cinema cars the two vehicles carried no outward designations other than red painted, roof mounted boards with white block lettering reading: LNER/PATHE CINEMA COACH.

Travelling post office vehicles

The usual arrangement has been that TPO vehicles are maintained by the railway company but new construction and alterations are paid for jointly by the Post Office and railway company. The newest TPO vans in the LNER fleet at Grouping were those built by the GNR, the others being clerestory roof, gas-lit NER vans built 1902–4 and GER six-wheelers which were up to 35 years old. After Grouping there were frequent complaints from the Post Office as to the general condition and poor heating of the older vehicles, their concern increasing after the Charfield accident of October 1928 which saw fire break out in the gas-lit vehicles of the Leeds–Bristol mail train. While the Post Office had put pressure on the LNER in 1924/5 to build new sorting vans for the London–Norwich and London–Leeds TPOs, no major changes were made to the LNER's stock of TPO vans until 1932. In the meantime there had been changes to the services, with the switch in 1925 of the North Eastern TPO sorting van from the 8.25 pm from Kings Cross to the 10.25 pm to Edinburgh and the introduction in 1929 of the Liverpool Street–Peterborough mail trains, routed via Bury St Edmunds.

Before then the first LNER design TPOs had appeared during 1929, under the 1927/8 CBP. These three vans were striking in appearance as the upper part of one body side was built out to accommodate the various sorting cabinets and lockers. This was to keep the vehicles within gauge and to a maximum width of 8 ft 6 in in the days before clearance for 9 ft 3 in width vehicles on the East Coast main line. At its narrowest the body of the Dia 131 vans was 7 ft 7 in. They were built on 60 ft underframes, with light type 8 ft 6 in bogies and had straight roof ends. They had mail bag delivery brackets and a pick up net on one side and their facilities included a lavatory, wardrobe and overhead steam pipes for heating the interior. Nos 2260/86, 2339 went into service on the North Eastern TPO, the 10.25 pm Kings Cross–Newcastle and corresponding return working.

In June 1932 the Traffic Committee agreed to proposals discussed with the Post Office for the replacement of gas by electric lighting in TPOs, on the basis that the Post Office would meet 75% of the costs for conversion. Of the LNER fleet of 29 vehicles, only the three 1929 vans had electric lighting and the others included some ancient examples, ten being six-wheelers of between 30 and 47 years service, the oldest being GER vans built in 1886 and 1890. Under the new arrangements only the six most modern gas-lit vans were converted to electric lighting and the ten six-wheelers were to be withdrawn; the latter and two others were to be replaced by seven new TPO vans, the Post Office meeting the difference in cost between new six wheelers and bogie vans! The requirements were to be taken into account in the 1933 CBP.

As a result of these changes, the three Dia 131 vans were transferred to the GE section during 1933 for use between Liverpool Street and Peterborough and their delivery and collection equipment was removed. They were used on these services well into the mid 1960s, No 70278 being reported on the East Coast main line during 1967.

The new TPO vans authorised in the 1933 CBP were of two types, Dias 164 and 165, the later differing only by having a secure cupboard for valuable packets. They had 8 ft 6¾ in wide bodies without the projections of the 1929 vans. Mail bag delivery brackets and a collection net were fitted on all seven vehicles. Staff comforts included an electric urn and a gas oven. The seven vans were allocated to the London–York–Edinburgh and North Eastern TPOs. The Post Office pressed for the replacement of the seven remaining gas-lit TPO vans and further Dia 164 vehicles were built. Two, Nos 4202/3, replaced NER vehicles on the Kings Cross–Leeds TPO and although nominally completed to the 1937 CBP were authorised in advance and built in 1936. The five other TPO vans were spruced up for a few more months service before being replaced during 1937 by new vans Nos 4206/7, to replace two GNR clerestory vans of 1902 on the Kings Cross–Leeds workings, and 2440–2 which displaced the remaining pre Grouping vans in the East Coast circuits.

All TPOs on the LNER were withdrawn in September 1940 and a number of changes to workings took place on restoration of services from May 1946. The Leeds service did not reappear and the displaced TPOs were transferred to the GE section to work the 6.25 pm Norwich–Liverpool Street, this working picking up mail en route. The van returned as a bag tender on the 4.25 am Liverpool Street–Norwich.

In September 1945, the joint ownership of TPOs in the Newcastle–Bristol service was terminated and the eight vans involved were distributed between the LNER and LMS. However, the LNER had built a new steel panelled stowage van, Dia 342, early in 1946 and an official Doncaster photograph shows it as No 30281 in the joint stock but it was soon renumbered as 70640 and indeed may never have left the works under its first identity. This vehicle was built on the new standard 52 ft 2½ in underframe adopted for non-vestibuled stock. More TPO vans were constructed during 1949/50 to Dia 356, Nos 70641–6. These were also steel panelled and had 60 ft underframes and double bolster bogies; they were of similar layout to the Dia 164 vans but without net apparatus. They were allocated to the Newcastle–Bristol and East Anglian services.

Two other stowage vans – or tenders – were produced. The first was a conversion of a standard 51 ft 1½ in Dia 284 passenger brake van. This came about as a result of the Gidea Park accident of 2 January 1947 when a stowage van and sorting van were written off. The conversion involved the fitting of offset gangways and two pairs of sliding doors to each side, the new diagram being 357. In the mid 1960s this van, numbered 70561, was being used on a Leeds–Kings Cross working. The second conversion of a passenger brake van was of a Dia 129 vehicle, No 70268, rebuilt as a TPO tender in the early 1950s.

The TPO vans had the LNER standard varnished teak finish and customary lettering and numbering. In addition, before 1930, the designation ROYAL MAIL was applied in 4 in blocked and shaded characters midway on the bodysides and just below the waistline. After 1930, 7 in lettering was used in the same position, arranged as follows: ROYAL G(cipher)R MAIL. the cipher and crown changing with the monarch. The late fee box was GPO red with G(cipher)R and LETTER BOX above the slot, as well as the legend 'Letters posted here…'

The LNER design TPOs remained on much the same duties through the 1950s and 1960s, but the arrival from 1968 of a new series of BR Standard sorting and stowage vans reduced their ranks. The nets had been removed earlier from some vans such as 70290/4/6/7/302 and 70290/5/8/9

Below Six-wheeled BZ E70705E, at St Pancras in 1967.

were withdrawn by 1970. Further deliveries of new stock caused the remaining prewar vans to be withdrawn by 1973 and of the postwar vans only 70641/3 remained by the end of 1973.

Bullion van No 11050

In 1949 a standard 61 ft 6 in brake third, No 16373 to Dia 114 of 1929, was converted to a bullion van on Dia 362. The bodyside panelling was extended in the style of the existing pattern to leave only the end compartment. The ceiling, floor, ends and sides of the extended van section were lined with steel plate and the toplights were of obscured glass with grilles behind. The carrying capacity was ten tons. The security guard's compartment, with two seats, was made full width, with access doors to the main compartment only and the lavatory was retained. Dummy vestibules were fitted with faceplates. No 11050 was condemned during 1966.

Four/six-wheel passenger stock vans

Four-wheel vans (coded BY)
Dia 86   General purpose vans. Body 32 ft by 8 ft 11½ in. Eight tons load. Vertical matchboarding and ventilators. Oil lamps for lighting.

Dia 87   As above, but for milk churn traffic.
The following designs had high-roofed teak panelled bodies, similar in style to bogie vans.

Dia 120   For racing pigeon traffic and fitted with shelves for pigeon baskets. Body 32 ft by 9 ft. Five tons load. Ducket right-hand side. Dual fitted and built for Northern Scottish Area and GE section.

Dia 170   General service but generally as Dia 120. Body 31 ft 8⅝ in by 9 ft and lower in height than Dia 120. Underframes from Howlden passenger stock.

Dia 176   General service. Body 31 ft 11⅝ in by 9 ft. Underframes from Howlden passenger stock.
Dia 177 As Dia 176 but body 30 ft 10½ in by 9 ft.

Six-wheel vans (coded BZ)
In 1950 a steel panelled design was introduced, on Dia 358, the 80 vans being assembled at Stratford Works from parts manufactured at Darlington. The body was similar in style to contemporary passenger stock, its dimensions were 32 ft by 8 ft 11¼ in and it was provided with interior lighting and steam heating. The carrying capacity was five tons. There were 70 of this type still in traffic at the end of 1973 but only nine remained at the end of 1977 and all had gone by 1980.

Dynamometer car DE 320041

From 1927 Gresley had been keen that a modern locomotive testing plant should be built in Britain for use by the Big Four railways and the locomotive manufacturers. By 1936, it was left to the LNER and LMS jointly to construct a test plant and it was also agreed that a dynamometer car would be built for joint use at a cost of £40,000. In July 1937 it was decided that each company would build its own car but that the dynamometer and table should be standard with those in the Rugby test plant. The apparatus for the test plant and dynamometer cars was ordered during November 1938 and the construction of the LNER car was put in hand at Doncaster. Unfortunately, the part-completed car was burnt out in the fire of 1940. Its replacement was authorised in 1947 but not completed until 1951.

No DE320041, later renumbered in the BR series as DB 999500, was built on a 60 ft underframe and had a handsome steel panelled body with square cornered windows, generally similar in style to the contemporary passenger stock. The interior comprised a recording saloon, a general saloon and a pantry with gas cooking equipment. Heavy type 8 ft 6 in compound bolster bogies were fitted. One end had a normal Pullman type gangway and buckeye coupler, the other a dummy shield and the live drawbar for coupling to the engine on test. Despite completion of the Rugby test plant in 1951 the car was based at Darlington Works and was the preserve of Dynamometer Car Dan. It was transferred to the Railway Technical Centre at Derby in 1967.

The Chief General Manager's Saloon DE 902260
This unusual steel panelled vehicle was built at York in 1945, with body dimensions of 61 ft 6 in by 9 ft 3 in. It was gangwayed at one end with a verandah at the other. Light type 8 ft 6 in bogies were fitted by 1948, the earlier type being conjectural. The interior had a dining saloon seating twelve at the gangway end, then a kitchen, lavatory, office with four seats and a lounge at the verandah end with nine seats. Pressure ventilation was fitted and the saloon had a hand brake in addition to the normal vacuum braking. As late as March 1954 it remained in simulated teak livery as LNER 902260.

At a later stage this somewhat elusive vehicle had the verandah end panelled in and by 1980 had arrived on the Scottish Region at Perth. In 1980 it was moved to the West Highland line for use as an observation saloon on the Mallaig extension, acquiring the name *Lochaber* in the same year when it was also transferred to capital stock and numbered SC1999. It was successfully operated for the 1981–3 seasons, being joined by the former chief civil engineer's saloon described below, both being in LNER simulated teak livery by 1983. In 1984 the former CGM's saloon was purchased by Flying Scotsman Services and based at Carnforth, until sold in 1989 to the Great Southern and Western Railway Co for use in its 'Royal Scotsman' touring train for which purpose it was extensively rebuilt in 1990 and now runs on BR pattern B4 type bogies. It is referred to as Dining Car 2 and provides seating for sixteen diners.

Chief Engineer's Saloon DE 900580
This steel panelled, non-vestibuled vehicle, generally similar in outline to the contemporary passenger steel panelled stock, measured 60 ft 1½ in overall and 9 ft 3 in wide and was built at Doncaster in 1936. One end had an open balcony, from which end the interior had in sequence a saloon and a side corridor serving a lavatory, guard's compartment, bathroom and galley. At the other end of the corridor was a saloon with observation windows. As the chief engineer's vehicle it was based at Stratford.

By the early 1980s it was on the Scottish Region and was taken into capital stock in 1982 for use with the former chief general manager's saloon as a observation car on the Mallaig

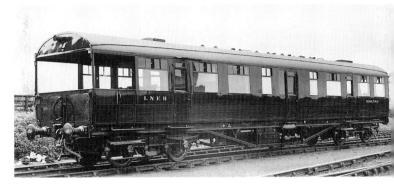

Above The Chief Engineer's Saloon 900580, at the balcony end, after overhaul in 1945. The balcony was later enclosed and the vehicle entered capital stock for a brief time in the 1980s.

Extension. During 1983 it was numbered 1998 and named *Loch Eil*. By 1984 it had been purchased by Flying Scotsman Services, subsequently passing to David Smith, and in 1992 was used on the internal passenger carrying line at Steamtown, Carnforth.

Other coaching stock vehicles
Also listed among the passenger stock diagrams were the following milk tank wagons and trucks for conveying mobile road tankers:

Dia 121 Four-wheeled glass-lined milk tank wagon. Capacity of tank, 2,000 gallons. Maximum weight 12 tons.
Dia 122 Four-wheeled glass-lined milk tank wagon. Capacity of tank, 2,000 gallons. Maximum weight 14 tons.

Dia 166 As above.

Dia 183 Six-wheeled truck for mobile road milk tanker.

Dia 184 Six-wheeled glass-lined milk tank wagon. Capacity of tank 3,000 gallons. Maximum weight 14 tons. Some converted from Dia 122.

Dia 220 Six-wheeled glass-lined milk tank wagon. Capacity of tank 3,000 gallons. Maximum weight 14 tons.

Dia 222 Six-wheeled glass-lined milk tank wagon. Capacity of tank 2,000 gallons. Maximum weight 12 tons. Conversions from Dia 121.

Dia 295 Six-wheeled truck for mobile road milk tanker.

Dia 323 Six-wheeled glass-lined milk tank wagon. 3,000 gallons/14 tons.

Dia	Type	Wheels	Dimensions	No built	Year	Running numbers
1	Special cattle van	4	21' 9" by 8' 7"	38	1924	477–82/94–9, 2201–26
2	Covered combination truck (CCT) (NE Dia 207)	8	45' by 8' 6"	25	1924	1201–25
3	CCT	8	As above	16	1927	1226–41
4	Horsebox	4	22' 1" by 8' 7½"	109	1936/7	2227–2335
5	Horsebox	4	As above	30	1938	Un-numbered; carried owners' name.
6	CCT	4	37' 6" by 8'	60	1939	1242–1301
7	CCT	8	52' by 8' 6"	12	1940 1950	1302–5/65–8 1306–64/9–72
8	Special cattle van	6	26' by 7' 10"	30	1944	731–60
9	Horsebox	4	24' 1" by 8' 3"	25	1954	2366–90

Diagram 9 was then adopted for horseboxes built in BR days at Earlestown for the LMR and other Regions and numbered in the LNER series 2391–2510.

Dia 325 As above.

Dia 333 As above.

The vehicles appeared in the building programmes as underframes only: the dairies owned the glass-lined, steel tank barrels.

Non-common user vehicles
Listed by diagram number, these vehicles having a series of their own, as listed below. They are not listed in the appendix. The Covered Combination Trucks had one separate number series, the horseboxes, special cattle vans another, neither being subject to transfer between sections or renumbering.

The East Coast royal train in LNER days
In 1924, the LNER reviewed the two royal trains it had inherited – the seven vehicles of the GER set and the eight-vehicle ECJS train. The recommendations made to the Board by the Traffic Committee were that the GER royal train should be disbanded and its vehicles converted for normal traffic while the East Coast train should be made suitable for all the journeys that royalty were likely to make on the LNER.

A pre-Grouping formation for the East Coast royal train was:

Bogie brake No 82, saloon No 1281, saloon No 3100, royal saloons Nos 395/6, saloon No 3099, saloon No 1280, bogie brake No 132.

Apart from the substitution of No 132 by standard ECJS full brake No 135 in 1922, this was to remain the arrangement for the time that the full royal train was operated.

Brief notes on the royal train vehicles are as follows:

No 395, His Majesty's saloon and No 396,
Her Majesty's saloon
The length over the body ends of both royal saloons was 67 ft. They were built in 1908 but Her Majesty's seems not to have entered service until the following year.

GNR saloons Nos 1280/1281
Built in 1906 as first-class saloons, 58 ft 6 in over body panels.

In their final days, No 41280 was designated 'Saloon for royal household staff and railway officers' and 41281, 'Saloon for royal household staff'.

GNR saloons Nos 3099/3100
With bodies 58 ft 6 in over the panels, built in 1908 for the royal train in which they were used by ladies in waiting and attendants.

Modifications were made to their interiors in 1924/5. In their final days, No 43099 was classed as 'Saloon for equerries and ladies in waiting' and No 43100 as 'Saloon for ladies in waiting and private secretaries'.

Royal train equipment/brake vans
To accompany Nos 395/6. a special 56 ft 6 in bogie brake van was built in 1908. This was No 82 in the ECJS list and was otherwise very similar to the earliest batch of ECJS bogie brakes. Renumbered 109 in 1929.

The royal train after 1924/5
The alterations to the royal train approved by the LNER involved the provision of a bath and dressing room in both Nos 395/6. In addition, all the furniture and furnishings were to be renewed, the interior redecorated and the vehi-

cles' running gear given a general overhaul. Not only that but No 396 was to be converted to Their Majesties' Saloon.

The total value of work approved on 31 July 1924 was £6,750 and White Allom's were engaged for certain interior alterations and the supply of new furnishings and fittings. Other structural and conversion work was the responsibility of York, Doncaster and Stratford shops.

No 396, as Their Majesties saloon, later used by HM the
Queen and HRH the Duke of Edinburgh
This was the first to be dealt with and it went into York Works on 7 August 1924. It was outshopped on 9 October the same year.

The interior was altered to provide a saloon, largely as before, and a private sitting-room in place of the bedroom/dining room while the remaining rooms alongside the internal corridor became the Queen's dressing room and the King's bath and dressing room.

The exterior was revarnished and the King's coat of arms replaced those of Queen Alexandra's and the Queen's ciphers were removed from the balcony doors.

No 395, as HM the Queen's saloon,
later HM the Queen Mother's saloon
No 395 was sent to Doncaster Works for modifications to be carried out in February 1925. Outshopped in the June of that year it was back again for detailed changes to be made in December, finally being released in July 1926.

The attendant's balcony was reduced in length, a new toilet provided next to it, and the dressing room remodelled entirely. A private saloon was created from the bedroom. All windows were replaced with new glass carrying HM Queen Mary's cipher.

The subsequent changes made at Doncaster from the end of 1925 included an increase in the length of the balcony at the expense of the saloon.

Until 1939 the royal train vehicles were stabled at Wellington sidings, Highgate but were then transferred to Doncaster Works.

The royal train to 1961
After the death of King George VI, No 395 became the royal saloon for HM Queen Elizabeth the Queen Mother and for the use of other members of the royal family when running in the complete royal train.

In 1954, it was decided to bring the livery of the East Coast vehicles into line with those of the former LMS royal train. The result was that the LNER royal train vehicles were repainted into the dark claret livery with black and vermilion lining out.

The last time that a complete East Coast royal train was operated was on 8 June 1961 to convey HM the Queen to the wedding of HRH the Duke of Kent at York Minster. Subsequently, all vehicles from the royal train fleet, except Nos 395/6 and 109, were withdrawn and scrapped.

Formation of the royal train
A November 1925 diagram showed the formation and numbering to be:
82J – 1280N – 3100N – 396J – 395 – 3099N – 1281N – 135

A list of the royal train vehicles held at Doncaster Works and dated 17 February 1961 showed the following:
109 – 41280 – 9171 – 396 – 43100 – 135 – 395 – 41281 – 43099

No 9171 was a standard LNER restaurant first (Dia 236), allocated, it would seem, from 1954 for royal train use and painted that year in royal claret livery.

CHAPTER 14
NUMBERING SCHEMES

LNER numbering schemes 1923–1925

It was decided in January 1923 that there would be no central control of passenger rolling stock, with the consequence that the individual sections or Areas would be responsible for their own stock and as a result would maintain their own number series. Instructions were issued during April 1923 concerning the numbering of coaching stock taken into the new organisation. All vehicles would retain their pre-Grouping numbers but a suffix letter would be added to denote the section to which they were allocated and which would be responsible for their maintenance. At this time former GER stock was renumbered, just to confuse matters. New stock, both to the constituent companies' designs and where built to the design of another company, was numbered in the existing series. The suffixes allocated were: East Coast stock – J; North Eastern Railway/Area – Y; North British Railway/Southern Scottish Area – B; Great Northern Railway/section – N; Great Central Railway/section – C; Great Eastern Railway/section – E; Great North of Scotland Railway/Northern Scottish Area – S.

In April 1924 it was decided by the chief mechanical engineer's office that new carriages to the LNER standard designs should be numbered in their own series from 10000 upwards. A suffix letter denoted the section to which they were allocated, using the suffix letters as had been applied to pre-Grouping vehicles and this included the East Coast stock. Therefore, for example, the vehicles forming the GE section Continental boat sets were numbered 10000E etc, the main series of East Coast thirds 10019J–49J and non-vestibuled vehicles for the Southern Scottish Area, 10263B–6B and so on. But the scheme made no distinction as between types or sections and Areas and was not satisfactory in having no real logic. There remains some confusion as to the complete application of the scheme as some vehicles that by rights should have received 100xx numbers did not and others referred to as having them in official documents did not actually carry the numbers. By the spring of 1925 numbers were being allocated to GE section quintuplets in the range from 10362E up to 106xxE.

In April 1925 a new numbering scheme was introduced by the LNER and the 100xx serials were discontinued, renumbering into the replacement series continuing until 1930.

LNER numbering scheme 1925–43

The new scheme was introduced in April 1925 and dispensed with the use of suffixes to pre-Grouping numbers as well as the 100xx series. From now onwards the owning Area or section was denoted by the first digit in the number, this prefix being added to the existing number. This was in similar manner to the locomotive numbering scheme brought in from early 1924 and the effect was as follows:

Section/Area	April 1923 numbers	April 1925 numbers
East Coast	12J/123J	112/1123
North Eastern	12Y/123Y/1123Y	212/2123/21123
Southern Scottish	12B/123B/1123B	312/3123/31123
Great Northern	12N/123N/1123N	412/4123/41123
Great Central	12C/123C/1123C	512/5123/51123
Great Eastern	12E/123E/1123E	612/6123/61123
Northern Scottish	12S/123S	712/7123

The numbers shown above are only for the purposes of illustration.

New standard stock was allocated the lowest available number in the various three, four and five-digit series but other isolated blocks of numbers were used in the five digit ranges. Individual numbers gave no indication of age. Numbers were reused so that destroyed or transferred vehicles' numbers might be allocated to their replacements.

The new scheme included five separate ranges of numbers:

1. Carriages.
2. Passenger brake vans.
3. Non-common user vans.
4. Horseboxes and special cattle vans.
5. Carriage trucks.

The separate series allocated to carriages and to passenger brake vans meant that there was duplication of numbers, as indeed there was with ranges 3–5 above!

Vehicles transferred from one Area or section to another were renumbered in the case of almost all standard LNER vehicles and usually – although not always – with pre-Grouping stock. Vehicles transferred from the East Coast stock to Areas or sections were renumbered. Sometimes vehicles were renumbered by the sections, for instance, the GE section renumbered Dia 27 open thirds used for dining from 61xxx to 61xx and restaurant cars from 61xx to 6xx. The Southern Scottish Area renumbered carriages transferred from first-class to composite.

The full range of numbers for carriages and passenger brake vans was as follows:

East Coast stock
Carriages: 10–19; 100–199; 1000–1999. Also 16431–16533: Nos 16431–3 originally had been 6431–3. Vans 10–19; 100–199; 1000–50.

North Eastern Area
Carriages: 20–29; 200–299; 2000–2999; 20000–26179. Vans 20–29; 200–299; 2000–2500.

Southern Scottish Area
Carriages 30–39; 300–399; 3000–3999; 30000–33000. Vans 30–39; 300–399; 3000–3200.

119

Southern Area – Great Northern section
Carriages 40–49; 400–499; 4000–4999; 40000–49419.
Vans 40–49; 400–499; 4000–4375.

Southern Area – Great Central section
Carriages 50–59; 500–599; 5000–5999; 50000–59349.
Vans 50–59; 500–599; 5000–5482.

Southern Area – Great Eastern section
Carriages 60–69; 600–699; 6000–6999; 60000–65369.
Vans 60–69; 600–699; 6000–6999; 60000–60023.

Northern Scottish Area
Carriages 70–79; 700–799; 7000–7963. Vans 70–79;
700–799, 7000–7159.

When the LNER took over responsibility for passenger
stock from the Midland & Great Northern Joint line after
October 1936, all vehicles, carriages, vans, CCTs and
horseboxes were given numbers in a new 8xxxx series but
remained lettered M&GN. In BR days the carriages were
renumbered within the GE pre-Grouping range.

LNER numbering scheme from 1943

In March 1939 the CGM met the Area Managers and the
central distribution of passenger rolling stock was contemplated, in a similar manner as the central control of freight
stock introduced previously on the LNER. Not all the
Areas were in favour and the outbreak of World War 2
delayed further development until an all-line operating
organisation was set up during 1942. This resulted in the
creation the same year of an office at York under a rolling
stock controller and proposals were submitted in March
1942 for a new all-line system of numbering coaching
stock vehicles. This was revised in August 1942 and a
further plan was submitted under the joint names of the
chief mechanical engineer, the rolling stock controller and
the chairman of the SPM Committee, meeting final
approval late in 1942.

Under the new scheme, LNER standard carriages and
passenger brake vans were renumbered by type and the
new numbers applied in order of the vehicles' diagram
numbers and, within the range allocated to the diagram
number, in the order North Eastern, Southern Scottish,
Great Northern, Great Central, Great Eastern and
Northern Scottish. Pre-Grouping carriages – and the
exceptions noted below! – retained their old numbers.
Unlike the renumbering of the company's locomotives,
there was no set day for the new numbering to be applied;
the process began in 1943 but some vehicles retained their
old numbers until early BR days. East Coast vehicles
retained their numbers, except as indicated below, new
East Coast stock taking 1xx and 1xxx series numbers, also
10–19 in the case of vans.

The numbering blocks were as follows:

Type		Series range	Highest number in 1954
Vestibuled stock			
East Coast*	carriages	100–199	157
		1000–1999	1998
	vans	10–19	19
		100–199	193
		1000–1020	1012

* The triplet restaurant cars numbered in the range
16431–16533 were renumbered 1401–33.

Type	Series range	Highest number in 1954
Catering vehicles	9000–9370	9217
Composite brakes	10000–10370	10174
Firsts and first brakes	11000–11370	11189
Thirds	12000–14225	13985
Third brakes	16000–17112	16873
Composites	18000–18741	18517

Passenger brake vans – vestibuled and non-vestibuled,
TPO vans

	70000–70999	70767

Motor car vans converted from passenger stock in BR days
were numbered 71000–71099

Type	Series range	Highest number in 1954
Non-vestibuled carriages		
Composite brakes	80000–80741	80421
Firsts and first brakes	81000–81370	81084
Thirds	82000–83112	82905
Third brakes	86000–87483	87333
Composites	88000–88741	88616

Gaps were sometimes – although not always – left in the
blocks of numbers where vehicles had been lost to enemy
action.

This was the overall series but the former indication by
Areas and sections was not to disappear completely.
Although there were blocks of numbers allocated in the
main scheme for 'short' vehicles, those vestibuled carriages
on 51 ft underframes, for some reason these were not
taken up with the result that the following retained their
1923–43 scheme numbers:

Open thirds Dia 26 23801/2 At least these were to all
intents and purposes pre-Grouping vehicles!
Composites Dia 190   42759–66
All vestibuled GE 'short' carriages:
6452–6/8/9/61–5/84,   6990/1,   60500–98/600–3,
61634–46/97–793, 61867–85, 61957–74, 62549–70/
98–623/30–49/55–65. 62748–84, 63291–319, 63801/
10–52/65/6/71–86. 63967–94.

In addition, electric multiple units built in LNER days
or to LNER designs were allocated numbers in the old
Areas/sections ranges. The Tyneside stock was renumbered from its former 24xxx series to 29xxx, the
Manchester–Glossop/Hadfield units took 'Great Central'
numbers 59401–8, 59501–8, 59601–8 and the Liverpool
Street–Shenfield stock 'Great Eastern' numbers
65201–92, 65401–92 and 65601–92.

The Tyneside stock had been allocated numbers in the
8xxxx series: 80222–89, 82452–82511 for the passenger
vehicles and the luggage vans, 70552/3.

After nationalisation, LNER carriages and vans
appeared from late 1948 with a prefix 'E' only to their
numbers – for example, E1234, but with the introduction
of BR Standard stock a suffix was added to the numbers to
indicate the Region responsible for maintenance, the
vehicle now becoming E1234E. From 1951 the Scottish
Region received its own allocation of passenger stock so
that former LNER vehicles in that Region's stock became,
for example, SC1234E. LNER vehicles reallocated to
another Region became, for example, M13927E.

APPENDIX 1
LIST OF LNER CARRIAGES

Introduction

THE Appendix lists the following vehicles: 1. All carriages and vans built for the LNER between 1923 and 1948, including cases where vehicles were rebuilt; 2. All carriages and vans built to LNER designs or outlines or rebuilt to same in BR days. It does not include the steam and diesel railcars built for the LNER after 1923 nor the electric multiple units. Details of milk tank wagons, trucks for mobile milk tanks and non-common user vehicles appear in Chapter 13 but not in the Appendix.

Diagrams

At first, the LNER standard vehicles were referred to by the drawing number for the particular type, eg 11857D or 4673N where D = Darlington and N = Doncaster drawing offices. During 1927 the chief mechanical engineer produced a diagram book for LNER standard carriages and vans (including milk tanks, steam and diesel railcars and electric multiple units) which was issued after incorporating comments from the SPMs. This diagram book began with Diagram 1 and numbers were progressively added over the years, a new number being allocated to each new design, until there were three books of diagrams, the highest numbered diagram being 376, this covering the conversion of vehicles in 1956. Some conversions were covered by new diagrams, some were not. Sometimes updated designs were allocated a new number, in other cases a suffix was applied, eg 27A and 27C. Even so, the diagram number was not universally used as a reference, the Carriage Working books often referring to vehicles by number series, eg the GN section book talked of 1241 series SLTs when describing Dia 95 cars.

Appendix – notes on format, listing and codes used:

Column No	Heading in table	Notes
1.	None	V – vestibuled design. No code for non-vestibuled.
2.	Type	( ) denotes articulated vehicles as twin, triplet, quadruplet, quintuplet. Semi-open denotes a vehicle with seating in an open saloon and side corridor compartments. Unclass denotes vehicle with seating used for first or third-class passengers. Lavatory composite – non-vestibuled vehicle with lavatories adjoining compartments Δ End door layout vehicle.
3.	Dia No	All vehicles are to LNER diagrams unless otherwise shown. * following a diagram number indicates that other vehicles were built to this diagram in some other year. After 1923 the bodies of articulated sets were generally on different diagrams, from 1935 the complete set was usually on one diagram.
4.	CBP Year	See Chapter 3 for details of carriage building programmes. The date given is the CBP under which the vehicles were ordered.
5.	Order No	Official LNER order number (Not applicable to vehicles of pre-grouping design).
6.	Dimensions	All overall dimensions, over body end panels and width over the panels.
7.	Compartments/seats	These are shown as 4:32 etc where 4 denotes the number of compartments and 32 the number of seats. † as a suffix denotes seating in open saloons, by number of saloons. Composite vehicles are shown as 2/5:14/48 where 2 is the number of first-class compartments, 5 the number of third-class. A coupé compartment is shown as ½.
8.	Built at	The following codes are used for builders: LNER works – DK Dukinfield; DL Darlington; DR Doncaster; SF Stratford; IV Inverurie; YK York. BR works – EH Eastleigh; Contractors – BHM Birmingham Railway Carriage and Wagon Co; CL Clayton Wagon Co; CM Cammell - Laird, later absorbed into Metropolitan Cammell; CR Cravens; GLO Gloucester RC & W Co Ltd; HN Hurst Nelson & Co Ltd; MET Metropolitan CW & Finance Co Ltd, later absorbed into Metropolitan Cammell; MID Midland RC & W Co Ltd; M-C Metropolitan Cammell Carriage Wagon & Finance Co Ltd; RYP R.Y. Pickering & Co Ltd.
9/10.	Running Numbers	The number first shown in column 9 is that allocated when new. Subsequent numbering is shown by brackets – (1234) for the first change of numbers, [5678] for the second change of number. For pre-Grouping carriages, the 1923 number is shown in column 10. For LNER standard vehicles, the numbers in column 10 are those allocated under the 1943 scheme and were carried until withdrawal.
11.	Notes	All vehicles are electrically lit. §§ Vehicle with gas cooking equipment. BS gangways-vehicle with British Standard gangways. LH left-handed brakes as built, otherwise RH right-handed. DEA destroyed by enemy action in World War 2 and withdrawn. W/O written off as a result of the accident indicated if the location is known. Accident replacement-vehicle built to replace similar written off in an accident or destroyed by fire. PV pressure ventilation and heating, as built. SP steel panelling, after 1945 all vehicles are steel panelled. Trans-vehicle transferred from East Coast to Area or section stock or between Areas and sections.

Carriages completed in 1923 to the LNER Carriage Building Programme for 1923 and to programmes of constituent companies

Type	Dia No	CBP Year	Dimensions	Comps/ Seats	Built At	Running numbers Original	1925	Braking	Notes
First	GC3Q4	1923	56' 0" × 8' 10½"	8: 64	DK	57, 976/7/9/80	557, 5976 etc	V	GCR design
First	NB145B	1923	49' 0" × 8' 6"	7: 56	YK	128–137	31994-32003	V	NER design
Second	¶300	1922	54' 0" × 8' 10"	10: 120	SF	6743/8/62/3/71 6777	same	A	GER design, GE dia No prefixed 14600 as above.
Second	¶300	1923	54' 0" × 8' 10"	10: 120	SF	6780/2/5/6, 6812/4/42/3	same	A	
Third	¶428	1922	54' 0" × 8' 10"	10: 120	SF	60435–40	same	A	GER design
Third	¶428	1923	54' 0" × 8' 10"	10: 120	SF	60447–51/4–6	same	A	GER design
Third	GC3B8	1923	56' 0" × 8' 10½"	9: 108	DK	777, 1218/9, 1596	5777, 51218 etc	V	GCR design
Third	NE178	1922	49' 0" × 8' 6"	8: 80	YK	239/45, 2155/93, 2206/49/58/74, 2290, 2360/83/4, 2643/56, 2761, 2876, 2903/39/83/8/94, 21207, 21471, 21764, 21769/74, 21883/92, 21918, 22014/42/54, 22062, 22115/21/72/6/98		D	NER design
Third	NB143B	1923	49' 0" × 8' 6"	8: 80	YK	2/3/6/12/8/9/26 33/6/40/65/71	32/3/6, 312 etc	V	NER design NER dia No 178 Initially in NE Area stock
Third	GNS 52S	1922	48' 0" × 8' 6"	7: 70	IV	427–30	7427–30	D	GNoS design
Brake third	GC3A10	1923	56' 0" × 8' 10½"	6: 72	DK	1513/4	51513/4	V	GCR design
	GC3A11	1923	56' 0" × 8' 10½"	6: 72	DK	1515–22	51515–22	V	GCR design
Brake third	¶542	1922	54' 0" × 8' 10"	7: 84	SF	62233–8	same	A	GER design
Brake third	¶542	1923	54' 0" × 8' 10"	7: 84	SF	62179–86	same	A	GER design
Brake third	NB146B	1923	49' 0" × 8' 6"	6: 60	YK	711–3/5–8/20/1	3711–3/5–8 etc	V	NER design
Composite	¶237	1922	54' 0" × 8' 10"	4/5≠ 40/60	SF	63231–4/41/2	same	A	GER design ≠ 1st/2nd class
Composite	¶237	1923	54' 0" × 8' 10"	4/5≠ :40/60	SF	63243–6	same	A	GER design ≠ 1st/2nd class
V First sleeping car	EC64B	1923	61' 6" × 9' 0"	10: 10	YK	159J/62J, 172–4/6J	1159/62/72–4/6	V	
V(First sleeper)	EC68*	1923	56' 2½" × 9' 0"	10: 10	DR	198J/200J	1198/1200	V	Twin sleeping cars
(First sleeper)			56' 2½" × 9' 0"	10: 10		199J/201J	1199/1201	V	
(Brake third)	GN218QQ	1922	55' 6¼" × 8' 6"	5: 50	DR	4001/11/21/31	44001/11 etc	V	Twin articulated
(Composite)			55' 6¼" × 8' 6"	3/4 :22/38	DR	4002/12/22/32	44002/12 etc	V	Twin articulated
(Brake third)	GN218RR	1922	55' 6¼" × 8' 6"	5: 50	DR	4041/51/61/71, 4081/91	44041/51 etc	V	Twin articulated
(Composite)			55' 6¼" × 8' 6"	2/5 :14/48	DR	4042/52/62/72, 4082/92	44042/52 etc	V	Twin articulated
Brake third	GN467A	1922	38' 1¼" × 8' 6"	5: 60	DR	8691, 8121¶	48691–4	V	
Third	/GN 467B¶		38' 1¼" × 8' 6"	7: 84	DR	8692, 8122¶	48121–4		
Third			43' 6" × 8' 6"	8: 96	DR	8693, 8123¶			
Third			43' 6" × 8' 6"	8: 96	DR	8694, 8124¶			

Above are London suburban quadruplets   Dia 467A GN type vehicles, Dia 467B LNER type vehicles

Type	Dia No	CBP Year	Dimensions	Comps/ Seats	Built At	Running numbers Original	1925	Braking	Notes
Composite	GN478	1922	43' 6" × 9' 0"	3 3rd/4 1st		8144/54	48144/54	V	86247/51 after 1943
Composite (1st/3rd)	Built DR		43' 6" × 9' 0"	4 1st/3 3rd :40/36		8143/53	48143/53		86246/50
Second			38' 1¼" × 9' 0"	7: 84		8142/52	48142/52		86245/9
Brake second			38' 1¼" × 9' 0"	5: 60		8141/51	48141/51		86244/8

Above are London suburban quadruplets 8141–4 8 ft bogies, 8151–4 8 ft 6 in bogies

Type	Dia No	CBP Year	Dimensions	Comps/ Seats	Built At	Running numbers Original	1925	Braking	Notes
Passenger brake van	GNS62S	1922	48' 0" × 8' 4"	–		131–4	7131–4	D	GNoS design
V Passenger brake van	GC1Y13	1923	56' 0" × 8' 10½"	–		5109–11 (1869–71)	51869–71	D	GCR design

List of LNER design carriages constructed by calendar year 1924–1953

Type	Dia No	CBP Year	Order No	Dimensions	Comps /Seats	Built At	Running numbers Original	1943	Notes

1924 – including carriages to pre-Grouping designs

LNER standard designs – all vacuum braked only

Type	Dia No	CBP Year	Order No	Dimensions	Comps /Seats	Built At	Running numbers Original	1943	Notes
First	46	1924/5	38	60' 0½" × 9' 3"	8: 64	DK	51855/6/7(4288), 51858	88283,82000, 88282/4	51855/7/8 to compos on Dia 283 51856 to all-third on on Dia 46
Third	58	1924/5	39	56' 0½" × 9' 3"	9: 108	DK	51722–5, 51851(41126), 51852–4	82363–6/2/7–9	
V Third	23★	1924/5	47	61' 6" × 9' 0"	8:48	YK	10019–32J (1000–13) [4462–4, 52041–3, 52083/¶/4/5, 3922, 52152/¶/3]	12039–41/92–7, 12019/–/99/60–4	¶1007/12- see Dia 23A. 52152 W/O Transfers 1930–7
V Toilet third	23A	conversion from Dia 23			3: 21	–	1007/12	12109/10	Converted to toilet third 1928, see text. Reverted to Dia 23
Brake third	59	1924/5	40	56' 0½" × 9' 3"	6: 72	DK	5978, 51715–21	86000–7	
V Brake third	40★	1924/5	44	61' 6" × 9' 0"	3: 18	YK	10118–23J (1055–60) [52094–9]	16166–71	Transfers 1935/6
V Composite	7★	1924/5	45	61' 6" × 9' 0"	2½/5 :15/30	YK	10151–6J (1061–6) [64132–4, 7766/81,1066]	18027–9/32/3/6	Transfers 1939/40
V Locker composite	8★	1924/5	46	61' 6" × 9' 0"	2½/4 : 15/24	YK	10168–76J (1067–75) [22253–5, 42800–5]	18037–44/–	Transfers 1938
V Brake composite	34★	1924/5	48	61' 6" × 9' 0"	2/2 :12/12	YK	10177/8J (1076/7) [52180/1]	10020/1	Transfers 1936/7
V First-class sleeping car	17★	1924/5	37	61' 6" × 9' 0"	10: 10	DR	10194–7J (1147/9, 1235/7)	1147/9, 1235/7	EC Dia 64B
V(Restaurant first)	12	1924/5	33	55' 2½" × 9' 0"	2† 36	DR	16431/41/51/61/71	1401/4/7/10/3	Triplet restaurant car sets
(Kitchen car)	13★			41' 0" × 9' 0"	–	DR	16432/42/52/62/72	1402/5/8/11/4	
(restaurant third)	14			55' 2½" × 9' 0"	2† 42	DR	16433/43/53/63/73	1403/6/9/12/5	
Brake third	72B★	1923	–	38' 1¼" × 8' 6"	5: 60	DR	8131, 8811/21/31/41/51/61/71		Later 48131–4, 48811–4 etc
Third	73★			38' 1¼" × 8' 6"	7: 84	DR	8132, 8812/22/32/42/52/62/72		1943 Nos 86360–3, 86364–7,
Third	74★			43' 6" × 8' 6"	8: 96	DR	8133, 8813/23/33/43/53/63/73		86368–71, 86372–5,
Third	75★			43' 6" × 8' 6"	8: 96	DR	8134, 8814/24/34/44/54/64/74		86376–9, 86380–3,

Above are London GN section suburban quadruplets Dias 72B, 73–75 also referred to as GN Dia 467B

86384–7, 86388–91

Type	Dia No	CBP Year	Order No	Dimensions	Comps /Seats	Built At	Running numbers Original	1943	Notes
Composite (1st/3rd)	71★	1923	–	43' 6" × 9' 0"	3 3rd/4 1st :36/40	DR	8894/904/14/24/34/44/54/64		Later 48894–1, 48904–1 etc
Composite (1st/3rd)	70★			43' 6" × 9' 0"	4 1st/3 3rd :40/36	DR	8893/903/13/23/33/43/53/63		1943 Nos 86255–2, 86259–56, 86263–60,
						DR			
Second	69★			38' 1¼" × 9' 0"	7: 84	DR	8892/902/12/22/32/42/52/62		86267–4, 86271–68, 86275–2, 86279–6,
Brake second	68B★			38' 1¼" × 9' 0"	5: 60	DR	8891/901/11/21/31/41/51/61		86283–80

Above are London GN section suburban quadruplets Dias 68B–71 also referred to as GN Dia 478

Type	Dia No	CBP Year	Order No	Dimensions	Comps /Seats	Built At	Running numbers Original	1943	Notes
V Bogie brake van	43★	1924/5	43	61' 6" × 9' 0"	–	YK	10233–9J (140[5270]/1–146)		70017/20/–/2–5

Vehicles to pre-Grouping designs

Type	Dia No	CBP Year	Dimensions	Seats	Built At	Running numbers Original	1925	Braking	Notes
V Third saloon	NB151B	1923	50' 6" × 8' 6"	3† 43	YK	165B/166B	3165/6	V	NER design
First	GC3Q4	1923	56' 0" × 8' 10½"	8: 64	DK	975C	5975	V	GCR design
V Open first	NB234B	1923	53' 6" × 9' 0"	2† 36	YK	1B, 4B, 12B	31867/70/8	V	NER design

Type	Dia No	CBP Year	Dimensions	Seats	Built At	Running numbers Original	1925	Braking	Notes
V Open first	NE204	1923	53' 6" × 9' 0"	2† 36	YK		2222/2976	V	NER design
V Brake first	NE200	1923	53' 6" × 9' 0"	2: 12	YK		22195, 23583	V	NER design
Second	300¶	1923	54' 0" × 8' 10"	10: 120	SF		6844/5	A	GER design
Third	428¶	1923	54' 0" × 8' 10"	10: 120	SF		60452/3	A	GER design
Third	GC3B8	1923	56' 0" × 8' 10½"	9: 108	DK	1659C/1660C	51659/60	V	GCR design
V Open third	LNER 26	1924	54' 0" × 8' 9"	2† 42	SF		23801/2	D	GER outline Ex- ambulance
V Third	445¶	1923	53' 6" × 8' 6"	7: 56	YK	2101E–2127E	61581–61607	D	NER design ¶ GE dia No
V Open third	NB150B	1923	53' 6" × 9' 0"	2† 42	YK	181B	3181	V	NER design NER dia 155
V Open third	NE155	1923	53' 6" × 9' 0"	2† 42	YK		2161, 2945	D	NER design
V Third	NE193	1923	53' 6" × 8' 6"	7: 56	YK		2239, 2354, 2378, 2486, 21035, 21598, 22085/93	V	NER design
Brake third	542¶	1923	54' 0" × 8' 10"	7: 84	SF		62187/8	A	GER design
V Brake third	NE209	1923	53' 6" × 8' 6"	3: 24	YK		2964, 21121	D	NER design
							22161, 22201	D	22161 W/O Eaglescliffe 1933
V Brake third	555¶	1923	53' 6" × 8' 6"	3: 24	YK	1051E–1060E	62504–13	D	NER design
Composite	237¶	1923	54' 0" × 8' 10"	4/5 : 40/60	SF		63151/75, 63247–54	A	GER design 1st/2nd composite
V Composite	249¶	1923	53' 6" × 8' 6"	2/5 :12/40	YK	861E–868E	63761–8	D	NER design
V Composite	GNS77S	1923	50' 6" × 8' 6"	3/3 : 18/24	YK	8S/11S	7876/7	D	NER design
Brake composite	NB153B	1923	57' 0 " × 8' 6"	2/4 : 16/40	YK	68B/74B/75B, –/82B/88B	32335/41/2/5, 32349/55	V	NER design
V Brake composite	NB256B	1923	58' 6 " × 8' 6"	2/3 : 12/18	YK	89–94	32356–61	V	NER design NER Dia 154
V Brake composite	NE174	1923	53' 6 " × 8' 6"	2/3 : 12/24	YK		2482/9, 22045	V	NER design

Type	Dia No	CBP Year	Order No	Dimensions	Comps /Seats	Built At	Running numbers Original	1943	Notes
1925 All vehicles vacuum fitted except those shown as ✷which were dual fitted as built									
First	47★	1924/5	42	51' 1½" × 9' 0"	7: 56	SF	10248–62B (31881/3/4/6–9 31893–5/7–9, 31902/3)	81000–12/–/3	31902 altered to composite on Dia 189 in 1935 and renumbered 32546 (88142)
V Open first	4	1924/5	68	61' 6" × 9' 0"	2† 42	DR	1220/1 10005Y (21509)	11035/6 11034	
V Open first	3	1924/5	59	61' 6" × 9' 3"	2† 42	SF	10008E (688) [52101]	11033	Continental boat set
			60				10009E (689) [31890]	11032	Continental boat set
V First	1★	1924/5	59	61' 6" × 9' 3"	7: 42	SF	10000/1E (6441/2) [4146/7]	11016/7	Continental boat set
			60				10002–4E (6443–5)	11022–4	Continental boat set
V First brake	30	1924/5	69	61' 6" × 9' 0"	3: 18	DR	10010Y (21130)	11045	RH
V Open second	22	1924/5	59	61' 6" × 9' 3"	2† 48	SF	10014/5E (695/6)	12000/1	Continental boat set
			60				10016/7E (6986/7) [2275/92]¶	13673/4	Continental boat set ¶Later converted to Dia 225, see text
V Second	21	1924/5	59	61' 6" × 9' 3"	8: 48	SF	10011E (6983) [2273]	12244	Continental boat set
			60				10012E (6984) [4172]	–	2273, 6985 later on Dia 115
							6985	12686	
V Second brake	35	1924/5	60	61' 6" × 9' 3"	4: 24	SF	10018E (62514)	–	Continental boat set
Third	56★	1924/5	49	51' 1½" × 9' 0"	8: 80	YK	10263–82B	82064–83	

Type	Dia No	CBP Year	Order No	Dimensions	Comps /Seats	Built At	Running numbers Original	1943	Notes
							(3671/2/5–9/81, 3688/90–3/5–8, 3723–5)		
							320/35/50/5/66/7, 3109/25/6/51/80, 3194/7, 3219/55/7/68, 3271/6/88	82023–42	
							10303–23Y		≠ For 1943 numbers see 82019 etc
							(22358, 21234[61891], 22323, 21169, 22199, 21603, 22353[61892], 22193[776], 21088/11, 22048, 22476, 22291[787], 21713, 21656, 22419[794], 22207[796], 22281, 21873, 21218, 22183)		
								82019/141/018/04/16/09/142/7, 82003/1/14/21//148/012/11, 82149/50, 82017/13/5/15	
			–			CL	22046/9/55/65/96 (60617–21)	82110–2/–/3	≠
			–			CR	22135/47, 22200/19 22242/79/92, 22348/59, 22396/450/551, 22940/1/3, (31028/2/30/4/42/40/15, 61889, 22359, 31035, 60622/3, 61890, 22941, 775)	82099/8/100/1/4/3/97/102 82139, 82020, 82114/5/40, 82022, 82146	≠
			–			RYP	3470/1/3–5	82059–63	
V Open third	27*	1924/5	75	61' 6" × 9' 0"	2† 48	DK	2389, 3315, 21772, 22170, 10113Y (22315)	12127–31 12128–30	
V Third	23*	1924/5	57	61' 6" × 9' 0"	8:48	YK	10033–68J, 1050/1 (1014–51) [–/42517–25, 31156–77, 52182, 4465–8/71/2/4/6]	12060–8, 12020–38/42–9	
								1014 W/O Welwyn 1935	Transfers 1930–8
							7485–8 (3683–6)	12015–8	
									Transferred CBP 1928/9
							10075/6Y (21127, 22347)	12004/12	
							21001/15, 21501, 22102/56, 22169/88/92, 22285/355/90	12002/3/5–11/3–14	≠
							5500–9	12071–3/–/5–80	
Brake third	62	1924/5	62	51' 1½" × 9' 0"	5: 50	YK	10324–47B (3477/9/80/3/4, 3486/7/91/2/4/7, 3501/52/70/92/4, 3497–9, 3601/2/4, 3605/14)	86018–41	
Brake third	62	1924/5	–	51' 1½" × 9' 0"	5: 50	CR	3616/9/22/7–9	86042–7	
V Brake third	40*	1924/5	70	61' 6" × 9' 0"	3:24	DR	10132–4C (5763–5) 10136Y (1112) [4935] 2223/4, 2243[1113] then 4939 62537–40 4740/53/4/7/8/64/79/82	16160–2 RH 16157 ≠ 16137/8/58 ≠ 16173/4/–/5 ≠ 16148–55	
V Brake third	38	1924/5	59	61' 6" × 9' 3"	4: 32	SF	62515	–	Continental boat set
			74		4: 24	SF	10149J (2243)	16120	
							10150J (1113) [22058]	16121	
							The transfers of Dia 40 10136Y and 2243 to East Coast stock took place in 1926, as exchanges for Dia 38 10149 and 1113.		
Composite	49*	1924/5	63	51' 1½" × 9' 0"	3/4 : 19/33	SF	32284/96, 32304/28	88000–3	
V First-class sleeping car	17*	1924/5	37	61' 6" × 9' 0"	10: 10	DR	10198–201J (1238/61/8/9) 1208–10	1208–10/38 1261/8/9	EC Dia 64B

Type	Dia No	CBP Year	Order No	Dimensions	Comps /Seats	Built At	Running numbers Original	1943	Notes
V Restaurant sleeping car	20★	1924/5	52	61' 6" × 9' 0"	6 berths /2 3rd compts¶	DR	10205–9J (1088–92)	1707–10/39	¶ conv to sleeping berths 1929
V Restaurant kitchen car	10★	1924/5	71	61' 6" × 9' 0"	1† 18	DR	22251	9001	§§
V Restaurant kitchen car (first-class)	10A★	1924/5	59 60	61' 6" × 9' 3"	1† 18	SF	10211E (676) [2865] 10212E (677) [2866]	9002 9003	§§ Continental set §§ Continental set Transfers 1935, became unclassed.
V Restaurant kitchen car (third-class)	16	1924/5	72	61' 6" × 9' 0"	2† 24	DR	10213Y (22206) 10214J (1224) [22265] then 52040–1931 10215J (1225)	9063 9064 9065	§§ §§ To NEA 1928 §§
V Restaurant pantry car(third-class)	15	1924/5	73	61' 6" × 9' 3"	2† 39	DR	1257 (2331) 1258	9061 9062	
Brake third	72★	1925/6	–	38' 1¼" × 8' 6"	5: 60	CL/	48321/31/41/51	86316/20/4/8	¶ Two trains CL, two MID
Third	73★			38' 1¼" × 8' 6"	7: 84	¶MID	48322/32/42/52	86317/21/5/9	
Third	74★			43' 6" × 8' 6"	8: 96		48323/33/43/53	86318/22/6/30	
Third	75★			43' 6" × 8' 6"	8: 96		48324/34/44/54	86319/23/7/31	

Above are London GN section suburban quadruplets

Type	Dia No	CBP Year	Order No	Dimensions	Comps /Seats	Built At	Running numbers Original	1943	Notes
Composite (1st/3rd)	71★	1925/6	–	43' 6" × 9' 0"	3 3rd/4 1st :36/40	CL/ ¶MID	48384/94/404/974	86207/11/5/9	¶ Two trains CL, two MID
Composite (1st/3rd)	70★			43' 6" × 9' 0"	4 1st/3 3rd :40/36		48383/93/403/973	86206/10/4/8	
Second	69★			38' 1¼" × 9' 0"	7: 84		48382/92/402/972	86205/9/13/7	
Brake second	68★			38' 1¼" × 9' 0"	5: 60		48381/91/401/971	86204/8/12/6	

Above are London GN section suburban quadruplets

Type	Dia No	CBP Year	Order No	Dimensions	Comps /Seats	Built At	Running numbers Original	1943	Notes
(Composite)#	76	1924/5	–	43' 6" × 9' 3"	4/3 : 40/36		63001/3/5/7/9/11, 63013/5/7/9/21/3, 63025/7/9/31/3/5, 63037/9/41/3/5/7, 63049/51/3/5/7/9, 63061/3/5/7/9/71, 63073/5/7/9/81/3, 63085/7/9/91/3/5, 63097/9/101/3/5/7, 63109/11/3/5	86396/401/6/11/6/21, 86426/31/6/41/6/51, 86456/61/6/71/6/81, 86486/91/6/501/6/11, 86516/21/6/31/6/41, 86546/51/6/61/6/71, 86576/81/6/91/6/601, 86606/11/6/–/6/31, 86636/41/6/51/6/61, 86666/71/6/81	
(Second)	77	1924/5	–	43' 6" × 9' 3"	8: 96		6501–58	86397/402/7/12/7/22, 86427/32/7/42/7/52, 86457/62/7/72/7/82, 86487/92/7/502/7/12, 86517/22/7/32/7/42, 86547/52/7/62/7/72, 86577/82/7/92/7/602, 86607/12/7/–/27/32, 86637/42/7/52/7/62, 86667/72/7/82	
(Composite)¶	78	1924/5	–	43' 6" × 9' 3"	4/4 : 48/48		63000/2/4/6/8/10, 63012/4/6/8/20/2, 63024/6/8/30/2/4, 63036/8/40/2/4/6, 63048/50/2/4/6/8, 63060/2/4/6/8/70, 63072/4/6/8/80/2, 63084/6/8/90/2/4, 63096/8/100/2/4/6, 63108/10/2/4	86398/403/8/13/8/23, 86428/33/8/43/8/53, 86458/63/8/73/8/83, 86488/93/8/503/8/13, 86518/23/8/33/8/43, 86548/53/8/63/8/73, 86578/83/8/93/8/603, 86608/13/8/–/28/33, 86638/43/8/53/8/63, 86668/73/8/83	
(Third)	79	1924/5	–	43' 6" × 9' 3"	8: 96		60000–57	86399/404/9/14/9/24, 86429/34/9/44/9/54, 86459/64/9/74/9/84, 86489/94/9/504/9/14, 86519/24/9/34/9/44, 86549/54/9/64/9/74, 86579/84/9/94/9/604, 86609/14/9/–/29/34, 86639/44/9/54/9/64, 86669/74/9/84	

Type	Dia No	CBP Year	Order No	Dimensions	Comps /Seats	Built At	Running numbers Original	1943	Notes
(Brake third)	80	1924/5	–	43' 6" × 9' 3"	6: 72		62000–57	86400/5/10/5/20/5, 86430/5/40/5/50/5, 86460/5/70/5/80/5, 86490/5/500/5/10/5, 86520/5/30/5/40/5, 86550/5/60/5/70/5, 86580/5/90/5/600/5, 86610/5/20/–/30/5, 86640/5/50/5/60/5, 86670/5/80/5	

Builders: CL Six trains – 63001–23 odd Nos; 6501–12; 63000–22 even Nos; 60000–11; 62000–11.
CR Five trains – 63025–43 odd Nos; 6513–22; 63024–42 even Nos; 60012–21; 62012–21.
HN Three trains – 63045–55 odd Nos; 6523–8; 63044–54 even Nos; 60022–7; 62022–7.
MET Seven trains – 63057–83 odd Nos; 6529–42; 63056–82 even Nos; 60028–41; 62028–41.
MID Five trains – 63085–103 odd Nos; 6543–52; 63084–102 even Nos; 60042–51; 62042–51.
RYP Three trains – 63105–15 odd Nos; 6553–8; 63104–14 even Nos; 60052–7; 62052–7.

Dias 76–80 London GE section suburban quintuplets Air-braked Into traffic with numbers in series 10362E–10652E
First/second-class, later all-third ¶ Second/third-class, later all-third.

Type	Dia No	CBP Year	Order No	Dimensions	Comps /Seats	Built At	Running numbers Original	1943	Notes
V Bogie brake van	43★	1924/5	59 60	61' 6" × 9' 0"	–	SF	6724 10246E (6725)	70018 70019	Continental boat sets

Vehicles to pre-Grouping designs

Type	Dia No	CBP Year	Dimensions	Seats	Built At	Running numbers Original	1925	Braking	Notes
V Composite	249¶	1923	53' 6" × 8' 6"	2/5 :12/40	YK	869E–880E	63769–80	D	NER design ¶ GE Dia

Type	Dia No	CBP Year	Order No	Dimensions	Comps /Seats	Built At	Running numbers Original	1943	Notes
1926 All vehicles vacuum fitted except those shown as ≠ which were dual fitted as built									
First	47★	1925/6	–	51' 1½" × 9' 0"	7: 56	MID	31904/7– 10/5/7/8/20	81014–22	
V First	2★	1925/6	109	61' 6" × 9' 0"	7: 42	DR	51651/2	11029/30	
Third	56★	1924/5	–	51' 1½" × 9' 0"	8: 80	BHM GLO	61616–25 3353/9/63/ 71/85/8/91, 3392, 3400/53	82116–25 82049–58	≠
						HN MET MET	3327/40/3/6/7 3326 21086, 21476/96, 21512, 21621	82044–8 82043 82002/6/7/8/10	
							21010/2, 21163, 21477/92, 22104/9/14/ 32/58/9/74, 22210 (3839/60, 3771, 3803/21/52, 3777, 3805/66/27/54/ 79/3781)	82091/4/84/7/9/92/85 82088/95/90/3/6/86	
						≠	21475, 21597, 22152, 22256/72 (4496/9, 4500–2)	82105–9	
							21009, 21136/67, 21469, 21718, 22124/55/71, 22220/49/52/89/95	82126/34/6/1/27/32, 82133/28/37/8/29, 82135/30/43–5	

Type	Dia No	CBP Year	Order No	Dimensions	Comps /Seats	Built At	Running numbers Original	1943	Notes
							(61856/64/86/61/ 57/62/3/58/87/8, 61859/65/60) 21175, 22264/99 (765/73/4)		
V Open third	27★	1925/6	110	61'6"×9'0"	3†48	DK	5524/5/7/8	12132–5	
V Third	23★	1924/5	57	61'6"× 9'0"	8:64	YK	5516–20	–/12087/–/8/9	
		1925/6	111			DK	61626–33	12101–8	≠
							4819/25/8/35/6	12050–4	
							1194/5 (42532/3)	12069/70	Trans 1935/6
							5510–5	12081–3/5/6	
V Locker third	24	1924/5	51	61'6"×9'0"	7:56	YK	1052–4 (750/1/3)	12111–3	Trans 1939
V Third	25	1925/6	107	52'6"×9'0"	7:56	SF	61634–46		
Brake third	63	1925/6	–	51'1½"×9'0"	5:50	CR	62543–8	≠	86878–81, as altered to Dia 254, 1938; 86048/9
Brake third	64	1925/6	–	51'1½"×9'0"	4:40	CL	3631/2/4/5/7/8/41/3 21002/3/5/6/8 (62668–71, 7571¶)	86050–7 86058–61, ¶86997	¶Converted to Dia 320, 1942 and reno 7571.
Brake third	65★	1925/6	149	51'1½"×9'3"	4:40	YK	317/29/42/3/ 52/62/79/85/99, 3107/20/72/7/84/ 5/98, 3216/31/3¶, 3287, 3331	86063–75/–/6–9	¶3233 to Dia 317 1940
Brake third	66	1925/6	–	51'1½"×9'0"	3:30	BHM	3645/7/51/3/4/6–8/61/3/5/7/8/70	86158–71	
V Brake third	36★	1925/6	114	61'6"×9'0"	6:48	DR	5750–2/62, 7631/62	16000–5	
V Brake third	39	1925/6	112	61'6"×9'0"	4:32	YK	4788/90/3/5, 4800/13/5	16123–9	
V Brake third	40★	1924/5	70	61'6"×9'0"	3:24	DR	5741–9	16130/–/1–4/–/5/6	
							62541/2	16176/7	≠
		1925/6	112			YK	22154, 22202	16139/40	
							112–5/38– 40/2/3/5–8/50 (52044/5, 755/63, 52100, 3934, 52091, 3938/95, 31003, 31198/9, 31201, 4934)	16163/4/78/9 16172/41/65/42–7, 16156	
V Brake third	42	1925/6	108	52'6"× 9'0"	3:24	SF	62549/50		≠
V Composite	6★	1925/6	65	61'6"×9'0"	3½ /4: 21/32	YK	63792–800	18008–16	≠
			115				51869/70	18000/1	
V Composite	7★	1925/6	65	61'6"×9'0"	2½ /5: 15/40	YK	7878/9 (32376/7)	18017/8	
			115				51871	18019	
							151/4/5/6/7/8/62/3/83 (789, 52046/7, 790, 58100–3, 64131)	18030/20/1/31/22–5, 18026	Transfers 1930–9
							7880/1	18034/5	
V Locker composite	8★	1925/6	116	61'6"×9'0"	2½ /4: 15/32	DR	184/6/8/9 (7762–5)	18046–9	Transfers 1938/9
Brake composite	54	1925/6	–	51'1½"×9'0"	2/2 : 16/20	CL	32364/7	80012/3	
V Brake composite	31	1925/6	66	61'6"×9'0"	2/4 : 12/32	YK	5547–9	10000–2	
			117			DR	5550–2	10003–5	
V Brake composite	33	1924/5	66	61'6"×9'0"	2/3 : 12/24	YK	22287, 32279	10014/5	
V Brake composite	34★	1924/5	66	61'6"×9'0"	2/2 : 12/12	YK	1078–87 (42881/2, 2328, 1081¶/2¶, 24680¶, 42883, 24681¶, 1086¶, 24683¶)	10017/8/6, 16852¶, 16853¶/47¶, 10019, 16848¶/9¶,16850¶	¶Converted to third brake from 1942.
			117			DR	1098¶/9, 1105/10/25/6	16851¶, 10027–31	
Composite	49★	1925/6	–	51'1½"×9'0"	3/4	MID	32331/6/62/3	88004–7	

Type	Dia No	CBP Year	Order No	Dimensions	Comps /Seats	Built At	Running numbers Original	1943	Notes
V Composite sleeping car	20★	1925/6	121	61' 6" × 9' 0"	: 19/33 6 berths /2 3rd compts¶	DR	63782–91 1093–7	88008–16/– 1776, 1848/89/–, 1097	≠ ¶ conv to sleeping berths 1929
V (First-class sleeping car) V (First-class sleeping car)	18 18A 19	1925/6	122	56' 2½" × 9' 0"	10 berths 9 berths 10 berths	DR	1202/33 1204 1203/5/34	Sleeping car twins: 1202/3, 1204/5, 1233/4 1204 with shower bath	
Brake third	72★	1925/6	–	38' 1¼" × 8' 6"	5: 60	MET	48361/71	86332/6	¶ One set MET
Third	73★			38' 1¼" × 8' 6"	7: 84	/MID¶	48362/72	86333/7	one set MID
Third	74★			43' 6" × 8' 6"	8: 96		48363/73	86334/8	
Third	75★			43' 6" × 8' 6"	8: 96		48364/74	86335/9	
Above are London GN section suburban quadruplets									
Composite (1st/3rd)	71★	1925/6	–	43' 6" × 9' 0"	3 3rd/4 1st :36/40	MET /MID¶	48984/94	86220/4	¶ One set MET one set MID
Composite (1st/3rd)	70★			43' 6" × 9' 0"	4 1st/3 3rd :40/36		48983/93	86221/5	
Second	69★			38' 1¼" × 9' 0"	7: 84		48982/92	86222/6	
Brake second	68★			38' 1¼" × 9' 0"	5: 60		48981/91	86223/7	
Above are London GN section suburban quadruplets									
Passenger brake van	43★	1924/5	67	61' 6" × 9' 0"	–	YK	160–162 7135–7 (342–4)	70026–8 70000–2	Transferred 1928/9 CBP
V Passenger brake van	44	1925/6	119	56' 6" × 9' 0"	–	DK	153–9	70029–35	
Passenger brake van	67★	1925/6	126	51' 1½" × 9' 0"	–	DK	31, 6686–90	70070–5	≠
General van four-wheeled	86★	1925/6	125	32' 0" × 8' 11½"	–	SF	6231–52	70079–70100	≠

1927 All vehicles vacuum fitted except those shown as ★which were dual fitted as built

Type	Dia No	CBP Year	Order No	Dimensions	Comps /Seats	Built At	Running numbers Original	1943	Notes
First	48★	1926/7	148	51' 1½" × 9' 3"	7: 56	YK	31875/7, 31901/11/62, 31985, 32024/ 30/1/63, 32076/ 78/82/93, 32113, 32128/9/32/9/ 49/51 6446–51	81025–8/36–40/–, /81041–3/–/4/–/–, 81045/–/–/6 81048–53	

32063/93, 32128/9/39/49 converted to composites on Dia 189 in 1935 and renumbered 32547–52 (88142–7)

Type	Dia No	CBP Year	Order No	Dimensions	Comps /Seats	Built At	Running numbers Original	1943	Notes
V First	2★	1925/6	109	61' 6" × 9' 0"	7: 42	DR	1130/1 (4151, 52048)	11028/31	Trans 1930
V Brake first	29★	1926/7	152	61' 6" × 9' 3"	5: 30	DR	4203/4/6	11042–4	LH
Second	55	1926/7	–	51' 1½" × 9' 3"	8: 80	GLO	6988/9	82360/1	Later thirds to Dia 57
Third	57★	1926/7	–	51' 1½" × 9' 3"	8: 80	CL	3819/20/4/ 9/30/2/3/5–7	82268–77	
						CR	61647–86 311/28/31/89, 3169/79/86, 3195/6, 3217	82310-49 82168/70/1/9/286, 82287/191/5/6, 82203	
						GLO	21047, 21143/78, 21622, 21872, 22052, 22318/85 (3749, 21143, 3806, 21622, 21872, 3831, 3858, 3791)	82303, 82153, 82264, 82155/7, 82305, 82285, 82304	
						HN	21103/15, 21867, 22145/87, 22221/32/88, 22331/43 (52027, 21115, 52028, CLC 573, CLC 572, 52029, CLC 571, 52030, CLC 570, 22343)	82306, 82152, 82307, M14961E, M14960E, 82308,/–, 82309, M14958E, 82162	

Type	Dia No	CBP Year	Order No	Dimensions	Comps /Seats	Built At	Running numbers Original	1943	Notes
						MET	3235/51, 3338/58/68/9, 3642, 3722/53/8–60/2–8/70/2–6, 3778–80/2–98, 3801/4/12–4	82205/8/17–21/5–9 82230–42	
						RYP	21118/25, 22101 (3767/95, 3808) 3840–5/7	82235/58, 82302 82278–84	
		1927/8	205			YK	21022, 21206, 21714, 22127/68, 22290, 22325/60 /1/70/87	82151/4/6/8–61, 82163/7/6/4	≠
V Third	23*	1925/6	111	61' 6"X 9" 0"	8: 64	YK	4840/4/9/55/8, 5521/2	12055–9/90/1	
V Open third	28*	1926/7 1927/8 1926/7	–	61' 6¼" × 9' 3"	3† 64	MET	42463/4/6/72/6 42481/2/9/90 5529–33	12223–7 12228–31 12232–6	All-steel
Brake third	61*	1926/7	161	51' 1½" × 9' 3"	5: 50	DK	3745/6/8/50–2/4–6	86008–16	
Brake third	65*	1926/7	149	51' 1½" × 9' 3"	4: 40	YK	21633, 21790 (7572¶/3) Transfers 1935 3644, 3731–4/6/7/8/41–3 62571–90 Detail differences from rest on this Dia	86984¶, 86156 ¶ converted to Dia 317 in 1940 86116–26 86134–53	
		1927/8	207			YK	22313, 22369 (7574) 3275/7/9/83, 3332/3/6, 3341/4/60/2/5/ 73/7/83/4, 3387, 3408/29/48, 3454	86062, 86157 Transferred 1935 86080–3/6–94, 86096–8, 86100, 86106–8/10	
V Brake third	37*	1926/7	153	61' 6"X 9" 3"	5: 40	DR	4706–8/19	16006–8/–	
V Brake third	41*	1926/7	146 173	52' 6"X 9" 3"	3: 24	YK DR	62556–70 62551–5		62569 DEA
Lav Composite	50*	1926/7	150	51' 1½" × 9' 3"	3/4 : 19/33	YK	63266–75 32344/73, 32436/54/6/8	88069–76/–/7 88019/22/3/5/7/9	
			175			DR	63276–90	88078–92	
Composite	51*	1926/7	176	51' 1½" × 9' 3"	4/3 : 32/30	SF	32459–67	88104–12	
V Composite	9*	1926/7	174	52' 6"X 9" 3"	2/4½ : 12/36	DR	63801/2		63802 withdrawn by 1943
Brake composite	52	1926/7	165	51' 1½" × 9' 3"	2/3 : 16/30	DK	32468–75	80000–7	
Brake composite	53	1926/7	177	51' 1½" × 9' 3"	2/2 : 16/20	SF	32476–9	80008–11	
V Brake composite	32*	1926/7	178	61' 6"X 9" 3"	2/3 : 12/24	DR	480/1	10011/2	
V First-class sleeping car	17*	1925/6	118	61' 6" × 9' 0"	10 berths	DR	1316–9		
V Restaurant kitchen car (first-class)	10*	1925/6	120	61' 6" × 9' 0"	1† 18	DR	681 (2867)	9000	§§ Transferred 1935, became unclassed
Brake third	72*	1927/8	–	38' 1¼" × 8' 6"	5: 60	MID	47921/31/41/51	86300/4/8/12	
Third	73*			38' 1¼" × 8' 6"	7: 84		47922/32/42/52	86301/5/9/13	
Third	74*			43' 6" × 8' 6"	8: 96		47923/33/43/53	86302/6/10/4	
Third	75*			43' 6" × 8' 6"	8: 96		47924/34/44/54	86303/7/11/5	

Above are London GN section suburban quadruplets

Type	Dia No	CBP Year	Order No	Dimensions	Comps /Seats	Built At	Running numbers Original	1943	Notes
Composite (1st/3rd)	71*	1927/8	–	43' 6" × 9' 0"	3 3rd/4 1st :36/40	MID	47964/74/84/94	86191/5/9, 86203	
Composite (1st/3rd)	70*	1927/8	–	43' 6" × 9' 0"	4 1st/3 3rd :40/36		47963/73/83/93	86190/4/8, 86202	
Second	69*	1927/8	–	38' 1¼" × 9' 0"	7: 84		47962/72/82/92	86189/3/7, 86201	

Type	Dia No	CBP Year	Order No	Dimensions	Comps /Seats	Built At	Running numbers Original	1943	Notes
Brake second	68*	1927/8	–	38' 1¼" × 9' 0"	5: 60		47961/71/81/91	86188/2/6, 86200	

Above are London GN section suburban quadruplets

Type	Dia No	CBP Year	Order No	Dimensions	Comps /Seats	Built At	Running numbers Original	1943	Notes
(Composite)#	81*	1927/8	–	43' 6" × 9' 3"	4/3 : 40/36	CL	63120–3	86686/91/6/701	
(Second)	82*	1927/8	–	43' 6" × 9' 3"	8: 96	CL	6560/59/62/1	86687/92/7/702	
(Composite)¶	83*	1927/8	–	43' 6" × 9' 3"	4/4 : 48/48	CL	63116–9	86688/93/8/703	
(Third)	84*	1927/8	–	43' 6" × 9' 3"	8: 96	CL	60058–61	86689/94/9/704	
(Brake third)	85*	1927/8	–	43' 6" × 9' 3"	6: 72	CL	62058–61	86690/5/700/5	

Above are London GE section suburban quintuplets Air-braked # First/second-class, later all-third. ¶ Second/third-class, later all-third.

Type	Dia No	CBP Year	Order No	Dimensions	Comps /Seats	Built At	Running numbers Original	1943	Notes
Passenger brake van	67*	1925/6	126	51' 1½" × 9' 0"	–	DK	6691–3	70076–8	≠
V Passenger brake van	45*	1926/7	–	61' 6"× 9' 0"	–	CM	163–170	70039–45/–	All-steel
General van four-wheeled	86*	1925/6	125	32' 0" × 8' 11½"	–	SF	6253–82	70101–30	≠
Milk van four-wheeled	87	1926/7	160	32' 0" × 8' 11½"	–	SF	6283–96	–/70132–6/–/8–44	

1928 All vehicles vacuum fitted except those shown as ≠ which were dual fitted as built

Type	Dia No	CBP Year	Order No	Dimensions	Comps /Seats	Built At	Running numbers Original	1943	Notes
First	48*	1927/8	206	51' 1½" × 9' 3"	7: 56	DK	31872/3, 31912/4	81023/4/9/30	
V Semi-open first	5*	1926/7	151	61' 6" × 9' 3"	5† 42	DR	4231/2/4	11039–41	
V First	1*	1928/9	245	61' 6" × 9' 3"	7: 42	YK	441 31940–3	11015 11011–4	
V Brake first	136	1927/8	191	61' 6" × 9' 3"	3: 18	YK	4162/3	11046/7	
Third	57*	1927/8	205	51' 1½" × 9' 3"	8: 80	YK	21177, 22370/61 325/38/49/59/ 61/8/9, 376, 3101/31/46/9/53, 3154/60/2/74/92, 3201 3205/8/12/5/21/ 49/59, 3260/4	82165–7 82169/72–8, 82180–8/94, 82197/9–202, 82204/7/11–3	≠
V Third	115*	1928/9	277	61' 6"× 9' 3"	8: 64	YK	3953–62 5395, 5602/ 5/6/8/14/6, 5618/20/3/4/35/7	12494–12503 12612–12624	
V Open third	28*	1927/8	–	61' 6¼" × 9' 3"	3† 64	MET	5534–40	12237–43	All-steel
Brake third	60*	1926/7	162	51' 1½" × 9' 3"	6: 60	DK	21113, 22167/277	M22536/7/5 after 1950	≠
							Transferred to CLC as 575, 586, 574 1930, 1932, 1930		
Brake third	133	1926/7	209	51' 1½" × 9' 3"	6: 60	YK	21750, 22060/92	–/M22538/9 after 1950	
							Transferred to CLC as 588/7/9 1932		588 DEA
Brake third	61*	1926/7	161	51' 1½" × 9' 3"	5: 50	DK	3757	86017	
Brake third	65*	1927/8 1928/9	207 252	51' 1½" × 9' 3"	4: 40	YK	3375, 3992/4, 31002/10/2/6/7 62608/9	86095, 86127–33 86154/5	
Brake third	119*	1928/9	253	51' 1½" × 9' 3"	3: 30	YK	31018/9/20/ 31/3/6/7, 31043/6/56/8/9/62	86777–89	
V Brake third	41*	1927/8	192	52' 6"× 9" 3"	3: 24	DR	62598–62607		
V Brake third	40A*	1927/8	193	61' 6"× 9" 3"	3: 24	DR	1262–4 (4940, 767/8)	16194/7/8	
								Transferred 1937, 1939/39	
Lav Composite	50*	1927/8	210	51' 1½" × 9' 3"	3/4 : 19/33	DK	32323/34/46/51, 32480–93	88017/8/20/1, 88030–43	
Composite	51*	1927/8	211	51' 1½" × 9' 3"	4/3 : 32/30	DK	32277, 32310/1	88101–3	
		1928/9	258				32513–6 63261–5	88113–6 88117–21 40 first-class 63265 push-pull	
V Composite	9*	1927/8	194	52' 6"× 9" 3"	2/4½ : 12/36	YK	63810–22		
V Locker composite	116*	1927/8	195	61' 6" × 9' 3"	2½/4 : 15/32	YK	1292 (7780), 1293/4	18163–5	
V Sleeper third	95	1928/9	278	61' 6" × 9' 3"	7: 28 /56	YK	1241–56	1241/4/5/6/9/52–6 ambulance train use WW2 1243 DEA	

After 1948 Nos 1242/7 remained as sleeper thirds, as did Nos 1248/50/1 which became 1519/26/7. Nos 1252–4 returned from wartime use as 1528–30. No 1245 scrapped. Nos 1241/4/6/9/55/6 rebuilt as restaurant cafeteria cars in 1954 as M 9209–14E – see under 1954.

Type	Dia No	CBP Year	Order No	Dimensions	Comps /Seats	Built At	Running numbers Original	1943	Notes
V Restaurant kitchen car (first-class)	10C*	1927/8	196	61' 6" × 9' 3"	1† 18	DR	43040, 51770/1	9008–10	
V Restaurant pantry car (third-class)	112*	1927/8	198	61' 6" × 9' 3"	2† 39	YK	42972	9066	
V(Restaurant first)	12B*	1927/8	199	55' 2½" × 9' 3"	2† 36	DR	46191	9052	Triplet restaurant car set
(Kitchen car)	13*			41' 0" × 9' 0"	–		46192	9053	
(restaurant third)	14A*			55' 2½" × 9' 3"	2† 42		46193	9054	
V(Restaurant first)	12A*	1927/8	199	55' 2½" × 9' 3"	2† 36	DR	16481/91	1416/9	Triplet restaurant car sets
(Kitchen car)	13*			41' 0" × 9' 0"	–		16482/92	1417/20	
(restaurant third)	14A			55' 2½" × 9' 3"	2† 42		16483/93	1418/21	1419–21 W/O Goswick 1947

16481–3, 16491–3 were the White Allom cars

Type	Dia No	CBP Year	Order No	Dimensions	Comps /Seats	Built At	Running numbers Original	1943	Notes
V(Restaurant first)	12B*	1928/9	262	55' 2½" × 9' 3"	2† 36	DR	16501/11	1422/5	Triplet restaurant car set
(Kitchen car)	13*			41' 0" × 9' 0"	–		16502/12	1423/6	
(restaurant third)	14A*			55' 2½" × 9' 3"	2† 42		16503/13	1424/7	
Brake third	72*	1928/9	–	38' 1¼" × 8' 6"	5: 60	MID	47841/51	86292/6	
Third	73*			38' 1¼" × 8' 6"	7: 84		47842/52	86293/7	
Third	74*			43' 6" × 8' 6"	8: 96		47843/53	86294/8	
Third	75*			43' 6" × 8' 6"	8: 96		47844/54	86295/9	

Above are London GN section suburban quadruplets

Type	Dia No	CBP Year	Order No	Dimensions	Comps /Seats	Built At	Running numbers Original	1943	Notes
Composite (1st/3rd)	71*	1928/9	–	43' 6" × 9' 0"	3 3rd/4 1st :36/40	MID	47884/94	86183/7	
Composite (1st/3rd)	70*	1928/9	–	43' 6" × 9' 0"	4 1st/3 3rd :40/36		47883/93	86182/6	
Second	69*	1928/9	–	38' 1¼" × 9' 0"	7: 84		47882/92	86181/5	
Brake second	68*	1928/9	–	38' 1¼" × 9' 0"	5: 60		47881/91	86180/4	

Above are London GN section suburban quadruplets

Type	Dia No	CBP Year	Order No	Dimensions	Comps /Seats	Built At	Running numbers Original	1943	Notes
General van four-wheeled	120*	1927/8	212/25 267	32' 0" × 9' 0"	–	SF	6801–14 6815–29	70194–70207 70208–22	≠
Passenger brake van	129*	1927/8	213	51' 1½" × 9' 0"	–	YK	2178/99, 2246, 2306	70251–4	≠
V Passenger brake van	111*	1927/8	204	52' 6" × 9' 0"	–	YK	6739–48	70145–54	
V Passenger brake van	43*	1927/8	203	61' 6"× 9' 0"	–	DR	4184–90 5201–7	70003–9 70010–6	
V Passenger brake van	45*	1926/7	–	61' 6"× 9' 0"	–	CM	35, 37 6700 171–93	70036/7 70038 70047–69	All-steel

1929 All vehicles vacuum fitted except those shown as ✹which were dual fitted as built

Type	Dia No	CBP Year	Order No	Dimensions	Comps /Seats	Built At	Running numbers Original	1943	Notes
First	48*	1929/30	322	51' 1½" × 9' 3"	7: 56	DK	51655/6	88316, 81047	51655 altered in 1938 to a composite on Dia 306.
V First	141*	1928/9	–	52' 6" × 9' 3"	6: 36	MET	6452/3		Cromer sets
Third	57*	1928/9	248	51' 1½" × 9' 3"	8: 80	DK	3970/1/4–85 61687–96	82288–82301 82350–9	
V Open third	27A*	1928/9	246	61' 6" × 9' 3"	2† 64	DR	4152 5541–6	12176 12177–82	
						MET	61705/6 (6100/1)	–/12185	Cromer sets 6100 W/O 1940
V Third	115*	1928/9	277	61' 6"× 9' 3"	8: 64	YK	21183, 21478, 22136, 22178 22208/36/66, 22352/62, 22461	12250/9/60/64–7, 12274–6	
V Third	141*	1928/9	–	52' 6"× 9' 3"	7: 56	MET	61697–61704		Cromer sets
V Brake third	37A*	1929/30	313	61' 6"× 9" 3"	5: 40	DR	41346–50	16064–8	
V Brake third	114*	1928/9	249	61' 6"× 9" 3"	4: 32	YK	41351–4 52201–12	16363–6 16371–82	16373 to bullion van on Dia 362, 1949
V Brake third	41*	1928/9	250	61' 6"× 9" 3"	3: 24	YK	62610–5		
			–			MET	62616–23		Cromer sets
V Brake third	40A*	1928/9	251	61' 6"× 9" 3"	3: 24	YK	3986/7/9–91 120 (31197)	16189–93 –	W/O 1938/9
Composite	51*	1929/30	329	51' 1½" × 9' 3"	4/3 : 40/30	DK	63833–6	88124–7	
Composite	110*	1929/30	328	51' 1½" × 9' 3"	4/3 : 40/30	DK	63831/2	88122/3	First/second compos Later on Dia 51

Type	Dia No	CBP Year	Order No	Dimensions	Comps /Seats	Built At	Running numbers Original	1943	Notes
Lav Composite	50★	1928/9	259	51' 1½" × 9' 3"	3/4 : 19/33	DK	32494–32512	88044–62	
V Composite	6★	1928/9	254	61' 6"× 9" 0"	3½/4 : 21/32	YK	51872–7	18002–7	
V Composite	9★	1928/9	–	52' 6"× 9" 3"	2/4½ : 12/36	MET	63823–30		Cromer sets
V Locker composite	116★	1928/9	255	61' 6" × 9' 3"	2½/4 : 15/32	YK	121 (7768)	18162	Transferred 1939
V Brake composite	32★	1928/9	256	61' 6"× 9" 3"	2/3 : 12/24	DR	32517–9 63781	10006–8 10013	
V Brake composite	127★	1928/9	257	61' 6"× 9" 3"	2/2 : 12/16	YK	122	10036	
V Sleeper third	109★	1929/30	287 307	61' 6" × 9' 3"	7: 28 /56	YK	1270–2/6–84 1285–91		
V Restaurant kitchen car (first-class)	10B★	1927/8	197	61' 6" × 9' 3"	1† 18	YK	678–80 (21474¶, 31929, 680)	9004–6 ¶ unclassed	§§ Transfers 1934/39
V Restaurant kitchen car (first-class)	10C★	1927/8 1928/9	196 260	61' 6" × 9' 3"	1† 18	DR	51772/3 51774/5 682/3 42969 1222/3	9011/2 9013/4 9017/8 9007 9019/20	
			–			MET	6119/20 (651/2)	9015/6	Cromer sets
V Restaurant kitchen car (unclassed)	11★	1929/30	306	61' 6" × 9' 3"	2† 30	DR	43041	–	

Converted for use in ambulance train 1943/4 and served overseas. Not returned until 1953 when it was rebuilt as a restaurant cafeteria car M 9217E. See under 1954.

Type	Dia No	CBP Year	Order No	Dimensions	Comps /Seats	Built At	Running numbers Original	1943	Notes
V Restaurant pantry car (third-class)	112★	1929/30	261	61' 6" × 9' 3"	2† 39	DR	1189 (42998)	9067	Transferred 1940
(Third)	124★	1928/9	263	51' 1½" × 9' 3"	8: 80	DR	44181/91	88153/5	Articulated twins
(First)	126			51' 1½" × 9' 3"	7: 56	DR	44182/92	88154/6	Later on Dia 242
(Third)	105★	1928/9	263	51' 1½" × 9' 3"	8: 80	DR	44172/44202	86791/3	Articulated twins
(Brake third)	125★			51' 1½" × 9' 3"	5: 50	DR	44171/44201	86790/2	
(Third)	105★	1929/30	332	51' 1½" × 9' 3"	8: 80	DR	44301	82372	Articulated twin
(Third)	106★			51' 1½" × 9' 3"	8: 80	DR	44302	82373	
(Lav compo)	123★	1929/30	332	51' 1½" × 9' 3"	3/4 : 23/39	DR	44272	88135	Articulated twin
(Third)	124★			51' 1½" × 9' 3"	8: 80	DR	44271	88134	
(Lav compo)	108★	1929/30	332	51' 1½" × 9' 3"	3/4 : 23/39	DR	44212/22	80071/3	Articulated twins
(Brake third)	107★			51' 1½" × 9' 3"	4: 40	DR	44211/21	80070/2	
Brake second	102	1928/9	264	51' 1½" × 9' 3"	3: 30	YK	62800–11	80014/8/22/6/30/4, 80038/42/6/50/4/8	
Composite¶	103			43' 5" × 9' 3"	4/2 : 40/20		64000–11	80015/9/23/7/31/5, 80039/43/7/51/5/9	
Third	104			43' 5" × 9' 3"	7: 70		61800–11	80016/20/4/8/32/6, 80040/4/8/52/6/60	
Third	105★			51' 1½" × 9' 3"	8: 80		61812–23	80017/21/5/9/33/7, 80041/5/9/53/7/61	
Brake second	102	1929/30	334	51' 1½" × 9' 3"	3: 30	YK	62812/3	80062/6	
Composite¶	103			43' 5" × 9' 3"	4/2 : 40/20		64012/3	80063/7	
Third	104			43' 5" × 9' 3"	7: 70		61824/5	80064/8	
Third	105★			51' 1½" × 9' 3"	8: 80		61826/7	80065/9	

Above are London GE section Hertford line quadruplets   Air braked   ¶The Dia 103 composites were first/second-class, later all-third

Type	Dia No	CBP Year	Order No	Dimensions	Comps /Seats	Built At	Running numbers Original	1943	Notes
Brake third	72★	1928/9	–	38' 1¼" × 8' 6"	5: 60	CR	47821/31	86284/8	
Third	73★			38' 1¼" × 8' 6"	7: 84		47822/32	86285/9	
Third	74★			43' 6" × 8' 6"	8: 96		47823/33	86286/90	
Third	75★			43' 6" × 8' 6"	8: 96		47824/34	86287/91	

Above are London GN section suburban quadruplets

Type	Dia No	CBP Year	Order No	Dimensions	Comps /Seats	Built At	Running numbers Original	1943	Notes
Composite (1st/3rd)	71★	1928/9	–	43' 6" × 9' 0"	3 3rd/4 1st :36/40	CR	47864/74	86175/9	
Composite (1st/3rd)	70★	1928/9	–	43' 6" × 9' 0"	4 1st/3 3rd :40/36		47863/73	86174/8	

Type	Dia No	CBP Year	Order No	Dimensions	Comps /Seats	Built At	Running numbers Original	1943	Notes
Second	69*	1928/9	–	38' 1¼" × 9' 0"	7: 84		47862/72	86173/7	
Brake second	68*	1928/9	–	38' 1¼" × 9' 0"	5: 60		47861/71	86172/6	

Above are London GN section suburban quadruplets

Type	Dia No	CBP Year	Order No	Dimensions	Comps /Seats	Built At	Running numbers Original	1943	Notes
Brake third	72A*	1928/9	–	38' 1¼" × 8' 6"	5: 60	¶	47741/51/61/71	86340/4/8/52	
Third	73A*			38' 1¼" × 8' 6"	7: 84		47742/52/62/72	86341/5/9/53	
Third	74A*			43' 6" × 8' 6"	8: 96		47743/53/63/73	86342/6/50/4	
Third	75A*			43' 6" × 8' 6"	8: 96		47744/54/64/74	86343/7/51/5	

Above are London GN section suburban quadruplets

Type	Dia No	CBP Year	Order No	Dimensions	Comps /Seats	Built At	Running numbers Original	1943	Notes
Composite (1st/3rd)	71A*	1929/30	–	43' 6" × 9' 0"	3 3rd/4 1st :36/40	¶	47784/94/804/14	86231/5/9/43	
Composite (1st/3rd)	70A*	1929/30	–	43' 6" × 9' 0"	4 1st/3 3rd :40/36		47783/93/803/13	86230/4/8/42	
Second	69A*	1929/30	–	38' 1¼" × 9' 0"	7: 84		47782/92/802/12	86229/33/7/41	
Brake second	68A*	1929/30	–	38' 1¼" × 9' 0"	5: 60		47781/91/801/11	86228/32/6/40	

Above are London GN section suburban quadruplets ¶ Two trains built by BHM, one each CR and M–C

Type	Dia No	CBP Year	Order No	Dimensions	Comps /Seats	Built At	Running numbers Original	1943	Notes
(Composite)#	81*	1928/9	–	43' 6" × 9' 3"	4/3 : 40/36	CL	63128–31/6–9	86706/11/6/ 21/6/31/6/41	
(Second)	82*	1928/9	–	43' 6" × 9' 3"	8: 96		6563–70	86707/12/7/22/ 7/32/7/42	
(Composite)¶	83*	1928/9	–	43' 6" × 9' 3"	4/4 : 48/48		63124–7/32–5	86708/13/8/23/ 8/33/8/43	
(Third)	84*	1928/9	–	43' 6" × 9' 3"	8: 96		60062–9	86709/14/9/24/ 9/34/9/44	
(Brake third)	85*	1928/9	–	43' 6" × 9' 3"	6: 72		62062–9	86710/5/20/5/ 30/5/40/5	

Above are London GE section suburban quintuplets Air-braked # First/second-class, later all-third ¶ Second/third-class, later all-third.

Type	Dia No	CBP Year	Order No	Dimensions	Comps /Seats	Built At	Running numbers Original	1943	Notes
V PO sorting van	131	1927/8	279	60' 1½" × 8' 6"	–	YK	2260/86, 2339 (6130–2)	70277–9	Trans 1933
General van four-wheeled	120*	1928/9	267	32' 0" × 9' 0"	–	SF	6830–9	70223/–/4–31	6831 DEA
		1929/30	325			YK	6840–7/8/(772), 6850	70232–4/–/5–9/40 ≠	
V Passenger brake van	113*	1928/9	265	61' 6"× 9' 0"	–	DR	5208–12 149	70176–80 70193	
			266			YK	5213/4 4028/34/40/1/59, 4171/9/92/3	70181/2 70160–4, 70172–5	4040/1 converted to cinema cars from 1935/6–42

1930 All vehicles vacuum fitted except where shown

Type	Dia No	CBP Year	Order No	Dimensions	Comps /Seats	Built At	Running numbers Original	1943	Notes
V First	1*	1929/30	308	61' 6" × 9' 3"	7: 42	DR	31869/76/82	11002/3/6	
			–			CR	31879/80/5/91, 31906/16	11004/5/7–10	
V First Δ	139	1930/1	357	61' 6" × 9' 3"	6: 36	DR	1132/3	11048/9	'Super firsts'
V First	140*	1930/1	376	52' 6" × 9' 3"	6: 36	YK	6454–9		6457 DEA
V Semi-open first	5*	1930/1	377	61' 6" × 9' 3"	5† 42	YK	4100	11038	
V Brake first	142*	1930/1	379	61' 6" × 9' 3"	4: 24	DR	22611	11062	Leeds–Glasgow set
V Open third	27A*	1929/30	311	61' 6" × 9' 3"	2† 48	YK	21084, 21212, 21508, 21954, 22238/73, 22314/71, 22410/71	12136/7/46–9, –/12150–2	22314 converted to buffet car on Dia 185, 1930.
							315/37/45/57 61707–10 (6102–5)	12163/6/7/70 12186–9	
V Open second¶	27B	1929/30	311	61' 6" × 9' 3"	2† 48	YK	697¶	12201	¶ Open third to Dia 27A, 1942.
V Open third	27A*	1930/1	382	61' 6" × 9' 3"	2† 48	YK	22660	12153	Leeds–Glasgow set
V Third	141*	1929/30	309	52' 6"× 9' 3"	7: 56	YK	61714–21		
V Second¶	141A*				7: 56		6990/1		¶ Third to Dia 141, 1942
V Third	115*	1929/30	310	61' 6"× 9' 3"	8: 64	YK	358/64/77/82/6, 392/5/7, 3102, 3114/43/67/70	12451/2/4/6/8, –/61–3/5/8/9, 12465/8/9/71	392 DEA

Type	Dia No	CBP Year	Order No	Dimensions	Comps /Seats	Built At	Running numbers Original	1943	Notes
		1930/1	358			YK	1114–9 (42526–31)	12599–12604	Transferred 1937
		1930/1	–			M–C	22333–5	12268–70	
V Brake third	146★	1929/30	312	52' 6"x 9' 3"	3: 24	DR	62630–9		
		1930/1	385			DR	62640–3		
V Open brake third	135	1929/30	316	61' 6" × 9' 3"	1† 32	YK	22271, 22350	16404/5	
V Brake third	114★	1930/1	314	61' 6"x 9" 3"	4: 32	YK	21059	16244	
							3293, 3310/25, 3337/50/4/7/64, 3370/2	16314–21/–/3	3370 W/O Carlisle 1931
			359			YK	1107/9 (52093, 3993)	16370/46	Trans 1935
			384				4941–7	16351–7	
							21863, 22226, 22383	16245–7	
			–			BHM	22384, 22654	16248/9	
							3485/9, 3607/8, 3615/8/60/2/6/9, 3673/82	16326–31/–/3, 16334–7	
V Brake third	40A★	1929/30	315	61' 6"x 9" 3"	3: 24	YK	3379/80	16187/8	
		1930/1	–			BHM	22364–8	16182–6	
							5773/4	16195/6	
Third	57★	1929/30	323	51' 1½" × 9' 3"	8: 80	DK	3176/82/7/9, 3202/45/52/6, 3274/85/6	82189/90, 82192/3/8, 82206/9/10/4–6	
Brake third	117	1929/30	330	51' 1½" × 9' 3"	5: 50	DK	5771/2	86766/7	
Brake third	65★	1929/30	324	51' 1½" × 9' 3"	4: 40	YK	3386/9, 3404, 3452/8/88/96/9	86099, 86101, 86105/9/11–4	
Brake third	128★	1929/30	324	51' 1½" × 9' 3"	4: 40	YK	62624–9	86806–9/–/11	
		1930/1	397				3687/9	86798/9	
Brake third	119★	1928/9	331	51' 1½" × 9' 3"	3: 30	YK	3610/2	86771/3	
V Composite	130★	1929/30	317	61' 6"x 9' 3"	3½/4 : 21/32	YK	32378/81/90/1, 32429	18269/70/2/3/5	
		1930/1	–			CR	22428–31	18166–9	
V Composite	137★	1930/1	364	61' 6"x 9' 3"	2½/5 : 15/40	DR	1259/60	18360/1	
V Brake composite	134★	1929/30	318	61' 6"x 9" 3"	2/4 : 12/32	YK	21643, 22248	10046/7	
V Brake composite	32★	1929/30	319	61' 6"x 9" 3"	2/3 : 12/24	YK	32524–6	10009/–/10	32525 W/O Carlisle 1931
V Brake composite	143★	1930/1	387	61' 6"x 9" 3"	2/3 : 12/24	DR	22652	10058	Leeds–Glasgow set
V Brake composite	127★	1930/1	–	61' 6"x 9" 3"	2/2 : 12/16	BHM	32531/2	10034/5	
Lav Composite	50★	1929/30	327	51' 1½" × 9' 3"	3/4 : 19/33	DK	32443/55/7	88024/6/8	
		1930/1	398			DK	32520–3	88063–6	
Brake Composite	118	1929/30	326	51' 1½" × 9' 3"	2/4 : 16/40	DK	32527/8	88082/3	
		1930/1	399			DK	32533/4	80326/7	Converted for push-pull working on Dia 318 1940
V First-class sleeping car	138	1930/1	361	61' 6'" × 9' 3"	10: 10	DR	1152–5		PV
V Sleeper third	109★	1930/1	356	61' 6" × 9' 3"	7: 28 /56	YK	1296–1305		
V Restaurant kitchen car (first-class)	11★	1929/30	320	61' 6" × 9' 3"	2† 30	DR	31922/3	9023/4	
V Restaurant kitchen car (third-class)	145	1930/1	392	61' 6" × 9' 3"	1† 18	DR	22650	9093	Leeds–Glasgow set
V Buffet car	185	–	–	61' 6" × 9' 3"	1† 24	YK	22314	9154	Converted from Dia 27A open third, built 1930
(Third)	105★	1929/30	333	51' 1½" × 9' 3"	8: 80	DR	52502/12	86795/7	Articulated twins
(Brake third)	125★			51' 1½" × 9' 3"	5: 50	DR	52501/11	86794/6	
(Third)	124★	1929/30	333	51' 1½" × 9' 3"	8: 80	DR	52522/32	88198, 88200	Articulated twins
(First)	126			51' 1½" × 9' 3"	7: 56	DR	52521/31	88197/9	Later on Dia 242

Type	Dia No	CBP Year	Order No	Dimensions	Comps /Seats	Built At	Running numbers Original	1943	Notes
(Lav compo)	108★	1929/30	332	51' 1½" × 9' 3"	3/4 : 23/39	DR	44232/42/52/62	80075/7/9/–	Articulated twins 44261/2 W/O
(Brake third)	107★			51' 1½" × 9' 3"	4: 40	DR	44231/41/51/61	80074/6/8/–	Hatfield 1939
(Third)	105★	1929/30	332	51' 1½" × 9' 3"	8: 80	DR	44311	82374	Articulated twin
(Third)	106★			51' 1½" × 9' 3"	8: 80	DR	44312	82375	
(Lav compo)	123★	1929/30	332	51' 1½" × 9' 3"	3/4 : 23/39	DR	44282/92	88137/9	Articulated twins
(Third)	124★			51' 1½" × 9' 3"	8: 80	DR	44281/91	88136/8	
(Composite)#	81★	1930/1	–	43' 6" × 9' 3"	4/3 : 40/36	M–C	64051/3/5/7	86746/51/6/61	
(Second)	82★	1930/1	–	43' 6" × 9' 3"	8: 96		6571–4	86747/52/7/62	
(Composite)¶	83★	1930/1	–	43' 6" × 9' 3"	4/4 : 48/48		64050/2/4/6	86748/53/8/63	
(Third)	84★	1930/1	–	43' 6" × 9' 3"	8: 96		60070–3	86749/54/9/64	
(Brake third)	85★	1930/1	–	43' 6" × 9' 3"	6: 72		62070–3	86750/5/60/5	

Above are London GE section suburban quintuplets Air-braked # First/second-class, later all-third ¶ Second/third-class, later all-third.

Type	Dia No	CBP Year	Order No	Dimensions	Comps /Seats	Built At	Running numbers Original	1943	Notes
V Passenger brake van	111★	1929/30	321	52' 6"X 9' 0"	–	DR	6749–53	70155–9	
V Passenger brake van	113★	1930/1	363	61' 6"X 9' 0"	–	DR	117/8	70191/2	
General van four-wheeled	120★	1929/30	325	32' 0" × 9' 0"	–	YK	6849, 6851–4 (773–6) 767–71	70239 70247/8/–/50 70241–5	≠ ≠

1931 All vehicles vacuum fitted

Type	Dia No	CBP Year	Order No	Dimensions	Comps /Seats	Built At	Running numbers Original	1943	Notes
V First	1★	1930/1	–	61' 6" × 9' 3"	7: 42	CR	22356/7	11000/1	
V First Δ	147	1930/1	357	61' 6" × 9' 3"	6: 24¶	DR	1134/5 (54750/1)	11064/5	'Super firsts' PV Trans 1939 11064 W/O Goswick 1947 ¶ Later 36 seats
V Semi-open first	5★	1930/1	377	61' 6" × 9' 3"	5† 42	YK	21254	11037	Leeds–Glasgow set
First	48★	1930/1	396	51' 1½" × 9' 3"	7: 56	DK	31919/27/8, 31930/2	81031–5	
V Brake first	149★	1930/1	378	61' 6" × 9' 3"	4: 24	DR	4110	11069	
V Open third	27A★	1930/1	382	61' 6" × 9' 3"	2† 48	DR	5554/5 61711 (6118) 321/53	12183/4 12190 12164/9	
			401						
V Open third	150	1930/1	383	61' 6" × 9' 3"	2† 48	DR	4175/6	12927/8	
V Third	141★	1930/1	380	52' 6"× 9' 3"	7: 56	YK	61722–31		
V Third	115★	1930/1	381	61' 6"× 9' 3"	8: 64	YK	21187, 21208, 21229/55/96, 21319/68, 21401/37, 21699, 21724/95, 22491/2/9, 22500/25, 22565, 22942, 23567	12251–9/61–3, 12277–84	
							4173/4	12504/5	
							334/73/84/7	12450/3/7/9	
							1320–3 (52183–6)	12625–8	Trans 1938
			–			M–C	22336–8, 3112/32/40/68, 3171/90, 3214, 3236/48/50/61, 3267/84/91/4, 3307/17/9–21, 3324/49/56/74, 3378/95	12271–3 12464/6/7/70, 12472–93	
Brake third	128★	1930/1	397	51' 1½" × 9' 3"	4: 40	DK	3694/9, 3735/9/44/7	86800–5	
V Brake third	114★	1930/1	384	61' 6" × 9" 3"	4: 32	YK	4948–52 3406/35 1108/60/1	16358–62 16324/5 16396–8	
			424				3370	16322	Accident replacement

Type	Dia No	CBP Year	Order No	Dimensions	Comps /Seats	Built At	Running numbers Original	1943	Notes
Lav Composite	50★	1930/1	398	51' 1½" × 9' 3"	3/4 : 19/33	DK	32529/30	88067/8	
V Composite	9★	1930/1	386	52' 6" × 9" 3"	2/4½ : 12/36	YK	63837–46		
V Composite	130★	1930/1	–	61' 6" × 9' 3"	3½/4 : 21/32	CR	32441/2	18276/7	
V Brake composite	143★	1930/1	387	61' 6" × 9' 3"	2/3 : 12/24	DR	4236/7	10065/6	
V Third-class sleeping car	148	1931/2	426	66' 6" × 9' 3"	8: 32 berths	YK	1336–44/6		
V Restaurant kitchen car (first-class)	144★	1930/1	389	61' 6" × 9' 3"	1† 18	DR	42787/8 51776/7	9068/9 9070/1	
V Restaurant kitchen car (unclassed)	11★	1930/1	390 425	61' 6" × 9' 3"	2† 30	DR	31924/6 31935	9025/– 9027	Accident replacement for former M & NB car W/O Carlisle 1931
			391				42783		

Nos 31924/6/35, 42783 converted for use in ambulance trains 1943/4. Nos 31924/35 returned to service but Nos 31926 and 42783 served overseas and not returned until 1953 when they were rebuilt as a restaurant cafeteria cars M 9215/6E. See under 1954.

Type	Dia No	CBP Year	Order No	Dimensions	Comps /Seats	Built At	Running numbers Original	1943	Notes
V Restaurant pantry car (third-class)	151★	1930/1	393	61' 6" × 9' 3"	2† 39	DR	42784–6 1309–11	9094–6 9100–2	
Passenger brake van	129★	1930/1	400	51' 1½" × 9' 0"	–	DR	6764–83	70255–74	Pigeon vans 70268 to TPO tender
V Passenger brake van	113★	1930/1	395	61' 6" × 9' 0"	–	DR	4136–9	70165–8	

1932 All vehicles vacuum fitted

Type	Dia No	CBP Year	Order No	Dimensions	Comps /Seats	Built At	Running numbers Original	1943	Notes
V First Δ	156	1931/2	433	61' 6" × 9' 3"	6: 24¶	DR	1136/7	11074/5	'Super firsts' PV
V Open third	27A★	1930/1	382	61' 6" × 9' 3"	2† 48	DR	61712/3 (6119/20) 3888/9	–/12192 12174/5	
V Third	141★	1930/1	380	52' 6" × 9' 3"	7: 56	YK	61732–6		61736 W/O 1937
V Third Δ	155★	1931/2	437	61' 6" × 9' 3"	7: 42	YK	1352/4/5/78, 1384/97–9	13003–5/–, 13006–9	1378 DEA
V Brake third	146★	1930/1	385	52' 6" × 9' 3"	3: 24	DR	62644–9		
V Brake third	114★	1931/2	440	61' 6" × 9" 3"	4: 32	YK	4936/8 3930/3	16349/50 16338/9	
V Composite	9★	1930/1	386	52' 6" × 9" 3"	2/4½ : 12/36	YK	63847–52		
V Brake composite	134★	1930/1 1931/2	388 446	61' 6" × 9" 3"	2/4 : 12/32	YK DK	63853–60 494/5	10050–7 10048/9	
V Brake composite	143★	–	424	61' 6" × 9" 3"	2/3 : 12/24	YK	32525	10064	Accident replacement
V First-class sleeping car	157★	1931/2	430•	66' 6'" × 9' 3"	10: 10	DR	1156/7		PV
V Composite sleeping car	160	1931/2	454	66' 6'" × 9' 3"	6/3 : 6/12	DR	32322	1100	PV (part)
V (First-class sleeping car)	161	1931/2	431	56' 2½" × 9' 3"	10 berths	DR	1183/5		Sleeping car twins
V (Third-class sleeping car)	162				7 compts : 28 berths		1184/6		
V Passenger brake van	113★	1931/2	450	61' 6" × 9' 0"	–	DK	5219/20	70186/7	
V Passenger brake van	154	1930/1	394	52' 6" × 9' 0"	–	YK	6754–63	70280–9	

1933 All vehicles vacuum fitted

Type	Dia No	CBP Year	Order No	Dimensions	Comps /Seats	Built At	Running numbers Original	1943	Notes
V First Δ	172★	1933	485	61' 6" × 9' 3"	6: 36	DR	22116 1139	– 11087	'Super firsts' PV (1139 only)
V Semi-open first	173	1933	486	61' 6" × 9' 3"	5† 42	DR	1138	11104	
V Open third	27A★	1933	503	61' 6" × 9' 3"	2† 64 2† 48	DR	21301–4 175 (744)	12138–41 –	PV
V Third	115★	1933	504	61' 6" × 9' 3"	8: 64	YK	167 (42516), 168	12598, 12716	167 trans 1936 168 PV

Type	Dia No	CBP Year	Order No	Dimensions	Comps /Seats	Built At	Running numbers Original	1943	Notes
V Third	141*	1933	505	52' 6" × 9' 3"	7: 56	YK	61737–61 61783		61753 DEA Replacement for GER vehicle lost in fire
		–	464						
V Brake third	174*	1933	490	61' 6" × 9" 3"	3: 24	DR	3969/88 62651–4 1265 (62847)	16478/9 16480/1/–/3 16493	Transferred 1941
V Open brake third	169	1933	502	61' 6" × 9' 3"	1† 52	DR	43500–9	16467–76	Tourist stock 43509 PV
V Brake third	114*	1933	491	61' 6" × 9" 3"	4: 32	DK	3940/63/5–8	16340–5	
V Brake third	178*	–	517	61' 6" × 9" 3"	6: 36	DK	52219	16505	Accident replacement
Composite	163	1931/2	474	51' 1½" × 9' 3"	4/3 : 40/30	DK	65000	88140	Alpax carriage
V Composite	9*	–	463	52' 6" × 9' 3"	2/4½ : 12/36	YK	63865/6		Replacement for GER vehicles lost in fire
V Brake composite	127*	1933	493	61' 6" × 9" 3"	2/2 : 12/16	DK	21671/87	10032/3	
V Brake composite	175*	1933	494	61' 6" × 9" 3"	2/4 : 12/32	DK	32556–8	10097–9	
V Restaurant kitchen car (first-class)	144*	1933	495	61' 6" × 9' 3"	1† 18	DR	1218 (660), 1219	9079/82	
V Buffet car	167*	1933	500	61' 6" × 9' 3"	1† 24	YK	32372	9126	§§
V Buffet car	168*	1933	500	61' 6" × 9' 3"	1† 24	YK	43510–9	9144–53	§§ Tourist stock
V (Open third)	171	1933	–	52' 0¹⁄₁₆" × 9' 3"	1† 56	BHM	45001/2, 45011/2, 45021/2, 45031/2, 45041/2, 45051/2, 45061/2, 45071/2, 45081/2, 45091/2,	13142–61	Tourist stock Articulated twins
V (Open third)				52' 0¹⁄₁₆" × 9' 3"	1† 56	M–C	45101/2, 45111/2, 45121/2, 45131/2, 45141/2, 45151/2, 45161/2, 45171/2, 45181/2, 45191/2	13162–81	
V TPO sorting van	164*	1933	480	60' 1½" × 8' 6¾"	–	YK	2155–7	70290–2	
V TPO sorting van	165	1933	481	60' 1½" × 8' 6¾"	–	YK	2151–4	70300–3	
V Passenger brake van	113*	1933	496	61' 6" × 9' 0"	–	DK	5216–8/21–3	70183–5/8–90	
Brake van four-wheeled	170*	1933	499	31' 8⅝" × 9' 0"	–	DR	5228–45	70304–21	
Brake van four-wheeled	176	1933	499	31' 8⅝" × 9' 0"	–	DR	4140–4 5224–7	70328–32 70333/4/–/6	
Brake van four-wheeled	177	1933	499	31' 8⅝" × 9' 0"	–	DR	5246–9	70337–40	

Dias 170/6/7 – underframes from GNR Howlden passenger stock

1934 All vehicles vacuum fitted

Type	Dia No	CBP Year	Order No	Dimensions	Comps /Seats	Built At	Running numbers Original	1943	Notes
First	48*	1933	497	51' 1½" × 9' 3"	7: 70	DK	6460	81054	
V First	140*	1933	507	52' 6" × 9' 3"	6: 36	DR	6461/2		
V First Δ	172*	1934	555	61' 6" × 9' 3"	6: 36	DR	1131	11088	'Super first' PV
V Third Δ	155*	1933	488	61' 6"× 9' 3"	7: 42	YK	3100/35/44/56, 3161/88/91/3 1306 (3864), 1308 (3865), 1313–5 (3867/8/71), 1327/8 (3872/4), 1329–31/48–51	12929–36 12962 12963 12964/5/7. 12968/70, 12996–13002	
V Third	141*	1933	508	52' 6" × 9' 3"	7: 56	YK	61762–93 61866–73 61874–81		61866 W/O 61874 DEA
		1934	533						
			558						
V Third	115*	1934	508	61' 6" × 9' 3"	8: 64	YK	1435–40 (2926–31) 1441–72	12245–8/–/9 12717–48	Trans 1938/9 2930 W/O
V Open third	27A*	1933	503	61' 6" × 9' 3"	2† 64 2† 48	YK	21305–8 327/46/88/96/8 61850–5 (6121–4, 6125[24137], 6126)	12142–5 12165/8/71/2/– 12193–6/62/97	21308 welded u/f 398 W/O

138

Type	Dia No	CBP Year	Order No	Dimensions	Comps /Seats	Built At	Running numbers Original	1943	Notes
		1934	534		2† 48		1140/1 (61995/6)	12198/9	Trans 1938
V Open third	182*	1934	576	52' 6" × 9' 3"	2† 39	YK	61882/3		
V Open third	186*	1934	559	61' 6" × 9' 3"	1† 64	YK	43600–19/64	13354–73, 13417	Welded u/fs
			560				3390/3/4	13350–2	
							21309	13218	13369 converted to a cafeteria car at Eastleigh on this number in 1952
V Brake third	40A*	1933	490	61' 6" × 9" 3"	3: 18	DR	22180/1	16180/1	BS gangways
V Brake third	146*	1933	509	52' 6" × 9' 3"	3: 18	DR	62655–8		62658 W/O
		1934	535			YK	62659–62		
V Brake third	114*	1933	510	61' 6" × 9' 3"	4: 24	DR	52233–42	16383–92	
		1934	564			YK	1228–30/2/6	16399–16403	
							1231 (24675)	16313	Trans 1941
V Brake third	178*	1933	511	61' 6" × 9' 3"	6: 36	DK	52220–32	16506–18	
V Brake third	37A*	1933	512	61' 6" × 9' 3"	5: 30	YK	52213–8	16089–94	
V Brake third	174*	1934	562	61' 6" × 9' 3"	3: 18	YK	1000–5/44 (7556–9, 764/6, 7560)	16496–9/4/5, 16500	
									Trans 1938/9
V Open brake third	179*	1934	–	61' 6" × 9' 3"	1† 48	BHM	22267–70	16532–5	Tourist stock
Lav composite	50*	1933	498	51' 1½" × 9' 3"	3/4 : 19/33	DK	63867–70	88093–6	
V Composite	9*	1933	513	52' 6" × 9" 3"	2/4½ : 12/27	YK	63871–4		
		1934	536				63875–8		
V Composite	130*	1933	492	61' 6" × 9' 3"	3½/4 : 21/32	YK	63861–4	18302–5	
							32385, 32401/53, 32559–61	18271/4/8–81	
V Brake composite	143*	1934	568	61' 6" × 9" 3"	2/3 : 12/18	DK	1127	10074	
V First-class sleeping car	157*	1934	537	66' 6"' × 9' 3"	10: 10	DR	1165–8		PV
V Restaurant kitchen car (first-class)	144*	1934	523	61' 6" × 9' 3"	1† 18	DR	653	9073	
			538				51778	9072	
							1216/7	9080/1	
V Restaurant kitchen car (first) (unclassed)	11*	1934	539	61' 6" × 9' 3"	2† 30	DR	31868, 31902	9021/2	
			524				42782	9029	
V Restaurant kitchen car (composite)	187*	1934	541	61' 6" × 9' 3"	1†/1† :12/18	DR	32535–7	9155–7	
V Restaurant pantry car (third-class)	151*	1934	540	61' 6" × 9' 3"	2† 39	DR	1226/7	9098/9	
V Buffet car	168*	1934	–	61' 6" × 9' 3"	1† 24	BHM	21604–7	9136–9	§§ Tourist stock
V (Open third)	180*	1934	–	52' 0¹/₁₆" × 9' 3"	1† 56	M–C	21261/2, 21263/4,	13182–97	Tourist stock
V (Open third)				52' 0¹/₁₆" × 9' 3"	1† 56		21265/6, 21267/8, 21269/70, 21271/2, 21273/4, 21275/6		Articulated twins
V Passenger brake van	113*	1934	573	61' 6" × 9' 0"	–	DK	4145–7	70169–71	

1935 All vehicles vacuum fitted, except where shown

Type	Dia No	CBP Year	Order No	Dimensions	Comps /Seats	Built At	Running numbers Original	1943	Notes
V Open first	197	1934	577	52' 6" × 9' 3"	2† 33	YK	6463/4		
V First	140*	1934	556	52' 6" × 9' 3"	6: 36	YK	6465		
V First	1*	1935/6	615	61' 6" × 9' 3"	7: 42	YK	52401	11021	
Second	204	1935/6	–	54' 1½" × 9' 3"	10: 120	CR	6575–99	82403–27	Ilford stock Air braked
V Open second	27B*	1935/6	651	61' 6" × 9' 3"	2† 48	YK	698¶, 6994	12202/3	¶ Lettered RC Both to Dia 27A 1942.
V Open third	27A*	1935/6	621	61' 6" × 9' 3"	2† 48	YK	23803–10	12154–61	
V Open third	182*	1934	561	52' 6" × 9' 3"	2† 39	YK	61884/5		

Type	Dia No	CBP Year	Order No	Dimensions	Comps /Seats	Built At	Running numbers Original	1943	Notes
V Open third	186*	1934	559	61' 6" × 9' 3"	1† 64	YK	43620–63	13374–81/–, 13382–13416	43628 W/O Goole 1941, u/f reused – see O/N 1154. 43610/6/20/38/9, 43650/1 to ambulance trains WW2, returned to service as open thirds
		1935/6	594				22501–16	13219–25/–, 13226–33	22508 W/O Westborough 1941
			622				52243–56	13535–48	
							52257–9	13549–51	
							23814–25	13234–45	
							3142/55	13344/6	
							7405/6	13619/20	
V Third	115*	1935/6	619	61' 6" × 9' 3"	8: 64	YK	1474–82	12749–57	
							4971–92	12506–27	
			–			BHM	41031–48	12528–45	
							52260–8	12629–30/–/1–6	52262 W/O 1941
							23853–98	12285–12330	
V Third Δ	155*	1935/6	620	61' 6"× 9' 3"	7: 42	YK	1483–1506	13010–33	
			–			M–C	3873/6/85, 3905, 3915/21/4/8/9/36, 3939/41–4/8/64, 3998/9, 31005–9, 31011/3	12969–95	
							1545–78	13041–8/–, 13049–73	1553 W/O by 1938
V Third	141*	1935/6	623	52' 6" × 9' 3"	7: 56	DK	61957–9		
Third	203	1935/6	–	54' 1½" × 9' 3"	10: 120	RYP	60074–60100	82376–82402	Ilford stock Air braked
V Brake third	174*	1934	562	61' 6" × 9" 3"	3: 18	YK	1045–9 (7561, 1046, 62844–6)	16501/2, 16491/–/2/3	Trans 1940/1 62845 W/O
V Brake third	146*	1934	563	52' 6" × 9' 3"	3: 18	YK	62663–5		
V Open brake third	191	1934	565	61' 6" × 9' 3"	1† 32	YK	43560–75	16540–55	43561/7/9 to ambulance trains WW 2.
V Open brake third	196*	1935/6	595	61' 6" × 9' 3"	1† 48	YK	21213–6, 23826–48	16588–16614	
V Open brake third	179*	1935/6	–	61' 6" × 9' 3"	1† 48	BHM	21217/9/20/1 31096/9, 31100, 31111	16528–31 16536–39	Tourist stock
V Open brake third	217	1935/6	626	52' 6" × 9' 3"	1† 24	DK	62748/9		
Brake third	202	1935/6	–	54' 1½" × 9' 3"	7: 84	RYP	62074–99	86812–37	Ilford stock Air braked
V Composite	190	1934	570	52' 6" × 9" 3"	4/2 : 24/12	DR	42759–66		SP
V Composite	9*	1934	566	52' 6" × 9" 3"	2/4½ : 12/27	YK	63879–86		
		1935/6	628				63967–82		63979 W/O 1940
V Composite	130*	1934	567	61' 6" × 9' 3"	3½/4 : 21/24	YK	32275/86, 32306	18267/8/–	32306 W/O Castlecary 1937
		1935/6	–			M–C	23918–47	18170–99	
		1935/6	–			BHM	51878–94	18282–98	
							7761/70/1	18313–5	
Lav composite	50*	1934	569	51' 1½" × 9' 3"	3/4 : 19/33	YK	63887–90	88097–88100	
Composite¶	205	1935/6	–	54' 1½" × 9' 3"	4/5 : 40/60	GLO	64058–81	82428–51	Ilford stock Air braked ¶ 1st/2nd class
V First-class sleeping car	157*	1935/6	601	66' 6'" × 9' 3"	10: 10	DR	1211–4		PV
V Restaurant kitchen car (first-class)	144*	1935/6	602	61' 6" × 9' 3"	1† 18	DR	654	9074	
							1215 (659)	9078	Trans 1938
			605				655–7	9075–7	
V Restaurant kitchen car (composite)	187*	1935/6	606	61' 6" × 9' 3"	1†/1† :12/18	DR	32564/5	9158/9	

Type	Dia No	CBP Year	Order No	Dimensions	Comps /Seats	Built At	Running numbers Original	1943	Notes
V Restaurant pantry car (third-class)	151★	1935/6	630	61' 6" × 9' 3"	2† 39	DR	1542 (43003), 1543/4	9097 9103/4	Trans 1940
V (Restaurant first)	201	1935/6	646	56'2½" × 9' 2¼"	2† 28¶	DR	1583		Triplet set 'Silver Jubilee'
V (Kitchen car)				45' 11" × 9' 2¼"	–		1584		¶ Later 34 seats
V (Restaurant third)				56' 2½" × 9' 2¼"	2† 48		1585		
V Buffet car	167★	1935/6	596	61' 6" × 9' 3"	1† 24	YK	21608–11 648	9111–4 9133	§§ §§
V Buffet car	168★	1935/6	–	61' 6" × 9' 3"	1† 24	BHM	21612 31097/8, 31103/8	– 9140–3	§§ Tourist stock §§
V (Third)	194	1934	571	51' 11¾" × 9' 3"	7: 42	DR	45402/12/22/32/42, 45452/62/72/82/92, 45502/12/22/ 32/42/52	16557/9/61/3, 16565/7/9/71, 16573/5/7/9/81, 16583/5/7	
V (Brake third)	195			51' 11¾" × 9' 3"	4: 24	DR	45401/11/21/31/41, 45451/61/71/81/91, 45501/11/21/ 31/41/51	16556/8/60/2, 16564/6/8/70, 16572/4/6/8/80, 16582/4/6	

Dias 194/5 were steel - panelled articulated twins originally formed with composites to Dia 190 as eight five-car sets

Type	Dia No	CBP Year	Order No	Dimensions	Comps /Seats	Built At	Running numbers Original	1943	Notes
(Lav compo)	193	1934	572	55' 6¼" × 9' 3"	3/4 : 22/38	DR	44332/42/52/62, 44962/72/82/92	80085/7/9/91, 80093/5/7/9	Articulated twins
(Brake third)	192			55' 6¼" × 9' 3"	5: 50	DR	44331/41/51/61 44961/71/81/91	80084/6/8/90, 80092/4/6/8	
(Composite)	210★	1935/6	640	55' 6¼" × 9' 3"	2/5 : 14/48	DR	52542/52/62	80179/81/3	Articulated twins Marylebone
(Brake third)				55' 6¼" × 9' 3"	6: 60	DR	52541/51/61	80178/80/2	suburban services
V (Semi-open first)	200	1935/6	646	56' 2½" × 9' 3"	4† 30¶	DR	1582		Twin set 'Silver Jubilee'
V (Brake first)				56' 2½" × 9' 3"	5: 20	DR	1581		¶ Later 24 seats
V (Third)	199	1935/6	646	56' 2½" × 9' 3"	7: 42	DR	1586		Twin set 'Silver Jubilee'
V (Brake first)				56' 2½" × 9' 3"	5: 30	DR	1587 (1588)		

The 'Silver Jubilee' was formed of the twin to Dia 200, the restaurant triplet to Dia 201 and the twin to Dia 199 until 1938 when the third-class twin was converted to a triplet with the addition of a new third in 1938 and previous No 1587 became 1588.

Type	Dia No	CBP Year	Order No	Dimensions	Comps /Seats	Built At	Running numbers Original	1943	Notes
V (Open third)	180★	1935/6	–	52' 0¹⁄₁₆" × 9' 3"	1† 56	M–C	31101/2, 31104/5,	13198–13211,	Tourist stock
V (Open third)				52' 0¹⁄₁₆" × 9' 3"	1† 56		31106/7, 31109/10,	–/–	Articulated twins
							31112/3, 31114/5,		
							31116/7, 31118/9		31118/9 W/O
V Passenger brake van	198★	1934	573	61' 6" × 9' 0"	–	DK	112/3 (4198/9), 114–116	70363/4, 70383–5	SP 112/3 trans 1938/9
V Passenger brake van	207	1935/6	573	58' 6" × 9' 0"	–	DR	4197	70396	
V Passenger brake van	208	1935/6	573	56' 6" × 9' 0"	–	DR	4194–6	70397–9	

Nos 4197. 4194–6 on recovered underframes from sleeping cars Nos 1410, 1146/8/51 – built 1908 for GN/NE Joint Stock (1410) and 1910 for ECJS (rest)

Type	Dia No	CBP Year	Order No	Dimensions	Comps /Seats	Built At	Running numbers Original	1943	Notes
Brake van four-wheeled	170★	1934	635	31' 8⅝" × 9' 0"	–	DR	5255–60	70322–7	

1936 All vehicles vacuum fitted, except where shown   • Special 1935/6 programme
Vehicles ordered in January 1936 under Government assistance programme

Type	Dia No	CBP Year	Order No	Dimensions	Comps /Seats	Built At	Running numbers Original	1943	Notes
V First △	172★	1935/6	608 665	61' 6" × 9' 3"	6: 36	DR	125–131 1579/80 31871/4/96, 31900/13/21	11089–95 11096/7 11077–82	
V Open first	262★	1935/6	616 692	61' 6" × 9' 3"	2† 42	YK	1473 52402/3	11127 11124/5	
							1588 (1704)	11128	Reno 1938
V First	1★	1935/6	615	61' 6" × 9' 3"	7: 42	YK	6467	11025	Continental boat set
V Semi-open first△	219★	1935/6	648	61' 6" × 9' 3"	5† 42	YK	6468	11113	Continental boat set
		• 1935/6	657				4101	11109	
V Open first	218	1935/6	649	61' 6" × 9' 3"	2† 28	YK	689 (6491)	11107	Continental boat set
V First	140★	•1935/6	556	52' 6" × 9' 3"	6: 36	YK	6466		DEA 1940
First	48★	1935/6	693	51' 1½" × 9' 3"	7: 70	YK	6469–82	81055–68	

141

Type	Dia No	CBP Year	Order No	Dimensions	Comps /Seats	Built At	Running numbers Original	1943	Notes
V Brake first Δ	221	1935/6	617	61' 6" × 9' 3"	3: 18	DR	1541	11114	
V Second	115	1935/6	647	61' 6" × 9' 3"	8: 48	YK	6992,	12687,	Continental boat set
							6993 (61997)	12705	Both thirds after 1942.
V Third	115★	• 1935/6	659		8: 48	YK	1523	12758	
							4992	12527	
		1935/6	–			BHM	23899–23917	12331–49	
							7407–10/31–4	12708–15	
							#41049–58	12546–55	
							#711, 791	12706/7	
V Third Δ	155★	1935/6	620	61' 6" × 9' 3"	7: 42	YK	3281, 3399,	12938/9/41–3,	
							3403/5/23, 3430/55,	12945–9/–,	
							3613/36/48,	12950–61/6	
							3674, 3740/99,		3674 W/O Castlecary
							3800/7,		1937
							3809/10/22/6/34/49/53,		
							3857/69		
							1507–13	13034–40	
						M–C	#1601–54	13074–87/–/–/9–13126	
							#3280, 3330,		
							3402/28	12937/13790/12940/4	
V Open third	27C★	1935/6	–	61' 6" × 9' 3"	2† 48	CR	#41059/60	12217/8	
							#22250,	12204–9	
							#24130–4		
							#1655–7	12215/6/9	Trans 1938
							(41029/30, 6125),		
							#1658–60	12220–2	
V Open third	186★	1935/6	–	61' 6" × 9' 3"	1† 64	BHM	23973–97	13271–95	
			–			M–C	#24083–90,	–/13296–13302/19–35	
							24108–24		
							52269–75	13552–8	
							3972	13353	24083 W/O
			–			BHM	#23948–64,	13246–62,	Westborough 1941
							#24125–9	13336–40	
							#310/80	13341/2	
			–			M–C	#24091–24106	13303–18	
			–			BHM	#23965–72	13263–70	
V Open third	216	1935/6	639 661	52' 6" × 9' 3"	1† 52	YK	60500–18 60519–52		
V Brake third	146★	1935/6	607 667	52' 6" × 9' 3"	3: 18	YK	62751–60 62761–6		
V Brake third Δ	212★	1935/6	624	61' 6" × 9" 3"	4: 24	YK	3270/2/96,	16668/9/–/71/2	
							3311/8		3296 W/O Castlecary
									1937
							1514–22	16702/3/–/5–10	
		1935/6	–			BHM	#41363/4	16700/1	
							#3108, 3269/92,	16666/7/70/3/4,	
							3476, 3571,	16676–80/3	
							3846/59, 3901/9,		
							3914/45		
							#1661–6	16711–4/– 5	1665 W/O by late 1938
			–			M–C	#3595, 3919/35/47,	16675/81/2/4,	
							31004/14/21/3–7/9,	16685–95	
							31032/8/44		31044 W/O
									Castlecary 1937
V Brake third	114★	1935/6	650	61' 6" × 9" 3"	4: 24	YK	62750 (62516)	16726	Converted on Dia 292 as brake second for 'Hook Continental' set, 1938 and re-numbered.
			694			YK	41359/60	16367/8	
							7584/5	–/16395	
V Brake third	178★	• 1935/6	658	61' 6" × 9" 3"	6: 36	YK	1539	16527	
		1935/6	658				41361/2	16503/4	
V Brake third	37A★	1935/6	663	61' 6" × 9" 3"	5: 30	YK	24022–66	16009–34/–/5–52	
							41355–8	16069–72	
V Composite Δ	211★	1935/6	627	61' 6" × 9" 3"	3/4 : 18/24	YK	32282, 32300	18370/1	
							1524–31	18435–9/–/40/–	
			697				32301/5/7–9,	18372–7/9/80	
							32312/30/2		

Type	Dia No	CBP Year	Order No	Dimensions	Comps /Seats	Built At	Running numbers Original	1943	Notes
Lav composite	244	1935/6	–	51' 1½" × 9' 3"	2/5 : 13/41	CR RYP	63892–63917 63918–47 63898–900 ≠	88201–26 88227–48/–/9–51	63940 DEA Stratford 1940
Composite¶	215	1935/6	637	51' 1½" × 9' 3"	2/6 : 20/60	DK	63891	88148	¶ 1st/2nd composite
V Brake composite	175*	1935/6	629	61' 6" × 9" 3"	2/4 : 12/24	YK	42872–6 1532–8	10104/–/–/6/7 10134–40	
V First-class sleeping car	157*	1935/6	670	66' 6" × 9' 3"	10: 10	DR	1591/2		PV 1592 converted to Bayonet car 1944, afterwards returned to sleeping car.
V Restaurant kitchen car (first-class)	144*	1935/6	672 717	61' 6" × 9' 3"	1† 18	DR DR	1597–1600 #1667–72	9083–6 9087, 1668–72	
V Restaurant kitchen car (composite)	187*	1935/6	673	61' 6" × 9' 3"	1†/1† :12/18	DR	32566/7 7960	9160/1 9162	
V Buffet car	167*	1935/6	702	61' 6" × 9' 3"	1† 24	YK	24079–82	9115–8	
(Brake third)	210*	1935/6	640	55' 6¼" × 9' 3"	6: 60	DK	45201/11/21/31, 45241/51/61/71, 45281/91/301/11, 45321/31/41/51/61	80100/2/4/6/8, 80110/2/4/6/8, 80120/2/4/6/8, 80130/2	
			675				45561/71/81/91, 45601, 45611/21/31/41/51, 45661/71/81/91, 45701, 45711/21/31/41	80134/6/8/40/2, 80144/6/8/50/2, 80154/6/8/60/2, 80164/6/8/70	
			640				52571/81	80184/6	
(Composite)			640	55' 6¼" × 9' 3"	2/5 : 14/48	DK	45202/12/22/32, 45242/52/62/72, 45282/92/302/12, 45322/32/42/52/62	80101/3/5/7/9, 80111/3/5/7/9, 80121/3/5/7/9, 80131/3	
			675				45562/72/82/92, 45602, 45612/22/32/42/52, 45662/72/82/92, 45702, 45712/22/32/42	80135/7/9/41/3, 80145/7/9/51/3, 80155/7/9/61/3, 80165/7/9/71	
			640				52572/82	80185/7	

Dia 210 to form articulated twins – composite/brake third. GC section sets for Marylebone suburban services.

Type	Dia No	CBP Year	Order No	Dimensions	Comps /Seats	Built At	Running numbers Original	1943	Notes
(Composite)	213*	1935/6	641	55' 6¼" × 9' 3"	3/4 : 22/38	DK	52592, 52602/12	80189/91/3	
(Brake third)			641	55' 6¼" × 9' 3"	5: 50	DK	52591, 52601/11	80188/90/2	

Dia 213 to form articulated twins for Marylebone suburban services.

Type	Dia No	CBP Year	Order No	Dimensions	Comps /Seats	Built At	Running numbers Original	1943	Notes
(Composite)	214*	1935/6	642	55' 6¼" × 9' 3"	4/3 : 30/28	DK	52622/32/42	80201/3/5·	
(Brake third)			642	55' 6¼" × 9' 3"	6: 60	DK	52621/31/41	80200/2/4	

Dia 214 to form articulated twins for Marylebone suburban services.

Type	Dia No	CBP Year	Order No	Dimensions	Comps /Seats	Built At	Running numbers Original	1943	Notes
V TPO sorting van	164*	1937	723	60' 1½" × 8' 6¾"	–	YK	4202/3	70296/7	4203 body DEA at Wood Green, 1945 and rebuilt under order No 1185.
V Passenger brake van	198*	•1935/6	656 664	61' 6" × 9' 0"	–	YK YK	4148–50 5271–3 4221–32 798 1000–10	70360–2 70377–9 70365–76 70380 70386–91/–/1007–9, 70305	SP 1006 W/O

1937 All vehicles vacuum fitted, except where shown
Vehicles ordered in January 1936 under Government assistance programme

Type	Dia No	CBP Year	Order No	Dimensions	Comps /Seats	Built At	Running numbers Original	1943	Notes
V First Δ	172*	1936	711#	61' 6" × 9' 3"	6: 36	YK	#1678/9	11098/9	
V First	1*	1937	764	61' 6" × 9' 3"	7: 42	YK	41241–3	11018–20	
V Open first	237	1937	786	61' 6" × 9' 3"	2† 36¶	YK	6483	11117	'East Anglian' set ¶ Three saloons, 1938

143

Type	Dia No	CBP Year	Order No	Dimensions	Comps /Seats	Built At	Running numbers Original	1943	Notes
V Brake first	149★	1936	712#	61' 6" × 9' 3"	4: 24	YK	#4164/5	11070/1	
V Observation saloon	232	1937	809	51' 9" × 9' 2¼"	1: 16	DR	1719/29		PV 'Coronation'
V Third	141★	1935/6	718	52' 6" × 9' 3"	7: 56	YK	61960–74		
V Open third	239	1937	786	61' 6" × 9' 3"	2† 48	YK	60553	13675	'East Anglian' set
V Third Δ	155★	special 1937	724 –	61' 6" × 9' 3"	7: 42	YK GLO	3144 1749–52	12931 13128–31	Special replacement
V Open third	27C★	1936	–#	61' 6" × 9' 3"	2† 48	CR	#24135/6/8–40	12210–4	
V Third	115★	1937	–	61' 6" × 9' 3"	8: 48	BHM	60654–60 24390–24438	12688–94 12350–61/–/2–97	24402 DEA 1942
V Open third	186★	1937	–	61' 6" × 9' 3"	1† 64	M–C	43665–43730 52285–96 394, 3145	13418–68/–, 13470–5/–/6–82 13559–70 13343/5	
V Open brake third	196★	1936 1937	713# –	61' 6" × 9' 3"	1† 48	YK CR	#24141–4 #52276/7 3220/73 43576–89 52297–52302	16615–8 16649/50 16621/2 16635–42/–/4–8 16651–5	
V Brake third	37A★	1937	770	61' 6" × 9" 3"	5: 30	YK	41062–7	16058–63	
V Brake third	114★	1937	771	61' 6" × 9" 3"	4: 24	YK	24291–24336 31214/5	16250/1/–/2–94 16347/8	24293 DEA Middlesborough 1942–u/f reused for O/N 1150.
V Open brake third	240	1937	786	61' 6" × 9' 3"	1† 36¶	YK	62767/8	16721/2	¶ Three saloons from 1938
V Brake third Δ	212★	1935/6	–#	61' 6" × 9" 3"	4: 24	M–C	#31041/5/55/60	16696–9	
V Composite Δ	211★	1935/6 1936	697 714#	61' 6" × 9' 3"	3/4 : 18/24	YK YK	32321/71/5 #32382/6 #1680–8	18378/82/3 18385/6 18442–9, 18441	
V Composite	9★	1935/6 1937	698 805	52' 6" × 9' 3"	2/4½ : 12/27	YK	63983–94 63291–4		
V Composite	137★	1935/6	699	61' 6" × 9' 3"	2½/5 : 15/30	YK	42757/8	18316/7	
V Composite	130★	1937	773	61' 6" × 9' 3"	3½/4 : 21/24	YK	24337–66	18200–19/–/20–28	24357 DEA 1942
Composite	51★	1935/6	668	51' 1½" × 9' 3"	4/3 : 40/30	DK	63944–7	88128–32	
Composite¶	110★	1935/6	669	51' 1½" × 9' 3"	4/3 : 32/30	DK	63948/9	88132/3	¶First/second-class compos, later on Dia 51.
V Brake composite	175★	1935/6 1937	700 776	61' 6" × 9" 3"	2/4 : 12/24	YK YK	24067–78 7913 24387–9 42777–80 51866–8	10077–88 10133 10089–91 10100–3 10112–4	
V Brake composite	143★	1935/6	701	61' 6" × 9" 3"	2/3 : 12/18	YK	42877–80 51895 1589/90	10067–70 10073 10075/6	
V Brake composite	127★	1936	715#	61' 6" × 9" 3"	2/2 : 12/12	YK	#1689–97	10037–45	
V First-class sleeping car	227★	1936 1935/6	716# 670	66' 6" × 9' 3"	10: 10	DR DR	#1673–7 1593		PV PV
V Composite sleeping car	223	1935/6	671	66' 6" × 9' 3"	5/3 : 5/18	DR	1594–6		PV
V Restaurant kitchen car (first-class¶)	236★¶	1937 1937	780 786	61' 6" × 9' 3"	1† 18	DR YK	658 677	9185 9170	'East Anglian' set ¶Converted to third-class, 1938 and re-designated Dia 264.
V Restaurant kitchen car (third-class)	238	1937	786	61' 6" × 9' 3"	1† 24	YK	699	9172	'East Anglian' set
V Restaurant kitchen car (third-class)	241	1935/6	674	61' 6" × 9' 3"	2† 24	DR	42789–92	9173–6	§§

Type	Dia No	CBP Year	Order No	Dimensions	Comps /Seats	Built At	Running numbers Original	1943	Notes
V Kitchen car	226	1937	779	61' 6" × 9' 3"	–	DK	24282–4	9163–5	§§
V Buffet car	167★	1937	761	61' 6" × 9' 3"	1† 24	YK	24275–81	9119/–/21–5	
							43138	9127	
							51769	9128	
							641–4/9/50	9129–32/4/5	
(V Open brake third)	228	1937	755	56' 2½" × 9' 2¼"	1† 30	DR	45801	9166	'West Riding Limited' set Articulated twin SP PV
(V Open third/ kitchen car)				56' 2½" × 9' 2¼"	1† 12	DR	45802	9167	
(V Open first)	229	1937	755	56' 2½" × 9' 2¼"	1† 24	DR	45811	11115	'West Riding Limited' set
(V Open first)				56' 2½" × 9' 2¼"	1† 24	DR	45812	11116	Articulated twin SP PV
(V Open third)	230	1937	755	56' 2½" × 9' 2¼"	1† 30	DR	45821	9168	'West Riding Limited' set
(V Open third/ kitchen car)				56' 2½" × 9' 2¼"	1† 12	DR	45822	9169	Articulated twin SP PV
(V Open third)	231	1937	755	56' 2½" × 9' 2¼"	1† 42	DR	45831	16719	'West Riding Limited' set
(V Open brake third)				56' 2½" × 9' 2¼"	1† 24	DR	45832	16720	Articulated twin SP PV
(V Open brake third)	228	1937	755	56' 2½" × 9' 2¼"	1† 30	DR	1711/21/31		'Coronation' sets Articulated twin SP PV
(V Open third/ kitchen car)				56' 2½" × 9' 2¼"	1† 12	DR	1712/22/32		
(V Open first)	229	1937	755	56' 2½" × 9' 2¼"	1† 24	DR	1713/23/33		'Coronation' sets
(V Open first)				56' 2½" × 9' 2¼"	1† 24	DR	1714/24/34		Articulated twin SP PV
(V Open third)	230	1937	755	56' 2½" × 9' 2¼"	1† 24	DR	1715/25/35		'Coronation' sets
(V Open third/ kitchen car)				56' 2½" × 9' 2¼"	1† 12	DR	1716/26/36		Articulated twin SP PV
(V Open third)	231	1937	755	56' 2½" × 9' 2¼"	1† 42	DR	1717/27/37		'Coronation' sets
(V Open brake third)				56' 2½" × 9' 2¼"	1† 24	DR	1718/28/38		Articulated twin SP PV

1711–8, 1721–8 for the 'Coronation'; 1731–8, the spare set for the high-speed trains. 1737/8 W/O Huntingdon, 1951.

Type	Dia No	CBP Year	Order No	Dimensions	Comps /Seats	Built At	Running numbers Original	1943	Notes
(Composite)	210★	1935/6	675	55' 6¼" × 9' 3"	2/5 : 14/48	DK	45752/62/72	80173/5/7	
(Brake third)				55' 6¼" × 9' 3"	6: 60	DK	45751/61/71	80172/4/6	
(Composite)	213★	1935/6	676	55' 6¼" × 9' 3"	3/4 : 22/38	DK	52652/62/72	80195/7/9	
(Brake third)				55' 6¼" × 9' 3"	5: 50	DK	52651/61/71	80194/6/8	

Dia 213 to form articulated twins for Marylebone suburban services.

Type	Dia No	CBP Year	Order No	Dimensions	Comps /Seats	Built At	Running numbers Original	1943	Notes
(Composite)	214★	1935/6	677	55' 6¼" × 9' 3"	4/3 : 30/28	DK	52682/92, 52702	80207/9/11	
(Brake third)				55' 6¼" × 9' 3"	6: 60	DK	52681/91, 52701	80206/8/10	

Dia 214 to form articulated twins for Marylebone suburban services.

Type	Dia No	CBP Year	Order No	Dimensions	Comps /Seats	Built At	Running numbers Original	1943	Notes
(First)	242★	1937	795	51' 1½" × 9' 3"	7: 56	DK	52752/4/6/8/60/2/4, 52766/8/70/2/4/6	88157/9/61/3/5/7, 88169/71/3/5/7/9/81	
(Third)				51' 1½" × 9' 3"	8: 80	DK	52751/3/5/7/9/61/3, 52765/7/9/71/3/5	88158/60/2/4/6/8, 88170/2/4/6/8/80/2	

Dia 242 to form articulated twins for Marylebone suburban services.

Type	Dia No	CBP Year	Order No	Dimensions	Comps /Seats	Built At	Running numbers Original	1943	Notes
V TPO sorting van	164★	1937	787	60' 1½" × 8' 6¼"	–	YK	2440–2	70293–5	
							4206/7	70298/9	
V Passenger brake van	198★	1935/6	664	61' 6" × 9' 0"	–	YK	799, 7100	70381/2	SP
Passenger brake van	129★	special	749	51' 1½" × 9' 0"	–	YK	6784	70275	For racing pigeon traffic

1938 All vehicles vacuum fitted

Type	Dia No	CBP Year	Order No	Dimensions	Comps /Seats	Built At	Running numbers Original	1943	Notes
V First Δ	257	1938	841	61' 6" × 9' 3"	6: 24¶	DR	1850/1	11118/9	'Flying Scotsman' sets PV¶ Later 36 seats
V First	140★	1937	802	52' 6" × 9' 3"	6: 36	YK	6484		
V Open first	262★	1937	765	61' 6" × 9' 3"	2† 42	YK	41251/2	11122/3	
V Semi-open firstΔ	219★	1937	766	61' 6" × 9' 3"	5† 42	YK	41261–3	11110–2	
							24289	11108	

145

Type	Dia No	CBP Year	Order No	Dimensions	Comps /Seats	Built At	Running numbers Original	1943	Notes
V Open first	289	1938	848	61' 6" × 9' 3"	6† 24	YK	6485/6	11134/5	'Hook Continental' set PV
V Semi-open first Δ	290	1938	848	61' 6" × 9' 3"	6† 24	YK	6487	11136	'Hook Continental' set PV
First	252	1937	–	51' 1½" × 9' 3"	7: 56	RYP	31934/8	81071/2	SP
V Brake first Δ	263	1937	767	61' 6" × 9' 3"	5: 30	YK	52404/5	11132/3	
V Brake first	142	1937	768	61' 6" × 9' 3"	2: 12	YK	24290	11063	
V Brake first	149	1937	769	61' 6" × 9' 3"	4: 24	YK	4166/7	11072/3	
V Second Δ	288	1938	848	61' 6" × 9' 3"	7: 42	YK	6995	13686	'Hook Continental' set PV
V Open second	287	1938	848	61' 6" × 9' 3"	8† 48	YK	6996–8	13683–5	'Hook Continental' set PV
V Brake third Δ	285	1938	848	61' 6" × 9" 3"	6: 36	YK	62515	16725	'Hook Continental' set PV

(Second brake No 62516 in this set to Dia 292 was a conversion from Dia 114, No 62750)

Type	Dia No	CBP Year	Order No	Dimensions	Comps /Seats	Built At	Running numbers Original	1943	Notes
V Third	199	1938	854	45' 11" × 9' 3"	6: 35	DR	1587		'Silver Jubilee' SP, PV

Additional vehicle to form triplet with twin third brake built in 1935.

Type	Dia No	CBP Year	Order No	Dimensions	Comps /Seats	Built At	Running numbers Original	1943	Notes
V Third	141*	1937	803	52' 6" × 9' 3"	7: 42	YK	60554–60603		60599 W/O Knebworth 1943
V Third Δ	155*	1938	840	61' 6" × 9' 3"	7: 42	YK	1720	13127	
		1937	–			GLO	1753–62	13132–41	
V Third Δ	256	1938	840	61' 6" × 9' 3"	7: 42	DR	1842–9	13676–81/–/2	'Flying Scotsman' sets PV
V Third Δ	298*	1938	859	61' 6" × 9' 3"	7: 42	YK	1763–1802	13708/–/ 10–20/–/21– 46	1763/4/6 fitted with single bolster bogies to dwg No 15448N 1764 W/O Goswick 1947, 1776 DEA 1942.
V Third	115*	1937	–	61' 6" × 9' 3"	8: 48	BHM	24439–78	12398–12423/–/ 4–37	
		1938	–				41151–92	12556–97	
			–				56000–39	12644–66/–/7–72, –/12673–81	56023/30 W/O
			–				60654–63	12688–97	
		special	–				60664	12698	
V Open third	186*	1938	–	61' 6" × 9' 3"	1† 64	M–C	3328/45/51	13347–9	
							43731–82	13483–13534	
							56850–95	13571–13616	
							761/2	13617/8	
Lavatory third	265*	1938	–	54' 1½" × 9' 3"	8: 65	CR	60665–60710	82512–57	SP
Third	276*	1938	–	51' 1½" × 9' 3"	8: 80	RYP	60744–60	82619–35	SP
V Brake third	37A*	1938	837	61' 6" × 9" 3"	5: 30	DR	41381–7	–/16074–9	
							62785–98	16095–16108	62786/9/91/2/3/8 ambulance trains WW2, returned to service as brake thirds.
V Brake third Δ	212*	special	815	61' 6" × 9" 3"	4: 24	YK	1730	–	W/O
V Brake third Δ	261*	1938	838	61' 6" × 9" 3"	4: 24	DR	1840/1	16723/4	'Flying Scotsman' sets PV
V Brake third	146*	1937	804	52' 6" × 9' 3"	3: 18	YK	62769–98		62779 DEA, u/f used again
V Open brake third	196*	1938	–	61' 6" × 9' 3"	1† 48	CR	3115/50	16619/20	
							43548–59	16623–34	
							57700–9	16656–65	57706 reb as Dia 326, 1942 –32 seats.
Brake third	246	1937	794	51' 1½" × 9' 3"	6: 60	DK	52303–18	86838–53	
		1938	849			DK	57300–3	86854–7	
V Locker Δ composite	251	1937	775	66' 6" × 9' 3"	3/3½ : 12/21	YK	1740–8	18387/8/–/90–4	
		1938	843			DR	1854–7	18395–8	'Flying Scotsman' sets PV
V Composite Δ	259	1938	853	61' 6" × 9' 3"	3/4 : 12¶/24	DR	1858/9	18399, 18400	'Flying Scotsman' sets PV ¶ Later 18 seats
V Composite Δ	211*	1937	774	61' 6" × 9' 3"	3/4 : 18/24	YK	32370/9	18381/4	
V Composite	137*	1937	772	61' 6" × 9' 3"	2½/5 : 15/30	YK	51896–8	18320–2	

Type	Dia No	CBP Year	Order No	Dimensions	Comps /Seats	Built At	Running numbers Original	1943	Notes
V Composite	130*	1938	862			YK	64103–18	18324–39	
		1937	773	61' 6" × 9' 3"	3½/4 : 21/24	YK	24367–86	18229–42/–/4–8	
V Composite	9*	1938	863			YK	64101/2	18306/7	
		1937	805	52' 6" × 9" 3"	2/4½ : 12/27	YK	63295–63319		
V Restaurant kitchen car (first-class¶)	236*¶	1937	780	61' 6" × 9' 3"	1† 18	DR	678	9171	Anthracite-electric cooking equipment ¶Converted to third-class, 1938 and re-designated Dia 264. 'Hook Continental' set
V Restaurant kitchen car (first-class¶)	291	1938	848	61' 6" × 9' 3"	1† 12	YK	676	9198	'Hook Continental' set
V Restaurant kitchen car (second-class)	286	1938	848	61' 6" × 9' 3"	1† 18	YK	694	9197	Later third-class
V Restaurant kitchen car (third-class)	268	1937	782	61' 6" × 9' 3"	2† 24	DR	24285	9194	Anthracite-electric cooking equipment
V Restaurant pantry car (third-class)	151*	1937	762	61' 6" × 9' 3"	2† 39	DR	1698–1703	9105–10	
V Restaurant kitchen car (composite)	266	1937	781	61' 6" × 9' 3"	1†/1† :12/18	DR	32388/95, 32424	9186–8	Anthracite-electric cooking equipment
							7963	9189	Anthracite-electric cooking equipment
V Restaurant kitchen car (unclassed)	267	1937	783	61' 6" × 9' 3"	2† 24	DR	24286	9190	Anthracite-electric cooking equipment
		1938	867			DR	32302/3/93	9191–3	'Flying Scotsman' sets
V Buffet lounge car	258	1938	842	66' 6" × 9' 3"	1† 20	DR	1852/3		PV Converted by BR to buffet cars
(Composite)	214*	1937	796	55' 6¼" × 9' 3"	4/3 : 30/28	DK	52544	80213	
		1938	850			DK	53700/2/4/6	80215/7/9/21	
(Brake third)		1937	796	55' 6¼" × 9' 3"	6: 60	DK	52543	80212	
		1938	850			DK	53701/3/5/7	80214/6/8/20	

Dia 214 to form articulated twins for Marylebone suburban services.

Type	Dia No	CBP Year	Order No	Dimensions	Comps /Seats	Built At	Running numbers Original	1943	Notes
(First)	242*	1937	795	51' 1½" × 9' 3"	7: 56	DK	52778/80/2	88183/5/7	
		1938	851			DK	52800/2/4/6	88189/91/3/5	
			872			DK	32733/5	88150/2	
(Third)		1937	795	51' 1½" × 9' 3"	8: 80	DK	52777/9/81	88184/6/8	
		1938	851			DK	52801/3/5/7	88190/2/4/6	
			872			DK	32732/4	88149/51	

Dia 242 to form articulated twins for Marylebone suburban services – order Nos 795/851; Glasgow and Edinburgh – order No 872.

Type	Dia No	CBP Year	Order No	Dimensions	Comps /Seats	Built At	Running numbers Original	1943	Notes
(Brake third)	278	1938	873	51' 1½" × 9' 3"	4: 40	DK	32736/8/40/2	86926/8/30/2	
(Third)		1938	873	51' 1½" × 9' 3"	8: 80	DK	32737/9/41/3	86927/9/31/3	

Dia 278 to form articulated twins for Glasgow and Edinburgh suburban services.

Type	Dia No	CBP Year	Order No	Dimensions	Comps /Seats	Built At	Running numbers Original	1943	Notes
(Third)	247	1937	–	51' 1½" × 9' 3"	8: 80	RYP	32700/2/4/ 6/8/10	86859/61/ 3/5/7/9	SP
(Brake third)		1937	–	51' 1½" × 9' 3"	4: 40	RYP	32701/3/5/ 7/9/11	86858/60/ 2/4/6/8	SP

Dia 247 to form articulated twins for Glasgow and Edinburgh suburban services.

Type	Dia No	CBP Year	Order No	Dimensions	Comps /Seats	Built At	Running numbers Original	1943	Notes
(First)	248	1937	–	51' 1½" × 9' 3"	7: 56	RYP	32712/4/6	88252/4/6	SP
(Third)		1937	–	51' 1½" × 9' 3"	8: 80	RYP	32713/5/7	88253/5/7	SP

Dia 248 to form articulated twins for Glasgow and Edinburgh suburban services.

Type	Dia No	CBP Year	Order No	Dimensions	Comps /Seats	Built At	Running numbers Original	1943	Notes
(First)	249	1937	–	51' 1½" × 9' 3"	7: 56	RYP	32718	81069	SP
(First)		1937	–	51' 1½" × 9' 3"	7: 56	RYP	32719	81070	SP

Dia 249 to form articulated twin for Glasgow and Edinburgh suburban services.

Type	Dia No	CBP Year	Order No	Dimensions	Comps /Seats	Built At	Running numbers Original	1943	Notes
(Third)	250	1937	–	51' 1½" × 9' 3"	8: 80	RYP	32720/2/4/6	86871/3/5/7	SP
(Brake third)		1937	–	51' 1½" × 9' 3"	5: 50	RYP	32721/3/5/7	86870/2/4/6	SP

Dia 250 to form articulated twins for Glasgow and Edinburgh suburban services.

Type	Dia No	CBP Year	Order No	Dimensions	Comps /Seats	Built At	Running numbers Original	1943	Notes
(First)	253	1937	–	51' 1½" × 9' 3"	7: 56	RYP	32728/30	88258/60	SP
(Composite)		1937	–	51' 1½" × 9' 3"	4/3 :32/30	RYP	32729/31	88259/61	SP

Dia 253 to form articulated twins for Glasgow and Edinburgh suburban services.

Type	Dia No	CBP Year	Order No	Dimensions	Comps /Seats	Built At	Running numbers Original	1943	Notes
(Lav Third)	269★	1938	–	55' 6¼" × 9' 3"	8: 74	M–C	24518/20	86882/4	SP
(Brake third)			–	55' 6¼" × 9' 3"	4: 40	M–C	24519/21	86883/5	SP

Dia 269 to form articulated twins for Darlington–Saltburn service.

Type	Dia No	CBP Year	Order No	Dimensions	Comps /Seats	Built At	Running numbers Original	1943	Notes
(Third)	270★	1938	–	55' 6¼" × 9' 3"	9: 90	BHM	24530/2	82591/3	SP
(Third)			–	55' 6¼" × 9' 3"	9: 90	BHM	24531/3	82592/4	SP

Dia 270 to form articulated twins for Darlington–Saltburn service.

Type	Dia No	CBP Year	Order No	Dimensions	Comps /Seats	Built At	Running numbers Original	1943	Notes
(Lav composite)	271★	1938	–	55' 6¼" × 9' 3"	2/6 : 16/54	M–C	24572/4	88262/4	SP
(Lav composite)			–	55' 6¼" × 9' 3"	2/6 : 13/57	M–C	24573/5	88263/5	SP

Dia 271 to form articulated twins for Darlington–Saltburn service.

Type	Dia No	CBP Year	Order No	Dimensions	Comps /Seats	Built At	Running numbers Original	1943	Notes
V(Restaurant first)	255	1938	839	56' 2½" × 9' 3"	6† 36	DR	16521/31	1428/31	Triplet restaurant car sets
(Kitchen car)				45' 11" × 9' 3"	–		16522/32	1429/32	
(Restaurant third)				56' 2½" × 9' 3"	2† 42		16523/33	1430/3	'Flying Scotsman' sets PV
Passenger brake van	129★	special	788	51' 1½" × 9' 0"	–	YK	6791	70276	
V Passenger brake van	245★	1937	777	61' 6" × 9' 0"	–	YK	2426–39	70412–25	Racing pigeon traffic
							4233–47	70456–70	
		1938	870		–		4213–20	70448–55	
V Passenger brake van	260★	1937	777	61' 6" × 9' 0"	–	YK	312/20/1	70515–7	SP
		1938	844		–	DR	1012/3	70550/1	
			870		–	YK	322/3/8/9/31, 333/4/6/8/40, 346/7	70518–29	Racing pigeon traffic
V Passenger brake van	282	1937	778	52' 6" × 9' 0"	–	YK	6785–90/7	70554–60	

1939 All vehicles vacuum fitted

Type	Dia No	CBP Year	Order No	Dimensions	Comps /Seats	Built At	Running numbers Original	1943	Notes
V First	1★	1939	956	61' 6" × 9' 3"	7: 42	DR	6489/90	11026/7	
V Open first	262★	1938	857	61' 6" × 9' 3"	2† 42	YK	24485/6	11120/1	
							6488	11126	
							1862	11129	
V Brake first	149★	1938	858	61' 6" × 9' 3"	4: 24	YK	24487–9	11066–8	BS gangways
V Brake first	300	1939	958	61' 6" × 9' 3"	3: 18	DR	4168–71	11137–40	
							55230	11141	
Lavatory third	265★	1938	–	54' 1½" × 9' 3"	8: 65	CR	60711–43	82558–90	SP
Third	276★	1938	–	51' 1½" × 9' 3"	8: 80	RYP	60761–7	82636–42	SP
V Open third	302	1939	959	61' 6" × 9' 3"	1† 64	DR	3342/55/76, 3802/11/5/6/8	13774–81	
V Third Δ	298★	1938	859	61' 6" × 9' 3"	7: 42	YK	1803–21	13747–55/–, 13756–64	1812 DEA 1942
		special	903			YK	3674, 31083/90	13687/91/2	Accident replacements
		1939	946			YK	31001/47/50, 31145/51/4/62, 31175, 31200, 31202–4, 31211/2/6–9	13688–90, 13693–5/–, 13697–13707	31154/62/75, 31200/2 BS gangways 31162 W/O
V Third	115★	1939	947	61' 6" × 9' 3"	8: 48	YK	24590–24601	12438–49	
							43783–9	12605–11	
							56040–3	12682–5	
							60774–9	12699–12704	
Brake third	294★	1938	866	51' 1½" × 9' 3"	4: 40	YK	62821–30	86949–58	SP
V Brake third	37A★	1938	837	61' 6" × 9" 3"	5: 30	DR	24480–4	16053–7	
							41388–90	16080–2	
		1939	952			YK	41391–6	16083–6/–/8	
							62831–6	16109–14	
V Brake third	114★	1938	860	61' 6" × 9" 3"	4: 24	YK	24490–24509	16295/–/6–8 16309, –/16310–2	24495/9 BS gangways 24491, 24506 DEA
		1939	954			YK	43151	16369	
							57458/9	16393/–	

Type	Dia No	CBP Year	Order No	Dimensions	Comps /Seats	Built At	Running numbers Original	1943	Notes
V Brake third	174★	1939	960	61' 6" × 9" 3"	3: 18	DR	24662	16477	
							62837–62843	16484–16490	
V Brake third Δ	297★	1938	861	61' 6" × 9" 3"	4: 24	YK	1822–5	16738–42	
		special	904			YK	3296, 31044	16727/30	accident replacements
			962				3823/56, 31048,	16728/9,	3856, 31135,
							31123/7/35,	16731–3/–,	31221–3 BS gangways
							31220–3	16734–7	31135 DEA 1940
							1865	16742	
V Brake third Δ	301★	special	944	61' 6" × 9" 3"	3: 18	YK	31197	16767	accident replacement
V Open brake third	303	1939	963	61' 6" × 9' 3"	1† 48	DR	31226/7	16775/6	
V Open brake third	308	1938	942	61' 6" × 9' 3"	1† 48	YK	31864/5	16845/6	Tourist stock
Lav composite	299★	1938	877	51' 1½" × 9' 3"	3/4 : 19/33	YK	64119–23	88311–5	SP
V Composite	130★	1938	863	61' 6" × 9' 3"	3½/4 : 21/24	YK	24510–7	18249–56	
		1939	948			DR	24602–11	18257–66	
V Locker Δ composite	279	1938	868	66' 6" × 9' 3"	3/3½ : 18/21	DR	1838/9	18401/2	
V Composite Δ	296	1938	869	61' 6" × 9' 3"	3/4 : 18/24	DR	1831–7	18409–15	
		special	905			DR	32306	18403	accident replacement
		1939	933				32368,	18404–8	BS gangways
							32430/1/4/44 1860/1	18416/7	
V Composite	305★	1939	977	61' 6" × 9' 3"	3½/4 : 21/24	YK	58107–11	18420–4	SP In five–car sets with Dia 304 twins.
V Brake composite	175★	1938	864	61' 6" × 9" 3"	2/4 : 12/24	YK	42884–6	10108–10	
							58700–2, 64124–30	10115–7, 10118–24	
							1826–30	10141–5	
V Kitchen car	293	1938	865	61' 6" × 9' 3"	–	DK	32568	9199	Anthracite-electric cooking equipment
V Restaurant buffet car	275	1937	784	61' 6" × 9' 3"	2† 30	DK /DR	24287/8	9195/6	
V (Open third)	307	1938	941	52' 0¹⁄₁₆" × 9' 3"	1† 56	YK	32770/2/4/6	13782/4/6/8	Tourist stock SP
V (Open third)				52' 0¹⁄₁₆" × 9' 3"	1† 56		32771/3/5/7	13783/5/7/9	Articulated twins
V (Brake third)	304★	1939	967	52' 0" × 9' 3"	4: 24	YK	53500/2/4/6/8, 53510/2/4/6/8	16785/7/9/91/3, 16795/7/9, 16801/3	
V (Third)				52' 0" × 9' 3"	7: 42	YK	53501/3/5/7/9, 53511/3/5/7/9	16786/8/90/2/4, 16796/8, 16800/2/4	

Dia 304 comprised steel- panelled articulated twins originally formed with composites to Dia 305 as five, five-car trains

(First)	272	1938	874	51' 1½" × 9' 3"	7: 56	DK	32745/7/9/51	80291/3/5/7	
(Brake third)		1938		51' 1½" × 9' 3"	5: 50	DK	32744/6/8/50	80290/2/4/6	

Dia 272 to form articulated twins for Glasgow and Edinburgh suburban services.

(Third)	273	1938	875	51' 1½" × 9' 3"	8: 80	RYP	32753/5/7/9	86919/21/3/5	
(Brake third)		1938		51' 1½" × 9' 3"	5: 50	RYP	32752/4/6/8	86918/20/2/4	

Dia 273 to form articulated twins for Glasgow and Edinburgh suburban services.

(First)	274	1938	876	51' 1½" × 9' 3"	7: 56	DK	32760	88280	
(Composite)		1938		51' 1½" × 9' 3"	4/3 :32/30	DK	32761	88281	

Dia 274 to form articulated twins for Glasgow and Edinburgh suburban services.

(Lav Third)	269★	1938	–	55' 6¼" × 9' 3"	8: 74	M–C BHM	24522/4/6/8 24548/50/2/4, 24556/8/60/2/4, 24566/8/70	86886/8/90/2 86894/6/8, 86900, 86902/4/6/8, 86910/2/4/6	SP
(Brake third)			–	55' 6¼" × 9' 3"	4: 40	M–C BHM	24523/5/7/9 24549/51/3/5, 24557/9/61/3/5, 24567/9/71	86887/9/91/3 86995/7/9, 86901, 86903/5/7/9, 86911/3/5/7	SP

Dia 269 to form articulated twins for Darlington–Saltburn service.

(Third)	270★	1938	–	55' 6¼" × 9' 3"	9: 90	BHM	24534/6/8/40/2, 24544/6	82595/7/9, 82601, 82603/5/7	SP

149

Type	Dia No	CBP Year	Order No	Dimensions	Comps /Seats	Built At	Running numbers Original	1943	Notes
(Third)			–	55' 6¼" × 9' 3"	9: 90	BHM	24535/7/9/41/3, 24545/7	82596/8, 82600/2, 82604/6/8	SP

Dia 270 to form articulated twins for Darlington–Saltburn service.

Type	Dia No	CBP Year	Order No	Dimensions	Comps /Seats	Built At	Running numbers Original	1943	Notes
(Lav composite)	271*	1938	–	55' 6¼" × 9' 3"	2/6 : 16/54	M–C	24576/8/80/2/4, 24586/8	88266/8/ 70/2/4/6, 88278	SP
(Lav composite)			–	55' 6¼" × 9' 3"	2/6 : 13/57	M–C	24577/9/81/3/5, 24587/9	88267/9/71/ 3/5/7, 88279	SP

Dia 271 to form articulated twins for Darlington–Saltburn service.

Type	Dia No	CBP Year	Order No	Dimensions	Comps /Seats	Built At	Running numbers Original	1943	Notes
V Passenger brake van	245*	1937	777	61' 6" × 9' 0"	–	YK	4248–53	70471–6	
		1938	870		–		5274–80	70499–70505	
		special	878		–		5281–3	70506–8	
					–		1011	70514	Accident replacement
V Passenger brake van	260*	1937	777	61' 6" × 9' 0"	–	YK	312/20/1	70515–7	SP
		1938	844		–	DR	1012/3	70550/1	
			870		–	YK	322/3/8/9/31, 333/4/6/8/40, 346/7	70518–29	
Passenger brake van	284*	1938	871	51' 1½" × 9' 0"	–	YK	6792–6	70561¶/2/3/–/4	6795 W/O ¶70561 converted in 1949 to a PO stowage van, Dia 357.

1940 All vehicles vacuum fitted

Type	Dia No	CBP Year	Order No	Dimensions	Comps /Seats	Built At	Running numbers Original	1943	Notes
V Open first	262*	1939	951	61' 6" × 9' 3"	2† 42	YK	1863/4	11130/1	
V First Δ	172*	1939	957	61' 6" × 9' 3"	6: 36	DR	31931/7/44/5	11083–6	
Third	104*	special	1094	43' 5" × 9' 3"	7: 70	SF	61800		80016 Replacement body in quadruplet set – original damaged Ware 1940.
Third	276*	1939	970	51' 1½" × 9' 3"	8: 80	YK	24652–61	82609–18	SP
V Brake third	178*	1939	953	61' 6" × 9' 3"	6: 36	YK	57450–7	16519–21/–/3–6	
V Brake third Δ	297*	1939	962	61' 6" × 9' 3"	4: 24	YK	1866–84	16743–61	
V Brake third Δ	301*	1939	955	61' 6" × 9' 3"	3: 18	YK	31224/5	–/16768	31224 W/O
V Composite	130*	1939	975	61' 6" × 9' 3"	3½/4 : 21/24	YK	58104–6	18299–18301	
						YK	64135–9	18308–12	
V Composite	137*	1939	964	61' 6" × 9' 3"	2½/5 : 15/30	DR	42793/4	18318/9	
						DR	58117/8	–/18323	58117 DEA 1943.
						DR	64140–59	18340–4/–, 18346–59	64145 DEA, u/f used Order No 1153.
V Composite	305*	1939	977	61' 6" × 9' 3"	3½/4 : 21/24	YK	58112–6	18425/6/–/7/8	SP In five-car sets with Dia 304 twins.
Lav composite	299*	1939	968	51' 1½" × 9' 3"	3/4 : 19/33	YK	24617–38	88285–88306	SP
Composite	311*	1939	972	51' 1½" × 9' 3"	4/3 : 32/30	YK	57800–3	88323–6	SP In five-car sets with Dia 312 twins.
V Brake composite	143*	1939	965	61' 6" × 9' 3"	2/3 : 12/18	DR	24663–7	10059–63	
						DR	42887/8	10071/2	
V Brake composite	175*	1939	961	61' 6" × 9' 3"	2/4 : 12/24	YK	24612–6	10092–6	
						YK	64160–7	10125–32	
			974			YK	42892	10111	Accident replacement
V Brake composite	316	1939	966	61' 6" × 9' 3"	3/3 : 18/18	DR	42889–91	10156–8	
V (Brake third)	304*	1939	967	52' 0" × 9' 3"	4: 24	YK	53520/2/4/6/32, 53534/6/8/40/2	16805/7/9/11/3, 16815/7/9/21/3	
V (Third)				52' 0" × 9' 3"	7: 42	YK	53521/3/5/7/33, 53535/7/9/41/3	16806/8/10/2/4, 16816/8/20/2/4	

Dia 304 comprised steel-panelled articulated twins originally formed with composites to Dia 305 as five, five-car trains

Type	Dia No	CBP Year	Order No	Dimensions	Comps /Seats	Built At	Running numbers Original	1943	Notes
(Third)	312*	1939	973	51' 1½" × 9' 3"	8: 80	YK	54001/3/5/7/9, 54011/3/5	86968/70/2/4/6, 86978/80/2	

Type	Dia No	CBP Year	Order No	Dimensions	Comps /Seats	Built At	Running numbers Original	1943	Notes
(Brake third)		1939		51' 1½" × 9' 3"	6: 60	YK	54000/2/4/6/8, 54010/2/4	86967/9/71/3/5, 86977/9/81	

Dia 312 comprised steel-panelled articulated twins originally formed with composites to Dia 311 as four, five-car trains for Manchester suburban services.

Type	Dia No	CBP Year	Order No	Dimensions	Comps /Seats	Built At	Running numbers Original	1943	Notes
(Lav composite)	309	1939	976	51' 1½" × 9' 3"	3/4 : 23/39	YK	45841/51	88317/9	
(Third)		1939		51' 1½" × 9' 3"	8: 80	YK	45842/52	88318/20	
(Lav composite)	313	1939	976	55' 6¼" × 9' 3"	2/5 : 14/48	YK	45862/72	80323/5	
(Brake third)		1939		51' 1½" × 9' 3"	6: 60	YK	45861/71	80322/4	

Dia 309/13 comprised steel-panelled articulated twins to form one eight-car train for Kings Cross outer suburban services.

Type	Dia No	CBP Year	Order No	Dimensions	Comps /Seats	Built At	Running numbers Original	1943	Notes
(Lav composite)	–	1939	980	51' 1½" × 9' 3"	3/4 : 23/39	YK	GN section	–	
(Brake third) Order cancelled	–	1939		51' 1½" × 9' 3"	5: 50	YK	GN section	–	
(Third)	105★	special	982	51' 1½" × 9' 3"	8: 80	DR	44152	82371	Accident replacement
(Third)	106★			51' 1½" × 9' 3"	8: 80	DR	44151	82370	Articulated twin
V Passenger brake van	260★	1939	984	61' 6" × 9' 0"	–	YK	6851–6	70533–8	SP
V Passenger brake van	315	1939	983	61' 6" × 8' 11½"	–	YK	4254–75 5286/7	70477–81/–/ 3–98 70511/2	SP Later shown as Dia 245

1941 All vehicles vacuum fitted

Type	Dia No	CBP Year	Order No	Dimensions	Comps /Seats	Built At	Running numbers Original	1943	Notes
V Third Δ	298★	1940	1099	61' 6" × 9' 3"	7: 56	DR	1371/2/4–7/9, 1381	13765–72	
Brake third	294★	1939	969	51' 1½" × 9' 3"	4: 40	YK	24639–51	86936–48	SP
Brake third	319	1939	979 1025	51' 1½" × 9' 3"	6: 60	YK YK	43259–64 43265–70	86985–90 86991–6	SP
V Brake third	37A★	1940	1008	61' 6" × 9' 3"	5: 40	YK	62848–52	16115–9	
V Brake composite Δ	314	1939	999	61' 6" × 9' 3"	2/3 : 12/18	DR	32447/8/50 1885–91	10146–8 10149/50/–, 10152/–/4/5	BS gangways 1887 W/O 1889 W/O Kings Cross 1945
(Composite)	108★	special	981	51' 1½" × 9' 3"	3/4 : 23/39	DR	44132	80081	Accident replacement Articulated twin
(Brake third)	107★			51' 1½" × 9' 3"	4: 40	DR	44131	80080	
(Brake third)	310★	1939	980	51' 1½" × 9' 3"	5: 50	YK	45881/91/901, 45911/21/31	80298, 80300/2, 80304/6/8	SP
			1027			YK	45941/51/61, 45971/81/91	80310/2/4, 80316/8/20	
(Composite)			980	51' 1½" × 9' 3"	3/4 : 23/39	YK	45882/92/902, 45912/22/32	80299, 80301/3, 80305/7/9	SP
			1027			YK	45942/52/62, 45972/82/92	80311/3/5, 80317/9/21	

Dia 310 comprised steel-panelled articulated twins for Nottingham and West Riding districts used with Dia 319 brake thirds

Type	Dia No	CBP Year	Order No	Dimensions	Comps /Seats	Built At	Running numbers Original	1943	Notes
(Composite)	76★	special	1022	43' 6" × 9' 3"	4/3 : 40/36	SF	63067	86561	New body, original DEA.
V Passenger brake van	245★	1940	1017	61' 6" × 9' 0"	–	YK	2443 4050–3/5–7, 4060/1/3–72, 4074/6 5288	70426 70427–47 70513	SP
V Passenger brake van	260★	1940	1018	61' 6" × 9' 0"	–	YK	3000/1 6857–62/6	70530/1 70539/40/–/ 2–4/8	SP

1942 All vehicles vacuum fitted

Type	Dia No	CBP Year	Order No	Dimensions	Comps /Seats	Built At	Running numbers Original	1943	Notes
(Brake third)	85★	special	1029	43' 6" × 9' 3"	6: 72	SF	62066	86730	New body, original DEA.
(Brake third)	102★	special	1030	51' 1½" × 9' 3"	3: 30	SF	62804	80030	New body, original DEA.
V Brake third Δ	301★	1940	1009	61' 6" × 9' 3"	3: 24	YK	30020–4 7125–30	16762–6 –/16769–73	7125 W/O
V Restaurant pantry car (third-class)	321★	1939	971	61' 6" × 9' 3"	2† 38	DR	1892/4/7		Entered traffic as open firsts with the pantry locked out of use.

Type	Dia No	CBP Year	Order No	Dimensions	Comps /Seats	Built At	Running numbers Original	1943	Notes
V Composite	305*	1940	1010	61' 6" × 9' 3"	3½/4 : 21/24	YK	41007/8 58119–24	18418/9 18429–34	SP
V (Brake third)	304*	1940	1011	52' 0" × 9' 3"	4: 24	YK	45403/5/7/13 53544/6/8/50, 53552/4/6/8/60, 53562	16777/9/81/3 16825/7/9/31/3, 16835/7/9/41/3	
V (Third)				52' 0" × 9' 3"	7: 42	YK	45404/6/8/14 53545/7/9/51, 53553/5/7/9/61, 53563	16778/80/2/4 16826/8/30/2/4, 16836/8/40/2/4	

Dia 304 comprised steel-panelled articulated twins originally formed with composites to Dia 305 as two, five-car trains for the GN section and six, five-car trains for the GC section.

Type	Dia No	CBP Year	Order No	Dimensions	Comps /Seats	Built At	Running numbers Original	1943	Notes
V Passenger brake van	260*	1940	1018	61' 6" × 9' 0"	–	YK	3002 6863–5/7	70532 70545–7/9	SP

1943 All vehicles vacuum fitted

Type	Dia No	CBP Year	Order No	Dimensions	Comps /Seats	Built At	Running numbers Original	1943	Notes
Lav composite	299*	1940	1012	51' 1½" × 9' 3"	3/4 : 19/33	YK	24685–8	88307–10	SP
Composite	311*	1940	1013	51' 1½" × 9' 3"	4/3 : 32/30	YK	45958/9	88321/–	SP Replacements for war-damaged stock 45959 W/O- u/f used for new Dia 370 vehicle.
V Restaurant pantry car (third-class)	321*	1939	971	61' 6" × 9' 3"	2† 38	YK	1893/5/6/8–1900		Entered traffic as open firsts with the pantry locked out of use.
(Brake third)	312*	1940	1015	51' 1½" × 9' 3"	6: 60	YK	44421/31/41/51	86959–65	SP
(Third)				51' 1½" × 9' 3"	8: 80	YK	44422/32/42/52	86960–6	

Dia 312 comprised steel-panelled articulated twins for Kings Cross–Hitchin–Cambridge trains, working with Dia 311 composites.

Type	Dia No	CBP Year	Order No	Dimensions	Comps /Seats	Built At	Running numbers Original	1943	Notes
(Brake third)	322	1940	1016	55' 6¼" × 9' 3"	6: 60	YK	80328, 24689	80328/30	SP
(Lav composite)				55' 6¼" × 9' 3"	4/3 : 25/25	YK	80329, 24690	80329/31	SP Articulated twins
V Passenger brake van	245*	1940	1073	61' 6" × 9' 0"	–	YK	70740/50–66		70752 DEA Ilford 1944 70753 W/O
V Passenger brake van	260*	1940	1059 1061	61' 6" × 9' 0"	–	YK	70741–9/67		
Composite	205	special	1028	54' 1½" × 9' 3"	4/5 : 40/60	YK	64075	82445	New body, original DEA.

Type	Dia No	CBP Year	Order No	Dimensions	Comps /Seats	Built At	Running numbers	Notes

1944 No vehicles added to stock

1945 All vehicles vacuum fitted

Type	Dia No	CBP Year	Order No	Dimensions	Comps /Seats	Built At	Running numbers	Notes
V First	334	special	1139	61' 6" × 9' 3"	6: 36	DR	1531 (11142)	The prototype Newton carriage
V Third	329*	1944	1144	63' 0" × 9' 3"	7: 42	DR	1347	
V Passenger brake van	327*	1944	1123	61' 6" × 9' 0"	–	YK	70584–70626	Deal body panelling

1946 All vehicles vacuum fitted

Type	Dia No	CBP Year	Order No	Dimensions	Comps /Seats	Built At	Running numbers	Notes
V First	332*	1940	1003 1062 1128	63' 0" × 9' 3"	6: 36	YK	132–142 (11168–78)	These orders had been author-sed under the 1940 CBP and were for two firsts, two firsts and seven firsts respectively. As completed they were to post war design.
V Third	336	1944	1125	61' 6" × 9' 3"	7: 42	YK	1353/6–65/7–9, 1370–83/6–8	1370 W/O Goswick 1947
V Third	329*	1946	–	63' 0" × 9' 3"	7: 42	BHM	1013–42	First of the order for 263 Dia 329 thirds from BHM.

152

Type	Dia No	CBP Year	Order No	Dimensions	Comps /Seats	Built At	Running numbers	Notes
V Open third	330*	1944	1126	63' 0" × 9' 3"	1† 64	YK	13791–8	
V Brake third	331	1944	1127	63' 0" × 9' 3"	3: 18	YK	149–58 (149–16871, 151–16873)	
V Brake third	146*	special	1141	52' 6" × 9' 3"	3: 18	YK	62779	New body to original design, using old u/f. 62779 had been DEA Temple Mills 1944.
V Brake third	343	special	1150	63' 0" × 8' 11¼"	4: 24	DL	16854	New body to postwar design, using u/f of 24293 Dia 114, DEA Middlesbrough, 1942.
		special	1151			DL	16855	New body to postwar design, using u/f of 31135 Dia 297, DEA Stratford, 1940.
V Composite	328*	1944	1124	59' 6" × 9' 3"	3/3 : 18/18	YK	143–146 (143, 18510–2)	
V Passenger brake van	327*	1944	1123	61' 6" × 9' 0"	–	YK	70627–33	Deal body panelling
		special	1142			YK	70634	New body to Dia 327, using u/f of 70753 Dia 245, DEA Ilford 1944.
		special	1152			DL	70635	New body to Dia 327, using u/f of 16073 Dia 37A, DEA Wood Green 1945.
		special	1153			DL	70636	New body to Dia 327, using u/f of 64145 Dia 137, DEA Marylebone 1944.
Bread van	335	special	1186	51' 1½" × 8' 9½"	–	DR	70637	Replacement for bread van No 3138 W/O 1945 and used u/f of 60599 Dia 141, W/O 1943
		special	1187	51' 1½" × 8' 9½"	–	DR	70639	Replacement for bread van No 303 W/O 1945 and used u/f of 63940 Dia 244, DEA 1940
V PO sorting van	164*	special	1185	60' 1½" × 8' 6¾"	–	YK	70297	New body to original design, using old u/f. 70297 had been DEA Wood Green 1945.
V PO stowage van	342	1947	1188	52' 4" × 8' 6"	–	DR	(30281) 70640	First number allocated in joint LMS/LNER stock

1947 All vehicles vacuum fitted

Type	Dia No	CBP Year	Order No	Dimensions	Comps /Seats	Built At	Running numbers	Notes
V First (with ladies' retiring room)	348	1946	1189	63' 0" × 9' 3"	5: 30	YK	1326–8	PV 'Flying Scotsman' sets
Third	339*	1946	–	52' 4" × 9' 3"	8: 80	RYP	82643–69	Initial order was for 50, reduced to 35, balance delivered 1948.
V Third	336	1944	1125	61' 6" × 9' 3"	7: 42	YK	1366	
V Third	329*	1946	–	63' 0" × 9' 3"	7: 42	BHM	1043–96, 1101–4, 1111–24, 1400/34/5, 1439–72/4–8/82–4	Continuation of the order for 263 Dia 329 thirds from BHM. 1441 W/O Goswick 1947
		1946	1177			YK	1006/8–10	
			1192			YK	1000–5, 1604–7	PV 'Flying Scotsman' sets
V Third (with ladies' retiring room)	349	1946	1193	63' 0" × 9' 3"	6: 36	YK	1608–10	PV 'Flying Scotsman' sets
V Brake third	346*	1946	1195	63' 0" × 9' 3"	4: 24	YK	1901–4	PV 'Flying Scotsman' sets
V Open third	330*	1944	1126	63' 0" × 9' 3"	1† 64	YK	13799–13805	
V Open third	350*	1946	1194	63' 0" × 9' 3"	2† 48	YK	1982–4	As dining cars PV 'Flying Scotsman' sets
V Open third	337	special	1154	61' 6" × 9' 3"	2† 48	DL	13860	New body to postwar design, using u/f of 43628 Dia 186, burnt out at Goole 1941.
Lav composite	338*	1946	–	52' 4" × 9' 3"	3/4 : 19/33	CR	88327–78	
V Composite	328*	1944	1124	59' 6" × 9' 3"	3/3 : 18/18	YK	147/8 (18513/4)	
		1946	1191				1195–7, 1206 (18515–7)	PV 'Flying Scotsman' sets
V Brake composite	345*	1946	–	63' 0" × 9' 3"	2/3 : 12/18	M–C	1140–3/6/8/58 (10169–72, 1146/–, 1158)	1148 W/O Penmanshiel 1948

Type	Dia No	CBP Year	Order No	Dimensions	Comps /Seats	Built At	Running numbers	Notes
V Third-class sleeping car	347*	1948	1240	66' 6" × 9' 3"	12: 16	DR	1348	
V Passenger brake van	344*	1946	1180	63' 0" × 9' 0"	–	YK	10–12	To work in 'Flying Scotsman' sets

1948 All vehicles vacuum fitted

Type	Dia No	CBP Year	Order No	Dimensions	Comps /Seats	Built At	Running numbers	Notes
V First	332*	1946	1174	63' 0" × 9' 3"	6: 36	YK	1312–5/8/20–5 (11179–89)	
V Open first	351*	1946	1175 1190	63' 0" × 9' 3"	2† 42	YK	1959–71 1956–8	As dining cars As dining cars PV 'Flying Scotsman' sets 1960 PV
V Third	329*	1946	–	63' 0" × 9' 3"	7: 42	BHM	1479–81/5–1513, 1523/9, 1540/2/3, 1545–69 13806–52	Continuation of the order for 263 Dia 329 thirds from BHM. 1498 W/O Penmanshiel 1948
		1946	1177			YK	1011/98, 1385/9–94, 1574–8, 1601–3	
V Open third	350*	1946	1178	63' 0" × 9' 3"	2† 48	YK	1988–98	As dining cars
V Brake third	346*	1946	1179	63' 0" × 9' 3"	4: 24	YK	1905–36	1905–7 PV 'Junior Scotsman' sets 1905–36 later converted to Dia 376.
V Composite	328*	1946	1176	59' 6" × 9' 3"	3/3 : 18/18	YK	16856–60 1228–32/6/9/40, 1243–6/8/50–6, 1262–7/73/4	
		1949	1176 1219			YK	18450–6 1207/15/8/24	PV 'Junior Scotsman' sets
V Brake composite	345*	1946	–	63' 0" × 9' 3"	2/3 : 12/18	M–C	1144/5 (10173/4), 1150/1, 1160/1/3/4/9, 1170/1/5/7–9, 1180/7/8–90/2–4	
Third	339*	1946	–	52' 4" × 9' 3"	8: 80	RYP	82670–7	
			–			CR	82678–88	
Brake third	340*	1946 1947	–	52' 4" × 9' 3"	4: 40	M–C	86998–87027 87028–54	
Lav composite	338*	1946	–	52' 4" × 9' 3"	3/4 : 19/33	CR	88379–88426	
V Kitchen car	353*	1946	1196	63' 0" × 9' 3"	–	DR	1943–5 1946	'Flying Scotsman' sets All with anthracite-electric cooking equipment
V Buffet lounge car	352	1948	1197	63' 0" × 9' 3"	1† 8¶	DR	1705/6	PV 'Flying Scotsman' sets Rebuilt by BR in 1959 as conventional buffet cars, with gas equipment and seating 24.
V Third-class sleeping car	347*	1948	1240	66' 6" × 9' 3"	12: 16	DR	1349–51	PV
V Passenger van	344*	1946	1180	63' 0" × 9' 3"	–	YK	13–19 100–8/10	To work in 'Flying Scotsman' brake and 'Junior Scotsman' sets

1949 All vehicles vacuum fitted

Type	Dia No	CBP Year	Order No	Dimensions	Comps /Seats	Built At	Running numbers	Notes
V First	332*	1949	1217 1256/73	63' 0" × 9' 3"	6: 36	YK	1306–8 115–31, 1099, 1105/7–10, 1125–39, 1579/80	PV 'Junior Scotsman' sets
V Open first	351*	1949	1218	63' 0" × 9' 3"	2† 42	YK	1972–4	As dining cars 'Junior Scotsman' sets
First	341	1948	–	52' 4" × 9' 3"	7: 56	CR	81073–84	
V Third	329*	1949	1220	63' 0" × 9' 3"	7: 42	YK	1106, 1514–8, 1570–3	PV 'Junior Scotsman' sets
			1274			YK	13861–13895	
			1282			YK	13896–13900	
		1948	–			BHM	13853–9	Completion of the order for 263 Dia 329 thirds from BHM.
V Open third	350*	1949	1221	63' 0" × 9' 3"	2† 48	YK	1985–7	As dining cars 'Junior Scotsman' sets

154

Type	Dia No	CBP Year	Order No	Dimensions	Comps /Seats	Built At	Running numbers	Notes
Third	339*	1946	–	52' 4" × 9' 3"	8: 80	CR	82688–92	
V Brake third	346*	1949	1222	63' 0" × 9' 3"	4: 24	YK	1937–42	Later converted to Dia 376.
V Composite	328*	1948	1176	59' 6" × 9' 3"	3/3 : 18/18	YK	1249/75	
		1949	1176				18457/8	
			1219			YK	1226/7	PV 'Junior Scotsman' sets
			1258			DR	1524/5, 1680–2	
V Third-class sleeping car	347*	1948	1240	66' 6" × 9' 3"	12: 16	DR	1352	PV
		1949					1354	PV
V Restaurant kitchen car (first-class)	354*	1949	1208	63' 0" × 9' 3"	1† 18	YK	1655–7	Anthracite-electric cooking equipment
V Restaurant pantry car (third-class)	355*	1949	1209	63' 0" × 9' 3"	2† 38	YK	1330–5/45	
Brake third	340*	1949	1257	52' 4" × 9' 3"	4: 40	YK	87068–87127	
		1948	–			M–C	87055–67	
V Kitchen car	353*	1948	1196	63' 0" × 9' 3"	–	DR	1947–9	All with anthracite-electric cooking equipment
		1949					1950–3	
V PO sorting van	356*	1949	1245	60' 1½" × 8' 6"	–	DR	70641	
		1949	1266			DR	70642–5	

1950 All vehicles vacuum fitted

Type	Dia No	CBP Year	Order No	Dimensions	Comps /Seats	Built At	Running numbers	Notes
V First	332*	1950	1279	63' 0" × 9' 3"	6: 36	YK	11143–67	
V Third	329*	1950	1282	63' 0" × 9' 3"	7: 42	YK	1611–4/7–37 13901–85	13905/77 W/O
Third	339*	1950	–	52' 4" × 9' 3"	8: 80	RYP	82693–82710	87202–10 allocated to the Scottish Region as new
V Brake third	346*	1950	1288	63' 0" × 9' 3"	4: 24	DR	1661–6/89–95, 1730, 1822–5, 1840/1, 1865–74 16861–70	1690/1, 1868/72 converted in 1956 with two sleeping compartments
V Composite	328*	1950	1280	59' 6" × 9' 3"	3/3 : 18/18	YK	18459–18508	
V Brake composite	345*	1950	1281	63' 0" × 9' 3"	2/3 : 12/18	YK	10159–68	
V First-class sleeping car	359	1950	1275	66' 6" × 9' 3"	11: 11	DR	1257–60/92	PV
V Restaurant kitchen car (first-class)	354*	1950	1287	63' 0" × 9' 3"	1† 18	DR	1216/7/9/22/3, 1597–1600/67	Anthracite-electric cooking equipment
V Passenger brake van	344*	1950	1283	63' 0" × 9' 0"	–	YK	141/3–6/53–7, 159–63	
V PO sorting van	356*	1949	1266	60' 1½" × 8' 6"	–	DR	70646	
Brake van six-wheeled	358	1950	1284	32' 0" × 8' 11¼"	–	DL /SF	70647–70726	

1951 All vehicles vacuum fitted

Type	Dia No	CBP Year	Order No	Dimensions	Comps /Seats	Built At	Running numbers	Notes
Third	339*	1950	–	52' 4" × 9' 3"	8: 80	RYP	82711–42	Allocated to the Scottish Region as new
		1950	–			GLO	82743–82803	82743–65 allocated to the Scottish Region as new
		1951	1337			DR	82813–82893	82880–93 allocated to the Scottish Region as new
Brake third	340*	1950	–	52' 4" × 9' 3"	4: 40	M–C	87128–77	87128–71 allocated to the Scottish Region as new
		1951	1342			YK	87228–97	
Brake third	361	1950	–	52' 4" × 9' 3"	5: 50	M–C	87178–87227	87178–87202 allocated to the Scottish Region as new
		1951	1343			YK	87298–87327	87310–27 allocated to the Scottish Region as new
Brake composite	360*	1950	–	52' 4" × 9' 3"	2/4 : 16/40	BHM	80332–91	80332–42 allocated to the Scottish Region as new
Dynamometer car	367	–	1147	61' 6" × 9' 3"	–	DR	DE 320041 (DB 999500)	Amsler recording equipment Pullman vestibule one end

Type	Dia No	CBP Year	Order No	Dimensions	Comps /Seats	Built At	Running numbers	Notes
1952 All vehicles vacuum fitted								
Third	339*	1950	–	52' 4" × 9' 3"	8: 80	GLO	82804–12	
Lav composite	338*	1950	–	52' 4" × 9' 3"	3/4 : 19/33	BHM	88427–96	88427–49 allocated to the Scottish Region as new
		1952	1372			DR	88497–88516	
		1951	–			BHM	88541–88610	88599–88610 allocated to the Scottish Region as new
Lav composite	370	1952	special	51' 1½" × 9' 3"	3/4 : 19/33	DR	88523	New body to postwar design, using u/f of 45959 Dia 311.
Brake composite	360*	1951	–	52' 4" × 9' 3"	2/4 : 16/40	BHM	80392–80421	80417–21 allocated to the Scottish Region as new
V Third-class sleeping car	368	1950	1335	66' 6" × 9' 2¼"	11: 22	DR	1760/1	PV
		1951	1349			DR	1762–4	Attendant's compartment
V Third-class sleeping car	369	1950	1336	66' 6" × 9' 2¼"	12: 24	DR	1765–7	PV
		1951	1348			DR	1768–70	Completed 2 August 1952
1953 All vehicles vacuum fitted								
Lav composite	338*	1952	1372	52' 4" × 9' 3"	3/4 : 19/33	DR	88517–22	
Composite	371	1952	1372	52' 4" × 9' 3"	3/4½ : 24/44	DR	88524–40	Allocated to the Scottish Region as new Completed 22 August 1953
Third	372	special	–	54' 1½" × 8' 11¼"	8: 96	YK	82894–9	New bodies on Ilford stock u/fs. For LT & S section
Brake third	373	special	–	54' 1½" × 8' 11¼"	6: 72	YK	87328–33	New bodies on Ilford stock u/fs. For LT & S section
Lav composite	374	special	–	54' 1½" × 8' 11¼"	3/1† :19/40	DR	88611–6	New bodies on Ilford stock u/fs. For LT & S section
Open third	375	special	–	54' 1½" × 8' 11¼"	2†: 80	DR	82900–5	New bodies on Ilford stock u/fs. For LT & S section

As built, vehicles to Dias 372–375 formed six, four-car sets

Type	Dia No	CBP Year	Order No	Dimensions	Comps /Seats	Built At	Running numbers	Notes
1954								
V Restaurant cafeteria car	–	–	Not known	61' 6" × 9' 0"	2† 18	EH	9209 (1241), 9210 (1244), 9211 (1246), 9212 (1249), 9213 (1255), 9214 (1256), 9215 (31926), 9216 (42783), 9217 (43041)	Conversions from ambulance vehicles which were originally Dia 95 sleeping cars – 1241 – 56–and Dia 11 restaurant cars 31926 etc.

Allocated when new to the London Midland Region as M 9209E – M 9217E   Propane/butane gas cooking equipment

LNER TELEGRAPHIC CODES FOR COACHING STOCK

The LNER's coaching stock telegraphic code was widely used in official communications, particularly on the railway telegraph, but was not painted on the vehicles themselves until after 1942. The code was adopted by BR and officially used in simplified form until the early 1980s, the suffixes to denote lavatories and/or vestibules, LV and V, being dropped soon after Nationalisation.

The basic code for vacuum braked, bogie stock was as follows, being supplemented by suffixes after the basic code to specify particular stock.

Saloons	First-class	SF
	Third-class	ST
	Invalid	SI

Vestibuled carriages		
Restaurant kitchen	First	RF
cars	Composite	RC
	Either class	RU
	Third	RT
	Triplet	RTS
	Pantry third	RTP
	Buffet car	RB
	Kitchen only	RK

Sleeping cars	First-class	SLF
	First-class (twin)	Twin SLF
	Composite	SLC
	Composite (twin)	Twin SLC
	Third-class (non-pantry)	SLT
	Third-class (pantry)	SLTP
	Third-class, 22 berths (with pantry)	SLTTP
	Third-class, 24 berths (non-pantry)	SLTT

Open stock	First-class	FO
	Composite	CO
	Third-class	TO
	Third-class brake	BTO
	Semi-open first	Semi FO
	Second-class	SO

Tourist stock	Third open	TTO
(bucket seats)	Third open (twin)	Twin TTO
	Brake third open	TBTO

Corridor stock	First-class	FK
(L suffix added to	First-class brake	BFK
denote lavatory)	Second-class	SK
	Composite	CK
	Composite brake	BCK
	Third-class	TK
	Third-class brake	BTK

Non-vestibuled stock		
	First-class	F
	First-class (lavatory)	FL
	First-class brake	BF
	First-class brake (lavatory)	BFL
	Composite	C
	Composite (lavatory)	CL
	Composite brake	BC
	Composite brake (lavatory)	BCL
	Third-class	T
	Third-class (lavatory)	TL
	Third-class brake	BT
	Third-class brake (lavatory)	BTL

Articulated stock This was referred to by the prefix of the word 'Twin', 'Triple', 'Quad', 'Quint', as appropriate.

| Post Office vehicles | PO sorting van | POS |
| | PO tender | POT |

Passenger vans (brake vans)		
	Four-wheeled	BY
	Six-wheeled	BZ
	Bogie (without gangways)	B
	Bogie (with gangways)	BG
	For racing pigeon traffic (braked)	BP
	Milk van (braked)	BM

| Miscellaneous vans | Parcels and miscellaneous vans | PMV |

The various suffixes added were as follows:

	Dual brake fitted	D
	Westinghouse air brake	W
	Pullman vestibule	PV, later PG
	British Standard vestibule	BS
	BS with Pullman adaptors	A
	Vestibule-type not specified	V
	Locker	G

Thus an open first, with dual brake and BS gangway would be FODBS

Six-wheeled passenger stock was denoted by an X as a prefix, eg XF, XC, XT.

Later BR codes for vehicles featured in this book were:

	Kitchen buffet car	RKB
	Cafeteria car	CAF
	Restaurant cafeteria car	RCAF
	First-class (loose chairs)	RFO
	Third-class (loose chairs)	RTO

ACKNOWLEDGMENTS

IN preparing this book as a thorough revision of *Gresley's Coaches*, published in 1973, a number of people were immediately helpful in offering their assistance and, as time went on, many more contributed immensely.

I am most grateful to everyone who provided me with facilities, information and photographs.

The custodians of the major archives relating to LNER carriages are the Public Record Office, Kew and the National Railway Museum. The staff at Kew were always ready to provide the material requested and it was a pleasure to work there. Similarly, too, at the National Railway Museum where I would like to thank Andrew Dow, Head of Museum for the facilities made available and also his colleagues, in particular, Phil Atkins, the Librarian, Mike Blakemore and Mike Rutherford.

An early approach to Dr Geoffrey Hughes was most fruitful and he made a number of valuable suggestions as to useful contacts. As a result, I was able to contact Norman Newsome whose paper, *The Development of LNER Carriage and Wagon Design*, first read before the Institution of Locomotive Engineers on 10 March 1948, was an indispensable starting - point for this work. The subsequent correspondence and meeting with Mr Newsome were extremely valuable and his particular contribution has already been mentioned in the Preface. I am really most grateful to him. From Geoff Hughes also came an introduction to Geoff Goslin, Secretary of the Gresley Society, and I would like to thank him for his contribution, also Wilf Wells, Secretary of the LNER Study Group, and through his good offices I was grateful for much useful information on particular vehicles, thanks to Group members, John Dawson and Harry Wilson. Wilf also provided some much needed lists from the Guy Hemingway archive and was invaluable in affording me access to the records of the late Stephen Gradidge.

I would like to thank Peter Trewin, Secretary to the British Railways Board, for giving permission for me to examine records held at the Public Record Office but not normally available for inspection.

Of other well-wishers and providers of greatly appreciated information and photographs, my thanks go to Michael Brooks, Murray Brown, John Dawson, Robert Humm (for his kindness in loaning me archive illustrative material), John Lloyd, David Lowther, David Percival, Dick Riley, Graham Stacey and to RAS Marketing, Brian Stephenson, Ron White.

In the preparation of *Gresley's Coaches*, I recorded my thanks to the then Chief Mechanical Engineer of British Railways Eastern Region for permission to visit Doncaster Works to examine the records held there prior to 1968. At Doncaster, Messrs D. Haines of Doncaster paintshop and Boyd of the drawing office were extremely helpful in answering numerous enquiries. The Works Manager at the then British Rail Engineering Ltd's York Works gave me permission to visit the works where several staff took great trouble in unearthing material relating to LNER days. John Vidal, formerly with J. Stone & Co, provided me with some fascinating detail relating to the important development of electric cooking and pressure ventilation equipment supplied to the LNER by J. Stone.

Not least, I would like to thank my family, Carol, Edmund and Georgia and my Mother, for their patience in putting up with my long absences, researching or glued to the indispensable Mac, and for their many helpful suggestions and unstinting interest.

References

The principal sources of reference were those held at the PRO, in particular the LNER Board Minutes, the minutes of the Joint Meeting of the Locomotive and Traffic Committee, the minutes of the Traffic Committee and the minutes of the meetings of the Superintendents and Passenger Managers, in each case during the LNER period, or in the case of the SPM meeting, from 1921. There are a number of LNER Secretarial papers held at Kew covering diverse subjects, as well as those of the former Hotels Executive of the British Transport Commission, to which reference has been made. At the National Railway Museum, quite the most interesting fresh material on hand were the instructions issued by the Chief Mechanical Engineers of the LNER from 1923–1948 relating to carriage and wagon matters.

I have already, I hope, paid tribute to the value of the paper given to the I Loco E by Norman Newsome in 1948. Also of value was the unpublished manuscript, *A History of the Doncaster Plant Works* by J.E. Day, kindly made available by the Borough Librarian of Doncaster. The Post Office allowed me access to information relating to TPO vehicles operating on the GNR and the LNER.

Finally, many useful references have come from study of the following journals: *The Engineer, The LNER Magazine, The Locomotive Magazine, the Railway Engineer, The Railway Gazette, The Railway Magazine, The Railway Observer, Railway World and Trains Illustrated.*

Photographic credits

The following photographs are reproduced by courtesy of the respective photographers or owners of collections:
the late W. J. V. Anderson/Rail Archive Stephenson: page 65 (top); David Lowther: pages 20 (lower), 29 (lower), 66 (lower), 70 (upper), 78 (both), 82 (centre and lower left), 87 (top), 90 (centre), 106 (both), 107 (top);P. Mulholland/North Eastern Railway Coach Group: page 23 (upper); National Railway Museum: pages 8, 9 (top), 10, 11, 12 (bottom), 15 (top), 17 (left), 18 (bottom), 19, 20 (top), 26 (bottom), 30 (upper), 34, 37 (upper), 47 (upper), 48 (bottom), 50, 53 (lower), 56 (bottom), 59, 64, 66 (lower), 67 (lower), 70 (lower), 71, 75 (bottom), 81 (top), 82 (top), 89, 90 (top), 91 (upper and centre), 92 (bottom), 94, 96, 99 (top), 102, 103 (top), 105 (bottom), 107 (bottom), 115 (top,left and lower); Ken Nunn Collection/Locomotive Club of Great Britain: pages 15 (lower), 17 (right), 25 (top), 55, 63, 77 (upper); C. H .S. Owen: page 87; David Percival: pages 16, 20, 32, 39, 42, 43, 44 (upper), 48 (lower), 55 (both), 69 (bottom), 71 (top), 72, 81 (bottom), 92 (top), 104, 105 (top), 107 (centre), 108, 109 (both), 110 (centre), 111, 112 (all), 113 (both), 116; RAS Marketing: frontispiece (both), pages 21, 23 (upper), 25 (bottom), 27, 28, 29 (upper), 30, 49, 58, 66 (upper), 69 (upper), 72 (lower), 73, 97, 100, 115 (top,right); Real Photographs/ G. W. Goslin: page 33(upper); R. C. Riley: pages 41, 47 (upper), 48, 57, 88; the following drawings from Norman Newsome's paper to the Institution of Locomotive Engineers are reproduced by kind permission of the Institution of Mechanical Engineers page 18(top), 35(both), 81(centre).

INDEX

Accidents and train fires 18, 36, 39,
  68, 104, 121
All-steel carriages
  for ECJS 13
  for NBR 15
  later development of and
    proposals for 12, 17, 19, 20, 22,
    34, 94, 101
  proposals for, 1914 18
Aluminium, use of 19, 34, 36, 94
Anthracite-electric cooking equipment 81, 83, 105
Articulation of carriages 12, 19, 59,
  95, 97, 99
Axlebox, roller bearing 35, 68, 69

Bogies
  Great Northern Railway 13, 111
  Gresley Spencer- Moulton 12, 19,
    34 *et seq*, 53, 54, 64, 80, 106,
    114
  Other LNER 35, 102, 106
Braking systems,
  of high-speed trains 64, 68
  use of and unification of
    23, 33, 34, 45, 57
Bread vans 112
Bucket seats 36, 44, 47, 95, 96
Buffet cars, use of 28, 80, 85, 96
Bulleid, O. V. S. 13, 17, 33, 34, 95

Cafeteria cars 44, 87
Carriage Diagram Numbers 23, 24,
  42, 121 *et seq*
Carriages
  bodies, 10, 12, 13, 15, 17, 21, 94,
    96
  cost of, 63, 94, 96
  materials, 13, 17, 18, 19, 20, 21,
    31, 35, 39, 66, 94, 95, 96, 103,
    111
  methods of building, 13, 21 *et seq*,
    35, 63, 66, 94, 95
  riding of 19, 60, 63
Cheshire Lines Committee, carriages
  built for and transferred
  to 44, 50, 53
Cinema cars 113
Couplers and couplings
  articulation 18
  buckeye 9, 13, 34
  screw 34, 35

Destination boards, indicators and
  roller blinds 41, 63, 96, 114
Dimensions, standardisation of
  and changes to 32 *et seq*, 36, 42,
  49, 74, 80, 101, 115

East Coast Joint Stock and East
  Coast Stock 8, 10, 23, 25, 26, 58
  et seq, 93, 107
East Coast Joint Stock Committee
  and East Coast companies'
  managers 8, 9
East Coast Royal Train 118
Electric cooking equipment 19, 25,
  30, 58, 75, 77, 79, 81, 87
Electric heating, experiments with 37
Electric lighting 12, 30, 34, 37, 115
Electric water heating 74, 89
Electrification schemes
  GN suburban 25, 26, 53, 55, 102
  Manchester/Sheffield 31, 120
  Shenfield and GE generally 26,
    31, 52, 55, 102, 110, 120
  Tyneside 28, 120
Enemy action, rolling stock losses 31,
  100, 112
English Electric Company Ltd, The
  18

Gangways
  British Standard 33, 45, 46, 47
  Pullman-type 9, 33
Gas cooking equipment
  oil-gas 79, 85.95
  propane gas conversions 85, 86
Gas-lighting in rolling stock 12, 50,
  115
Great Northern and North Eastern
  Railway, differences of opinion 9,
  15
Great Northern Railway
  Development of carriage design 9,
    10, 12
  Involvement with ECJS 8, 9, 10
Great Northern/North Eastern Joint
  Stock 13
Gresley, Herbert Nigel, Sir 8, 11, 17,
  18, 23, 28, 81, 94, 102, 116

Heating systems, steam 9, 34, 37, 92
High-speed trains of the LNER 28,
  62 *et seq*, 68 *et seq*,
  proposed and actual use postwar
  65
  proposed Hull-Liverpool trains
  70
Howlden E. F. 9

Interior decor and finishes 38, 58,
  63, 66, 73, 76, 83, 91, 95, 97, 103,
  106, 109
Interior fittings 38, 49, 58, 63, 66,
  73, 78, 82, 101, 106, 108, 113

Lavatories 36, 66

Lettering and numbering
  BR 41, 53, 120
  ECJS 119
  LNER 40, 53, 74, 119 *et seq*
Liveries
  BR 40, 41, 47, 92, 101, 104, 106,
    108, 118
  LNER imitation teak finishes 19,
    40, 96, 99, 103, 104, 106, 117
  LNER special 63, 67, 69, 83, 86,
    95, 96, 116
  LNER standard 19, 39, 40, 54,
Locomotive Testing Plant, Rugby
  116
London and North Eastern Railway
  Carriage building and repair work-
    shops
    Cowlairs Works 8, 15, 20, 21
    Darlington Works 21
    Doncaster Works 8, 9, 11, 20, 21,
      22, 31, 34, 58, 102, 104, 116
    Dukinfield Works 15, 21, 52, 85
    Faverdale Works 101
    Inverurie Works 15
    Shildon Works 20
    Stratford Works 15, 20, 21, 116
    Walker Gate Works 15, 20
    York Works 8, 13, 15, 20, 21, 22,
      34, 58, 101, 102, 104
  Carriage building and repair work-
    shops: production facilities 20
  Carriage Building Programmes
    19, 23 *et seq*, 42, 55, 112
  Competition with LMS 24, 58, 90
  Constituent companies' design
    policies 12 *et seq*
  Difficulties in 1930s 24, 27
  Drawing offices 17, 121
  Organisation and management of,
    16, 17, 120
  Postwar planning 19, 68, 101 et
    seq
  Royal train 118
  Superintendents and passenger
    managers 16, 17, 23, 33, 42,
    60, 68, 80
  Telegraphic code for coaching
    stock 157
LNER catering vehicles modernised
  by BR 85-88, 96

Midland & GN Joint passenger stock
  21, 120
Midland & North British Joint
  Services 93
Milk tank wagons 117

Newsome, N. 17, 19, 24, 66, 94, 95,
  158

Newton, Sir Charles 101, 102
Non-common user vehicles 117, 119
North Eastern Railway
    design policies 10, 11, 13
    involvement with ECJS 8, 10, 11, 13
Numbering schemes 74, 119 *et seq*

Paint, types of 39-41
Plywood, use by the LNER 36, 95
Pre-Grouping stock inherited by LNER- four and six-wheeled 17, 28, 50
Pressure ventilation, development and use of 19, 37, 61, 63, 77, 91, 105
Production totals of LNER passenger stock 22, 110
Provision of special passenger facilities on-board trains
    Cinema cars 113 *et seq*
    Continental boat trains 73, 74, 78
    East Coast trains 58 *et seq*, 106
    Hairdressing salon 60, 62, 71
    Ladies' retiring rooms 60, 71, 106
    Radio and records 61
    Shower baths 89, 92
    Speed recorders, Flaman 63
Pullman cars on LNER 78, 86
Push-pull services 31, 52 *et seq*,

Restaurant car services, wartime withdrawal of 85
Rexine, use of 36, 38, 49, 63, 66, 76, 78, 91, 92, 95, 113
Roofs, finish of 41, 96, 102, 103

Seating 32, 36, 58, 66, 73, 82, 95, 102
SHAEF train 92
Steel panelling: use of 19, 36, 40, 96, 97, 99, 102, 103

Teak, use of 94, 96
Third-class sleeping cars 89, 90, 108
Thompson, Edward 20, 102, 104
Train services: East Coast main line general
    24 *et seq*, 28, 29, 41-44, 58 et seq, 65, 68, 79, 84, 92, 94, 102, 104
    'Capitals Limited', The 106
    'Coronation', The 65 *et seq*
    'Flying Scotsman', The 44, 58 *et seq*, 84, 105
    Kings Cross-Newcastle 26, 37, 58, 60, 65, 71, 84
    'Northern Belle', The 60 *et seq*,
    'Silver Jubilee', The 62 *et seq*
    sleeping car services 89-93
    'Talisman', The 69, 107
    to Scarborough 28
Train services: GC section
    cross- country 26, 31, 42, 68, 70,

Marylebone suburban 28, 53
    'South Yorkshireman', The 107
Train services: GE section
    Boat trains including the 'Hook Continental' 25, 29, 44, 73, 77
    Cross-country 26
    East Anglian local 28, 29, 99
    East Anglian main line 25, 26, 27, 28, 33, 73, 74, 107
    London suburban 24, 26, 34, 49 *et seq*, 99, 113
Train services: GN section
    Cambridge line 53, 99
    Kings Cross-Leeds 26, 31, 43, 45, 84, 114
    Lincolnshire 26, 53
    London inner suburban 49 *et seq*
    London outer suburban 53, 99
    'West Riding', The 68 *et seq*
Train services: LT&S section of ER 52, 99, 104, 109
Train services: North Eastern Area
    Cross-country incl York-Swindon 26, 33, 85
    Darlington-Saltburn 99
    Leeds-Glasgow 26, 45, 83, 114
    Newcastle-Middlesbrough 29, 85
Train services: Northern Scottish Area 45, 84
Train services: Southern Scottish Area
    Aberdeen/Edinburgh-St Pancras 26, 31, 93
    Edinburgh-Aberdeen 28, 43, 84
    Edinburgh-Glasgow 26, 27, 42
    Edinburgh suburban 50, 99
    Glasgow-Fort William/Mallaig 84, 85
    Glasgow suburban 29, 50, 52, 99
Types of carriages: East Coast Joint Stock
    articulated sleeping cars 1922/3 13, 89
    elliptical roofed stock 1906 8 *et seq*, 11
    'Flying Scotsman' 1893 sets 8
    'Flying Scotsman' 1914 sets 13, 58, 62
    Royal Train 118
        six-wheeled stock 10
        twelve-wheeled stock 10, 11
Types of carriages: Great Central Railway 15
Types of carriages: Great Eastern Railway 15
Types of carriages: Great Northern Railway
    articulated gen service stock 53
    gen service elliptical roofed vestibuled stock 11, 12,
    Leeds quintuplet set 13, 79
    vehicles for EC Royal train 118
Types of carriages: Great North of Scotland Railway 15
Types of carriages: North British Railway 15, 79

Types of carriages: North Eastern Railway
    designs built after 1923 14, 24
    general service stock 13
    vestibuled, with matchboard panelling 8, 12, 13
Types of non-passenger carrying coaching stock: LNER
    bullion van 115
    dynamometer car 115
    four and six-wheel vans 34, 115
    passenger brake vans 111 *et seq*
    pigeon vans 111 *et seq*
Types of non-vestibuled carriages: LNER
    'Alpax' 34, 94
    articulated 53, 99
    electric multiple-units 28, 31, 52
    postwar 101 *et seq*
    standard 51ft 25, 49 *et seq*
    steam railcars 25,
    suburban quadruplet 24, 26, 39, 49, 53
    suburban quintuplet 24, 26, 39, 49, 57
Types of vestibuled carriages: LNER
    all-steel 1927/8 94
    articulated 26, 59, 62, 65, 69, 71, 84, 89, 93, 95, 97
    catering vehicles 25, 27, 28, 36, 59, 73, 79 *et seq*, 105, 118, 119
    'East Anglian' 1937 set 76
    high-speed stock for 'Silver Jubilee', 'Coronation' and 'WestRiding' 28, 29, 62-70
    'Hook Continental' 77
    postwar 101 *et seq*
    sleeping cars 25, 26, 36, 89-93, 102, 104, 108
    standard 52ft 6in 74 *et seq*, 120
    standard 61ft 6in 17, 32 *et seq*
    Tourist stock 27, 28, 44, 95

Underframes and running gear
    finish of 21, 41
    LNER standard 20, 21, 34, 43
    pre-Grouping 9, 13
United States, influence of and from on carriage design 8, 11, 12, 13, 102
Upholstery 38, 49, 58-60, 61, 63, 66, 69, 71, 73, 76, 78, 81, 83, 91, 103

Varnishing procedures 17, 21, 39, 105

Wedgwood, Ralph, Sir 16, 17, 24, 27, 60, 62, 65, 76, 85, 90
Welding 21, 34,
Wheels and wheelsets 41
Whitelaw, William 24, 28
Windows
    double-glazed 19, 36, 63, 66, 71, 77, 105
    standard 32, 33, 81, 96, 97, 101, 102, 111